The Ethnic Dimension in American History

Second Edition

THE ETHNIC DIMENSION IN AMERICAN HISTORY

Second Edition

James Stuart Olson

Sam Houston State University

ST. MARTIN'S PRESS • New York

Editor: Louise H. Waller
Manager, publishing services: Emily Berleth
Publishing services associate: Kalea Chapman
Project management: Beckwith-Clark, Inc.
Art director: Sheree Goodman
Cover design: Circa 86, Inc.

Library of Congress Catalog Card Number: 92-62720
Copyright © 1994 by St. Martin's Press, Inc.
All rights reserved. No part of this book may be reproduced,
stored in a retrieval system, or transmitted by any form or
by any means, electronic, mechanical, photocopying, recording,
or otherwise, except as may be expressly permitted by the applicable
copyright statutes or in writing by the Publisher.
Manufactured in the United States of America.
87654
fedcba

For information, write:
St. Martin's Press, Inc.
175 Fifth Avenue
New York, NY 10010

ISBN: 0-312-08934-1

To my mother, Faith Wendfeldt (Asbjornsen) Olson

Preface

I am one-half Norwegian, one-quarter Swedish, and one-quarter English, although the English portion was diluted way back in the colonial period by a lone French Canadian. I married a woman who is one-half Swiss-German and one-half Anglo-Irish, which makes my children a polyglot mix of western Europeans. I am not very good at multiplying fractions, so I have not figured out their exact ethnic proportions. My odyssey with American pluralism is the rule rather than the exception. Most people who have lived in the United States for even a short period of time also have friends and acquaintances with a similar variety of ethnic backgrounds. And the American past, at virtually every turn in our history, profoundly reflects that pluralism, as will, no doubt, the American future.

I remain convinced today, as I was in 1979 when St. Martin's Press published the first edition of *The Ethnic Dimension in American History*, that although the forces of assimilation are extremely powerful, shifting coalitions of racial, ethnic, religious, and cultural values continue to create a highly pluralistic society. Given the immigration from South America and Asia during the 1980s, that diversity is even more complex today. And I still firmly believe that ethnicity is the central theme in American history, more important than the lack of an aristocracy, the existence of the frontier, the abundance of natural resources, the entrepreneurial impulses, or the isolated security behind two oceans. From the earliest confrontations between native Americans and

Europeans in the early 1600s to the 1993 bombing of the World Trade Center by Muslim fundamentalists, ethnic diversity continues to shape public debate.

Readers familiar with the first edition of *The Ethnic Dimension in American History* will notice several major changes in the second edition. This book is shorter, and the material that has been most notably compressed deals with eighteenth- and nineteenth-century ethnic history. Those changes allow for more coverage of recent American ethnic history, which has become especially complex with the arrival in the United States of new groups from Central America, South America, the Caribbean, Middle East, South Asia, Southeast Asia, East Asia, and the Pacific.

The first edition was also written from the perspective of the late 1970s in the United States, a time when ethnic conflict seemed on the wane because of the achievements of the civil rights movement and the country's preoccupation with Vietnam, economic malaise, and political scandal. But in the 1980s and early 1990s—because of the mass immigration from new parts of the world, continuing discrimination against African Americans, Latino and Latina Americans, and native Americans, and the rise of multiculturalism as an educational and political issue—ethnicity has reasserted itself as a central theme in public policy debates. The second edition of *Ethnic Dimension* addresses these recent developments.

I grew up in Los Angeles in the 1950s and 1960s, and I started college in 1965, just a month after the Watts riots. Wisps of smoke were still rising from burned out buildings when I got on the Greyhound bus at the terminal on Main Street to go away to school. Twenty-seven years later, my parents left Los Angeles in May 1993, selling their forty-five-year-old house in a neighborhood that police had quarantined during the recent rioting. In between there were nearly three decades of civil rights movement, rhetoric about equality, ethnic studies programs, and federal and state legislation allegedly to make sure that the riots of 1965 never happened again. Today, in 1993, we had better take a close look at our cities and our reservations; if we ignore them we are doomed to a future with more riots and fear and pain. Maybe history really is the study of how we do not learn from the past. I hope not.

My thanks to those who commented on the manuscript and whose help I value. They include Ballard Campbell of Northeastern University, Leonard Dinnerstein of the University of Arizona, Joseph J. Parot of Northern Illinois University, and David M. Reimers of New York University. Any errors are my own and not attributable to these reviewers.

James S. Olson

Contents

Introduction

They keep coming to the United States, one wave of immigrants after another, just as they have done for generations, except today the points of origin are different. Instead of the Great Migration waves from northern and western Europe and then from eastern and southern Europe, they are now leaving Haiti, Cuba, Mexico, Central America, Indochina, the Middle East, the islands of the Pacific, East Asia, South America, and Africa, escaping problems and searching for opportunities. And we keep worrying about them, wondering what impact they will have on American culture, whether they will be able to fit in and assimilate, and whether the economy will be able to absorb them. As it has always been, American public policy—both domestic and foreign—continues to be affected at every turn by ethnic issues. The Los Angeles riots of 1992, the plight of the Haitian boat people, the debates over bilingual education, the rise in hate crimes, the fear of ethnic gangs in urban areas, the toll AIDS is taking on minority groups, the academic controversies over political correctness, the Gulf War, starvation in Somalia, and the horrors of what was formerly Yugoslavia are only the most recent examples. For several generations historians said it was the existence of the frontier that made the United States so distinctive, but it was immigration and ethnicity that have had the longest and most consistent impact on American history and American values.

Although ethnic loyalties created stability within individual groups, they often generated competition, fear, and instability for the society as

1

a whole; so Americans constantly searched for ways of fulfilling their egalitarian ideals without dissolving their community. For more than three centuries, Americans have been preoccupied with their diversity, worried about whether the centrifugal force of race, religion, language, and national origin would eventually split the country apart. The traditional and most rigid approach to diversity was "Anglo-conformity," the conviction that American society would survive only if newcomers adopted the values of the white Protestant majority. In the Dawes Act of 1887, for example, Congress tried to force native Americans to become small farmers by breaking up reservation land into small holdings. Such American groups as the Know-Nothing party of 1850s, the American Protective Association of the 1890s, the Ku Klux Klan in the 1920s, and the "English-only" movements of the 1980s and 1990s have tried to force Anglo-Protestant values on Jewish, Catholic, Buddhist, and Muslim immigrants. Even Yankee, French, and "liberal" Catholics in the nineteenth century worked to Americanize immigrants as quickly as possible in order to prevent the church from being identified as a "foreign institution." Throughout the Southwest, teachers discouraged Mexican-American children from speaking Spanish in school. The minorities, of course, resented Anglo-conformity. Surrendering their religion to Protestants or their language and spiritual values to other Americans would have left them naked in a strange cultural environment, unable to interpret or adapt to the new values around them. So the idea of Anglo-conformity, though popular among some American groups, was not a realistic approach to the problem of diversity.

The middle ground in the debate over American diversity was the "melting-pot" ideal. The most naive proponents of this ideal were confident that a new culture would quickly emerge in the United States. In *The Melting Pot* (1909), English playwright Israel Zangwell described his vision of it:

> . . . where a thousand mammoth feeders come from the ends of the world to pour in their human freight. Ah, what a stirring and a seething—Celt and Latin, Slav and Teuton, Greek and Syrian, black and yellow. . . .

By embracing every group and expecting the emergence of a new culture, the melting-pot ideology was more generous than Anglo-conformity and more in tune with notions of freedom and opportunity. The naiveté of the melting-pot ideal came in its assumption that the new culture would appear quickly, fusing every race, color, religion, language, and nationality group into a new whole. For complete assimilation to have taken place, ethnic groups would have had to discard their cultural heritage, intermarry freely, lose their sense of national and religious peoplehood, and encounter no prejudice from other Americans. Obviously, assimilation stopped short of rapid amalgamation, even though mass culture, mass education, economic prosperity, and geographic mobility have touched most people living in the United States. For most immigrants, assimilation would take several generations. Now, more than eighty years since Zangwell's prediction, the melting pot he envisioned remains only a dream.

Distinctions based on race, religion, and class continue to sustain strong group identities. For many Americans—especially African Americans and to a lesser extent other people of color—there has been relatively little marital assimilation. Discrimination based on color largely barred these people from the most personal relationships with whites, so divisions based on color remain the most visible separation in American society. Most Americans identify themselves in broad ethnic terms as whites, African Americans, native American, Asians, or Hispanic Americans. Within broad categories based on color, Americans also group themselves along religious lines. Millions of whites, proud of their Protestant, Catholic, or Jewish heritage, deliberately confine intimate relationships to members of their religious group. Asians and Indians may group themselves on the basis of Christian or non-Christian beliefs, and Hispanic Americans divide into Protestant and Catholic groups. And finally, within color and religious groupings, class divisions further retard assimilation. A new "underclass" of desperately poor people alienated by extreme poverty from the rest of society exists in many urban and rural areas. Some Puerto Ricans in the South Bronx, some African Americans in South Central Los Angeles or on Chicago's South Side, some Mexican Americans in East Los Angeles, and some whites in Appalachia are so emotionally and culturally isolated that they feel affinities only for others in their racial, religious, and class status. Because of social ostracism, personal choice, or unconscious emotional needs, then, most Americans still claim membership in an ethnic community. The melting pot may be bubbling, but it is still a long way from creating an America of one race, one religion, and one culture. Pluralism, not complete assimilation, is the reality of life in the United States.

Recognition of that reality gave rise to the idea of cultural pluralism, the extreme opposite of Anglo-conformity. Accepting everyone's right to political and economic opportunity, cultural pluralists also proclaimed the right of each ethnic group to sustain its own identity. In the 1980s and 1990s, advocates of cultural pluralism exalted ethnic differences as the genius of American society, for although ethnic diversity guaranteed cultural conflict, it also prevented class conflict by dividing workers along cultural lines. Promoting equality and diversity, cultural pluralists were far more tolerant of ethnic differences than were supporters of Anglo-conformity. Advocates of bilingual education, for example, reject the English-only movement and argue that immigrant children must first learn to manipulate their own language—in terms of reading and writing—before they can hope to learn English well. And in schools and colleges across the country we celebrate diversity. Cultural pluralism implies, of course, the indefinite survival of ethnic subcultures and their inevitable accompaniments, suspicion and prejudice. But its supporters also claim that their existence will continue to guarantee a vigorous and politically healthy debate over the meaning of democracy and opportunity in America.

Part I
RED, WHITE,
AND BLACK
IN EARLY AMERICA

In the sixteenth century, political, economic, and religious upheavals were disrupting the lives of millions of people in western Europe. Nation-states were emerging in Spain, Portugal, France, and England as local monarchs extended their territorial authority; entrepreneurs were searching for lucrative business opportunities; and frustrated people were about to rebel against the Catholic Church. The convergence of nationalism, the Commercial Revolution, and the Reformation shook Europe to its foundation and sent thousands of people across the Atlantic in a search for economic opportunity and religious security.

North America's first colonists had to cope not only with a harrowing ocean voyage and often hostile inhabitants, but also with their own religious rivalries and political expectations. Virginia had its "starving time"; the Plymouth colonists braved a horrible winter in flimsy wooden huts; and New England shuddered in fear during King Philip's War. Eventually the colonists adjusted to the environment, transforming scarcity into abundance and hope into confidence. On the shores of the New World, America played host to cultural pluralism and individual rights; both concepts were destined to become ideological standards for the world.

Cultural pluralism revolved around religious diversity. Compared with the rest of the world, British North America seemed an island of toleration in a vast sea of bigotry—even though Congregationalists,

Presbyterians, Anglicans, and Catholics were hardly known for open-mindedness. Because America was settled by many groups, political loyalty was never identified with any one set of religious beliefs. There was, to be sure, a powerful Protestant spirit, but in the absence of a national church, American culture was nonsectarian. Love of country never implied love of a particular church.

Religious pluralism led slowly to toleration. Jews, Catholics, Friends (Quakers), Separatists, Congregationalists, Presbyterians, Baptists, Methodists, Dutch Reformed, Lutherans, and German Reformed all competed for converts, but no single group had an absolute majority. All were minorities, and to protect its own security each had to guarantee the security of others. Tolerance evolved slowly, even tortuously. Virginia prohibited Jewish immigration in 1607; Governor Peter Stuyvesant of New Netherland imposed discriminatory taxes on Jewish merchants in the 1650s; and Pennsylvania tried to prevent Jews from voting in 1690. The Maryland Toleration Act of 1649, which promised freedom of worship for all Christians, was temporarily repealed in 1654. Massachusetts expelled Roger Williams and Anne Hutchinson for heresy in the 1630s and persecuted Quakers throughout the 1600s. Nor was any love lost between Anglicans and Scots-Irish Presbyterians in the South. Still, each denomination drifted toward toleration out of necessity, and crusades to win converts were largely voluntary affairs by the late 1700s. Freedom of religion was becoming a hallmark of American democracy.

As the colonists came to terms with diversity, they institutionalized the natural rights theory of John Locke—that governments were only temporary compacts protecting individual claims to life, liberty, and property. The colonists believed that power was evil, governments dangerous, and restrictions on political power absolutely necessary. Such basic American concepts as separation of powers, checks and balances, federalism, and a bill of rights would eventually circumscribe power and exalt the individual rather than state or church. Offering abundant land, economic opportunity, and geographic mobility, the New World reinforced individualism, and natural rights became the secular religion of America. The European colonists worshiped God in different ways but paid homage to themselves with remarkable consistency: they possessed "unalienable" rights, and the purpose of government was to sustain those rights.

Early American politics inaugurated the first successful colonial rebellion in modern history. By 1776 the colonists had concluded that England was fulfilling Locke's warnings about the dangers of concentrated political power. They believed the writs of assistance, the Sugar Act of 1764, the Stamp Act of 1765, the Townshend Acts of 1767, the

Tea Act of 1773, and the Intolerable Acts of 1774 violated individual rights. Parliament had thereby surrendered its legitimacy as a government of the colonies. The Declaration of Independence and later the Constitution formally established natural rights as a basis for governance.

The colonial period, then, established freedom of religion—with its implied respect for cultural pluralism—and the natural rights philosophy as standards for American society. Nothing would test those standards more severely than racial, ethnic, and religious diversity. When nationalism unified Americans politically, ethnic pluralism divided them culturally. At the same time the natural rights philosophy promised justice and equity to everyone. The tensions between cultural pluralism and egalitarianism would be the central dynamic in United States history.

If the eighteenth century gave America its cultural and political values, the nineteenth century tested them. Caught up in vast economic and social change, the young republic had to decide whether pluralism and liberty applied to all races as well as all religions. The community horizons of the early Protestants were challenged by profound ethnic changes. In the eighteenth century, cultural conflict had largely involved white Protestants, and cultural pluralism had implied toleration for each Protestant denomination. But in the nineteenth century, Catholic immigration from Ireland, Germany, and Quebec frightened Protestants, who had only recently learned to live with one another. At the same time whites had to decide whether African Americans, native Americans, Mexican Americans, and Chinese were entitled to freedom and equality. Americans would pass through the crucibles of cultural conflict and civil war searching for answers to those questions, and their basic values would emerge intact and expanded, ideologically more pervasive than they had been in 1776.

Economic changes created new subcultures in the United States. The transition from a mercantile and subsistence-farming economy to industrial production, commercial farming, and resource extraction stimulated demand for land and labor, and millions of immigrants were drawn into that expanding economy. With jobs in the Northeast and land in the West, America seemed a beacon of opportunity, toleration, and freedom to small farmers and artisans in western Europe and southeastern China. Few social movements in modern history compare with the migration of eighteen million people to the United States between 1820 and 1900. The Great Migration was like the eruption of a huge social volcano, and it transformed the human landscape throughout the Western world.

Economic unrest was the driving force behind emigration. Because of the smallpox vaccine, the introduction of the American potato, and the absence of protracted war, Europe's population increased dramatically: from 140 million in 1750, to more than 260 million in 1850, to nearly 400 million by World War I. Farm sizes dwindled, and many younger sons and laborers had to give up hope of ever owning their own land. As huge mechanized farms appeared in the United States and oceanic transportation improved, American wheat became competitive in European markets. World grain prices and the income of millions of small farmers declined. Except for the tragic potato blight in Ireland, these changes occurred little by little, year after year. To supplement their incomes, European farmers had to find extra work in the winter. Many began traveling to cities—Bergen, Amsterdam, Christiania, Copenhagen, Hamburg, Bremen, Antwerp, Vienna, or Prague—to look for jobs. Some became a migrant people long before they migrated to the United States.

Just as opportunities in agriculture were diminishing, changes in the industrial economy eliminated other occupations. When cheap Canadian and American timber entered Europe in the nineteenth century, many jobs in the lumber industries of Scandinavia and Germany disappeared. Shipbuilding in Canada and the United States eliminated more jobs in northern Europe. Factories supplanted production of goods by independent artisans. Working longer hours for less money to compete with the mass-produced goods of American, English, and German factories, these independent artisans grew dissatisfied with the present and anxious about the future. After the 1870s, millions of industrial workers immigrated to America looking for better jobs and higher wages in the Northeast and Midwest. Except for the Irish, immigrants were not typically the most impoverished people of Europe; chronically unemployed members of the proletariat and peasants working large estates usually did not emigrate. Both vision and resources were needed for such a drastic move. It was status-conscious workers and small farmers who traded Old World problems for New World opportunities.

Appetites whetted by the advertisements of railroads hungry for workers, steamship companies for passengers, and new states for settlers, they came from the British Isles, France, Germany, the Netherlands, Scandinavia, and China. The Irish left from Queenstown, in Cork Harbor, or crossed the Irish Sea on packet ships and departed from Liverpool; the Scots boarded immigrant vessels at Glasgow; the English and Welsh traveled by coach or rail to Liverpool and left from there; the Germans made their way to Antwerp, Bremen, or Hamburg; and the Scandinavians left first from Bergen, Christiania, or Goteborg for Liverpool, and from there sailed to America. Immigrant mortality rates in these sailing ships were extremely high. After weeks or months at sea in crowded holds, they landed in one of six places: the Maritime

TABLE 1
IMMIGRATION FROM WESTERN EUROPE, 1820–1900

	1820s	1830s	1840s	1850s	1860s	1870s	1880s	1890s	Total
England	14,055	7,611	32,092	247,125	222,277	437,706	644,680	216,726	1,822,272
Scotland	2,912	2,667	3,712	38,331	38,769	87,564	149,869	44,188	368,012
Wales	170	185	1,261	6,319	4,313	6,631	12,640	10,557	42,076
Ireland	50,724	207,381	780,719	914,119	435,778	436,871	655,482	388,416	3,869,490
Canada	2,277	13,624	41,723	59,309	153,878	383,640	393,304	3,311	1,051,066
France	8,497	45,575	77,262	76,358	35,986	72,206	50,464	30,770	397,118
Germany	6,761	152,454	434,626	951,667	787,468	718,182	1,452,970	505,152	5,009,280
Belgium	27	22	5,074	4,738	6,734	7,221	20,177	18,167	62,160
Netherlands	1,078	1,412	8,251	10,789	9,102	16,541	53,701	26,758	127,632
Switzerland	3,226	4,821	4,644	25,011	23,286	28,293	81,988	31,179	202,448
Denmark	169	1,063	539	3,749	17,094	31,771	88,132	50,231	192,748
Sweden	91	1,201	13,903	20,931	37,667	115,922	391,776	226,266	794,665
Norway					71,631	95,323	176,586	95,015	451,647
TOTAL	89,987	438,016	1,403,806	2,358,446	1,843,983	2,437,871	4,171,769	1,646,736	14,390,614

Provinces of Canada, Boston, New York, Philadelphia, Baltimore, or New Orleans. From Canada they traveled down the St. Lawrence to the Great Lakes or caught vessels to Boston; from the Atlantic ports most of them made rail, wagon, or steamboat connections to the interior; and from New Orleans they went up the Mississippi River and scattered out along its tributaries. The Chinese immigrants left from Canton, Hong Kong, and Macao, stopped over for a period in Hawaii, and sailed on to San Francisco.

Before 1890, most immigrants were white Protestants. Hardworking and literate, they scattered widely throughout the country, getting good jobs in the cities and building prosperous farms in the hinterland. Most Americans welcomed them, and they in turn welcomed the religious toleration, political liberty, and economic opportunity they found in the United States. On the other hand, the immigration of Irish, German, and French-Canadian Catholics, as well as Chinese Buddhists, tested the American commitment to pluralism. Themselves affected by dislocations of industrialization and mobility—and without the traditional moorings of a powerful central government, a state church, or extended kinship systems—millions of Americans were afraid of the Catholic influx. Rumors of papal conspiracies and priestly orgies became common, as did discrimination against Catholics. Chinese immigrants encountered similar fears. Few Americans had any idea of how to incorporate these immigrants into the society.

While the Great Migration was generating cultural controversy, the westward movement was creating disputes involving Indians and Mexicans on the frontier. German, Scandinavian, English, and Scots-Irish farmers moved into the Ohio Valley, the southeastern forests, and west of the Mississippi. In the Treaty of Paris ending the American Revolution, Britain ceded its land east of the Mississippi River, and in 1803 President Thomas Jefferson added the Louisiana Purchase. Spain sold Florida in 1819. Britain ceded all of Oregon below the forty-ninth parallel in 1846; and after the Mexican War, the Treaty of Guadalupe Hidalgo gave Texas, New Mexico, Arizona, California, Nevada, Utah, and part of Colorado and Wyoming to the United States. The American empire now stretched from ocean to ocean. Native Americans were pushed to the west and Mexicans whose ancestral homes were in the west had new difficulties. Both peoples faced the pressures of immigration of tens of thousands of whites, and eventually both lost their land. Their plight also tested the reality of freedom and equality in American life.

Finally, southern society confronted the natural rights philosophy. During the American Revolution the hypocrisy of fighting for freedom while ignoring slavery was clear, and first in New England and then throughout the North slavery was attacked. Many Southerners began defending it as a positive good that made possible an advanced stage of civilization for part of the population. There was little room for compromise, because the economic and social imperatives of slavery—the need to control a large black population in order to make use of its involuntary labor—rendered natural rights irrelevant in most planters' minds. During the Missouri debates of 1819 and 1820 regarding the status of slavery in new states, the North and South became sharply divided over the question of slavery, especially over its expansion into western territories. The Liberty party in 1840 and the Free-Soil party in 1848 campaigned to keep slavery out of the West, while Southerners in the Democratic party wanted desperately to see slavery expand. The sectional crisis deepened in the 1850s and then exploded into civil war.

Meanwhile, immigration was having significant effects in the Northeast. One indication was the emergence of clandestine fraternities. In 1849, right-wing Protestants organized the Supreme Order of the Star Spangled Banner, a secret society complete with oaths, signs, and ceremonial garb. Described as Know-Nothings because of their refusal to talk about their activities, they called for immigration restriction, strict naturalization laws, discrimination against Catholics, and exclusion of Chinese. Renaming themselves the American party in 1854, they organized politically and did spectacularly well in areas where Irish Catholic immigrants were settling, taking control of the Massachusetts state government and winning local elections throughout the Northeast. Other shifts in political loyalty occurred. Throughout the nineteenth century, poor immigrants were drawn to the Democratic party—descended from Jefferson's Republican party—because of its cultural diversity and sympathy for working people. But because of the increasing numbers of Irish Catholics in the party during the 1850s, many immigrant Protestants, especially the British and Scandinavians, began looking for a new political vehicle.

They found it when the Republican party was formed in the 1850s. By supporting tariffs, a sound currency, a national bank, and internal improvements, the Republicans won the loyalty of conservative businessmen; by condemning slavery and opposing its expansion into the western territories, they were joined by abolitionists and Free-Soilers; by tacitly supporting stricter naturalization laws to keep new immigrants from voting, they gained the support of anti-Catholic nativists who feared foreigners; and by calling for free homesteads in the West, they won the support of English, Scandinavian, Dutch, and German farmers in the Midwest. The Republican party represented everything the South feared—abolition, free soil, a national bank, protective tariffs, and internal improvements, any or all of which might create an economic alliance between the North and the West. When the Republican candidate, Abraham Lincoln, won the election of 1860, the South panicked and seceded from the Union. The Civil War had begun.

For Northerners the Civil War became a crusade against slavery, a reaffirmation of the American commitment to equality and toleration. The Emancipation Proclamation of 1863, the Thirteenth, Fourteenth, and Fifteenth amendments to the Constitution, and the Civil Rights Act of 1866 all extended political rights to African Americans. Cultural pluralism and the natural rights philosophy were sounding again, this time in a much broader context. Politics and society did not yet reflect those ideals: anti-Catholicism would rise again; Native Americans and Mexican Americans were losing their land; the Chinese were about to be excluded permanently from the United States; and with the end of Reconstruction in 1876, African Americans were consigned to a social and economic lower class for years to come. Still, American values had survived controversy and the most terrible war the world had ever seen. They were durable enough to remain a hope, if not yet an all-embracing actuality.

Chapter One

The First Americans

Although small bands of Europeans or Asians may have crossed the oceans to the Americas, most native Americans, scholars argue, descended from Siberian hunters who migrated to North America many thousands of years ago. Between 40,000 and 32,000 B.C.E., the onset of the Ice Age created huge glaciers that froze up millions of cubic miles of ocean water, dropping the worldwide sea level by hundreds of feet. The shallow ocean floor of the Bering Sea surfaced, leaving a land bridge (called Beringia) more than a thousand miles wide connecting eastern Asia with Alaska. Vegetation grew on what had once been the ocean floor, and animals from Siberia and Alaska slowly occupied the new land. Nomadic Siberian hunters followed the big game, and each season their villages moved farther east until, thousands of years later, after several shorter "ice ages," the migration was complete. "Siberians" became "Americans."

For the next fifteen thousand years native American hunters spread across the Western Hemisphere, from the Arctic Circle to the tip of South America, and from the Pacific to the Atlantic. Separate bands split repeatedly from one another, and as people in different regions adapted to the land and the varying climates, their ways of organizing life and looking at the world proliferated into hundreds of different cultures. Some tribes remained nomadic, dependent on the natural environment, while others learned to grow their own food and liberated themselves from the need to search for it constantly. This agricultural revolution led to more sedentary lifestyles, increases in food production and population, social and religious development, and more complex divisions of labor based on sex and status. Some of the agricultural communities developed elaborate social, economic, and political systems.

On the Eve of Colonization

Throughout United States history white people have stereotyped native Americans as "Noble Red Men," innocent children of nature, or fierce bloodthirsty savages. But in fact, when European settlers first came to the New World, the native American communities had advanced far beyond their Siberian ancestors. Native American societies in 1500 c.e. ranged from the primitive foraging tribes of southern California to the advanced Aztec and Inca civilizations of Mexico and Peru. Although some historians and anthropologists believe the land may have supported several million people, most agree that on the eve of colonization there were probably one to two million Indians living in what is now the United States. They were divided into more than six hundred separate groups speaking more than two hundred languages, and occupied seven major regions: the northeastern woodlands, the southeastern forests, the Great Plains, the Great Basin, the northern plateau, the southwestern desert, and the Pacific coast.

The nations of the Northeast lived between the Mississippi River and the Atlantic coast, north of the Carolinas and the Ohio River Valley. In New England they included the Penobscots, Pennacooks, Pequots, Narragansetts, Mohegans, Massachusetts, and Wampanoags. In the Hudson River Valley the Five Nations of the Iroquois Confederacy—composed of the Mohawks, Oneidas, Onondagas, Cayugas, Senecas, and later the Tuscaroras—reigned supreme. And between the Great Lakes and the Ohio River were the Eries, Conestogas, Sauk and Fox, Ottawas, Kickapoos, Shawnees, Chippewas, Peorias, Menominees, and Miamis. Except for the buffalo hunters of the Illinois plains and the nomadic foragers of the far north, they lived in settled agricultural villages and cultivated corn, squash, and beans in communal gardens. They lived in wigwams or bark houses separated by streets and surrounded by protective stockades, and they hunted game for both food and clothing. Except for the highly centralized Iroquois Confederacy of New York and the Algonquian-based Illinois Confederacy, each nation was independent.

The southeastern nation lived between the Mississippi River and the Atlantic coast and south of the Ohio River Valley. They included the

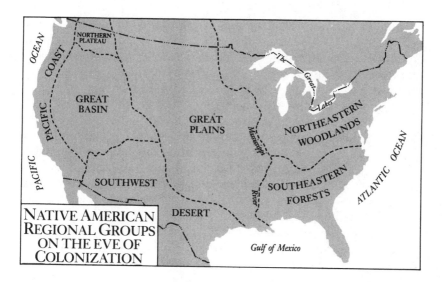

NATIVE AMERICAN REGIONAL GROUPS ON THE EVE OF COLONIZATION

Cherokees of North Carolina and Tennessee; the Seminoles, Timucuas, and Calusas of Florida; and the Choctaws, Chickasaws, Creeks, and Alabamas on the Gulf Coast. Most were sedentary farmers who raised corn, beans, and tobacco; hunted small game; and gathered nuts, seeds, and wild rice. They lived in farming towns of mud-plaster homes.

A different native American society emerged on the arid short-grass plains of what are now the Dakotas, Montana, Wyoming, eastern Colorado, western Kansas, Oklahoma, and the Texas panhandle. The Blackfeet, Dakotas, Sioux, Crows, Cheyennes, Arapahos, Comanches, Pawnees, and Kiowas were nomadic hunters whose social and economic life revolved around the buffalo herds. Bearing their portable tepees, they were constantly on the move. The buffalo provided them with meat, which they ate fresh or dried. Buffalo skins gave them their blankets, moccasins, clothes, and covering for their homes. Buffalo hair and tendons became thread and string for their bows. The buffalo stomach became a water bottle. Buffalo horns were used as cups and spoons. The hunters even turned the buffalo tongue into a hair brush and buffalo fat into hair oil. The sixteenth-century acquisition of the horse from the Spaniards vastly increased their range, improved the success of their hunts, and reinforced their nomadism.

For the Indians who lived in the Great Basin, the area between the Rocky Mountains and the Sierra Nevadas that includes present-day Utah, Nevada, southern Idaho, eastern Oregon, and eastern California, life was primitive. Water was precious, agriculture difficult, and the people extremely poor. Roving bands of Utes, Paiutes, Gosiutes,

Monos, Panamints, Paviotsos, and Shoshones populated the region. With little agriculture there were no permanent villages, and small groups of extended families subsisted on small game, berries, roots, nuts, seeds, and insects. Here survival was problematical and prosperity unknown.

The plateau Indians—Flatheads, Spokanes, Yakimas, Nez Percés, Wallawallas, Chinooks, Modocs, and Klamaths—lived between the Rockies and the Cascade Mountains. The heavily wooded mountains and high plains of western Montana, Idaho, and eastern Washington were a generally nonagricultural environment. Most tribes hunted for small game, gathered berries and roots, and fished for the giant salmon. Relatively poor and politically decentralized, they lived in semipermanent villages along the major salmon rivers and streams.

Two cultures developed in the Southwest. One was the Navajo, which rose to power at the "four corners" junction of Utah, Arizona, New Mexico, and Colorado; the other, the Apache, was dominant in southeastern Arizona and southwestern New Mexico. Both were fierce, nomadic hunters who often raided neighboring settlements. They lived in tepees when moving through open country and in brush shelters in the mountains.

The second southwestern culture comprised the sedentary, even urban societies of the Hopi, Zuñi, and Pueblo of Arizona and New Mexico. Despite dry weather they raised corn, squash, and beans. They also domesticated poultry, sheep, and cattle; wove cloth; and into rocky hillsides built towns of multistoried adobe dwellings. Labor was specialized, social structure complex, and the culture as sophisticated as any in the United States.

Two more groups appeared on the Pacific coast. In southern California more than a hundred tribes—including the Yuroks, Salinas, Athapascans, Miwoks, and Chumosh—lived in nomadic villages and gathered acorns, seeds, shellfish, roots, and berries. Most were excellent artisans. In northern California, Oregon, and Washington another coastal culture included the Chinooks, Umpquas, Coos, and Tolowas. Though these groups were nonagricultural, an abundant supply of fish and game permitted the development of stable communities. They built gable-roofed plank homes and, unlike most other Indians, believed in private property.

Native American cultures had enormous variety. While the Plains Indians wore buffalo skins and the Basin Indians not much at all, the Pueblos were highly skilled weavers of blankets and clothing. The Plains and California Indians were nomadic, but the Iroquois and the Zuñis lived in permanent, settled communities. Most northeastern, southeastern, and southwestern tribes raised corn and squash, while other tribes were hunters or gatherers. The Utes lived in primitive lean-tos and the Pueblos in multistoried buildings. Some Indians worshiped the "Master of Life"; others paid homage to ancestors, animal spirits, or the elements. Thus when the European settlers arrived, there were already hundreds of different ethnic groups in America.

Native Americans and Europeans: The Cultural Confrontation

The misunderstanding and persistent friction between New World natives and Old World immigrants grew out of competitive, mutually exclusive perspectives. White settlers mainly wanted to make a better living for themselves; they intended to use the wilderness, to convert nature into property, status, and security. The land was not sacred to them, and the earth had no transcendent meaning. But for native Americans the environment was holy, possessing a cosmic significance more important than its material riches. They viewed the earth as a gift of the gods that had to be protected and worshiped. Consequently the Indians lived in a symbiotic relationship with the environment, using resources without exhausting them. Chief Smohalla of the Wanapum tribe expressed this view of the environment when he said:

> God . . . commanded that the lands and fisheries should be common to all who lived upon them; that they were never to be marked off or divided, but that the people should enjoy the fruits that God planted in the land, and the animals that lived upon it, and the fishes in the water. God said he was the father and earth was the mother of mankind; that nature was the law; that the animals, and fish, and plants obeyed nature, and that man only was sinful.
>
> You ask me to plow the ground! Shall I take a knife and tear my mother's bosom? Then when I die she will not take me to her bosom to rest.
>
> You ask me to dig for stone! Shall I dig under her skin for her bones? Then when I die I cannot enter her body to be born again.
>
> You ask me to cut grass and make hay and sell it, and be rich like white men! But how dare I cut off my mother's hair?*

The use and ownership of land was the source of the most important environmental conflict between native Americans and Europeans. Impatient with native American economic values, whites considered Indian land-use methods inefficient, incapable of getting the most out of the soil. That fact alone, some believed, justified taking the land— peacefully if possible, but violently if necessary.

*Fourteenth Annual Report of the Bureau of American Ethnology (1896), pt. 2, p. 721.

In addition, the idea of private property was alien to most Indians; giving one person exclusive, perpetual control of land was as inconceivable to them as giving one person the air or sky. The Reverend John Heckewelder, a Moravian minister, complained about an Indian's horses eating grass on his land. The Indian said:.

> My friend, it seems you lay claim to the grass my horses have eaten, because you had enclosed it with a fence: now tell me, who caused the grass to grow? Can you make the grass grow? I think not, and nobody can except the great Manni-to. He it is who causes it to grow both for my horses and for yours! See, friend! The grass which grows out of the earth is common to all; the game in the woods is common to all. Say, did you never eat venison and bear's meat?. . . . Well, and did you ever hear me or any other Indian complain about that? . . . Besides, if you will but consider, you will find that my horse did not eat all your grass. †

This view was inconceivable to most of the settlers, and they began almost at once to displace the Indians, pushing them toward the vacant land of the West.

The ethnocentrism of the Europeans also guaranteed conflict with native Americans. Convinced of their own religious and moral superiority, the Europeans approached native Americans from two different but equally destructive social perspectives. Some looked on the Indians as savages requiring no more ethical consideration than the beasts of the field. By denying Indian humanity and creating negative stereotypes they could rationalize the economic and military assaults on native American society. But other Europeans accepted the humanity, if not the cultural equality, of the Indians. Instead of annihilating them, these colonists wanted to transform native Americans into settled farmers who believed in private property and Christianity. Though more humane than the other point of view, this missionary impulse proved equally detrimental to native American society.

There were, of course, exceptions to the rule. In 1635, Roger Williams enraged the civil magistrates of Massachusetts by denying their Puritan authority and accusing them of violating native American rights. Insisting that the Indians owned the land and could keep or dispose of it at will, Williams went against the grain of European opinion, and the Boston magistrates expelled him from Massachusetts. A half-century later, in Pennsylvania, the Quakers tried to pursue an even-handed policy toward native Americans. A persecuted people dedicated to nonviolence and the belief that all men and women were children

† John Heckewelder, *Account of the History, Manners, and Customs of the Indian Nations, Who once Inhabited Pennsylvania and the Neighboring States* (Philadelphia, 1819), p. 86.

This sketch of an Indian village in North Carolina, drawn by John White in 1590, reveals the complexity of native American society. (The Granger Collection)

of God, the Quakers wanted a colony in which everyone could live in harmony. They respected the Delaware Indians' right to the land and purchased it from them only after the most careful negotiations. Word spread, and in the 1690s and early 1700s the Tuscaroras, Shawnees, and Miamis all migrated to Pennsylvania. But as Scots-Irish Presbyterians, German Lutherans, and English Protestants pushed west and squatted on Indian land, traditional views triumphed in all the colonies.

Indian Resistance

Although the first years of colonial life were peaceful, the tranquility was short-lived. As soon as the Indians realized that more and more colonists would come to take more land, they began to resist. For years the Algonquain-speaking nations of Virginia and North Carolina, linked together in a loose alliance under the leadership of Powhatan, had assisted the Jamestown settlers. Important cultural exchanges took place from the very beginning of the Chesapeake colonies. While Europeans excelled in transportation and the use of iron for tools and weapons, the Indians were far more advanced in regional geographic knowledge and economic adjustment to the land. Members of the Powhatan nation were quick to make use of English kettles, traps, fishhooks, needles, and guns, and they passed on to the English their knowledge of fishing, of raising tobacco, corn, beans, squash, rice, and pumpkins, and of using herbs and dyes.

In 1622, the peace was shattered. Powhatan had died in 1618, and a more aggressive relative, Opechancanough, had replaced him. During the next few years, as tobacco production became more profitable, the white population increased. Political relations changed dramatically. Feeling the enormous pressures of white civilization, the Indians began to fear it. On March 22, 1622, they attacked colonial settlements throughout Virginia, killing 347 people and destroying dozens of villages. More than a third of the white settlers died. Throughout 1622 and 1623, the English settlers pursued the Indians relentlessly, crushed the Powhatan Confederacy, and annihilated most of the native Americans who had participated in the uprising. Rather than trying to assimilate the remaining peaceful Indians, the colonists imposed a scorched-earth policy. Arbitrary treaties and forced land sales removed the Indians still living in the eastern counties.

Sporadic conflicts erupted throughout the next few decades, most notably in 1644, when Opechancanough himself rebelled, but Virginia would never again be threatened with extinction. After Opechancanough's rebellion the Virginians dealt with the Indians differently.

Tired of wars and of native American resistance to English culture, the Virginians "reserved" land north of the York River as a permanent Indian homeland. For the next thirty years the reservation policy worked, and the two peoples even established a valuable fur trade. But it was only a temporary expedient. As the white population increased, pressure to open up the reservation land to settlement became increasingly strong. Convinced that the reservation policy was the only way to guarantee peace, Virginia Governor William Berkeley refused, but white settlers moved north anyway. Nathaniel Bacon, an English-born member of the colonial council, demanded the opening of reservation lands, greater militia protection for western settlers, and wars of extermination against the Indians. When Berkeley still refused, Bacon took matters into his own hands in 1676. Marching against Jamestown, his supporters slaughtered peaceful Indians along the way and burned the colony's leading settlement. Bacon's Rebellion was over by 1677, and so was Indian resistance in Virginia. Divided politically and vastly outnumbered by Europeans, native Americans were weakened militarily; and by 1680, with a thousand Indians left out of an original population of more than thirty thousand, the clash of cultures was over in Virginia.

In New England the pattern of European land pressure, tribal rivalries, and ethnic conflict was repeated. With a proud sense of mission the Puritans had set out to build the kingdom of God in the New World. Squanto, a Pawtuxet Indian, had helped the Pilgrims in 1620, and for a few years the hatred of the Narragansetts, Wampanoags, and Pequots for one another prevented Indian resistance. When a smallpox epidemic wiped out thousands of native Americans in 1633 and 1634, the Puritans interpreted it as an act of God, proof that Christianity would triumph in the New World. But the Pequots were not convinced. They had moved into southern New England late in the 1500s, and ever since the founding of Massachusetts and Connecticut, they had worried about Puritan expansion. Occasional acts of mutual brutality occurred between 1631 and 1636; but in 1637, when the Pequots allegedly killed several whites in Connecticut, the colonists retaliated with a vengeance. It was a bloody affair. Puritan armies drove to Long Island Sound, shooting and burning more than six hundred Pequots. By 1638 the Pequots were nearly destroyed.

Some forty years later New England experienced one of the most savage racial conflicts in American history. Born in 1616 near what is now Warren, Rhode Island, King Philip became chief of the Wampanoags in 1662. Resentful of white settlements, violations of land titles, and assaults on individual native Americans, he attacked on July 4, 1675. Joined by the Narragansetts, Nipmucs, and Penobscots, the Wampanoags eventually destroyed twenty New England towns and

Edward Hicks' painting of William Penn's treaty with the Indians illustrates the careful, magnanimous approach the Quakers adopted in their relations with native Americans. (The Granger Collection)

killed more than three thousand people. It was only a temporary victory, however, for in the battle of Great Swamp in December 1675, Philip saw a thousand of his warriors die. He too was killed late in 1676. By 1678 a colonial army had cleared southern New England of Indians, opening the area to white settlers.

In the South the conflict continued. Along the coastal plains of North Carolina, the Tuscaroras had lived peacefully for years, raising hemp, corn, and orchard fruits; but despairing of white encroachment on their land, they killed 130 colonists in 1711. Exploited in the fur trade and frightened of white immigration, they joined the Creeks, Catawbas, Appalachees, and Santees and killed more than four hundred colonists. Not until the Cherokees joined the whites in 1716 did the rebellion end. The Yamasees and Creeks retreated into the wilderness.

Tension between Indians and whites was intensified by Anglo-French rivalry. Both France and England wanted the Ohio Valley, and the Indians were caught in the middle. Except for the Iroquois, most Indians were loyal to the French because the French did not pose quite the threat of the English. French settlements in Canada were not nearly as large as the English colonies; and because the French were more interested in trade and commerce than in agriculture, they did not usually push the Indians off their land. The centralized authority of the Roman Catholic Church and its interest in converting Indians guaranteed more humane treatment than that generally provided by English Protestants. It was only natural for the Indians to cast their lot with the French.

During the eighteenth century the French and the English fought four colonial wars in North America: King William's War (1689–1697), Queen Anne's War (1702–1713), King George's War (1740–1748), and the French and Indian War (1754–1763). In each case the English and most of the Iroquois fought the French and other northeastern nations. Not until 1763 did the French admit defeat and cede Canada. The Iroquois reaped the prestige and spoils of victory, but thousands of English, Scots-Irish, and German settlers began pouring across the Appalachians to take land from defeated "French-loving" Indians. Settlement pressures and unscrupulous land speculators angered the Indians, especially Pontiac, chief of the Ottawas. In 1763, he led the Ottawas, Delawares, Miamis, Kickapoos, and Shawnees against white settlements in the Ohio Valley. To mollify Pontiac and relieve the pressure on the western nations, the British Parliament issued the Proclamation of 1763, prohibiting further white settlement in the region. After three more years of fighting, Pontiac signed a peace treaty with England. Except for some nations in upstate New York and along the Gulf Coast, most of the Indians had been pushed from the Eastern Seaboard. Between 1766 and 1776 Indian relations improved with the British government and deteriorated with the colonists, and during the American Revolution most Indians would consider England their ally, again joining the loser in an international conflict.

The Indians had resisted the colonists almost from the beginning, but their resistance was doomed to failure. For one reason, the European population dwarfed them. Except for the first half of the seventeenth century, the Indians were always outnumbered. They might win some battles but they could never win the wars. Worse, they had no immunity to European diseases. Smallpox, influenza, scarlet fever, whooping cough, and diphtheria decimated Indian communities. Between 1607 and 1776, the European and African population in the British colonies grew to about 2.5 million people while the Indian population dropped to about 600,000. Even when Indians had temporary superiority in numbers, intertribal rivalries—often exploited by the colonists—prevented the formation of effective, long-lasting confederacies. Finally, the westward shift of the white economy destroyed the Indians' habitat and upset the ecological balance of their communities. As the white population increased, the small game disappeared, the buffalo herds were slaughtered, and the land itself was denied them.

In spite of all this, native Americans continued to resist European civilization in many ways, and the presence of whites never resulted in acculturation. Historians and pulp writers have immortalized resistance, and in the colonial period the Powhatan tribal uprisings of 1622 and 1644, the Pequot War of 1637, King Philip's War of 1675, the Tuscarora War of 1711–1712, the Yamassee War of 1715, and Pontiac's Rebellion of 1763 symbolize the Indian refusal to accept white encroachments passively. Some nations remained as cultural islands in the colonial society, usually confined to reservations; but even there, where white missionaries had unfettered opportunities to Europeanize the native Americans, they clung tenaciously to their own culture.

Chapter Two

The European Migration

The Colonial Period

The Europeans who moved to the New World were a special people, courageous enough to face an unknown wilderness, restless enough to leave the ties of home, and confident enough to believe they could succeed in such a daring enterprise. Some left Europe to escape poverty or persecution, others to save souls or reform the world. Most came to America to plant the Kingdom of God and build a better life. In 1624, the Dutch established a trading post on the Hudson River in New York. Spanish and Portuguese Jews, Belgian Protestants, Puritans from Massachusetts, French Huguenots, and Africans all lived in New Amsterdam before the English took over in 1664. The Swedish West India Company deposited Finns and Swedes along the Delaware River in 1638. New Sweden was annexed by New Netherland in 1655. Early America was a polyglot society, but for all this diversity, three groups dominated the early migrations: English, German, and Scots and Scots-Irish settlers came in such large numbers that by 1776 they were the most visible and influential people in the thirteen colonies.

The English were the most numerous of the colonial contingent. Since the early Middle Ages, English economic life had been remarkably stable, but the rise of a money economy and inflation created new social problems. Landlords increased rents to compensate for higher prices; and because commodity prices were not keeping pace with those of manufactured goods, tenant farmers were squeezed between their incomes and costs. At the same time, the Commercial Revolution created a class of business entrepreneurs looking for profits. Highly successful in textiles, banking, and foreign trade, they anxiously sought new investments and were willing to assume great risks. Their pursuit of wealth, along with the desires of more humble people for a better life, created a fascination with colonization. If the lower and middle classes were willing to settle abroad, the merchant capitalists would finance them.

England was also the scene of intense religious debate in the seventeenth century. Ever since the 1530s, when Henry VIII rejected Roman Catholicism, the Church of England had been a powerful institution. England was a spiritual battleground. Roman Catholics balked at Henry's break with Rome, and the Quakers rejected political, social, and religious authority. They believed that all human beings were equal and that by discovering the "Inner Light" to God, they could find their way to heaven, with or without an institutional church. Zealous Anglicans persecuted both groups, and many Catholics and Quakers looked to America as an escape. Puritanism was another powerful force. Committed to cleansing the social order of evil and corruption, they rejected the hierarchical structure of the Church of England, repudiated free will for predestination, and believed in the inherent evil of human nature. Eventually some Puritans decided that England was not ripe for purification and that perhaps in America a perfect community could be realized.

The Puritans began settling Massachusetts when a small band of Separatists colonized Plymouth in 1620. The Great Migration began with the settlement of Boston in 1629. Eventually the Puritans dominated cultural life in Rhode Island, Massachusetts, Connecticut, and New Hampshire. The Roman Catholic outpost in the New World was Maryland, where George Calvert, Lord Baltimore, established a colony in 1633 for his persecuted brothers and sisters. Anglicans poured into all thirteen colonies, but they were especially concentrated in New York and along the southern coast of Virginia, North Carolina, South Carolina, and Georgia. Finally, under the leadership of William Penn, Quaker settlers colonized the Middle Colonies—New Jersey, Delaware, and Pennsylvania.

In spite of their religious differences, the English colonists shared a common perspective. They were flexible and innovative, able to look beyond tradition and custom. America's characteristic pragmatism originated with them. In England they had accepted a rigid class structure as the natural order of things, but America undermined it. It was more easily undermined because the one social class that did not join the great migration was English nobility. Well-to-do landowners, political officials, merchants, and clergymen in America had risen from humble circumstances; their ties to the yeomanry were fresh. The upper class was fluid, and poor people hoped to enter it themselves.

A belief in progress reinforced their expectations. Many came as indentured servants. Because of labor shortages, large landowners and merchants recruited workers by advertising the great opportunities of life in America. Prospective colonists agreed to work a certain number of years in return for passage to America, room and board, and severance pay after fulfilling their contract. Since land was easy to acquire, most ended up as independent farmers, a status that would have been impossible for them in England. The middle class was always expanding and the servant class constantly changing as newer immigrants replaced liberated indenturers. Membership in the lower class seemed a temporary station. Faith in upward mobility became part of the national ideology. By the time of the American Revolution, there were 1.2 million people of English descent in the thirteen colonies.

The second European contingent in colonial America was the Germans. William Penn invited German pietists—Quakers, Moravians, Mennonites, and Dunkers—to settle in Pennsylvania, where he promised cheap land and religious freedom. Several thousand German Quakers settled in Pennsylvania in the 1680s and 1690s; and early in the 1700s, when news of Pennsylvania's rich soil spread across the continent, thousands of German Lutherans and Reformed settlers made the journey. By 1776, there were nearly 250,000 people of German descent in Pennsylvania and New Jersey and scattered through western Maryland, Virginia, North Carolina, South Carolina, Georgia, and upstate New York.

The Germans became a prosperous people. To this day southeastern Pennsylvania is known as Dutch Country, as *Deutsch* was their language and *Deutschland* their home. With large barns, neat houses, clean yards, flower gardens, well-built fences, and fine cattle, German farms were models of thrift and profit. Feudal obligations in Germany, often requiring peasants to work several days each week for the landlord, pressed hard on small farmers, and to support their families they extracted everything the land could yield. It was no wonder they worked hard. In America, with fine land and no landlords, they made their farms the most productive in the New World. And because of their desire to be self-reliant, they preferred subsistence, self-supporting farming over the large commercial farms or plantations of the English and Scots-Irish, which were dependent on export markets.

The Germans settled in groups, kept to themselves, and did not assimilate easily. Because their homeland was divided into separate principalities, they lacked a national perspective, and their political loyalties remained locally oriented. Years of war had left them wary of strangers, and the petty princes of Germany had made them suspicious of politicians. The English saw them as reluctant to associate with non-Germans, remaining loyal to their language, churches, and communities. German immigration was not entirely welcome among the English majority. Germans constituted one-third of the Pennsylvania population by 1776, and even Benjamin Franklin was afraid German customs might triumph there. In 1753, he remarked:

> Why should the Palatine Boors be suffered to swarm into our settlements, and by herding together, establish their language and manners, to the exclusion of ours? Why should Pennsylvania, founded by the English, become a colony of Aliens, who will shortly be so numerous as to Germanize us instead of our Anglifying them . . . ?

English colonists required the Germans to take loyalty oaths, and during the colonial wars suspected them, erroneously, of being pro-French. For the most part, however, the two groups kept their distance.

The third major group of colonial immigrants was the Scots-Irish. Nearly 300,000 of them left northern Ireland for the colonies in the 1700s. For centuries England tried to subdue Ireland, but the Irish resisted. When James I assumed the throne in 1603, he invited the Scottish Lowlanders to settle in Ulster, promising them low rents, long leases, and religious toleration. They jumped at the chance. Between 1610 and 1640, more than 40,000 Lowland Scots crossed the Irish Sea to colonize Ulster. Other Lowlanders emigrated after 1660. The Scots were Presbyterians who embraced the Calvinist belief in God's decision to redeem a few and damn everyone else. They objected to regal ceremonies, clerical elitism, and hierarchical church governments. When they arrived in Ulster, they took out their religious frustrations on the native Irish Catholics. By 1650, more than 600,000 people were dead, most of them Catholics, and in the process the English and Scots almost destroyed the Irish political and social order.

The Scots learned to drain the marshes, and by planting American potatoes they increased agricultural production enormously. Throughout the meadows of northern Ireland the Scots grazed sheep and built a prosperous textile industry. Dairy farms and cattle ranches flourished. Presbyterian ministers came with the settlers, and by 1680 the Lowlanders had built a new life for themselves. But as the Ulster economy matured, it competed with vested interests in England. Alarmed about shrinking markets and falling prices, English merchants and landowners persuaded Parliament in the 1690s to close England to Irish cattle and dairy products. English textile manufacturers lobbied for the Woolens Act, which eliminated foreign markets for Irish cloth by restricting exports to the British Isles. The textile industry in Ulster collapsed.

More hardships were in store. Throughout the eighteenth century, famines plagued Irish and Scots-Irish farmers alike; in the winter of 1740–1741 nearly 500,000 people starved to death. To recoup their losses, Anglican landlords broke Scottish land leases and raised rents. Tithes on the land, already offensive because they were destined for the Church of England, rose with the rents. Persecution made matters worse. The Test Act of 1673 required Presbyterians to pledge allegiance to the Church of England as a prerequisite for holding civil and military positions, teaching school, or attending college. Presbyterians were denied access to power and influence in English society. And during the reign of Queen Anne, in the early eighteenth century, the Anglican Church enforced religious conformity. English officials refused to recognize Presbyterian marriages, and couples were often prosecuted for "living in sin" even though they had been married for years. The Scots-Irish were outraged.

As in Germany, a contingent of ships' captains and real estate agents visited Ulster to promote emigration. The troubled Scots-Irish were ready listeners. If they could not pay their own way to America, the agents sent them as indentured servants. To farm tenants, the prospect of land ownership was irresistible. The exodus began in 1717. Most disembarked in Philadelphia, where free farmers headed west while indentured servants remained behind to fill their contracts. The price of land in southeastern Pennsylvania soon pushed them into Maryland, Virginia, and the Carolinas. By 1730 the Cumberland and Shenandoah Valleys were filling with Scots-Irish, and between 1730 and 1760 the Carolinas' population doubled as colonists moved east from the mountains to settle the Piedmont.

By 1776, the southern colonies were divided between the English settlements in the east and the Scots-Irish and German communities in the west. The Scots-Irish settled in separate communities, usually on the frontier, where they established their customs without resistance. Normal social intercourse between the Scots-Irish and the English did not often occur. That was fortunate. The Scots-Irish remembered Ulster and the Lowlands and had little affection for the English or their American cousins. And they were militantly Presbyterian. Wars against Ulster Catholics and Anglican discrimination against Presbyterians had only reinforced their religious commitment. Had they settled among Anglicans in the eastern cities rather than in the wilderness, there might have been more trouble between them.

Assimilation was retarded in colonial America because of language barriers, cultural diversity, and geographical segregation, but there were common bonds. For most colonists the journey to the New World was a one-way trip; they would never go home again. Continued immigration infused the old culture with new vigor, but loyalty to the Old World slowly decayed. The passage of time and the birth of native generations weakened emotional ties to Europe. For English, German, or Scots-Irish descendants, the New World was home.

Economic reality gave them a common perspective as well. Most Americans became small farmers with considerable independence of the ruling gentry. They owned land and enjoyed the security that accompanies property. Accepting what would later be called the Jeffersonian ideology of a nation of farmers and artisans, they saw themselves in democratic terms. Regardless of national origins, they were part of the middle class and shared an economic community of interest that often transcended ethnic differences, exerting similar effects on all the members of a class. The new Americans sensed a common destiny.

Finally, racial conflict and foreign enemies unified them. In the South all whites shared a racial unity transcending cultural differences, even though the English and Scots-Irish were much more willing to own slaves than were the Germans. Throughout the colonies, especially on the frontier, fear of Indians brought Europeans together. So did the Spanish presence in Florida and the French presence in Canada. In particular, the French and Indian War and the American Revolution united many colonists. The English-American community was deeply divided, but Germans and Scots-Irish supported the revolutionary cause. Germans harbored intense antiroyal sentiments and sympathized with colonial complaints about tyranny. Scots-Irish hatred of England was so intense that some British thought the American Revolution was essentially a Presbyterian rebellion. In every colony, and in virtually every engagement from Saratoga in 1777 to Yorktown in 1781, the Scots were the backbone of the revolutionary forces. An anonymous New England Tory described the Scots-Irish as the "most God-provoking democrats on this side of hell." The Revolution gave the three largest groups of European Americans a common cause.

British Protestants

The migration of British Protestants continued unabated after the American Revolution. The British Isles sent the largest number of immigrants to the United States. Between 1783 and 1924 more than eight million people emigrated from England, Scotland, Wales, and Ireland. More than two million British Canadians crossed the border.

The British Protestants rapidly adjusted to American society. British immigrants had, after all, peopled colonial America, and their religious values, cultural attitudes, and political institutions were the foundation of American society. Indeed, their beliefs in decentralized religious authority, individual liberty, hard work, and the dangers of concentrated power all had a place in the American political culture.

The English, Welsh, and Scots immigrants were not fleeing repression at home but were seeking their fortunes in America. Some of the Welsh and Highland Scots were poor, but most British Protestants decided that opportunities for economic success were too limited at home. Most brought money with them to America; they expected the return on their capital to be higher in the United States. By 1830 Great Britain was the most advanced industrial nation in the world, and most immigrants were skilled workers. When the Industrial Revolution reached America, the traditional labor shortage became even more acute. Demand for skilled workers produced high wages, and skilled immigrants found work in their own crafts. Unlike most immigrants, whose residence determined occupation, British Protestants settled where their skills could best be employed.

The British immigrants were readily accepted into American society. They were better off than other immigrants because they shared so much with the host society. In 1820, people of Anglo descent were the largest group in the society, and most Americans felt comfortable with them. Most of these immigrants were literate, and their command of the language enhanced acculturation. Yankee Americans respected their technical abilities, willingness to work hard, and commitment to success. Most of them joined Methodist, Baptist, Presbyterian, Congregational, or Episcopalian churches. Not surprisingly, their absorption into the larger society was rapid. Language and industrial skills helped them get good jobs and supervisory positions while other immigrants often spent years at the bottom of the occupational ladder. English families were often smaller than those of other groups; with fewer children to support, parents were more likely to save money, enjoy material security, and promote education. People admired England, despite the bitter feelings aroused by the American Revolution and the War of 1812. Its industrial wealth was the envy of other nations and its Parliament a beacon for the oppressed. Americans looked to England for models of municipal and industrial reform. In short, the United States functioned in a cultural framework that was largely British, and the immigrants prospered because of that special relationship.

They settled widely throughout the country and were more evenly distributed than any other group. Half of the English immigrants married within their group, but only one in six of the second generation did. They were already at home with other Americans through their

In this cartoon, entitled "The Lure of American Wages," John Bull, symbolic of Great Britain, tries to restrain people from going to America while Uncle Sam, across the sea, invites them to immigrate. (The Granger Collection)

relationships at work and school. Intermarriage completed the transition. It took somewhat longer for the Highland Scots and Welsh, who spoke Gaelic dialects, but it occurred relatively quickly nonetheless. Intermarriage with other European Protestants did not immediately destroy ethnicity, but after several generations the vast majority of people of British descent came to define themselves simply as Americans or as Americans with a regional (e.g., Yankee, Southerner) or religious focus.

The Irish

The Irish were the great exception to the Protestant migration. They had long been fighting British imperialism, and that struggle had assumed political and religious dimensions. In Ireland, after centuries of Anglo-Protestant persecution, religion and nationality fused. Indeed, the Gaelic word *Sassenach* meant both "Protestant" and "English." The attempt to anglicize Ireland created a dualism in Irish life: a deep, personal reverence for Roman Catholicism and a proud consciousness of Irish nationality. Members of the Irish Catholic clergy, like most of their parishioners, were poor, landless, and politically impotent. A siege mentality possessed both priests and peasants, and the Irish identified with the church as the central institution of their lives.

Savage economic problems also afflicted Ireland and precipitated the migration of four million Irish to the United States in the nineteenth century. During the Napoleonic Wars, European wheat production declined and prices rose, so Irish landlords put more land into wheat and raised the rents of Catholic tenants. When peace returned and European farming revived, prices collapsed and peasants were hard pressed to pay the higher rents. With grain prices plummeting, landlords turned most acreage back to pasture in hope of recouping their losses by raising sheep. They evicted Catholic peasants by the thousands, and between 1815 and 1825 more than 100,000 of them came to America. Then came the Great Famine. Potatoes had long been the dietary staple because they flourished in poor soil and yielded enough per acre to feed a family. But they were also a risky crop because yield fluctuations could mean life or death for millions. Crop failures occurred in 1817, 1822, and the 1830s, but a fungus destroyed the entire crop in 1845. The blight continued in 1846 and 1847, bringing starvation to a million people. For many survivors, American seemed the only option.

The Irish immigrants were unique. Most of them had little money and few skills, and even the more prosperous had only enough money to sustain them for a matter of weeks. The migration consisted of small peasant farmers whose only economic skills were primitive methods of raising potatoes and oats. Despite their poverty, the Irish possessed an ethnic culture that served them well in the United States. Theirs was a communal, "chain" migration in which the transplanting of Irish villages from the Old World to the New made for an ethnic solidarity unknown among most other immigrants. Because of the English elementary school program, probably half of the Irish immigrants were literate and most spoke English; and because of their political struggles against England, they were conditioned to Anglo politics and direct action. The Irish immigrants were a highly politicized people.

In many ways America intensified those feelings. American culture had a distinctly Anglo-Protestant flavor. There were no tax-supported Protestant churches in the country, but Yankees controlled wealth and power. In New England many Americans thought the Irish threatened Anglo-Saxon civilization. Irish immigration coincided with the democratic worship of the common man popular during the era of President Andrew Jackson, and Roman Catholicism seemed contradictory because it gave authoritarian power to the pope. Some Yankees questioned Irish allegiance, doubting that they could become "true

Americans" because dual loyalty to a religious monarchy and a liberal democracy seemed impossible. Also present in most northeastern cities was a small but vocal minority of Anglo-Irish Protestant immigrants, descendants of the English settlers who had colonized Ireland in the sixteenth and seventeenth centuries. Known as Orangemen, they were usually Episcopalians and Methodists after settling in America. Militantly anti-Catholic and anti-Democratic, they identified closely with Anglo-American Protestants. The immigrants transplanted their Old World rivalries to America. Conflicts between Anglo-Irish and Irish Catholic volunteer fire companies were frequent in Boston, New York, and Philadelphia; in 1870 and 1871, ethnic competition often erupted into open violence.

The Irish journey out of poverty was based on the family, urban politics, hard work, and a powerful sense of group identity. These characteristics sustained them in the early years. Poor and unaccustomed to urban life, the Irish suffered in the ghettos. Old mansions, stores, and warehouses were converted into crowded tenements, and many Irish lived in lean-tos and shacks made of tar paper or wooden crates. Raw sewage often flowed down the streets, and there was a constant battle against rats and lice, and cholera and tuberculosis were common. Most jobs paid poorly, and many of the poor turned to crime and prostitution.

One unique element of the Irish migration was the number of single women who made the journey. Because of the high death rates during the famine years, it was extremely difficult for young people to marry and start a family. Men postponed marriage because they could not make a living, and single adult women in Ireland increased to unprecedented numbers. Women who had jobs in cottage industries lost them to unemployed men. For many single women in Ireland, emigration was an act of empowerment, the only thing they could do to escape a lonely life as a maid or house servant. Roman Catholic nuns constituted a substantial portion of those single women. In the United States they played critical roles in Catholic institutional life, running the hospitals, schools, and orphanages that the church established to meet the needs of Catholic immigrants.

Yet the Irish family survived. In Ireland the father was always the head of the family, and he kept that role in America. But mothers were emotionally dominant in the family because they were more often at home to influence and discipline the children and because the Irish believed strongly in the virtues of motherhood. The spirit of the Irish home was moralistic; children were expected to be respectful and obedient. Given their scarce resources, Irish emphasis on family cohesion and mutual cooperation was strong. Kinship ties extended all the way through the father's relationships. Although family independence was a matter of great pride, people in need could call on paternal relatives for help and were expected to assist others when asked.

Political talent also served the Irish well. The Irish were equipped with centuries of experience in life-or-death political battles with the English. In Ireland mass and direct-action politics had gone on for years; and slowly, between 1820 and 1880, the Irish constructed their famous political machines, epitomized by Tammany Hall in 1880s New York and the Richard Daley machine in twentieth-century Chicago. Working through local parishes and saloons, Irish politicians first became street captains and later district and precinct leaders, aldermen, and state and national legislators. Using police, fire department, sanitation, and public works jobs as patronage, they attracted the loyalty of voters economically dependent on the political success of the machine. By championing the workingman, Irish Catholic politicians became very influential in the Democratic party. In New York, Boston, Cleveland, Chicago, Pittsburgh, Baltimore, St. Louis, and New Orleans, Irish political machines were powerful, and power is easily translated into respectability.

Second-generation Irish found skilled jobs in the construction industry and in factories; and although unskilled Irish workers had more difficulty finding skilled and white-collar jobs than did Protestant workers, enough succeeded to make the possibility real. A small business and professional elite of grocers, dry goods dealers, real estate brokers, attorneys, physicians, and commission merchants became the "lace-curtain" Irish. And all classes of Irish Americans were highly mobile in the nineteenth century. They had an intense drive for property ownership, and they established ethnic savings and loan associations—with such names as Flanagan, Hibernia, Emerald, Erin, Shamrock, and St. Patrick—to help them buy or build homes. They were prudent and thrifty, put their savings into the banks, sent wives and children to work, and finally bought their own homes in more respectable neighborhoods. The ghetto survived, but a constant stream of new immigrants—many of them also Irish—filled the vacuum.

The Irish also succeeded because they held on to their Old World identity. Throughout the nineteenth century they provided money to Irish revolutionaries, and they tried to use their leverage in the Democratic party to influence American foreign policy against England. During the controversy with England over the Oregon territory in 1844–1846, the Irish clamored for war. American Fenians—Irish-Americans dedicated to the liberation of Ireland—invaded Canada in 1866 hoping to weaken English power. Between 1914 and 1917 the Irish lobbied intensely to keep the United States out of World War I, and they bitterly condemned President Woodrow Wilson when the United States finally joined England against Germany. As late as the 1980s, pacifists in Northern Ireland were begging Irish Americans to stop sending money to finance the violence between Catholics and Protestants. Old World politics was a powerful ingredient in the New World ethnic nationalism of Irish America.

The Catholic Church solidified Irish Americans, and when success came they did not desert it. By sheer force of numbers the Irish clergy controlled the Catholic hierarchy in America, and the bond between the Irish clergy and parishioners was very strong. The local parish church in the center of the community was surrounded by homes, apartments, taverns, stores, and shops. The priests knew all the families, directed their church activity, and comforted them. For a son to enter the priesthood was a great honor to an Irish-American family. People were active in the parish, attending weekly mass, parochial schools, catechism classes, and frequent confessions; serving as altar boys and abstaining from meat on Fridays and from other worldly pleasures during Lent; and faithfully contributing money for the construction and maintenance of parish institutions. A compact, relatively close community, the parish was the emotional heart of Irish American life. These were the Irish Catholics—a separate community with a powerful ethnic nationalism based on their Gaelic heritage, their resistance to the British Empire, their New World experiences, and their Roman Catholicism.

The Dutch

The seventeenth-century Dutch empire stretched across the globe, from Newfoundland to West Africa to the East Indies, and in 1624 the Dutch West India Company planted a colony in North America. It purchased Manhattan Island from the Indians, named the settlement New Netherland, and extended the colony up the Hudson River in what is now New York State, down the Delaware River in New Jersey and Pennsylvania, and across the East River to Breuckelen (Brooklyn). Within forty years nearly ten thousand people lived there. But New Netherland never attracted enough settlers to remain independent of the surrounding English colonies. By 1664 more than fifty thousand Puritans were in New England and thousands of Anglicans were in Maryland and Virginia. Feudal Dutch patroonships along the Hudson River discouraged immigrants from coming because few wanted to become serfs in the New World. Conflict with the Indians also deterred settlement. The colony was a ripe plum that fell to an English fleet in 1664. New Netherland became New York.

Thousands of Dutch still came to America. Some Dutch Quakers and Mennonites moved to Pennsylvania in the 1680s; Dutch Labadists, members of a utopian sect, settled in Maryland in the 1680s; and thousands of Dutch farmers came in the 1700s. By 1776 nearly 100,000 Dutch were living in America, and from their original nucleus along the Hudson and Delaware rivers they settled throughout the Hudson Valley, the Mohawk Valley in upstate New York, the Passaic and Hackensack valleys of New Jersey, and in York, Bucks, and Adams counties in Pennsylvania. From there they moved out to western Pennsylvania and Kentucky.

They were a highly visible group. Compact rural communities and poor communications kept Dutch culture intact. Virtually every Dutch community had its Dutch Reformed Church and parochial schools offering services and education in the native language. Most members of the Dutch Reformed clergy serving in the United States were foreign-born, and they too helped preserve Dutch culture. Old World values were strong. In many parts of New Jersey and upstate New York, the Dutch often absorbed the English, Germans, or French Huguenots settling near them.

The Great Migration sent another 250,000 Dutch immigrants to America, 128,000 between 1820 and 1900 and another 120,000 between 1900 and 1924. By 1840 King William I controlled the Dutch Reformed Church and closely supervised church meetings and the training of ministers. When "Seceders" protested, the government broke up their meetings, jailed ministers, and arrested parishioners. Whole congregations fled to America.

Even more Dutch came looking for economic opportunity. They followed the colonial Dutch to New York City and the Hudson Valley, and they also settled in Michigan, Illinois, Wisconsin, and Iowa. Farms were small in Michigan, usually forty to eighty acres, but the Dutch, adept at draining swamps, purchased "poor" land at low prices and were able to accumulate equity in a short period of time. They tended to remain in settled areas, not moving on to new farms every few years. The largest Dutch communities developed in Kalamazoo and Grand Rapids, Michigan, and after the Civil War the Dutch pushed out to southwestern Minnesota, the Dakotas, western Iowa, eastern Nebraska, Montana, and Washington because of the availability of cheap land.

Eventually a split developed between the descendants of New Netherland and the immigrants of the Great Migration. More liberal and relaxed after two centuries in America, the old Dutch and the Dutch Reformed Church seemed strange to the new immigrants. Offering Holy Communion to nonmembers, sending children to public schools, and giving up Dutch-language services, the Dutch Reformed Church seemed to have lost touch with its Calvinist roots. In

1857, some of the new immigrants founded the Christian Reformed Church. Conservative and strict in the Calvinist tradition, it insisted on services in the Dutch language and on Dutch parochial schools; it condemned worldly amusements, the participation of women in church services, membership in secret lodges, and any trace of an ecumenical spirit.

By 1900, there were two Dutch communities in the United States. In the East the descendants of New Netherland were in a state of advanced assimilation. English was their mother tongue; public schools educated their children; the Dutch Reformed Church attracted a wide variety of Protestants; and marriages to English and German Protestants were the rule. Across the whole range of social relationships they were mixing with other Americans. But in the West the Christian Reformed Dutch held tenaciously to the Old World faith, speaking Dutch, attending church schools from kindergarten through Calvin College in Grand Rapids, and taking Dutch spouses more than 80 percent of the time. They were hardworking, ambitious, modest, pious, thrifty, and family oriented. The Dutch character was such that the immigrants flowed naturally into an ideological mainstream prepared by English Puritans and Scots-Irish Presbyterians.

The Germans

By 1820, colonial German society was rapidly acculturating in America, breaking out of the Old World patterns. As late as 1790, German was the daily language of immigrant communities, and Germans married Germans nearly 90 percent of the time. But after 1800, church registers were frequently written in English, and regular English services were introduced. Soon it became difficult to find a minister who could preach in both languages. The triumph of English was inevitable. Lutheran and Reformed churches ceased to be purely German institutions and opened their doors to English, Welsh, and Scots-Irish settlers.

But just as colonial German society seemed to be making the transition from acculturation to assimilation, the Great Migration began. Between 1820 and 1924, more than 5,700,000 people immigrated from Germany, perhaps 500,000 from Austria, 200,000 Germans from Alsace and Lorraine, 120,000 Russian Germans from the Volga River and Black Sea coast, and more than 270,000 people from Switzerland.

Before the 1880s the German community in the United States consisted primarily of religious dissenters, political refugees, and farmers. In 1805, Father George Rapp established a communist colony at Harmony, Pennsylvania, and in 1815 they moved to New Harmony, Indiana. In 1817, Joseph Baummler led 300 Germans to Zoar, Ohio, where their tiny community survived until 1898. After the Napoleonic Wars, several thousand German Mennonites settled in the Midwest. South of Cedar Rapids, Iowa, Christian Metz established the Amana colonies in 1842 for 800 German pietists. These colonies lasted well into the twentieth century. In the early 1870s, Germany—unified at last under Prussian dominance—began the *Kulturkampf,* "culture battle," annulling papal authority and abolishing Catholic orders and Catholic education. Some German Catholics emigrated to America. And after 1874, thousands of German Hutterites, an Anabaptist sect, came to the Dakotas, where even today they speak German.

Political problems inspired immigration even earlier. The Vienna Revolution of 1848 triggered peasant and burgher uprisings in Württemberg, Baden, the Rhineland, and Prussia. Most of the radicals demanded popular sovereignty and liberal reform. On May 18, 1848, liberals and radicals convened the Frankfurt Parliament to draft a constitution for a united Germany, but bitter divisions hurt the assembly. While they argued about the pace of change, whether to have a republic or a limited monarchy, and whether to create a unitary or federal government, the conservatives suppressed the rebellion. Perhaps five thousand rebellious "Forty-Eighters" fled to the United States. Democratic, anticlerical, and intensely nationalistic, men like Carl Schurz, Edward Salomon, and Jacob Müller stimulated the revival of German ethnicity in America.

But for every German who immigrated to America for religious or political reasons, a hundred came for economic reasons. Germany experienced economic changes just when rumors about the United States were attracting interest all over Europe. Population increases made life difficult for peasant families; American wheat depressed grain prices; periodic potato famines left thousands on the verge of starvation; factories centralized production and destroyed jobs for many artisans; and skilled workers left country villages and crowded into Vienna, Berlin, Hamburg, Breslau, Munich, and Dresden. From all over Germany workers headed for America: coal miners and heavy-metal workers left the Ruhr Valley; textile workers abandoned Saxony, Bavaria, Alsace, Lorraine, and Silesia; and glassworkers, cobblers, construction workers, leather workers, and cabinetmakers set out from Westphalia and Prussia.

German culture at first revolved around religion, language, and agrarian folkways. The German immigrants were a spiritual-minded people whose faith was strong; their churches institutionalized that faith, controlled behavior, and ordered community life in rural areas.

This was *Kirchendeutschen*—churches promoting German culture. Indeed, there was little need for other ethnic organizations because the churches played such a central role in community affairs. Life was hard in rural America. Settlers were troubled by Indians, the vagaries of nature, and general privation. Making a living consumed most of the immigrants' energies, and whatever time or resources remained went to the churches.

The German immigrants were also united in their conviction that language and faith were inseparable, that German was the best vehicle for expressing spirituality. When public schools appeared in the nine-teenth century, German farmers resented the intrusion of the state into their lives, feeling that the responsibility for educating children rested with parents. They associated value with production, the making of concrete goods; many looked on higher learning and the professions as wasteful. To them, Yankee commercialism was rude speculation, mak-ing money on the gullibility or misfortune of others. Through Lutheran, Reformed, or pietistic church schools, parents made sure their children were not "Anglicized." Founded to teach basic literacy, church schools preserved the German language and taught Biblical truth, safeguarding German faith and culture from the influence of Anglo-American values.

Finally, German culture in the early nineteenth century rested on Old World agrarian folkways; ruralism was a way of life, not just a way of making a living. Less restless than the English and Scots-Irish, the Germans had always looked for the best soil, for places where they could establish self-reliant permanent communities. In general, they were not inclined to purchase virgin land, clear it, and then sell it and move on. They placed great emphasis on having large patriarchal families and their grown children living close to home. It was common for parents to help young couples acquire farms of their own in the community; and because of the prevailing social stability, money was often lent interest free on the security of a handshake. Germans preferred family-size farms over plantations, intensive subsistence agriculture over commercialism, and free labor over slave labor.

By the middle of the nineteenth century, however, rural folkways began to yield to more secular interests. *Kirchendeutschen* for example, gave way to *Vereinsdeutschen* — German societies. New organizations fostering German traditions were formed: singing societies (*Sangerfeste*), militia companies, sharpshooting clubs, fraternal associations (Sons of Hermann, Order of the Harugari, Masons, and Oddfellows), literary clubs, mutual aid societies, theaters, beer halls, orchestras, and debating groups. Mid-century German immigrants no longer had their identities inextricably linked with the church. Community life for the German Catholics still revolved around the parish, but all the German immigrants were acquiring an identity as Germans that transcended older religious visions.

That was a complicated process. Of all the nineteenth-century immigrants, the German-speaking people were the least homogeneous. Linguistic, ideological, ethnic, regional, and finally religious differences set them apart from one another. Although they spoke German, each separate German duchy or state had enjoyed its own dialect. The most fundamental difference was between such Low German dialects as Dutch, Flemish, Friesian, and Prussian prevailing from Belgium and the Netherlands through Westphalia and Hanover to Prussia, and the High German dialects of Alsace, Bavaria, Austria, and Switzerland. So while the Germans shared a linguistic heritage, it was by no means a monolithic one.

There were also major regional differences based on ancient tribal origins and historical development. Swabian tribesmen had originally settled throughout southwest Germany in Alsace, Baden, Württemberg, and Switzerland. Bavarian tribesmen migrated to Bavaria, Austria, and Bohemia, and Franconians ended up in Austria. Upper Saxons made their way into Hanover and Brunswick; Lower Saxons into Saxony, Silesia, and Bohemia; and Thuringians into central Germany.

Upper Saxons and Belorussian Slavs mixed to become Prussians. The immigrants came from Alsace, Lorraine, Baden, Bavaria, Württemberg, Switzerland, Austria, Westphalia, the Palatinate, Hanover, Hesse, Holstein, Schleswig, Saxony, Thuringia, Silesia, Prussia, Pomerania, Posen, Brandenburg, and Brunswick, all of which had been independent kingdoms or duchies. If the immigrants had been asked their nationality, they would probably have called themselves by their origins in one of the German states, not by the name of Germany, especially before 1871.

In addition to these linguistic, tribal, and regional differences, the German immigrants were distinct from one another in terms of ideology and world view. The Forty-Eighters, for example, were liberal nationalists, deeply concerned with political philosophies and bitterly anticlerical; they blamed organized religion, Protestant but especially Roman Catholic, for the historic inability of Germany to unite. More devout Germans, of course, resented the Forty-Eighter hostility.

On another ideological level, the northern Germans by the mid-nineteenth century had accepted a lifestyle known as *Gesellschaft*, an accommodation to the more formal, anonymous values of an industrial, corporate world, while south Germans still lived in a world of *Gemeinschaft*, of traditional values such as village ruralism, familialism, and personalism. So while north Germans viewed southerners as hopelessly backward, south Germans viewed northerners as stiff and formal, materialistic and out of touch with life's more important qualities.

But the most profound differences were religious. Ever since the Protestant Reformation, Germany had been the scene of religious wars between Protestants, Catholics, and pietists. Between 1830 and 1865 most immigrants were Protestants, but after the American Civil War Catholics immigrated from southern and southwestern Germany in increasing numbers until they constituted half the incoming Germans in the 1800s. By contrast, most English, Scots, Welsh, and Scandinavian immigrants were Protestants, and practically all the Irish were Catholics. Religion and nationality were closely integrated for them. But for the Germans, religious loyalties divided the community and retarded pan-German ethnicity.

Gradually, however, a German melting pot emerged in America. Lutherans from the Rhineland married Lutherans from Bavaria, or Catholics from Silesia married Catholics from Westphalia. The children and grandchildren of these mixed marriages saw themselves as German Lutherans or German Catholics, losing in one or two generations the old vision of being Bavarian or Prussian or Silesian. Russian Germans, Swiss Germans, Alsatians, and Germans frequently intermarried, and their German-speaking children melted into the larger

German-American community. Because of the fluidity of the social structure, geographical mobility, and toleration of religious diversity, as well as their economic success, the German immigrants could not help becoming part of the larger society. With the arrival of each new generation the sense of being American became more pronounced. By 1900, the Prussian immigrants of 1880 and their children still felt intensely German, but descendants of colonial Germans who had emigrated out of western Maryland in 1790 possessed much weaker loyalties to German culture. Those same forces would work on the nineteenth-century immigrants as well. Just as the first generation acquired an ethnic nationalism, succeeding generations developed new role definitions based on residence, religion, politics, occupation, and income that would compete with nationality.

By 1900, most German-Americans were living in cities. Congregating at first in ghettos, they moved to the suburbs as soon as income permitted. New immigrants then replaced them in their downtown ghettos of Philadelphia or St. Louis or New York. In the suburbs upwardly mobile Germans lived near other Germans but were also surrounded by people of English, Irish, Welsh, Scots, or Scandinavian background. Their sense of community broadened to include middle-class residents of their neighborhoods. Complete assimilation was still not common, for in most of those areas the Germans married among themselves more than 60 percent of the time. But when German Lutherans married Scandinavian Lutherans, their children—or at least their grandchildren or great-grandchildren—considered themselves simply Lutherans again, or perhaps white Lutherans.

Political loyalties were also important, and German-Americans, whether Republicans or Democrats, often identified themselves with a party. Occupational patterns were important too. A fourth-generation machine-tool specialist from Milwaukee would regard his membership in the American Federation of Labor as an important part of his identity, perhaps as important as the fact that his great-grandfather had emigrated from the Rhineland in 1820. German culture was certainly intact in 1900, but the stage was set for important changes in the twentieth century.

The Scandinavians

New Sweden was the beginning of the Scandinavian presence in America, but it was not until the nineteenth century that large numbers of Swedes, Danes, Norwegians, and Finns crossed the Atlantic. Between 1820 and 1924 more than 750,000 Norwegians came to America, 580,000 of them after 1880. The Swedish migration was larger: more than 1.2 million Swedes settled in America. Perhaps 320,000 Danes immigrated, as did 300,000 Finns. Together they developed the upper Mississippi Valley.

There were important differences among the Scandinavians in terms of culture, language, and history, but in a number of ways they viewed life from a common perspective. After centuries of scraping a living out of rocky soil in a cold climate, they possessed a stoicism about life and a determination to hold out against its capriciousness. Scandinavians were dogged and tenacious, somewhat inflexible on moral questions and incredibly persevering on economic ones.

Before the American Civil War, thousands of people fled Scandinavia to trade the oppressive atmosphere of state Lutheranism for the freer environment of the United States. They were members of pietistic religious traditions emerging within the Lutheran Church. But after the Civil War, most people immigrated for economic reasons. The Scandinavian soil was either too moist or too rocky, the growing season too short, the winters bitterly cold and dark, and less than one acre in ten was arable. People wearied of life in rural mud homes, subsisting on potatoes and some meat in good times and rye bark or moss bread in bad times. Later in the century, as American wheat, Canadian timber, and English and American manufactured goods flooded Scandinavian markets, Scandinavian peasants, lumberjacks, and shipbuilders in search of work moved to Christiania, Stockholm, Copenhagen, and Helsinki; some then went on to America. Finland was not integrated into the Atlantic economy until the 1880s, but Finns began to emigrate then too. As steamship companies, railroads, and other immigrants littered Scandinavia with propaganda about America, the Great Migration began.

Most of the Scandinavians were not destitute, but they came determined to find in America the security that was disappearing in Europe. Until the 1880s most Scandinavian immigrants were farmers who settled in Michigan, Wisconsin, Illinois, Iowa, Minnesota, and the Dakotas. They carved out new lives on the great wheat fields of the northern prairies and forests where icy winters reminded them of home. Southern Wisconsin and northern Illinois contained more than 70 percent of the Norwegians in 1860, and from there they pressed into Minnesota, Iowa, and the Dakotas. During those first years they lived in sod houses or crude lean-tos and braved blizzards, dust storms, humid summers, and locusts, but the rough shelters soon gave way to log cabins and then to more substantial wood-frame homes.

After 1880, the Scandinavians increasingly settled in cities. Large Scandinavian colonies appeared in New York, Buffalo, Cleveland, Chicago, Duluth, Minneapolis, Des Moines, and in dozens of smaller cities in the North. Along the Great Lakes, Norwegian sailors were in great demand. Swedish painters, masons, machinists, carpenters, miners, and iron and steel workers filled the waiting industrial jobs, and second only to the British they supplied more skilled workers to the American economy than any other immigrant group. Because of their unusually high educational level, the Danes secured white-collar positions as clerks and sales personnel. The Finns had few industrial skills and took the hardest jobs as miners, lumberjacks, stevedores, and laborers clearing farms. The largest Finnish settlement developed around the huge copper mines in Hancock, Michigan, and other Finns worked in the iron mountains of the Mesabi range in Minnesota and in the western gold, silver, and coal mines. In the Great Lakes port cities they loaded freight, and large Finnish settlements appeared in the New England mill towns, especially Worcester and Fitchburg, Massachusetts.

The Swedes, Norwegians, Danes, and Finns had different levels of ethnic consciousness. Finns and Norwegians were more concerned about preserving Old World traditions, more dedicated to their own communities, and married compatriots more often than did the Danes and Swedes. These differences stemmed from their native cultures. In Denmark and southern Sweden small farms were mixed with large estates, all scattered around clustered village markets where peasants sold their produce and purchased goods from village artisans. These Scandinavians were commercial farmers functioning in a money economy. Because news, travelers, and goods from the outside world reached them through rail, steamship, and highway connections, the Danes and Swedes were more open to social change, strangers, and new ideas.

But in the heavily wooded forests and mountains of Norway and Finland each valley had a separate identity complete with variations in food, dialect, and customs. Homesteads were largely self-sufficient, and the commercial production of surpluses was limited. Extended families were close and so were neighbors throughout the valley. Less cosmopolitan than the Danish and Swedish peasants, as well as more isolated, the Norwegians and Finns were suspicious of strangers and conservative about social change. In the United States they held closely to people who spoke their language, worshiped in their churches, and joined their associations.

History contributed to immigrant identities. Denmark had enjoyed a national history since the Middle Ages, and Danish immigrants accepted nationality as a fact of life. So too did the Swedes, who had had national independence since 1523, when Sweden seceded from the Kalmar Union with Denmark and Norway. They felt no need to defend their national identity in America. It was markedly different, however, for the Norwegians and Finns. Sweden lost Finland to Russia in 1809;

and in the 1814 treaty of Kiel, Denmark, which had sided with Napoleon in the European conflict, was forced to cede Norway to Sweden. Trapped in a semicolonial relationship with Sweden, nineteenth-century Norwegians had a strong national consciousness, and immigrants carried that consciousness to the New World. When Norway peacefully achieved independence from Sweden in 1905, Norwegian Americans celebrated by forming the Nordmanns-Forbundet to strengthen Norwegian freedom.

Finland had been part of Sweden from the twelfth through the eighteenth centuries, and the language of the state bureaucracy was Swedish. Swedes controlled politics and looked down on the Finns as narrow-minded provincials. But Sweden ceded Finland to Russia during the Napoleonic Wars, and by the end of the nineteenth century the tsar was drafting Finns into the Russian army and trying to make Russian the official language. As a result of years of domination, nationalism pervaded Finland in the nineteenth century. Thus both the Norwegian and the Finnish immigrants arrived in the United States imbued with a sense of ethnic nationalism. The Danes, and to a lesser extent the Swedes, did not resist acculturation and assimilation. In 1890, for example, when only 8 percent of the Danes and 22 percent of the Swedes could be considered the dominant group in certain upper-midwestern counties, nearly 60 percent of the Norwegians and 70 percent of the Finns were dominant in certain areas. The Norwegians and Finns showed a far stronger inclination to settle among their compatriots. While Danes and Swedes enthusiastically supported the public school movement, Norwegians and Finns were more inclined to start parochial schools in conjunction with their Lutheran churches. And while half the Danes and perhaps 30 percent of the Swedes married outside their nationality, only 20 percent of the Norwegians and less than 10 percent of the Finns did. Well into the 1920s, Norwegian was the spoken language in numerous public and parochial schools, churches, homes, and businesses in many counties of the upper Midwest, as was Finnish in many mining and textile towns.

Of all the Scandinavians, the Finns were the most exclusive and group oriented. The American environment interacted with Finnish clannishness to create a cultural tenacity unknown among other Scandinavians. Many Americans—including some Scandinavian-Americans—were critical of the Finns. Part of the problem was economic. Because Finnish industrialization and the integration of Finland into the Atlantic economy did not begin until late in the nineteenth century, most Finns were unskilled workers and peasant farmers just when more and more German, Norwegian, Danish, Swedish, English, Scots, and Welsh immigrants were arriving with industrial skills. Many Americans considered the Finns a backward people and grouped them with the immigrants from southern and eastern Europe.

And in the Midwest, other Scandinavians looked down on the Finns. The Swedes, Norwegians, and Danes were all descendants of ancient Nordic tribes and took pride in Viking history. They were also able to understand one another's language. The Finns were descendants of ancient Magyar tribes that had emigrated out of Central Asia, and the Finnish language bore no resemblance to Swedish, Norwegian, or Danish. To other Scandinavians, Finns were a rather primitive people. But even if older Americans and Scandinavian immigrants had welcomed the Finns, Finnish ethnicity would still have led to group isolation. Language and cultural barriers, as well as an intense sense of nationalism, helped drive them together in the United States, but Finnish ethnicity also revolved around a strong impulse toward group integrity. Suspicious of others, Finns relied on Finns for security. Society was defined in terms of moral absolutes, usually on a class basis. For the Finns the economic world was divided between the *meikalainen* ("good working people") and the *herrat* ("bad aristocrats"), and the *herrat* would risk annihilation rather than surrender prerogatives to the *meikalainen*. Concluding that real mobility was impossible to achieve anywhere, some Finns withdrew to a rural environment, hoping there to work out their lives in peace.

By 1890 there were four Scandinavian "islands" in the United States, and because immigration from Sweden, Norway, Denmark, and Finland was just reaching its peak, the forces of assimilation were still weak. Like the British and German Protestants, the Scandinavians— except for the Finns—were generally well received in America. They were literate, white, Protestant, and socially conservative, and older Americans did not fear Scandinavian culture. Nativistic criticisms focused much less on Swedes, Norwegians, and Danes than on the Irish and German immigrants. But the prevailing hospitality did little to destroy Scandinavian self-reliance and clannishness, and large-scale assimilation would not occur until well into the twentieth century.

The French

In the colonial period France and England competed for supremacy in North America, the English moving down the Atlantic coast and the French, from the New France at Quebec, toward the Great Lakes. The Ohio River Valley became a point of contention, enough to trigger four colonial wars—King William's War, 1689–1697; Queen Anne's War, 1702–1713; King George's War, 1740–1748; and the French and

Indian War, 1754–1763. England prevailed in 1763 when war-weary France ceded Canada in the Treaty of Paris. Forty years later Napoleon completed the work of the Treaty of Paris by selling Louisiana to the United States for $15 million. After nearly two centuries, the Franco-American empire was gone.

But it was not the end of French culture in America. Over the centuries four separate waves of French immigrants came to the New World. Several thousand French Huguenots, fleeing religious persecution in France, relocated in America in the 1690s. More than seven thousand French Acadians were driven from Canada after 1755, many setting in Louisiana. Between 1820 and 1924 as many as 300,000 French-speaking immigrants from Europe came to the United States, and more than 400,000 French Canadians crossed the border to America.

The Huguenots were Calvinist reformers, a tiny Protestant colony in Roman Catholic France. Like the Puritans in England, Presbyterians in Scotland, Walloons in Belgium, and Reformed congregations in Holland and Germany, most were successful merchants and skilled artisans, the backbone of the French economy. They were a unique people—republicans in the age of absolutism, dissenters in a bastion of religious despotism. But in 1685, King Louis XIV launched anti-Huguenot persecutions throughout France, prohibiting Protestant services, burning Protestant publications, and closing Protestant chapels. Restrictions were placed on Huguenots becoming doctors, lawyers, teachers, or civil servants. Their property was confiscated and their civil rights were violated. Angry and afraid, more than 400,000 Huguenots left France in the 1690s.

Most settled in Holland and England, but several thousand came to America. Huguenot communities sprouted all along the Atlantic coast. Although no more than fifteen thousand Huguenots ever lived in America, some of the most famous families in United States history— the Bayards, Marions, Du Ponts, Delanos, and Reveres—were of Huguenot descent. Americans welcomed the Huguenots. Of all the non-English ethnic groups in early America, they assimilated the most quickly. As white Protestants who were successful and widely dispersed, they soon lost a separate identity. Highly educated, ambitious, and skilled entrepreneurs, they appreciated the social climate of America, the economic opportunity, and the religious freedom. Anglo-Americans appreciated them not only for their economic skills, but also as a Protestant people fleeing Roman Catholicism. Open acceptance encouraged assimilation. Learning English quickly, their children married Puritans in New England, Anglicans in New York and South Carolina, and Scots-Irish Presbyterians in the South and the West. By the early nineteenth century, the Huguenots hardly functioned as a self-conscious ethnic group.

The Acadians were the second wave of French-speaking immigrants. One of the oldest ethnic groups in North America, they are descendants of colonists who joined Samuel de Champlain's settlement at Port Royal on the Bay of Fundy in 1603. The new colony of Acadia expanded around the main settlement, and Acadians supported themselves by fishing, fur trading, and farming. But the cold, humid, windy winters and mosquito-infested summers made life difficult. Population growth was slow, and strong village kinship systems developed. The original families of the early seventeenth century became the Acadian clans of the eighteenth century. Roman Catholic in religion, Gallic in culture, and bound together in strong extended families, they were a highly insular community in North America.

After Queen Anne's War, England acquired Acadia from France, and for the next forty years the Acadians found themselves in an untenable position. England perceived them as potential traitors ready to rise and strike back in the name of France. When the Acadians refused to take a blanket loyalty oath to England at the outset of the French and Indian War, English politicians expelled them. The exile began in 1755, when there were probably fifteen thousand Acadians, and to this day Cajuns (Acadians who settled in Louisiana) call the exile *Le Grand Dérangement* ("the Big Upheaval"). Cramped into the dark holds of transport vessels, they were shipped out with only the possessions they could carry.

The Acadians were dispersed throughout the Old and New Worlds, wherever anyone would take them. Thirty years after the expulsion and more than twenty years after Spain acquired Louisiana from France, the Spanish government recruited sixteen hundred Acadians living in France to return to America, colonize the territory, and develop it economically. Seven expeditions deposited them in New Orleans in 1785, and from there they moved west to the bayous, rivers, swamps, and lakes of southwestern Louisiana. Loyal to their heritage, the Acadians became fishermen and fur trappers and cattle, cane, and cotton farmers. To this day, as the Cajuns trap the nutria and muskrat, gather shrimp, raise cattle, and grow rice and cotton and cane, links to early Louisiana and Acadia remain strong. From their early origins in France they had nurtured an independent spirit, and the powerful family clans of Acadia that were reconstituted in Louisiana helped reinforce their autonomy. Wronged historically and conscious of it, poor but independent, knitted into strong family networks, and isolated culturally and physically from the rest of the country, the Cajuns were deeply suspicious of outsiders, a separate people in nineteenth-century America. By

An artist's conception of the embarkation of the Acadians, who were herded onto ships with only the possessions they could carry. (Brown Brothers)

the 1990s there would be hundreds of thousands of Cajuns in Louisiana. Insular and proud, still Gallic and intensely Roman Catholic, Cajun America would continue to defy the melting pot, preferring instead the isolation of rural Louisiana.

Between 1820 and 1924 only 200,000 French-speaking immigrants settled in America. Given the total population of France, that was a small number. Because of the French Revolution, France was more open socially and politically than the rest of Europe, and there was a maturity to French culture; people were more satisfied with their environment. The population of rural France remained relatively stable and the pressures for land that were so strong elsewhere did not cause serious trouble. Not even the Industrial Revolution could disrupt cottage industry and rural family life in nineteenth-century France.

Most French immigrants were skilled workers and professionals. They settled in the major cities, and despite their Roman Catholicism the French encountered little hostility in America. The reason was partly demographic. French immigration averaged fewer than three thousand people each year; compared to the migrations from Ireland and Germany, it was inconsequential. At the same time, most of the French immigrants were craftspeople and professionals; Americans perceived them as economic assets. Furthermore, many Americans admired French culture. France had helped the colonies during the Revolution, and although many upper-class Federalists in the United States feared the French Revolution and resented Thomas Jefferson's love for France, most Americans shared his feelings.

French Canadians were the last group of French immigrants, a close-knit community bound together by strong kinship ties, language, and religion. Four colonial wars had left them with an Anglophobia rivaling that of the Irish. English rule only intensified French ethnicity. When Britain made English the national language, the French converted their own language into a cultural symbol; and when the English made known their preference for Protestantism, French-Canadian Catholicism became a badge of faith and community. Quebec separatism today is only the latest episode in a long struggle for independence. This was French Canada: a conquered people devoted to the French language, Roman Catholicism, and ethnic nationalism.

But economic life in Quebec was desperate. Outmoded farming techniques were depleting the soil, and the old French inheritance system that required subdivision of land among all children (and was still working well in France) reduced farms to small parcels that could not support a family. French Canadians looked south for jobs in lumber yards, canals, railroads, mines, quarries, harbors, mills, and factories of the United States. Whole villages were transplanted to the mill towns of New England; to the mines and steel mills of New York, Pennsylvania, and Ohio; to the copper and lead mines of Upper Michigan; to the automobile factories of Detroit; to the mines and farms of Minnesota; and to railroad labor gangs throughout the upper Midwest. By 1900 there were more than 500,000 French Canadians in New England alone. That number would eventually grow to 1.25 million by 1945, representing more than 15 percent of New England's 8 million people. Another 400,000 French Canadians lived in Michigan, 350,000 in New York, 300,000 in Illinois, and 125,000 in Minnesota—making it one of the more visible ethnic groups in the Northeast.

Like the Cajuns, the French Canadians resisted assimilation. What had happened in Quebec was the historical fusion of religion, language, and nationality. French was not simply the medium of culture to the French Canadians; it was a mystical badge of ethnicity and the "defender of the faith." French Canadians believed that the loss of their language implied loss of Roman Catholicism. The center of cultural life had thus been the French-speaking parish and parochial schools; they were bastions of Gallicism and Catholicism where religion, society, and politics mixed. The social climate of the United States further defined French-Canadian values. Americans welcomed craftspeople and professionals from France but worried about the French Canadians.

Poor and unskilled, ignorant of English, and concentrated into "Little Canadas," the French Canadians were a conspicuous and growing minority in the nineteenth century. Their Catholic loyalties and suspicion of public schools generated even more uneasiness. The nineteenth-century immigrants from France were often worldly and even rather secular about religion. But this was not true of the French Canadians, and they encountered the wrath of Know-Nothing activists in the 1850s and the Yankee sensitivities of other antiforeign groups in the 1890s.

This was Franco-America in the nineteenth century. The Huguenots had largely disappeared by the mid-1800s, victims of their Protestantism, urbanity, and economic prosperity. And the new immigrants arriving directly from France were readily accepted by a society starved for European French culture. The two main centers of American French culture were in New England and Louisiana, where French Canadians and the Cajun descendants of French Canadians lived separate lives in homogeneous communities. Both were close-knit people bound together by an ethnic culture that fused language, religion, family, and politics.

Chapter Three

Ethnicity and Manifest Destiny

Visions of land, lots of land, brought the first European colonists to America in the seventeenth century, and that same dream pushed their descendants across the continent in the eighteenth and nineteenth centuries. Obsessed with the spirit of Manifest Destiny, the United States acquired title to Texas, the Far West, and the Southwest in the 1840s. Millions of Americans wanted farms and ranches out west, and it became the express purpose of federal and state governments to assist and finance them. Because of the enormous capital investment required to build railroads, the governments donated land to help finance construction. The subsidies began in 1830 with the first state land grants and ended in 1871 when the federal government issued its final grant to the Texas & Pacific Railroad. Because of its access to the transportation network, railroad land was prime property, and the railroads sold it as quickly as possible to incoming settlers. The federal government also made it progressively easier for settlers to acquire land. The Homestead Act of 1862 provided 160 acres of free public domain land to a settler agreeing to live on the claim and make annual improvements.

The results of railroad construction and land legislation were dramatic. In 1840, only 1 percent of the non-Native American population of the United States—perhaps 175,000 people—lived west of the Mississippi River, but forty years later there were more than ten million people there, approximately 20 percent of the population. Between 1862 and 1904, settlers established titles to more than 755 million acres of land. The pioneers felt a God-given right to take up land in the west. Relatively few of them set out for the frontier hoping to kill the Native American or Mexican inhabitants living there. They simply wanted to "better themselves"—to leave something behind for their children. But the collective impact of millions of well-meaning settlers moving across the landscape with the backing of the government was a political and economic catastrophe for the native inhabitants of the American West.

Native Americans

Between 1776 and 1830, the United States reassessed its native American policy. Concerned during the Revolution about fighting Indians in the West and the English in the East, the government wanted Indians to resist British enticements and remain neutral. There were a number of isolated but serious confrontations, especially when British military officials encouraged the Indians to fight. Except for the Oneidas, the Iroquois nation was loyal to England, and on several occasions between 1777 and 1779, American troops invaded Iroquois territory. But generally the relationship between whites and Indians was tranquil. In 1777 and 1779, government officials repudiated attempts by speculators and white pioneers to settle on Indian lands in the Ohio Valley. The war had slowed the westward movement, and with fewer people crossing the mountains there were fewer confrontations; the government's policies seemed to be working.

Immediately after the Revolution, the government continued to be cautious in its Native American policies. American leaders hoped to avoid conflict with Indians in the West because it might divide Westerners and Easterners and threaten the young republic with political disintegration, especially if Britain and Spain tried to detach the western territories. American leaders therefore tried some conciliatory measures. It was, of course, only a temporary lull in the tension, for as soon as the mass migration of whites across the Appalachians began again, the conflict over land would reappear.

The hunger for land among white farmers was as insatiable as ever, and the government would have to respond by making way for those pioneers. The "backwardness" of native America was still used to justify taking land. A Baptist missionary journal argued in 1849 that native Americans were "deficient in intellectual and moral culture. . . . They do not furnish their share to the advancement of society, and the prosperity and wealth of the world. . . ." Such attitudes led inevitably to confrontation on the frontier. But at the same time, Europeans believed in Christian humanitarianism and the natural rights philosophy; missionaries as well as Jeffersonian idealists had to rationalize the taking of Indian land with their faith in natural rights. To these people, assimilation seemed an ideal solution. Transforming native Americans into settled farmers who could support a family on only a few dozen acres of land would liberate millions of acres for white settlement and uphold the natural rights philosophy. But this too proved destructive to the Indians. Assimilationists wanted them to abandon their religious beliefs, the hunter-warrior ideal, tribal government, and communal ownership of the land—in other words, to exchange their culture for that of white society.

After the Revolution the nations along the frontier were powerful, and the British agents still in the Ohio Valley could create trouble. In an effort to placate the native Americans, many argued that Indian land claims were sovereign and could be nullified only with Indian consent. In 1784, Congress negotiated the Treaty of Fort Stanwix, which reestablished peace with the Iroquois. And in 1785, the federal government concluded a treaty with the Cherokees guaranteeing their land claims and inviting them to send a representative to Congress. Two years later Congress promised in the Northwest Ordinance to respect native American rights in the Ohio Valley.

But these measures could not cope with the wave of settlers pouring across the Appalachians. By 1790 there were more than 35,000 settlers in Kentucky and nearly 75,000 in the Ohio Territory, and sporadic attacks on white settlements soon began. Whites demanded immediate assistance from the federal government, and President Washington dispatched troops to the Ohio Valley. There, on November 4, 1791, the Shawnees surprised the expedition and more than six hundred soldiers died, the worst single defeat United States forces were ever to suffer at the hands of native Americans. People roared for retribution. Three years later a military expedition led by General "Mad" Anthony Wayne defeated a large Shawnee force at the Battle of Fallen Timbers; the subsequent Treaty of Greenville of 1795 forced most of the Shawnees out of Ohio and into Indiana.

The Treaty of Greenville initiated a recurrent cycle in which native Americans, after resistance and military defeat, would surrender their land for guaranteed ownership of territory farther west. By 1810 there were 230,000 whites in Ohio, 406,000 in Kentucky, 260,000 in Tennessee, 25,000 in Indiana, 12,000 in Illinois, and 20,000 in Missouri. As white farmers cleared the forests, native Americans were hard pressed to maintain their lifestyles. Tecumseh, a Shawnee war chief, and his brother, a religious leader known as the Prophet, tried to unite the Great Lakes, Ohio Valley, and Gulf Coast tribes into a single military coalition. But the native Americans could not overcome centuries of tribal conflict; some would temporarily bolt the alliance to support the government or to fight each other, and some even sold their land. Between 1811 and 1813, troops under William Henry Harrison, governor of the Indiana Territory, relentlessly pursued Tecumseh and the Prophet, defeating their forces at the Battle of Tippecanoe in 1811 and killing Tecumseh in 1813 at the Battle of the Thames. After that, the northern tribes gradually yielded all their land east of the Mississippi River.

White idealists continued their crusade to remake native American culture. Throughout the early nineteenth century, War Department agents introduced European culture into native American villages, as did Protestant missionary groups such as the Society of United Brethren for Propagating the Gospel Among the Heathen and the American Board of Foreign Missions. Such people as Isaac McCoy, John Heckewelder, and Stephen Riggs wanted native Americans to accept the superiority of individualism over tribal communism, Christianity over native religions, commercial farming over hunting and subsistence agriculture, and English over their own tongues. Missionary boarding schools such as the Foreign Missionary School in Connecticut and the Choctaw Academy taught English, Christianity, Protestant views of morality, and European views of society and economics. Missionaries preached the same message to friendly tribes on the frontier, envisioning native American villages where Indians worked their own farms and worshiped each Sunday at a community church. They hoped to reform native American society, not only to save souls but to end the violence that was threatening native American survival as well as white expansion.

But most native Americans refused to oblige, believing that the Great Spirit had ordained to each race its own customs, land, languages, foods, and religions. In that the Indians cared about immortality and honorable behavior, they shared a broad perspective with the missionaries; but they wanted nothing of institutional Christianity. They considered their tribal customs more useful and humane than American individualism and found in their own culture the most sensible way of interpreting their environment. Some native Americans converted to Christianity, shed native dress for European clothes, attended mission schools, and tried to farm their own land. But once converted they were often outcast by their own people. The Chippewas ridiculed converts as "praying Indians," and Sioux warriors often physically abused them. And no matter how sincere or pious, Christian Indians were not accepted by whites. Caught between two cultures, many returned to their tribes rather than endure lives of social ostracism. When groups adopted the whites' faith but not white customs, their religions often became synthesized tribal and Christian beliefs. Many simply added God to an existing pantheon of deities or, like the Spokanes, mixed their medicine ceremonies with Christian prayers.

Whether the Indians adopted or repudiated white customs, missionaries realized by the early 1830s that native American culture was tenaciously resilient and that most native Americans had no intention of passively accepting European culture. Yet to white idealists Anglo-conformity seemed the only way to stop the seemingly endless violence on the frontier. Eventually the removal policies of Andrew Jackson, the reservation policies, and even the allotment policies would be concerned in part with changing Indian society, not just for the sake of change but to guarantee native American survival.

If noble, the sentiments of white idealists were naive. Even if the Indians had submitted to conversion, whites would still have wanted their land. By 1820, for example, there were hundreds of thousands of whites in Georgia, Alabama, and Mississippi. Much of the game on which native Americans relied had disappeared, and the old ways were difficult to maintain. Hoping to keep their land, some of the tribes tried to accommodate themselves to white society. In 1808, Cherokee leaders had formulated a legal code, and by 1821 the brilliant Cherokee Sequoyah had developed written characters for eighty-six Cherokee syllables. In 1828, the Cherokee nation began publishing its own newspaper; books, Bibles, hymnals, and tracts circulated widely throughout Cherokee society. Missionaries established new schools in Cherokee communities, and Protestant churches made more converts than ever before. The Cherokees fenced their farms, built comfortable homes, sold livestock commercially, and established a political system based on a written constitution, democratic elections, jury trials, and a bicameral legislature. But it was all in vain; most whites were more interested in their land than in cultural accommodation. With cotton production booming in the 1820s, tens of thousands of whites poured into the southeastern states and territories, and the Five Civilized Tribes, of which the Cherokees were one, were forced westward. Cultural accommodation could not counter economic expansion.

The Trail of Tears, 1830–1860

Since 1789, Americans as distinguished as Thomas Jefferson, George Washington, and John C. Calhoun had been suggesting that native Americans in the East be evicted to lands across the Mississippi River. Materialism and humanitarianism again made common cause. When Andrew Jackson entered the White House in 1829, the proposal gained a powerful advocate. He had made his reputation fighting Indians in the Southwest, trying to drive them across the Mississippi River. Indian attacks on white settlements would drive him to fury. At the same time he was concerned about the survival of native Americans and realized that as long as they remained in their traditional homelands, white assaults would continue. To open land for white settlement and to protect native Americans, President Jackson signed the Indian Removal Act in 1830.

In what is remembered as The Trail of Tears, 100,000 Indians were transported to Oklahoma. The peaceful Choctaws of the Deep South were first to go, marching in the winter of 1831. Many died of hunger and disease along the way. The Creeks were moved four years later after massive white attacks on them in Georgia and Alabama. The United States Army supervised the removal of the Chickasaws in 1837. The Cherokees fought removal in the federal courts, and the U.S. Supreme Court upheld their claims in 1832. Jackson refused to abide by the court decision. The Cherokees held out for several years, but in 1838 soldiers evicted them; four thousand died on the way west. Only the Seminoles resisted violently. Under Chief Osceola they waged a guerrilla war in the Florida Everglades between 1835 and 1842 that cost the government two thousand soldiers and $55 million. But they too were finally defeated and removed to Oklahoma in 1843.

Removal was equally relentless in the Ohio Valley. The Iroquois managed to stay in upstate New York, but since the defeat of Tecumseh in 1813 the fate of the other northern tribes had been sealed. The Ottawas, Potawatomis, Wyandots, Shawnees, Miamis, Kickapoos, Winnebagos, Delawares, Peorias, and the Sauk and the Fox had to leave. Only the Sauk and the Fox resisted. Under Chief Black Hawk they had been removed to Iowa in 1831, but they turned back a few months later. United States troops chased them across Illinois and Wisconsin and finally defeated them at the Battle of Bad Axe.

The removal treaties guaranteed perpetual ownership of the new land to the native Americans, but only a permanent end to the westward movement could have preserved their land tenure. That did not happen. With the acquisition of the Oregon Territory in 1846, thousands of American farmers poured into the Pacific Northwest. When a long winter killed much of the game, and a measles epidemic devastated several tribes in 1847 and 1848, the Cayuse attacked the Protestant mission of Marcus and Narcissa Whitman, killing them both. In 1853, a new territorial governor began placing various tribes on reservations to clear the way for a transcontinental railroad; the Yakimas revolted, and government troops did not subdue them until 1858. The Yakimas, Cayuses, Wallawallas, Nez Perces, Spokanes, and Palouses were all moved to reservations.

Robert Lindneux's painting of "The Trail of Tears" migration that followed
passage of the Indian Removal Act of 1830. (The Granger Collection)

The gold rush of 1849 brought disaster to the nomadic California
tribes. Massacres, epidemic diseases, and forced slave labor almost
destroyed them entirely. Their population declined from more than
100,000 people in 1849 to less than 15,000 in 1860.

When Mormon settlers entered the Great Basin in 1847, the lives of
the Utes, Paiutes, and Shoshones changed immediately. Mormon theology held native Americans in special esteem, seeing them as a rem-
nant of the lost tribes of Israel whom God had led to the New World
and had destined to become some day a mighty and noble civilization.
Mormon treatment of native Americans was more careful and diplomatic than that of most other whites. But as Brigham Young established
Mormon farming colonies in southern Utah, Nevada, California, Arizona, Wyoming, Idaho, and Canada, and thousands of non-Mormon
settlers came to the Salt Lake Valley in the 1850s, the white population
increased and native Americans lost much of their land. Construction
of the transcontinental railroad through Utah Territory nullified more
of their land claims. In the end the Utes, Paiutes, and Shoshones were
confined to barren reservations.

In 1848, when the Senate ratified the Treaty of Guadalupe Hidalgo
with Mexico, the United States took sovereignty over the southwestern
nations and their lands. Americans had traded with the Spanish and
Indians in the Southwest for years, and during the 1840s more white

settlers came to work the silver mines and establish cattle and sheep ranches. The Pueblos rebelled at Taos, New Mexico, in 1847 and killed several whites, but the uprising was quickly crushed. After that the Hopis, Zuñis, and Pueblos remained passively cooperative. Kit Carson and several hundred American troops attacked Navajos who had been raiding white settlements in 1864, and eventually they were marched several hundred miles to a reservation in eastern New Mexico; three years later the government transferred them back to Arizona. Except for the Apaches, the Indians of the Southwest were defeated by 1865.

The Final Conquest

Beginning in the 1860s, three developments sealed the future of native Americans. First, Congress passed the Homestead Act in 1862, and after the Civil War hundreds of thousands of white settlers took up 160-acre tracts of free land in the Dakotas, Montana, Wyoming, Colorado, western Kansas, western Nebraska, and Oklahoma. The mass migration imposed extraordinary pressures on the Plains Indians. Second, the completion of five transcontinental railroads, linking eastern manufacturers with western markets, made their situation worse because the roads sold parcels of their federal land grants to white farmers. The Union Pacific–Central Pacific line from Omaha to San Francisco was finished in 1869; farther north the Northern Pacific and the Great Northern railroads were completed in 1883 and 1893, passing through the Dakotas, Montana, Idaho, and Washington to link the Great Lakes with Puget Sound. And by 1884 two southern routes were completed. The Atchison, Topeka & Santa Fe ran from eastern Kansas to Los Angeles and the Southern Pacific connected New Orleans with the West Coast. Third, at the same time the railroads were being built, the buffalo slaughter became large-scale. Some public officials encouraged the hunts, hoping they would destroy the Plains economy and make it easier to force the Indians onto reservations. It worked. By 1883 the southern herd was wiped out and only remnants of the northern herd were surviving in Canada. The economy of the Plains Indians was in ruins.

Conflict began along the major trade and migration routes and later erupted wherever white settlers encroached on Indian land. Late in 1862, after repeated acts of fraud by traders and a massive increase in settlers along the Minnesota River, the Santee Sioux rebelled and killed several hundred whites. Panic spread throughout southern Minnesota, and thousands of people fled. Soldiers eventually dispersed the Sioux, capturing more than four hundred and driving others into Canada and the western Dakotas.

The southern Cheyenne in eastern Colorado also reacted to white settlers. After several skirmishes with whites in 1864, they agreed to a negotiated peace and quietly moved to a temporary camp at Sand Creek, Colorado. There, on November 29, 1864, soldiers under the command of Colonel John M. Chivington brutally attacked the Indians. In an orgy of violence they murdered three hundred Cheyennes, sparing none, not even women and children. A general war spread throughout eastern Colorado and western Kansas as enraged Cheyennes, Sioux, and Arapahos avenged the Sand Creek massacre. Not until 1868, when Lieutenant Colonel George A. Custer's Seventh Cavalry defeated the southern Cheyenne, did calm return temporarily to the Great Plains.

The wars intensified in the 1870s. In Idaho, Oregon, and Washington, troops extinguished the final resistance of the plateau nations. The Modocs went to the Oklahoma reservations in 1872, and a few years later the Flatheads and Bannocks moved to reservations in the Northwest. In 1877, after a dramatic attempt to escape to Canada, Chief Joseph and the Nez Percés were captured in northern Montana. The remnants of the Nez Percé nation went to Indian Territory in Oklahoma.

In the Southwest the city-dwellers and the Navajos were defeated by the 1870s, but the Apaches resisted fiercely. Between 1862 and 1886 they carried on a successful guerrilla war against white settlements, and not until 1886, when Chief Geronimo of the Chiricahua Apaches surrendered, did peace come to Arizona and New Mexico. Geronimo was sent to prison and the Apaches to reservations, where they depended for survival on supplies from the Department of the Interior.

Hostilities resumed on the Plains in 1874, when the discovery of gold in the Black Hills of South Dakota brought thousands of white miners. Only six years earlier the Sioux had been given "eternal" control of the area, but under intense political pressure the federal government hedged on its promise and asked them to leave. They refused, and the Department of the Interior ordered them out of the Black Hills. Still they refused, and government troops under Custer, now a general, and General George Crook left for the Dakotas. In one of the most famous battles in American military history, a combined force of Cheyenne and Sioux warriors led by Crazy Horse and Sitting Bull killed Custer and more than two hundred of his men at the Little Big Horn River in 1876. Inspired by revenge, white troops drove Sitting Bull into Canada and the Oglala Sioux to a South Dakota reservation. After more hopeless fighting, Crazy Horse surrendered in 1877 and the northern Cheyennes were moved to the Indian Territory. In fury and desperation Morning Star and Little Wolf led them off the reservation the following

Sitting Bull, warrior of the Dakota Sioux, slain in a melee at his home when Sioux authorities under federal contract came to arrest him. (The Bettmann Archive)

year and tried to make it back to ancestral lands in Montana. The flight captured national attention and touched the hearts of many whites, but troops soon returned those who were left to Oklahoma.

The last vestige of native American resistance disappeared after the murder of Sitting Bull in 1890. He returned to the United States from Canada in 1881 after government agents offered him amnesty. Under house arrest at Fort Randall for two years, he later moved to Standing Rock, Dakota Territory, before spending a year on tour with Buffalo Bill's Wild West Show. By 1888 he was openly opposing further Sioux land cessions, and after resisting arrest in 1890 he was shot to death by Indian police. News of his murder spread quickly through the Dakota Territory, and at Wounded Knee Creek, South Dakota, an angry Sioux warrior killed an army officer. In the ensuing melee enraged soldiers killed more than 150 Sioux men, women, and children. That tragedy formally closed a chapter in American history. Stripped of their land, the native Americans finally gave up and headed for the reservations. The wars were over.

Mexican Americans

Long before the arrival of Europeans, central Mexico developed one of the most advanced cultures in the New World. Between 1500 B.C.E. and 700 C.E. the Mayans enjoyed a sedentary life based on corn cultivation, city states, a fine transportation network, good educational programs, and an excellent water delivery system. They cleared the dense tropical jungle and raised surpluses of corn, beans, peppers, tomatoes, and squash. Mayan achievements included a hieroglyphic writing system, use of the zero in mathematics, accurate calendars, and astronomical observatories. They mined gold and silver, cut and polished precious gems, wove cotton into richly elaborate textiles, and created expressive pottery, murals, and mosaics. During the years of Mayan ascendancy Mesoamerica stood with the Near East, West Africa, and the Indus River Valley as a cradle of civilization.

Around 800 C.E., because of overpopulation, soil exhaustion, or both, Mayan cities declined, roads fell into disrepair, and tropical jungles reclaimed the corn fields. The Toltecs then rose to power. In architecture and metallurgy, if not in mathematics and science, they rivaled the Mayans, and their serpent god Quetzalcoatl was worshiped throughout Mexico and South America. Brilliant at its peak, Toltec civilization declined as quickly as it had developed. In the fourteenth century the Aztecs conquered the Toltecs, settled in the valleys, and built the city of Tenochtitlán. Eventually the Aztec empire had several urban centers and governed nearly nine million people. They flourished by clearing the land, irrigating the fields, terracing the hillsides, and constructing artificial islands in lakes. They raised corn, beans, tobacco, squash, tomatoes, potatoes, chili, and cotton; collected mangoes, papayas, and avocados; and domesticated dogs and turkeys. When Montezuma II assumed the throne in 1502, Aztec civilization was among the most advanced in the world.

The Spanish Origins

During the 1400s Portugal controlled commerce along the African coast and Italians monopolized the Near East trade. Spain considered diplomacy and even war to break those cartels until geographers suggested circling the globe. To assert its national glory, outdo the Portuguese, and destroy the Italian monopoly, Spain conducted worldwide explorations. Columbus made the first of four voyages to the New World in 1492, and in his wake a number of other Spanish *conquistadores* explored the Caribbean and Spanish Main, conquering the native American nations in the process. The Columbus family took control of the island of Hispaniola, and in 1514 Diego Velásquez began the conquest of Cuba. Juan Ponce de León had already established Spanish control over Puerto Rico, and he later explored the Bahama Islands and the coast of Florida. In 1519, Hernando Cortez and 700 men invaded Mexico. Spanish guns and horses gave Cortez military advantages, and Indian beliefs in the return of a bearded white deliverer provided an awesome—if temporary—psychological advantage. The Aztec policy of exacting tribute and practicing human sacrifice had left them with bitter enemies throughout Mexico. Cortez shrewdly exploited these enmities; in two years Montezuma was dead and the Aztec empire crushed. Between 1521 and 1540 Spain extended its authority throughout central and southern Mexico.

Spanish Catholicism was a zealous faith. Ferdinand and Isabella hoped to convert Indians and glorify Spain. The Spaniards also hoped to take Indian land and use their labor. The *encomienda* was a feudal covenant in which a Spaniard provided military protection and religious instruction to Indians in return for work. Encomienda Indians became an exploited lower class in New Spain (Mexico), laboring on farms, ranches, sugar mills, construction projects, and mines. Catastrophic declines in the native population, however, destroyed the encomienda. Between 1519 and 1600, measles, smallpox, diphtheria, whooping cough, and influenza reduced the Indian population from approximately twenty-five million to about one million. With less labor to exploit, Spaniards shifted from a labor-intensive to a land-intensive economy, gradually taking abandoned Indian property. Haciendas, or landed estates, replaced the encomiendas. Native civilization deteriorated, with Indians living at subsistence levels, tied to the haciendas by economic dependence, debt peonage, and force.

The class structure in Mexico reflected ethnic divisions. At the top were white European families, divided into Spanish-born *peninsulares* and Mexican-born *criollos*. At the bottom were Indian and black slaves, peons, and encomienda laborers. In between were *mestizos*—offspring of Spanish and Indian parents. In the 1500s, less than 10 percent of the colonists were women, so sexual contact between Spanish men and Indian women was common. The few mestizos born in wedlock were raised as Spaniards, part of the first criollo generation. Illegitimate mestizos remained in the Indian villages. They were ethnically distinct, neither Catholic nor Aztec, Spanish nor Indian. During the sixteenth century a mestizo middle class gradually emerged, and it eventually became the largest group in Mexico. In the towns and cities mestizos worked as domestic servants to criollos and peninsulares or unskilled dock and construction workers. Some became overseers on the haciendas, or labored as cowboys, sheepherders, or miners. Others were artisans. Thousands more became soldiers or went into sales or small business. Not as rich as whites but not as poor as Indians, mestizos were a unique consequence of the New World colonies—a new ethnic group.

The Borderlands: Expansion Northward

Late in the sixteenth century New Spain began expanding north. Catholic missionaries and mestizo soldiers carried out the borderlands colonization. Expeditions searched for gold, and conquest of local

Indians became the first stage in the settlement process. Since the fifteenth century Spain had looked on religious conversion as a "civilizing" force in the New World; but in the borderlands, native Americans appeared so "uncivilized," at least when compared to the Aztecs, that the civilizing role of the church assumed new importance. In California and Texas, the mission congregated them in residential communities near the church, and they learned to raise crops and livestock, work in industry, speak Spanish, and become Christians. The final stage began when soldiers remained in the north after their tour of duty. To service them, artisans and merchants settled near the missions and presidios (military outposts). Upper-class criollo or peninsulare women did not migrate, so mestizos became dominant, in numbers at least.

New Mexico became the first borderlands colony. Rumors of the fabulously wealthy "Seven Cities of Cibola" circulated in New Spain since 1519, and when Cabeza de Vaca returned from his ill-fated expedition to Florida in 1536, he amplified the excitement by spreading stories of gold-laden Indian societies to the north. In 1539 Fray Marcos de Niza explored western New Mexico in search of the cities, as did Francisco Coronado between 1540 and 1542. In 1581, several Franciscan friars began proselytizing the Indians in the north. Finally, geopolitical concerns inspired expansion. The Pacific voyages of Sir Francis Drake in the 1570s convinced Spain that England had located the legendary Northwest Passage; and to forestall any English presence in the area, New Spain sent colonists to New Mexico. Dominican missionaries established Santa Fe in 1609. When rich mineral deposits were not discovered, the missionary impulse became dominant. By 1680 New Mexico had twenty-five missions, encompassing nearly 100 villages and seventy-five thousand Indians. But Chief Popé and the Pueblos slaughtered hundreds of colonists and captured Santa Fe in 1680, which retarded the development of New Mexico for decades. Not until 1692, after years of bitter fighting, did Spain reconquer New Mexico, and it was not until 1706 that they founded Albuquerque.

Because of the danger of Indian attacks, the colonists lived in villages along the major rivers where water and presidios supported life. A cultural symbiosis occurred there. Like the Indians, the *nuevos mexicanos* (Mexican settlers) cultivated corn, beans, squash, and chili, but they added cotton and fruit, which the Indians quickly adopted. From the Indians the Spanish learned about irrigation and in return taught the Indians to raise sheep. Spaniards built churches in the Indian communities, and the Indians learned to speak Spanish and worship Christ. In 1800 there were eight thousand settlers in New Mexico—a well-to-do landowning class and an impoverished class of mestizo workers.

Arizona was settled more slowly because of the hostility of the Apaches and Navajos and the lack of water. The Jesuit priest Eusebio

Kino led an expedition deep into western Arizona in 1687. He worked closely with the Pima Indians and established a mission near Tucson after 1700. The Arizona economy depended on subsistence agriculture and sheep grazing, and the people lived in fortified towns; but with only two thousand colonists, the settlement remained underdeveloped throughout the Spanish colonial period.

Spanish colonization of Texas began after the French explorations of the Jesuit Father Marquette and Louis Joliet in 1673 and of Sièur de La Salle in 1682 had opened the Mississippi River. To counter French influence, New Spain founded Nacogdoches in 1716 and San Antonio in 1718. Cattle and cotton became the bases of the Texas economy; and because of the weakness of local Indians, the colonists (known as *tejanos*) were more scattered than in New Mexico. A tense rivalry existed in Texas until 1763, when Spain took Louisiana from France. Without the French threat, Spain's desire to colonize Texas waned, and as late as 1800 only thirty-five hundred Mexican settlers lived there.

The Spanish moved into California after hearing of Russian and English interest. The Franciscan priest Junipero Serra founded San Diego in 1769. Franciscans had established twenty other missions by 1823, including Los Angeles, Santa Barbara, San Jose, and San Francisco. California's rich natural resources and temperate climate made it the most prosperous borderlands colony. With the availability of good land and the Spanish inclination to make large land grants, the *ranchos* became powerful, independent economic units, much like the Mexican haciendas. Catholic missions and private ranchos dominated the California economy. The *californio* upper class consisted of large landowners and the clergy; the *cholo* middle class consisted of mestizo workers, soldiers, small farmers, and new settlers; and impoverished California Indians made up the lowest class. By 1800, a total of twenty-five thousand Mexicans were living in the borderlands.

From Spain to Mexico to the United States, 1810–1848

During the colonial period an immense social chasm developed between peninsulares and criollos. Resentment of peninsulares was so intense in New Spain that Indians, criollos, and mestizos subordinated their own ethnic differences in a united assault on European imperialism. Indians had always resented the power and self-righteousness of the Spanish settlers. When the general uprising against Spain began in 1810, Mexican Indians participated enthusiastically. Criollo resentment was both social and political. For centuries peninsulares had considered criollos crude and unsophisticated and had denied them political power. Although criollos obtained land and succeeded commercially, economic power did not translate into social or political influence because peninsulares controlled most positions in the government, army, and clergy. Despite their numerical superiority, criollos felt powerless, and late in the 1700s they began forming insurgent groups and talking of political separation from Spain.

Mestizos too were weary of Spanish domination and yearned for important civil and religious positions. Resentful of elites, they looked on peninsulares as the backbone of an exploitive upper class; removal of Spanish authority might lead to male suffrage, separation of church and state, and an economic revolution that would break up the large estates and distribute them among the poor. Mestizo cooperation with criollos was expedient at best, since the criollos too were seen as part of the upper class, but mestizos were nevertheless willing to join forces against Spain. In 1810, Father Miguel Hidalgo, the criollo son of a hacienda manager, launched the revolt against Spain, and eleven years later, Mexico was free.

Rebellion was already brewing in the borderlands in the early 1820s. Mexican liberals and conservatives had cooperated politically to destroy peninsulare dominance, but success exposed their differences. The conservatives were wealthy landowners, a political and social elite who believed in rule by the rich, the unity of church and state, and a strong central government. In 1834, they took control of the government and installed Antonio López de Santa Anna. He weakened the provinces by abolishing their legislatures, restricting the powers of municipal governments, and ousting local officials. Upset about the loss of local power, provincial leaders in the borderlands began considering rebellion against Mexico.

Their restlessness coincided with Anglo-American expansion. Between 1820 and 1848 thousands of Americans settled in the Southwest. The Santa Fe trail opened in 1822, and the economic relationship between the borderlands and central Mexico changed dramatically; it was easier now to obtain goods from the United States than from central Mexico. Nuevos mexicanos began drawing closer to the United States. A similar situation developed in California during the 1820s and 1830s, when American settlers established farms in the rich central valleys and merchants and shippers crowded into San Francisco to profit from the Pacific trade. Mexico encouraged American immigration during the 1820s by giving large land grants in Texas to men such as Stephen Austin. There were more than twenty-five thousand Americans in eastern Texas by 1830. Some married into local families, but most looked down on Mexicans as inferiors. American political loyalties flowed east to Washington, D.C., not south to Mexico City.

A coalition of discontented mestizos and Americans developed in all the borderland colonies. Texas was the first province to revolt against Mexico, and the rebellion there set in motion a chain reaction that eventually brought New Mexico and California into the United States. Attracted by the rich bottomlands of eastern Texas, thousands of settlers crossed the Louisiana border during the 1820s and started hundreds of cotton plantations. Mexican officials had encouraged the early settlers, but they became alarmed at the size of the immigration. To discourage American settlement, Mexico prohibited the importation of slaves into Texas and established customs houses and military presidios along the Texas-Louisiana border in 1830. But it was too late. After the conservative revolt of 1834 in Mexico City, Texans declared their independence. Despite an initial defeat at the Alamo mission in San Antonio in March 1836, a combined Texas army of Anglo Americans and tejanos, under the command of Sam Houston, defeated Santa Anna at the Battle of San Jacinto a month later. The subsequent Treaty of Velasco, which Santa Anna was forced to sign but Mexico never recognized, granted independence to Texas.

The Republic of Texas was not admitted to the Union for nine years, however, because many northern congressmen feared that five slave states might eventually emerge from Texas and give the south control of the Senate. But by 1845 the new expansionist Manifest Destiny ideology, which called for American sovereignty over the entire continent, had overcome all reluctance to accepting Texas. In 1845, in a joint session of Congress, the United States annexed the Lone Star Republic. Texas became the twenty-eighth state of the Union.

Mexico immediately severed diplomatic relations with the United States, but despite the breach between the two countries, late in 1845 President James K. Polk decided to try to purchase New Mexico and California. When Mexico bluntly refused, Polk ordered American troops into Texas south of the Nueces River hoping to create a military emergency. It was a pretext for acquiring the rest of the Southwest. After a brief clash between Mexican and American forces in a disputed area of southern Texas in May 1846, President Polk claimed that "Mexico . . . shed American blood upon American soil," and Congress declared war. California and New Mexico became United States territories soon afterward. On the eve of the war a group of Anglo-American and Mexican leaders in California, upset about the conservative triumph in Mexico, declared independence and launched the Bear Flag Revolt. When American military forces entered California, the revolt merged with the larger conflict, becoming one theater in the war with Mexico. American businessmen in Santa Fe convinced nuevo mexicano colleagues that the province would be more prosperous under

American control, and when General Stephen Kearny arrived in 1846 he met no resistance.

After months of bitter fighting, triumphant American troops entered Mexico City; and on February 2, 1848, the two nations signed the Treaty of Guadalupe Hidalgo. For $15 million the United States acquired California, Arizona, New Mexico, Nevada, Utah, and part of Colorado; and Mexico recognized American title to Texas. Manifest Destiny had triumphed.

Eighty thousand more people now lived in the United States. Concerned about the fate of Spanish-speaking Catholics in a white Protestant society, Mexican officials had inserted several guarantees into the Treaty of Guadalupe Hidalgo. Mexican residents had a year to decide their loyalties; if at the end of the year they had not declared their intentions, they would automatically receive United States citizenship. Only two thousand crossed the border; the others became Mexican Americans. Article IX, as well as a statement of protocol issued later, guaranteed their civil liberties, religious freedom, and title to their property. Despite the guarantees, however, the Fourteenth Amendment was still twenty years in the future. The federal government had promised a great deal, but it had little authority to enforce its will. An ethnic and religious minority in the Southwest, Mexican Americans would have difficulty enjoying their promised liberties.

Chinese Americans

Emigration has long been a part of Chinese history. As the New World opened, the Chinese went to Mexico, Peru, Brazil, and Canada until eventually perhaps ten million Chinese were scattered throughout the world. Between the gold rush of 1849 and the Chinese Exclusion Act of 1882, nearly 300,000, most from Kwangtung (Canton) Province in southeastern China, arrived in the United States. The population of China in 1850 was 400 million, and density along the coast averaged more than a thousand people per square mile. Agriculture was primitive and production never satisfied demand. Even when the harvest was good, rice had to be imported. Frequent river flooding and periodic crop failures further beset peasant life.

European imperialism complicated matters. Christian missionaries challenged the Confucian emphasis on family authority. British textiles entered Kwangtung, ruined local producers, and vastly increased unemployment. Anglo-Chinese wars stimulated racial violence between the English and the Chinese. And the Taiping Rebellion in the 1850s devastated southeastern China. The rebellion turned into a general uprising of several factions: discontented scholars denied admission to the civil service (and thus consigned to a life of menial work), merchants resentful of taxes imposed by British officials, Cantonese residents suffering from economic disruptions, troubled peasants wanting land reform, democrats hoping to destroy political tyranny, and Hakkas planning to blunt the power of the Cantonese. It was a social catastrophe; the rebellion and its suppression completely destroyed the rural economy and killed more than twenty million people. Desperate peasants began looking beyond China for new opportunities.

But amidst all these upheavals the Chinese family continued to order peasant life. A basic institution of social control, the clan tied families together in village economies where property was held in common, graveyards administered, and ancestral halls maintained. Individuals subordinated their personal interests to the authority of the extended family, and kinship patterns of elder male dominance continued throughout life. Peasants were intensely loyal to the family: it supplied their reason for being. The disruptions of the mid-nineteenth century tested that loyalty, as peasant farmers became more and more hard-pressed to support their families. In the end, family devotion pushed hundreds of thousands of peasants overseas.

Just as all these social and economic problems were developing in China, American merchants brought news of gold in California. Rumors spread, and the "Golden Mountain" and high wages in California seemed the answer to peasant troubles. The Chinese became sojourners, temporary immigrants who planned to work in America until they were fifty or sixty years old. Then they would return home bringing wealth and respect. During their years abroad, they hoped to make return visits to China several times, marry a woman selected by the clan, father many children, and help the family make ends meet. In America they would live frugally and send most of their money home to China. Emigration was not a turning away from their homeland but a defense of the family and the village, the only way to preserve the traditional order.

Chinese-American Society

By 1855 there were 20,000 Chinese immigrants in the United States, most of them in California. Of the 63,000 Chinese in America in 1870, more than 50,000 lived in California and nearly 10,000 in Idaho, Nevada, Oregon, and Washington. Ten years later there were 105,000 Chinese in America, 75,000 of them in California and 24,000 scattered throughout the western states. A few thousand Chinese immigrated to the Kingdom of Hawaii after the 1840s, and when the United States annexed Hawaii in 1898, they became Chinese Americans.

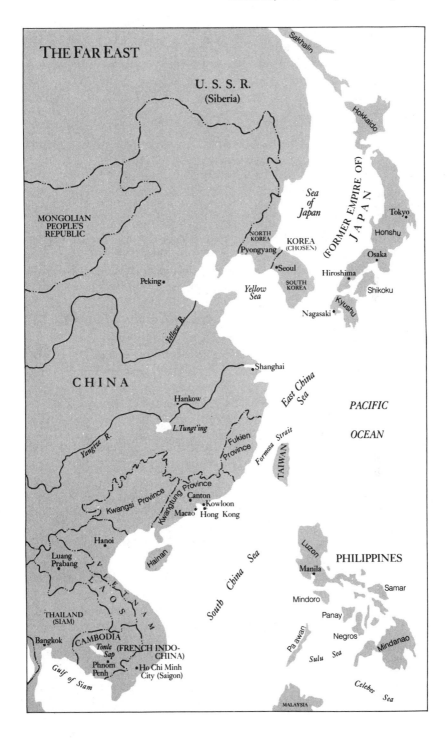

Although a few Chinese merchants found work supervising American trade with Asia, most early Chinese came looking for gold and worked in the mines. But whenever they made a large strike, jealous white miners drove them off their claims. When the shift to hydraulic extraction made mining more expensive, Chinese took jobs with the large mining companies. Thousands worked gold mines in Oregon, Idaho, and Montana; silver mines in Nevada and Arizona; and coal mines in Utah and Wyoming. Many Chinese were domestic servants, laundry workers, and restaurant owners; others were the backbone of the woolen, shoe and boot, and metal industries. After the Civil War the Central Pacific Railroad hired more than ten thousand Chinese workers to build the line from San Francisco to Utah. The Southern Pacific Railroad later employed them throughout the Southwest. Chinese could also be found building dams, levees, and irrigation systems in the San Joaquin and Sacramento River valleys. On the large wheat and fruit farms of California they were seasonal workers, the first generation of migratory laborers. Chinese truck gardeners and horticulturists were common in the West, and Chinese fishing villages dotted the Pacific Coast, where they processed and sold salmon, sturgeon, halibut, bluefish, redfish, flounder, shrimp, and abalone.

Because the Chinese saw their move as temporary rather than permanent, they brought few women along—only one immigrant in twenty was female. It was not customary for a Chinese woman to leave her family, and the men believed they would soon be returning anyway. Theirs was a "bachelor society." Not surprisingly, because of the lack of women and because of their reasons for leaving home, the Chinese returned home far more frequently than European immigrants. But most conspicuous was the resiliency of their social structure—the central place afforded the family. The Chinese sense of identity was powerful. Family and kinship relations were far more personal and important than in European societies. In Kwangtung whole villages were often inhabited by one family. The patriarchal order was strong, and clans were the basic unit of the economy, society, and local government. Even in death, through ancestor worship, family lineage continued. In terms of their origins and destiny, individuals were indistinct from their family backgrounds.

Once in America the Chinese did everything possible to reconstruct familiar social and political institutions, not only to ease their adjustment to the New World but to maintain emotional ties to China. Traditional clans became important in America too. Because there were only 438 distinct family surnames in China, it was relatively easy for immigrants to identify their clan, and those who shared the same surname associated closely. Leadership in China rested on village elders and the scholar-gentry; but since they did not migrate, the dominant figures in the immigrant communities were usually wealthy merchants. Stores were social centers for clan members as well as shelters for newcomers; merchants also offered charity to the old, the indigent, and the handicapped. Family elders in America served as proxy parents for new immigrants, and family associations provided guidance and discipline for the young. Clan ties directed settlement, and in the scattered colonies one or a few clans controlled local affairs. In San Francisco the Chan, Lee, and Wong families were dominant, as the Ong family was in Phoenix and the Chin family in Seattle. After World War II the Moi family rose to prominence in Chicago, as did the Yee clan in Detroit and Cleveland.

Overlapping and transcending clan authority were *hui kuan* associations, in which membership was determined by dialect and regional origins. Many different clans participated in each hui kuan, and these mutual aid societies played an important judicial role by mediating disputes between clans. In 1851, Cantonese immigrants in San Francisco formed the Sam Yup Company, a hui kuan association, and later in the year another group from Kwangtung established the See Yup Company. Chungsun immigrants formed the Yeong Wo Company and Hakka settlers the Yan Wo Company in 1852. The most powerful hui kuan association, the Ning Yeung Company, was formed in 1854; in 1862, others organized the Hop Wo Company. Known as the Six Companies, these hui kuan functioned as a quasi-government in San Francisco's Chinatown. They constructed large buildings to house their operations, and company representatives would greet new immigrants and take them to company headquarters. During the immigrants' first weeks in America the companies found places for them to live, lent money, found jobs, cared for the sick, adjudicated disputes, and helped return the dead to China for burial. In an age when public welfare was unknown, the Six Companies helped meet the social needs of Chinese immigrants.

Finally, there were the *tongs*. For more than a thousand years these secret associations had provided a form of social order independent of clan and hui kuan. Because of the tremendous loyalty expected in Chinese families, the country was atomized into hundreds of local elites lacking central direction. The Chinese could not unify because they were unable to transcend kinship, linguistic, and geographic differences. Secret societies, however, organized people without regard to these differences. People who failed civil service examinations joined tongs to get back at the government; angry tenants joined to punish landlords. During times of economic distress poor farmers, workers, and merchants joined to strike back at those who exploited them. In nineteenth-century China the tongs were a powerful social infrastructure—a clandestine linear system of political power organizing China along horizontal lines and helping to overcome family and language differences.

In America tong members chafed at the power of the merchant elite, whether clan or hui kuan leaders. The Suey Sing Tong repeatedly challenged the Wong family in San Francisco, and bloody battles between the On Yick Tong and the Yee clan were common. The secret societies were often involved in organized crime. In San Francisco's Chinatown the Hip Yee, Chee Kung, Wa Ting, and On Leong tongs controlled gambling, prostitution, heroin, and opium traffic. Rival tongs fought wars to control illegal businesses, resisted bitterly when the Six Companies tried to stamp out crime, and at times violently confronted prominent clan leaders who opposed their activities. Where clans or hui kuan were weakly organized, tongs provided health care and life insurance and welfare assistance to the sick, disabled, and unemployed. Along with the clans and hui kuan, the tongs provided Chinese America with an invisible government based on district and family loyalty, fear, and piety.

The Chinese formed one of the most self-contained immigrant communities in America. Clans, hui kuan, and tongs exerted great authority, nearly as much as in China. At the same time, most Chinese lived in urban ghettos where they were physically as well as culturally isolated. Not permitted to naturalize, they could not vote and had little power in local politics. Without the need to court their votes, local politicians ignored them. As a result, the Chinese had extraordinary control over their own affairs; the clans, hui kuan, and tongs were the real political power in Chinatown. While other immigrants struggled to gain access to the political establishment, the Chinese lived in a social and political island.

The Anti-Chinese Crusade

As nonwhite, non-Christian, and non-Western immigrants, the Chinese frightened many Americans. Treated as people of color, they experienced the discrimination meted out to blacks, native Americans, and Mexicans; as a religious minority they suffered the same indignities as German, Irish, and French-Canadian Catholics. Furthermore, as non-Western people they seemed strange, different from all other immigrants. Despite the general decline of nativism during the Civil War, an anti-Chinese movement developed soon afterward.

In the early nineteenth century American traders and missionaries had passed on negative images of the Chinese. In addition to ridiculing

Chinese tastes in food and music, Yankee traders living in China between 1780 and 1840 viewed the Chinese as backward people who were cruel, dishonest, immoral, and superstitious. And through sermons, books, magazines, and newspapers Protestant missionaries in China reinforced those images. To many Protestants the Buddhism, Taoism, and Confucianism of China were depraved religions and the Chinese faithful were heathens. Western society, with its emphasis on competitive individualism, embraced monotheism and took an emotional, evangelical approach to religion, seeing human affairs as a struggle between good and evil. Coming from a communal, ascetic culture, the Chinese were polytheistic, accepting many gods and relying periodically on different ones for assistance; there were gods and goddesses of war, wealth, fertility, agriculture, and rain. The Chinese found devotion to one and only one god a particularly narrow-minded perspective. They were not at all in tune with sectarianism; instead they tolerated all faiths and were even able to accept the deities of other people. Ignored by most Chinese, the missionaries became only more convinced of "Oriental paganism." Finally, many missionaries spread pornographic rumors, saying that sexual licentiousness was widespread throughout the country.

Nativism existed for economic reasons as well, especially among workers convinced that Chinese immigrants would depress wages and make jobs scarce. Business owners, however, favored Chinese immigration as a source of cheap labor; and in 1868, business triumphed when Congress ratified the Burlingame Treaty, which permitted unrestricted immigration of Chinese laborers to work on the transcontinental railroad. But when the Union Pacific–Central Pacific Railroad was completed in 1869, ten thousand Chinese workers had to look for other jobs and competed directly with American workers. Many Americans believed all Chinese were "coolies," slave laborers controlled by contractors who had "shanghaied" them to the United States. But while many Chinese laborers who left Hong Kong and Macao for South America and the West Indies did work as slaves, contract workers in the United States were permitted complete freedom of movement as long as they paid monthly installments on their passage debt. Whenever there were wage cuts or unemployment, native workers held the Chinese responsible. Labor unions began demanding immigration restriction.

Social and cultural misgivings also surfaced. Many Americans believed stereotypes about Chinese proclivities for gambling, prostitution, and opium smoking, and the crowded, physically deteriorating conditions in San Francisco's Chinatown seemed a source of crime and unrest. The lack of Chinese women frightened people who believed Chinese men were sexually attracted to white women. The Chinese were believed to be spreading leprosy, venereal disease, and other illnesses. Finally, Chinese culture seemed strange. The immigrants believed China was the center of the earth, the highest expression of human civilization, and that Westerners were the barbarians. Not that they said so, but Americans were outraged anyway. They were also suspicious about the tongs, clans, and hui kuan that made the Chinese communities so autonomous. Most Americans viewed the Chinese as an alien group that would never assimilate. Demands for immigration restriction grew more intense.

Discrimination became more common. Between 1852 and 1860 several counties in northern California expelled Chinese miners; and as the mining frontier moved north into Oregon, Washington, and Idaho, similar measures were passed there as well. In the 1870s, labor unions in California conducted anti-Chinese propaganda campaigns; and early in the 1880s, the state legislature denied the use of California employment bureaus to the Chinese and prohibited them from working on dam, levee, or irrigation projects. In 1854, a white man was convicted of murder on the eyewitness testimony of a Chinese worker, but the California Supreme Court overturned the decision on the grounds that "Mongolians" could not testify against whites. After that it was difficult to prosecute whites for anti-Chinese violence, and the Chinese had no legal avenues to express grievances. California prohibited Chinese children from attending public schools in 1860; and although state courts later ordered "separate but equal" facilities, local school districts refused to build new schools for Chinese children. Harassment laws were common. One San Francisco law prohibited carrying baskets on long poles, a common practice in Chinatown, and an 1873 ordinance required jailers to give short haircuts to all prisoners, cutting off the queues of Chinese men. Such laws resulted in second-class status for the Chinese in America.

Sporadic violence also occurred. On October 23, 1871, as Los Angeles police tried to end a feud about the status of a woman contractually bound as a worker to a hui kuan, two policemen were killed. Hearing the news, more than five hundred whites entered Chinatown, burned dozens of buildings, and lynched fifteen people. In 1876, a mob in Truckee, California, burned several Chinese homes and shot fleeing occupants. Ten months later vigilantes known as the Order of Caucasians murdered several Chinese in Chico, California. The 1877 riots in San Francisco destroyed thirty Chinese laundries. The worst race riot took place at Rock Springs, Wyoming, on September 2, 1885, when rampaging white miners murdered twenty-eight Chinese. Another riot occurred at Log Cabin, Oregon, in 1886. Muggings, beatings, and destruction of property were common.

Anti-Chinese riots erupted
in Denver, Colorado, in
1880. (Brown Brothers)

As nativist fears mounted, the immigration restriction movement
grew stronger. The Know-Nothing party called for an end to Chinese
immigration, and in 1855 the California legislature passed a tax of fifty
dollars for each Chinese worker brought into the state. Although difficult to enforce, the law's intent was clear. In 1870, California prohibited the immigration of Chinese women unless they could prove good
character, and other western states passed similarly punitive laws to
drive out the Chinese. Demands for exclusion were especially intense
during the depression of the 1870s, when a lull in railroad construction
brought thousands of unemployed Chinese workers back to California.
The Workingmen's party demanded restriction of the Chinese. All this
occurred just as immigration was swelling dramatically. More than
115,000 Chinese arrived on the West Coast in the 1870s, and another
50,000 came in 1881 and 1882. Under enormous pressure from western politicians and labor unions, Congress approved the Chinese
Exclusion Act in 1882 prohibiting future immigration from China.

From then until 1943, when China was once again permitted to send immigrants, the Chinese-American population declined as tens of thousands returned to Kwangtung. And for those remaining in the United States, the melting pot did not exist; assimilation was impossible. Most Americans were too suspicious of the Chinese, and the immigrants lived in their own world anyway. Politically inactive, culturally distinct, and economically independent of the general economy, Chinese America was an isolated entity in the United States.

Women in the West

Women—immigrants and native-born—went west for a variety of reasons. Most of them, of course, were farming women who wanted, like their husbands, to acquire more land and build a better life for their children and grandchildren. Some women migrated for religious reasons. Many Baptist, Methodist, Presbyterian, and Congregationalist women went west as missionaries to bring Christianity to native Americans and Protestantism to Spanish-speaking Roman Catholics. Other women, converted to Mormonism in the cities of the East or abroad in Great Britain or Scandinavia, went to Salt Lake City and from there to smaller towns and villages throughout the Great Basin to help build "Zion in the wilderness." Prostitutes settled in the mining camps and cattle towns to make a fast buck in those overwhelmingly male communities. And there were tens of thousands of seamstresses, laundresses, cooks, waitresses, maids, and teachers trying to make a living on the urban frontier.

Life was especially harsh for the women who crossed the plains and deserts in covered wagons and struggled to survive after finding a place to settle. They lived for years in dugouts or sod houses on the Great Plains and in lean-tos, small shacks, or cabins in the Far West. Money went first into farm equipment and livestock. Living conditions were far more crude than they had anticipated. Most of those women came from a sexist culture in the East, where domesticity rigidly defined their social and economic roles. But gentility was a luxury on the frontier. Women fought a constant war against mud and wind and dust before finally surrendering to it. They kept stoves hot all day long, summer and winter, for cooking, bottling, canning, washing clothes and dishes, and heating bathwater. And they often engaged in heavy farm labor alongside their husbands. The rigid divisions of labor so common back east tended to break down on the frontier.

It was a lonely existence. Farms were often widely scattered, allowing only rare opportunities to interact with women friends. Men frequently left home to pan for gold, deliver cattle or sheep to market, fight Indians, or engage in business and politics, or work for wages on ranches or in towns in order to buy the goods their farms needed. Often they were gone for months at a time. Women stayed behind to watch the farm and take care of the children. With their men gone, they worried constantly about enemy raids or bandits. Worst of all, however, was the excruciating, stifling loneliness. One woman farming out on the plains of western Texas wrote home to her mother, that "As long as I live I'll never see such a lonely country."

Chapter Four

African Americans in the Early Years

The Origins of Slavery

Slavery was both an economic and a social institution in America. With its fertile soil, long growing season, and navigable rivers, the South was ideal for a plantation economy. And with European demand for tobacco, rice, indigo, and cotton seemingly insatiable, commercial agriculture prevailed from the beginning. But commercial production of tobacco, rice, and cotton required a huge supply of cheap labor, and labor was scarce and costly. If southern farmers were to prosper, they needed workers who would not demand high wages, be inclined to leave the plantation, or aspire to higher callings. It seemed impossible that free laborers would meet these requirements, particularly when most colonists worshiped the twin ideas of success and individual opportunity. Slave labor seemed to offer a solution.

True, there were white indentured servants, and plantation owners were not above exploiting them. But servants proved unsatisfactory. They were expensive. They sometimes escaped to the cities, where it was difficult to trace them. And they worked out their contracts in a few years and were free to go.

Nor was enslaving native Americans the answer. There were simply not enough of them. Only about 700,000 were left by 1700, and not all of them were accustomed to a sedentary agricultural life. Nor, with their lack of immunity to European diseases, could native Americans survive contact with whites; epidemic death among native Americans was catastrophic. Finally, they knew the land and could escape with relative ease. An economy based on slave labor required an abundant supply of easily recognizable people conditioned to settled agriculture and immune to European diseases. Americans turned to Africa.

The relationship between slavery and prejudice is complex. Some scholars believe slavery created prejudice—that debilitating involuntary servitude led to misconceptions about race and color. Others argue that slavery reinforced preexisting beliefs about racial inferiority. From their earliest contact with Africans in the sixteenth century, the English responded negatively, first with surprise and then suspicion; and long before plantations had created a demand for slaves, the English were prejudiced toward black people.

Color was important. For centuries Western society has instinctively attached meaning to various colors. Red, for example, suggests anger, and green symbolizes envy. But the most powerful associations are those connected with black and white. Black has usually been linked with fear, evil, sin, death, and the unknown; white with purity, chastity, light, spiritual essence, and truth. Many people still think of white as good and black as bad. The 1992 edition of the *American Heritage Dictionary of the English Language* included in its definition of *black* the following; ". . . soiled; dirty; evil . . . disgraceful . . . cheerless and depressing; . . . marked by anger or sullenness; . . . deserving of censure or dishonor." But color association alone does not explain the origins of racism. Many Europeans fastened moral values to cultural differences. They examined African culture—homes, food, clothes, languages, and sexual practices—and decided that it was savage and primitive. They also disapproved of African religions. Sixteenth-century Protestantism left little room for toleration. To many Europeans, Africans were heathens, misguided children destined for hell. With its magic and mysticism, its worship of idols and ancestors, African religion seemed sacrilegious. Images of African heathenism reinforced white racism.

If the plantation created the need for involuntary servants, English racism turned American eyes to Africa as the source of slaves. That Africans were numerous, accustomed to settled agriculture, and relatively immune to European diseases made them even more likely candidates for slavery.

African slaves, yoked in pairs, are forcemarched to the coast, where slave ships wait to take them to America. (The Granger Collection)

The Atlantic Slave Trade

The first African slaves were taken by the Portuguese in 1443. The Portuguese began the transatlantic slave trade to supply their Brazilian sugar plantations. Late in the seventeenth century, after tobacco and sugar plantations were established in North America and the Caribbean, the English created the Royal African Company, ending the Portuguese and Dutch monopolies. From that time until its demise in the nineteenth century, the slave trade was dominated by the British.

There were three stages in the Atlantic slave trade. First, the slaves had to be captured, and European traders relied on other Africans to do this. Human bondage was nothing new to West Africa; for centuries West Africans had owned and traded slaves. But slavery was not a capitalist or a racist institution in West Africa. Most slaves were house servants who shared their master's race and whose opportunities for adoption or freedom were relatively good. Slavery was not the harsh, exploitive institution it became in the New World. And at first the slave trade was a casual affair; Africans sold their prisoners of war to the Europeans. By the eighteenth century, however, the trading had assumed economic importance and had become a major cause of war in Africa as coastal tribes competed to supply the New World plantations.

Moving captives from the interior to the coastal exchange posts was the second stage of the trade and was also handled by Africans. Along the way, slaves changed hands several times as African middlemen exacted their own profits. When they reached the coast, the Europeans bought them with rum, cotton cloth, guns, gunpowder, cowrie shells, brass rings, and pig iron.

After plying the African coast for several months acquiring cargo, the slave ship turned west and headed for America. This was the third stage—the "middle passage." Hundreds of slaves were crowded into the dark, damp holds of a slave ship for months at a time, with little or no exercise, subsistence diets, and no sanitary facilities. The mortality rate from flu, dysentery, pleurisy, pneumonia, and smallpox was devastating. Thousands died from "fixed melancholy," a form of mental depression so severe that its victims lost the will to live. Twenty percent of the captives did not survive the voyage. Since perhaps 10 million slaves were taken from Africa to all the colonies in the Western Hemisphere between 1600 and 1800, it can be assumed that millions died in transit. It was, as one European trader recalled, "a dreadful business."

Slavery in Colonial America

Dutch merchants delivered the first Africans to Virginia in 1619. At that time Africans were legally indentured servants, and they were released after seven to ten years of work. Between 1619 and 1660, however, laws prohibiting interracial sex and the possession of firearms by Africans began to appear in Virginia. The length of service for African servants was gradually increased, distinguishing them from white indentured servants. In 1661, the Virginia House of Burgesses called for lifetime servitude in certain cases and shortly thereafter declared that the children of lifetime servants inherited their parents' legal status. At first lifetime servitude was reserved for rebellious or criminal servants, but by 1700 it had become common throughout the country and meant hereditary servitude. Slave codes became more severe during the 1700s. Soon the law viewed slaves as property, people without civil liberties and subject to the absolute legal control of their masters.

Economic and social pressures hurt African Americans in the South. As tobacco, rice, and indigo plantations were developed, black indentured service seemed uneconomical. By requiring service for life, planters eliminated labor turnover and protected their investment. And as the African-American population increased, a sense of insecurity developed among whites. In the northern colonies, where African Americans were less than 5 percent of the population in 1750, there was little insecurity; but it was different in the South. African Americans comprised only 2 percent of the Virginia population in 1640, but they accounted for 31 percent in 1715 and over 40 percent in 1770. Similar situations prevailed in Maryland, the Carolinas, and Georgia. Whites feared the growth of the black population but believed it was economically necessary. Black indentured servitude was expensive and possibly dangerous. African-American servants would someday be free, as would their children. Whites worried about the prospects of having thousands of free African Americans living beyond the authority of the plantation. If all of them were slaves, however, they could be controlled absolutely and, supposedly, would be less threatening to the white community. Not surprisingly, during the last half of the eighteenth century whites transformed African-American labor, replacing indentured servitude with lifetime hereditary slavery.

Deterioration in the treatment of slaves was especially severe in the South. In New England slavery was comparatively mild; slaves joined the Congregational Church, had their marriages recognized by the state, and received limited educations. To a lesser extent, New Jersey, Delaware, and Pennsylvania treated slaves liberally. In New York City, where African Americans accounted for perhaps 15 percent of the population, racial tensions were more pronounced and the slave codes more severe. But for the middle colonies in general, with only 10 percent of the population black and the Quakers demanding humane treatment, race relations were better than in the South.

Changes in the status of African Americans came just as they were playing increasingly important roles in southern life. Since the climate and flora of West Africa resembled those of the South, Africans made conspicuous contributions to the economy. West Africans helped introduce rice cultivation to South Carolina, and Guinea corn was mixed with native American varieties. Experienced in animal husbandry, Africans were put in charge of the livestock. The use of gourds for drinking, grass and reeds for baskets and mats, and palmetto leaves for fans, brooms, and chairs all came from Africa. Familiar with swamps and marshes, Africans dominated fishing and passed on to Europeans their knowledge of temporarily poisoning rivers and streams with quicklime to catch fish. Europeans feared alligators, but Africans knew that, like the crocodiles back home, they could be used to protect livestock. They introduced the use of certain herbs and natural medicines to the colonies, dominated the fur trade as native American traders disappeared, and served in the colonial militias well into the 1700s.

The basis of the southern economy, slavery provided whites with a degree of economic security; but at the same time it robbed them of their emotional security, troubling their consciences and disturbing their sleep. Yet in an extraordinary paradox, slavery enabled white planters to join in the rhetoric of democracy; they could support civil rights for all whites, regardless of economic status, because Africans had come to occupy the bottom of the social ladder. With a readily exploitable slave caste, the whites could at least pay lip service to white democracy. Throughout southern history rich whites would manipulate the racial fears of poor whites, always holding out to them their elite social and political status as whites even though they were desperately poor. In this sense slavery permitted a plutocratic society to sustain a democratic ideology.

Slavery had profound effects on the entire American population, white people as well as blacks. In 1776, when the colonies rose up against England in defense of certain "unalienable" rights, more than 500,000 African Americans lived in bondage. Their plight would soon test the fabric of American values.

The American Revolution

The American Revolution was more than a political separation from England; it also released a set of ideological forces that would ultimately lead to the Civil War. By 1776 the colonists were maturing politically. From England they had inherited ideas of representative government, the evil nature of political power, and the unalienable rights of individuals, and when England violated those rights after 1763, the colonists became revolutionaries willing to resort to violence. In 1861, that spirit ignited the Civil War.

Throughout the eighteenth century Philadelphia Quakers had denounced slavery because of their egalitarian theology. The antislavery movement was also strengthened by the Enlightenment emphasis on reason and natural rights, which made legal justifications for slavery increasingly hollow. And evangelical Protestantism inspired a spirit of abolition in some northern circles by advocating charity toward all people. All these arguments had fallen on deaf ears until the Revolution. But then the inconsistency of denouncing oppression while condoning slavery began to weigh heavily on the Founding Fathers. How could Americans criticize English oppression when 500,000 people were slaves? After 1776 Thomas Paine, Benjamin Franklin, Thomas Jefferson, James Otis, John Adams, Noah Webster, and John Jay all condemned slavery.

The military service of thousands of blacks during the Revolution also pricked the conscience of America. Crispus Attucks, a runaway slave, was shot and killed during the Boston Massacre in 1770 and became the first American to die at the hands of British soldiers. Peter Salem and Salem Poore, both slaves freed to fight in the Continental Army, distinguished themselves at the Battle of Bunker Hill, as did Lemuel Haynes at the Battle of Ticonderoga and "Pompey" at the Battle of Stony Point. Manpower shortages forced state after state to free slaves who would volunteer to fight. Eventually more than five thousand African Americans fought with colonial forces, participating in every major engagement from Lexington in 1775 to Yorktown in 1781. Their service further exposed the hypocrisy of slavery within a revolution.

African Americans in the North

After the Revolution northern agriculture and industry became capital rather than labor intensive, relying on machines instead of people whenever possible. Because wheat, corn, and livestock farms as well as eastern factories did not depend on slave labor, the economic foundation of slavery crumbled. Nor was there a social rationale; the African-American population of the North was too small to threaten white society. There were only 75,000 blacks out of nearly 1.5 million northerners in 1776, and the ratio declined to only 250,000 out of 20 million northerners in 1860. Not often frightened by the African-American minority, whites did not resist abolition; vested social and economic interests had little to lose from it.

For all these reasons a powerful movement arose in the North. Quakers organized the first antislavery society in 1775, and in 1780 Pennsylvania provided for the gradual abolition of slavery. Massachusetts abolished slavery by court order in 1783, and the next year Connecticut and Rhode Island passed general abolition laws. New York and New Jersey enacted similar laws in 1785 and 1786, and in 1787 the Northwest Ordinance prohibited slavery in the Ohio Valley. After fierce debate in 1787, the Constitutional Convention outlawed the importation of slaves after 1807. The American Revolution brought freedom from England and, for African Americans in the North, freedom from bondage.

Legal freedom, however, did not mean equality. In Ohio, Indiana, and Illinois white settlers from the South segregated free blacks whenever possible. White workers there feared economic competition from blacks, and black youths were often placed in long-term apprenticeships closely resembling slavery. African Americans could not serve on juries or vote, and their immigration from other states was barred. Between 1807 and 1887 New Jersey, Connecticut, New York, Rhode Island, and Pennsylvania passed laws disfranchising African Americans. And throughout the North, African Americans were segregated in public facilities and widely discriminated against in the job market. The North was hardly the promised land.

Nevertheless, African Americans created meaningful lives for themselves. By 1860 there were more than 250,000 of them in the North; and although most were poor and restricted to menial jobs, several gained national recognition. Benjamin Banneker was a renowned astronomer and mathematician. Paul Cuffe, a businessman from Massachusetts, became a wealthy shipbuilder and an advocate of African-American rights. Phillis Wheatley, Jupiter Hammon, and Gustavus Vassa were prominent literary figures. David Walker, a free black who had moved to Boston in 1829, wrote *Walker's Appeal,* which called on southern slaves to rise up against their masters. Robert Young, Theodore Wright, Sojourner Truth, Harriet Tubman, David Ruggles, and Charles Remond were all well-known African-American abolitionists.

Perhaps the most famous of all was Frederick Douglass. Born at Tuckahoe, Maryland, in 1817, Douglass escaped from slavery in 1838 and taught himself to read while working as a laborer. In 1841, he spoke at a meeting of the Massachusetts Antislavery Society, captivated the largely white audience, and immediately became one of the most popular abolitionists in the country. Writer, lecturer, and editor of the abolitionist *North Star,* Douglass went on to be active in Republican politics during the Civil War and, before his death in 1895, a Washington official and United States consul general to Haiti. His autobiography, published in 1845, was widely read.

Facing racial prejudice, African Americans turn inward, relying on themselves for respect, recognition, and assistance. A number of early African American organizations opposed slavery and campaigned for equal rights. The National Negro Convention, the American Moral Reform Society for Improving the Condition of Mankind, the General Colored Associations, the African Civilization Society, the American League of Colored Laborers, and the National Council of Colored People demanded abolition of slavery and citizenship for African Americans.

But the most important organizations in the black community were the fraternal, mutual aid societies and the churches. The African Union Society, the Free African Society, the Black Masons, and the Negro Oddfellows supplied medical, educational, and burial services to their members as well as provided a forum for recognizing achievements and resolving disputes. Even more important was the church. Most African Americans were Methodists or Baptists because those churches permitted the ordination of black ministers. They began forming their own congregations late in the eighteenth century. In

1787, after being asked to occupy segregated pews at St. George's Methodist Church in Philadelphia, Richard Allen and Absolom Jones left and established the African Methodist Episcopal (AME) Church. In 1816, the independent AME churches in Pennsylvania, New Jersey, and Delaware joined into a national convocation and named Allen their bishop. African-American Baptist churches also emerged in the North between 1805 and 1810. Independent of white influence, they were influential forums where leadership could be developed and grievances freely expressed. In the process of selecting teachers, officers, ministers, and ecclesiastical representatives, parishioners exercised a franchise power that the larger society denied them. The churches actively promoted educational and fraternal programs. Richard Allen, for example, played a leading role in the Free African Society and the Black Masons. Thus when African Americans became active in their churches, they were also helping to build other social and economic institutions in their communities. Even in our own time, the most influential African-American leaders—including Martin Luther King, Jr. and Jesse Jackson—have come from the African-American churches.

African Americans in the South

The ideological revolution was stillborn in the South. A small but vocal antislavery movement developed in the upper South during the Revolution, but it died out after 1800. To most white Southerners, abolition was an ugly word. Slavery was justified as providing cheap labor and a means of controlling African-American workers.

Just as the economic need for slaves was disappearing in the North, southern dependence on cheap labor was increasing. With their soil exhausted and world markets glutted in the 1790s, tobacco farmers were searching desperately for a more lucrative crop. The Industrial Revolution stimulated demand for cotton, but the South could not fill it because removing seeds from the fiber was too expensive. Eli Whitney solved that problem in 1793 when he invented the cotton gin, a machine that removed the seeds without destroying the cotton fiber, and cotton quickly became the South's major cash crop. Production increased from four thousand bales in 1790 to more than five million bales in 1860. The southern plantation economy depended on having millions of slaves in the fields each day.

Southerners also opposed abolition for social reasons. By 1860 there were four million African Americans to only seven million whites in the South. In Virginia, Texas, and Arkansas whites outnumbered blacks by three to one, but in Mississippi and South Carolina blacks outnumbered whites. The population was divided almost equally in Louisiana, Alabama, Florida, and Georgia. The size of the minority population seemed ominous; whites were obsessed with fears of slave uprisings, and only slavery gave them absolute control over African Americans. Emancipation was unthinkable.

Because the United States was in general a Protestant, capitalistic, and states-rights society, there was no central authority—church or state—to ameliorate the condition of slaves. Slave status imposed severe pressures on African Americans. The decisions of whites often invaded the privacy of social and family life. African Americans were not permitted full decision-making power in their homes. They had to work in the fields even when their children were young, and African-American women were sometimes exploited sexually by white men. Children had to go to work at an early age, and family members could be sold separately at any time. Southern states outlawed any education for slaves, hoping that illiteracy would keep them dependent on their white owners.

Living conditions were primitive. At the age of ten or twelve, African American children went to work in the fields and would perform backbreaking tasks all their lives unless they were among a tiny group of skilled workers or domestic servants. Typical food rations for field hands were four pounds of pork fat, a peck of corn meal, and a small amount of coffee and molasses each week; they usually had one dress or two shirts and one pair of trousers; and they lived in damp, small shanty homes in the "quarters." There were few rewards and few incentives.

But slave owners had to provide a subsistence living for their property, if only to protect their own investment. Planters also had a vested interest in plantation stability because it boosted productivity; terribly unhappy slaves or slaves who hated an overseer were inefficient workers. Slaves resisted in many ways. To avoid field work, many convinced their masters that they were naturally lazy, clumsy, and irresponsible people from whom little could be expected. Other slaves injured farm animals, broke tools, and disabled wagons to postpone work. Some slaves even hurt themselves, inflicting wounds on their hands or legs, to avoid being overworked or sold. Feigning illness was common. Thousands of slaves also ran away, hoping to reach the North or Canada through the Underground Railroad—a group of whites and free blacks who assisted runaway slaves. And there were hundreds of slave rebellions. From the 1712 uprising in New York City, which killed nine whites, to Nat Turner's rebellion in 1831, which resulted in the death of sixty Virginia whites, discontented slaves often used violence to try to liberate themselves. Still, such rebellions were relatively rare; slave resistance was more often directed at ameliorating the conditions of slavery than at liberation.

Within the slave quarters, far from white society, was the world of African America. "From sundown to sunup" a special slave culture appeared—part American, part African—that eased the trauma of bondage, provided group solidarity and status, verbalized aggressions, and demonstrated love. The slaves' relationship with whites during the workday was secondary to their relationship with one another, and scholarly theories describing the slave personality only in terms of white society overlook the primary environment of the quarters. There blacks developed a language of their own, ethical and family values, positive self-images, and group unity.

Leisure time permitted slaves to play social roles different from those of driven servants. In the evenings they gathered to visit and gossip or to sing and dance; on Sundays and holidays they hunted, fished, gambled, attended church, or had afternoon parties. Most excelled at something—racing, storytelling, singing, dancing, preaching, or teaching—and enjoyed prestige from such talents. Leisure activities offered a respite from the drudgery of the fields, a liberation from the emotional pressures of bondage.

Music was central to slaves' lives and accompanied daily activities—work, play, and church services. It was functional and improvisational, symbolically related to group solidarity and individual aspirations. In their songs the slaves retained the form and spirit of their African origins, fashioning expressive modes for dealing with the New World. Spirituals and secular songs helped them express anger or despair that whites would not have tolerated in speech. One slave song went:

> See these poor souls from Africa
> Transported to America;
> We are stolen, and sold in Georgia,
> Will you go along with me?
> We are stolen, and sold in Georgia,
> Come sound the jubilee!
>
> See wives and husbands sold apart,
> Their children's screams will break my heart—
> There's a better day a coming,
> Will you go along with me?
> There's a better day a coming,
> Go sound the jubilee!*

*W.W. Brown, *Narrative of William W. Brown, A Fugitive Slave* (Boston, 1847), p. 51.

Often whites had no idea what the lyrics of slave songs implied, but to African Americans their meaning was quite clear.

By the eighteenth century a distinct African-American culture had appeared. Many African traditions survived. Carrying infants by one arm with the child's legs straddling the mother's hips was an Old World custom, as was coiling, a method of sewing woolen trays. Special styles for braiding hair came from Africa, as did the wearing of head kerchiefs by women. Except for isolated words (such as the West African "okay," which became "OK" to Americans) or the dialects of the most isolated African-American communities (such as the Sea Islanders of Georgia and South Carolina), few African words survived in America. People from all over West Africa were thrown together in a melting pot that used them ethnically. By the eighteenth and nineteenth centuries a fourth-generation African American had little sense of tribal origins.

But although slaves spoke English, it was an English unique in grammar, pronunciation, and morphology. Some fusion with their native tongues occurred. African-American English tended to eliminate predicate verbs, so that such statements as "He is fat" or "He is bad" became "He fat" or "He bad." Slave grammar neglected possessive constructions, saying "Jim hat" rather than "Jim's hat" or "George dog" rather than "George's dog," and it ignored gender pronouns and used "him" and "he" for both the masculine and the feminine. West African dialects had been similar to one another in structure, so in America the slaves used English words but placed them in a grammatical context that was both English and African in origin.

Religion too liberated slaves from the white world and allowed them to express their deep feelings. Slave religion made few distinctions between the secular and the spiritual, between this life and the next, and symbolically carried slaves back in history to more glorious times and forward into a more benign future, linking them with the cosmos and assuring them that there was justice in the universe. Except for proud first-generation Africans tenaciously holding to the faiths of their fathers, most slaves converted to fundamentalist Protestantism, but they imbued it with an emotional spirit all their own. African musical rhythms and dances, voodooism and folk culture, and grave decorations survived in African-American culture; and since the idea of being possessed by a spirit was common in West Africa, the revivalistic flavor of fundamental Protestantism—with its handclapping, rhythmic body movements, public testimonies, and conscious presence of the Holy Ghost—appealed to the slaves. Some white planters encouraged religion as a tool of social control, and white ministers preached bondage as the will of God. Patience, obedience, submission, gratitude—these were the themes of white-sponsored slave religion. Lunsford Lane, an escaped slave, recalled in 1848 that he had often heard white preachers tell slaves

> how good God was in bringing us over to this country from dark . . . Africa, and permitting us to listen to the sound of the gospel. . . . The first command-ment . . . was to obey our masters, and the second was . . . to do as much work when they or the overseers were not watching us as when they were.*

But the slaves were not fooled, and they adapted Christianity to their own needs. In white churches they went through the motions of rever-ent attention, but they were rarely taken in by the joyless message of white preachers bent on molding them into submission. Instead they used white services to visit with friends and family from other farms or plantations, which they could rarely do at other times because the rigid pass laws confined them to their masters' property.

When permitted to worship on their own, the slaves reinterpreted Christianity and enjoyed an autonomy denied them everywhere else. Rejecting Calvinist notions of predestination, unworthiness, sin, and damnation as well as the Pauline doctrine of dutiful obedience, slave spirituals sang of redemption, glory, freedom, change, and justice. African-American culture was not obsessed with guilt and depravity, and black preachers spoke of the spiritual equality of all people and God's uncompromising love for everyone. Threatened on all sides by a hostile environment, black slaves united the next world with this one and bound themselves into a single community, a "chosen people" loved by God. And this redemptive vision thrived even though white society repeatedly tried to tell them that they were the lowliest of human beings. Slave religion allowed slaves to vent the frustrations of bondage, united them in a sense of mission, and recognized them as individuals. Theirs was a spiritual world of deliverance, of Moses leading a special people out of bondage, and Jesus saving them from a corrupt world.

Slave folk tales and beliefs in voodoo, magic, and the world of spirits reinforced the role of religion. African cultures had always assumed that all life had direction and that apparently random events were part of a larger cosmic plan, which could be divined by reading the appropriate "signs" in nature and human affairs. Man was part of a natural pan-theon of life. All things had causes; if one could figure them out, they could be controlled. These ideas were not completely alien to Euro-peans either; beliefs in witchcraft, satanic influence, and magical heal-ings were still widely held. Slaves used folk beliefs and folk medicine to

*Lunsford Lane, *The Narrative of Lunsford Lane* (Boston, 1848), pp. 20-21.

heal the sick, and some folk practitioners were highly respected. Certain signs—an owl's screech, a black cat crossing one's path, the approach of a cross-eyed person—indicated bad luck ahead, which could be remedied by such devices as spitting, crossing fingers, turning pockets inside out, or turning shoes upside down on the porch. Dreams had great meaning. The world of magic and voodoo gave slaves a sense of power over their masters, for in the hexes, signs, and punishments of the supernatural they tried to control the behavior of whites and their own destiny. African folk culture offered a degree of power, a means of integrating life and transcending enslavement.

Finally, in the slave family African Americans found companionship, love, esteem, and sexual fulfillment—things the master-slave relationship denied them. Despite the breakup of families through the sale of slaves, white sexual exploitation of black women, and incursions on the authority of black parents, the family was the basic institution of slave society. Although antebellum slave society tolerated premarital sexual liaisons, adultery was strictly forbidden. Once two people had "jumped the broomstick," fidelity was expected. Typical slave households had two parents and were male dominated: the father exercised discipline and supplemented the family diet by hunting and fishing, and the mother was responsible for household duties and raising young children. Most slave marriages were sound—when husband and wife were allowed to remain together—and most African-American children traced lineage through their fathers rather than their mothers. That former slaves eagerly had their marriages legalized after the Civil War and searched the country over to reunite separated families confirms the loyalty of parents, children, and spouses.

African-American women found themselves in uniquely difficult circumstances. Because of their legal status as chattel, they were vulnerable to sexual exploitation by their white owners, and they were always faced with the threat of losing their husbands and children through sale. At the same time, as women, they lived in nuclear family settings where patriarchical authority was very real. A few radical historians have argued that slavery, by emasculating African-American men, truly liberated African-American women, but consensus opinion agrees that African-American women had to deal with the power of white men and black men on the plantations. Because of that reality, they developed complex networks of relationships with other African-American women, and that sense of sisterhood assisted them in dealing emotionally with their society.

Despite their ability to rise above the dehumanizing effects of slavery, African Americans were still embittered about their fate in the United States. Olaudah Equiano, an Ibo tribesman, expressed those feelings:

Well may I say my life has been
One scene of sorrow and of pain;
From early days I griefs have known,
And as I grew my griefs have grown.

Dangers were always in my path,
And fear of wrath and sometimes death;
While pale dejection in me reign'd
I often wept, my grief constrain'd.

When taken from my native land,
By an unjust and cruel hand,
How did uncommon dread prevail!
My sighs no more I could conceal.*

Slavery and the Civil War

Since the colonial period economic interest and political philosophy
had divided the North and the South. Committed to an agrarian economy and international export markets, the South had never seen the
need for a national bank, high tariffs, internal improvements, or any
other measures designed to stimulate industry. Most southern politicians preached laissez-faire, states' rights, and a strict interpretation of
the Constitution to prevent preferential treatment of northern manufacturers. With a mixed economy of farming, commerce, and manufacturing, the North favored protective tariffs, a strong national bank, and
federally financed internal improvements.

But when the issue of slavery was added to these differences, civil war
erupted. Slavery was the structural foundation of southern society. It
created a static caste system in the South, different from the more open
class system of the North. And slavery went against the ideas of democracy, equality, and freedom. Some Northerners attacked it as a moral
evil, while many Southerners defended it as a moral good, a way of
preserving white culture and introducing black people to Christian
civilization.

At first the national debate was limited. William Lloyd Garrison and
Frederick Douglass called for the immediate abolition of slavery, but
most Northerners were unwilling to sanction such a radical disruption
of southern life. Instead they opted for more gradual schemes. Formed
in 1816, the American Colonization Society campaigned to resettle
African Americans in Africa, and before the Civil War the society sent

*Gustavus Vassa, *The Interesting Narrative of the Life of Olaudah Equiano, or Gustavus
Vassa, The African* (London, 1794), p. 290.

several thousand people to Liberia. Most free African Americans detested the idea, claiming the right of any other native-born American to dignity and equality within the United States. Other Northerners wanted gradual abolition and compensation by the federal government to slaveholders for the loss of their property. The South would have none of it.

Most Northerners realized that immediate abolition, gradual abolition, and colonization were naive, unworkable approaches to the problem. They decided just to oppose the extension of slavery into the western territories, hoping to contain the "peculiar institution" in the Old South, where it might expire gradually. The Liberty party of 1840 and 1844, the Free-Soil party of 1848, and the Republican party— organized in 1854—committed themselves to that objective. But Southerners believed that for slavery and the plantation system to survive they would have to have access to fresh soil in the West.

The sectional strife also reflected attitudes toward the composition of American society. A minority of northern whites opposed the expansion of slavery into the territories because they believed slavery was immoral and that any measures strengthening it were similarly evil. But they were joined by millions of others who opposed the expansion of slavery for economic reasons—free white workers could not compete financially with slaves—or who disliked African Americans in general. Confining slavery to the South would guarantee free territories and a largely white society, where the entrepreneurial instincts of Yankee culture could flourish. Southern whites, convinced that containment of slavery was a first step toward its ultimate eradication, and terrified by the prospect of having four million former slaves in the South, insisted on the right to carry slaves into the territories, which the Dred Scott decision by the Supreme Court in 1857 permitted them to do. Southerners also realized that containment of slavery would guarantee the nationwide triumph of Yankee entrepreneurialism and its faith in technological change, material progress, and democratic egalitarianism. So in part the debate over free-soil politics was a cultural conflict between Yankee Northerners and white Southerners.

Between 1820 and 1860 every sectional crisis in the United States— the Missouri Compromise of 1820, the Mexican War of 1846, the Compromise of 1850, the Kansas-Nebraska Act of 1854, and the Dred Scott case of 1857—involved slavery in the territories. When the Republican candidate, Abraham Lincoln, won the presidential election of 1860 on a platform of free soil, protective tariffs, a national bank, and internal improvements, white Southerners felt threatened socially, economically, and philosophically. The South panicked and seceded from the Union.

The Civil War ultimately destroyed slavery and resolved, legally at least, the status of African Americans. At first Lincoln's objectives were narrowly defined. The Civil War had broken out, he thought, only because Southerners had insisted on carrying their slaves to the West; the North was fighting to prevent that and bring the South back into the Union. Preservation of the Union, not abolition, was the central issue. Suspicious of radical social change, Lincoln opposed abolition in the early months of the war. When General John C. Fremont entered Missouri in 1861 and freed the slaves, Lincoln angrily rescinded the order, and the next year he nullified General David Hunter's abolition order in Georgia, South Carolina, and Florida.

But a number of pressures transformed the Civil War into a struggle to preserve the Union and liberate the slaves. First, most Northerners, including the president himself, had anticipated a brief, conclusive war in which superior northern forces would overwhelm the Confederacy. But after staggering defeats at Bull Run and in the Shenandoah Valley in 1861 and 1862, a war of attrition developed. Lincoln hoped abolition might disrupt the southern economy by depriving the Confederacy of four million slaves.

Political and ideological concerns also pushed Lincoln toward emancipation. Republican abolitionists were steadily gaining strength by denouncing the hypocrisy of proclaiming democracy while condoning slavery. Radical Republicans including Thaddeus Stevens, Charles Sumner, Wendell Phillips, and Benjamin Wade insisted that Lincoln abolish slavery and were outraged when he repealed military abolition orders. Lincoln was in political trouble. Military defeats had dissipated his popularity, and a powerful wing of his own party was condemning his racial insensitivity. If he was to be renominated in 1864, Lincoln had to revive his popularity and attract Radical support. Abolition might do it. By appearing as a moral crusader rather than just a political leader, Lincoln hoped to shore up his crumbling political fortunes.

But regaining Radical Republican support posed another dilemma. Abolition would please the Radicals, but if Lincoln freed the slaves he would sacrifice the support of Democrats loyal to the Union in Delaware, Maryland, Kentucky, and Missouri—slaveowners who had opposed secession. Abolition might win renomination, but it would just as surely cost Lincoln the general election. Some way of satisfying Radical Republicans without alienating loyal slave-owning Democrats had to be found. Lincoln slowly moved toward partial emancipation. In the spring of 1862 he supported congressional abolition of slavery in the District of Columbia and in the territories. Finally, on January 1, 1863, Lincoln issued the Emancipation Proclamation, liberating only the slaves in the rebellious states. The 400,000 slaves in loyal border states remained slaves. Lincoln thus gained Radical support without estranging border Democrats. And in another brilliant political maneuver he selected Andrew Johnson, a loyal Tennessee Democrat, as his running mate in the election of 1864. He then went on to reelection.

In April 1865, the Union armies trapped General Robert E. Lee's troops near Appomattox Court House in Virginia. The Confederacy was finished and Lee surrendered. The national nightmare was over. More than 600,000 people and $15 billion had disappeared in the smoke of destruction; dreams were broken, faiths shattered, and lives wasted. The South was a pocked wasteland of untilled farms, broken machinery, gutted buildings, fresh graves, worthless money, and defeated people. Schools, banks, and businesses were closed; inflation was spiraling; and unemployment was on the rise. Only the former slaves were hopeful that a new age of liberty and equality was dawning.

Reconstruction

The status of African Americans in American society had become a national obsession. Were they to remain beasts of burden, slaves in everything but name, or were they to become full citizens protected by the Constitution?

Radical Republicans wanted to elevate the political status of African Americans in the South. Supporters of high tariffs, federal internal improvements, free homesteads in the West, and free soil, the Republicans had been unpopular in the South long before the war; now, to keep control of the federal government, they had to construct a southern political base. Former slaves would be the new constituency; the party of Lincoln, of freedom, would become the party of equality. By giving African Americans the right to vote and hold public office, the Republicans intended to preserve their ascendancy. Only then could they be sure that Congress would pass the tariffs and subsidies the business community needed. Northern entrepreneurs were also looking to the South as an economic colony, a source of raw materials and a market for finished products. Interested in the coal, iron, tobacco, cotton, and railroad industries of the South, northern investors wanted southern state legislatures to be Republican and pro-business. And many former abolitionists, now active among the Radical Republicans, wanted freedom converted into civil rights for the former slaves. Politics, economics, and ideology all combined to create a movement for African-American political liberty.

Thus during the Reconstruction period, the late 1860s and 1870s, Radical Republicans insisted on political rights for four million African

Americans. In March 1865, Congress created the Freedmen's Bureau to help them make the transition to freedom. The bureau sent thousands of doctors, nurses, lawyers, social workers, teachers, and administrative agents into the South to provide emergency food, jobs, housing, medical care, and legal aid to former slaves. Many white Southerners hated the bureau and called its agents "carpetbaggers," but the bureau played an invaluable role in the South. The Thirteenth Amendment, ratified in December 1865, extended the Emancipation Proclamation to the border states. Slavery was ended. Early in 1866, Congress passed the Civil Rights Act outlawing discrimination on the basis of race, and two years later the Fourteenth Amendment gave all African Americans citizenship and prohibited states from interfering with their civil liberties. In 1870, the Fifteenth Amendment gave them the right to vote.

White Southerners fought back. Some states elected former Confederate authorities to local and state offices. Mississippi refused to ratify the Thirteenth Amendment and was joined by Georgia, Texas, and Virginia in postponing ratification of the Fourteenth Amendment. State legislatures enacted "black codes" segregating African Americans in schools and public facilities, prohibiting them from carrying firearms or changing jobs, imposing strict vagrancy and curfew regulations on them, and making it virtually impossible for them to enter the skilled trades or the professions. In July 1866, when several hundred African Americans and Unionists held a rally in New Orleans to protest the Louisiana black code, state troops moved in and shot two hundred demonstrators, killing forty of them. Organized in 1865, the Ku Klux Klan relied on shootings, lynchings, torture, and intimidation to terrorize southern African Americans into political submission.

The presence of Union troups guaranteed Reconstruction. More than 700,000 African-American men gained the right to vote in 1870, and along with the so-called carpetbaggers (Northerners living in the South) and scalawags (white Southerners in the Republican party), they took over every southern government except Virginia's. Sixteen former slaves, including Hiram Revels and Blanche Bruce of Mississippi, entered the United States Congress, and hundreds of others took seats in the legislatures of South Carolina, North Carolina, Louisiana, Mississippi, Alabama, Arkansas, and Florida. Yet African Americans never dominated any state government, even though this period has been called Black Reconstruction.

Reconstruction governments in the South have sometimes been criticized as corrupt and incompetent. There was some corruption, to be sure, but the Reconstruction legislatures built the South's first public school system, eliminated debt imprisonment and property requirements for voting, repaired war-destroyed public buildings and roads, rebuilt railroads, repealed the black codes, enacted homestead laws, and tried to end discrimination in public facilities. Southern state governments were responding to the needs of poor people as well as rich, black as well as white.

Reconstruction collapsed as soon as Union troops left the South; African Americans did not have the economic independence to survive politically. Radical Republicans had worried about black economic status and had even considered breaking up the plantations and distributing land among African-American families. But the confiscation schemes never made it through Congress, probably because they so clearly represented an assault on private property. Although former slaves had gained the right to vote, they were economically dependent on propertied whites. When the troops left, whites exploited that dependence.

Nor were Republicans as concerned in 1877 about southern African Americans as they had been in 1865. Politically they felt more secure about the future because new states were entering the Union. Nevada had become a state in 1864, and Nebraska followed three years later. Colorado received statehood in 1876, and the Dakotas, Montana, Washington, Idaho, Wyoming, and Utah would soon apply. Republican members of Congress from the new states would more than make up for the loss of the African-American vote in the South. Removal of federal troops, disfranchisement of black Republicans, and the resurrection of the white aristocracy no longer seemed so potentially disastrous. Northern businesspeople began to think their economic interests might best be served by white Democrats. The civil rights momentum evaporated. By 1877 the federal government had withdrawn its troops and whites were back in power in the South. Reconstruction was over, and African-American voters would soon fall victim to poll taxes, literacy tests, and white primaries.

During Reconstruction southern African Americans had to adjust to their new freedom, and most did so simply by struggling to create a stable family life based on legal marriages, reunions, the purchase of land, and education. When the Union armies entered the South, they had established "contraband" camps where escaped slaves could live. Although the camps were makeshift and run by white soldiers who were often openly racist, African Americans used the camps enthusiastically to begin their new lives. At the Fortress Monroe, Craney Island, and City Point camps mass ceremonies were held to legalize slave marriages. Blacks longed for the sanctity and stability of family life that legal marriage held out for them. They also wanted desperately to find family members who had been sold away. One slave song proclaimed:

> I've got a wife, and she's got a baby
> Way up North in Lower Canady—
> Won't dey shout when dey see Ole Shady
> Comin', Comin',! Hail, mighty day.
> Den away, Den away, for I can't stay any longer:
> Hurrah, Hurrah! for I am going home. *

Newspapers abounded with personal classified ads of former slaves trying to locate loved ones. One reason African Americans wandered so widely throughout the South after emancipation was not because they were irresponsible or did not want to work but because they were searching for parents, spouses, and children. Family reunion was the first task of freedom. Next came land and education. Thousands sacrificed to acquire their own farms, despite opposition from local whites, and tens of thousands supported Freedmen's Bureau schools to help educate their children. Emancipation held out the hope of a normal life in the United States, and African American Southerners were determined to have it.

*Frank Moore, ed., *The Rebellion Record*, 11 vols. (New York, 1862–1864) 8:63.

Part I Conclusion

Ethnic America
in 1890

As the 1890s opened, American life seemed stable. People had resumed the normal business of life. After seventeen years of military conflict and political instability, the Civil War and Reconstruction were over. The Union was preserved, the states' rights philosophy defeated, and the noble experiment of African American civil equality ended. Americans were taking up where they had left off in 1860, conquering the continent and transforming the environment into material wealth and security. Approximately sixty million people were living in the United States by 1890, and the end of one era and beginning of another would have enormous consequences for all of them: for the twenty-three million people of British descent as well as for the other European and racial minorities.

African Americans were immediately affected by changes in the political and social climate. For thirty years they had been the focal point in the national debate over free soil, abolition, and equality. When the last federal troops left Florida, South Carolina, and Louisiana in 1877, there were approximately seven million African Americans living in the United States, 85 percent of them still in the South. Black communities existed in most northern states, and thousands of black farmers and cowboys had moved west, but most African Americans were still attached to the soil of the rural South. For fourteen years, between the Emancipation Proclamation of 1863 and the election of 1876, the Republican party had experimented with racial equality, trying through the Fourteenth Amendment, the Fifteenth Amendment, and the civil rights laws of 1866 and 1875 to give African Americans power at the ballot box. And as long as federal troops patrolled the South, the white descendants of the early English, Scots, Scots-Irish, and German settlers had put up with the reforms. But by 1877 northern Republicans had tired of their "southern strategy." New GOP votes were pouring in from the western states and the need for African-American votes was declining. Tired of the political instability generated by army troops and the Ku Klux Klan, and anxious to invest in the resources and labor of the South, northern business-owners called for an end to the experiment. The troops left, conservative white Dixiecrats resumed their former positions of power, and black Republicanism was dead. With neither capital nor land, southern blacks were poor and dependent once again on the power of the white upper class. Jim Crow laws were already appearing.

Changes were also affecting native Americans. The advance of Christian missionaries, environmental change, disease, and hundreds of thousands of white settlers had devastated the native American population. By 1890 there were only about 250,000 native Americans, most of them barely surviving on government reservations. Contemptuous of white values but unable to defend their traditional ways, some were turning to pan-Indian spiritual movements to deal with their new lives. From the Great Basin, the Sun Dance religion of the Utes and Shoshones was spreading to other native American communities; the gospel of the Ghost Dance was still affecting native Americans throughout the Plains; and from Mexico via the Mescalero Apaches, the peyote cult was gaining thousands of native American converts.

On the West Coast, nativism had resulted in the Chinese Exclusion Act of 1882. Because of rumors from missionaries and traders traveling in China and fears of their own, local officials were passing harassment laws against the Chinese, and the Workingmen's party in California was demanding deportation. For their part, the Chinese were working hard on railroads, commercial farms, construction projects, factories, and in their own businesses, governing their own community while earning enough money to return to the "Celestial Kingdom," where their families would forever live in prosperity and honor, free of the poverty and pain of peasant life.

And throughout the Southwest nearly 300,000 Mexican Americans were trying to keep hold of their land despite the influx of thousands of Anglo settlers. By 1890 the tejanos and californios were vastly outnumbered by Anglo farmers and were rapidly losing their land through fraudulent decisions by local judges, state legislatures, and public land commissions. In New Mexico the nuevos mexicanos still retained most of their land and a good deal of power in the territorial legislature, but large-scale Anglo immigration would soon develop, as it had earlier in California and Texas. Mexican Americans tried to save their land, but like native Americans, they would lose it; and like African Americans, they would become a low-income laboring people.

Disfranchised and poor, these minorities were on the defensive. In the South, people of British and German descent had wrested political power from black Republicans; on the Great Plains, British, German, and Scandinavian farmers had pushed Indians onto reservations; in California, English, German, and Irish workers had discriminated against the Chinese; and hundreds of thousands of white farmers, mostly of British and German descent, had acquired Mexican-American land.

Except in their attitudes toward nonwhites, there was little unanimity among white Europeans in the United States; they too were divided along ethnic lines in 1890. Scattered throughout urban America but concentrated in the Northeast were more than six million Irish Catholics. Still poor, ostracized socially because of their religion, and largely confined to poor housing downtown near the docks, warehouses, and railroad terminals or in peripheral shantytowns and "Paddy's Villages," they were a distinct ethnic community. Every major city had an Irish population, and the immigrants took great pride in being Irish and Roman Catholic. From the coal fields of Pennsylvania, where the Molly Maguires had fought discrimination, to the great railroad strikes of 1877, the Irish immigrants were working for a better standard of living. And from urban political machines they were about to strike back against Protestant assaults on their saloons, parochial schools, and Catholic charities.

Throughout rural and urban America there were more than eight million people of German descent. A diverse group of Lutherans, Calvinists, Catholics, and pietists from various provinces in Germany, they had possessed neither nationalistic nor religious unity, but by 1890 they were becoming more conscious of their German nationality. Mostly concentrated in rural villages and urban centers of the German belt and German triangle, and linguistically isolated from the rest of America, they too constructed their own ethnic world and exhibited an overwhelming inclination—in the first generation, at least—to marry other Germans.

The Norwegian, Swedish, Danish, Finnish, Dutch, Swiss, and French immigrants were too-recent arrivals in 1890 to be threatened by assimilation. Of the 1.2 million Scandinavians living on the farms and in the towns of Michigan, Wisconsin, Illinois, Minnesota, Iowa, and the Dakotas, more than 900,000 had arrived or been born since 1870. Although many of the New York and New Jersey Dutch had deep roots in the colonial period, most of the 80,000 Dutch in Michigan and Wisconsin had come to America since 1870, as had more than half of the 200,000 Swiss settlers in the Midwest. And the French community in the United States—500,000 French Canadians in New England and the Great Plains, 200,000 Cajuns in Louisiana, and 150,000 immigrants from France—was still separated by religion and language from the larger society.

For all these people the melting pot did not really exist in 1890. In schools, shops, and churches the Old World languages and customs were still flourishing; time and the passing of generations had not yet blurred the European past. Ethnic America in 1890 was still that—a nation of ethnic communities.

The most distinguishing feature of ethnic America in 1890 was the rise of the ethnic city. Rural agrarian America was disappearing into the urban industrial complex of the twentieth century. Cities were attracting all kinds of people with promises of jobs, freedom, anonymity, and excitement. It was an extraordinary time. New York City grew from sixty thousand people in 1800 to more than a million in 1860, and cities like Buffalo, Chicago, Cleveland, and Cincinnati were doubling their populations every decade. But American cities were totally unprepared to absorb millions of new inhabitants. Housing, sanitation, transportation, water and utilities, and police and fire services were far from adequate; as a result, crime, disease, crowding, and vice were common. Entrepreneur landlords began building tenements and converting stables, cellars, sheds, and warehouses into multifamily housing. Even in smaller cities Irish and French-Canadian shantytowns appeared on the outskirts as the immigrants found work in the mills and factories. Poverty, unemployment, and sickness were a rude shock for the immigrants as well as for better-established Americans. Whether it was the Chinese in San Francisco, the Scandinavians in Minneapolis, the Germans in St. Louis, the Irish in New York, or the French-Canadians in Boston, urban life was new and strange to them.

In Holyoke, Massachusetts, for example, the Irish immigrants of the 1840s worked in the city's textile and industrial economy, and soon after settling they established a Roman Catholic parish in what was once a center of English Congregationalism. Then, in the late 1850s, French-Canadians began moving in to take up jobs in the textile mills, and so did a few hundred German Lutherans. Soon there was a French Catholic parish in Holyoke as well as a German Lutheran church and a Catholic hospital, orphanage, and parochial school. Similar patterns occurred in other Massachusetts mill towns—Lowell, Lawrence, Fall River. In larger cities ethnic diversity increased between 1776 and 1890. In Rochester, New York, Irish Catholics had a parish in the

1820s; German Catholics, Lutherans, and Reformed were established in the 1830s; and a French-Canadian parish, a Reformed German-Jewish synagogue, and a Dutch Reformed church all came in the 1870s. In major metropolitan areas such as Boston the massive influx of the Irish in the 1840s transformed the physical landscape. They were followed by other immigrants who crowded into downtown Boston near the piers, warehouses, markets, and factories while the English, Scots, and Germans fled for quieter suburbs in the West End, South End, and Charlestown. Eventually, as the street railways reached into every area of the city, prosperous immigrants or their children headed for better homes in the suburbs, leaving the downtown slums for poorer, newer immigrants to fill. In a few years they too would be moving toward the suburbs and replaced by southern and eastern Europeans, then by southern blacks in the 1920s, 1930s, and 1940s, and by Puerto Ricans after World War II. In 1890 most Americans were still living in a rural, agrarian world, but the outlines of the future were clearly drawn.

Assimilation among these people was almost nonexistent in 1890 because a third immigrant generation had not yet appeared. Except for the Irish, the mass migration from Europe did not begin until the 1850s, and not until after the Civil War did it reach flood-tide proportions. Immigrants and their children were tightly bound into their own ethnic families, churches, and associations, and social contact outside work and business was infrequent. Still, acculturation was well under way by 1890. Despite vigorous attempts to preserve Old World ways, the adoption of some dimensions of American culture was inevitable. For the second generation the use of English became the rule, and the Old World tongue became a relic used only in speaking to parents or grandparents. As historian Marcus Hansen has written, members of the second generation often worked at acquiring at least the appearance of American culture. They spoke English with relish, quickly shed Old World costumes for the utilitarian, mass-produced clothing of America, and celebrated such holidays as the Fourth of July and Thanksgiving with patriotic fervor. They were also affected by the ideological flavor of American life and imbued with the American faith in progress, at least after the initial shock of migration and settlement had passed. They became enthusiastic supporters of Manifest Destiny, American democracy, and natural rights and popular sovereignty.

By 1890 the immigrants were also expanding their contacts with other white ethnic groups. They had long worked and done business with a wide variety of people, but their family and social contacts had been narrowly defined. That was slowly changing. As the immigrants made the transition to English, some contact with other groups occurred in the churches. When the German and Scandinavian churches switched to English-language services, some of the immigrants and their children began attending the Lutheran or pietist church closest to home. Industrialization and the rise of factories accelerated that trend. Over the course of the nineteenth century, home manufacturing declined as factory production increased. Men and women found themselves interacting at the workplace with individuals from other ethnic backgrounds. And as the public school movement spread throughout the country in the 1870s and 1880s, the Protestant ethnic parochial schools gradually disappeared and English, German, Scots, Danish, Norwegian, and Swedish children began attending the common school together. As the so-called street-car suburbs expanded out from the cities, the Germans, English, Irish, and Scandinavians fanned out to newer homes and apartments. Income as well as ethnic group came to determine residential patterns, and people from different cultural backgrounds found themselves living together as neighbors. That further encouraged cultural assimilation and led to the full assimilation that would occur in the twentieth century.

Finally, political controversy helped integrate the immigrant communities into the larger society. Across the United States—from the Irish ghettos of the East to the German Catholic centers in the Midwest and the tiny Dutch Catholic settlements in Michigan—Roman Catholics supported the Democratic party in 1880. English Protestants, Welsh Methodists, Scandinavian Lutherans, Irish Protestants, and Dutch Reformed were more likely to vote Republican. German pietists also voted Republican, while German Lutherans and Reformed broke the pattern by narrowly supporting the Democrats. In part the ethnic cleavage in American politics had an economic base. The Whigs and Republicans had traditionally reflected the interests of business and commerce, and—in an economy just beginning to industrialize— those of skilled craftsmen who were still either small businessmen themselves or the elite of the labor force in mining and manufacturing. Generally, businessmen of British descent believed the Republican party would best promote their economic needs. And in the 1860s and 1870s, when most of the Dutch, German, and Scandinavian farmers poured into the Midwest, the Republican party had favored free land through the Homestead Act. So among businessmen, skilled workers, and northern farmers the Republican party enjoyed strong support.

But in 1890, cultural values were as effective a barometer of political behavior as were economic interests. Ethnic groups supporting the Republican party were usually pietistic or evangelical in religion whereas more formal, ritualistic groups tended to support the Democrats. That is, the Baptists, Methodists, Presbyterians, Quakers, Scandinavian

Lutherans, and Scandinavian and Dutch Calvinists in the North were often Republicans, while Roman Catholics and high-church Lutherans were generally Democrats. Emphasizing formalism and priestly authority, the Catholics and German Lutherans viewed the world skeptically, as if secular affairs really were distinct from religious ones and people could do little to purify the world of corruption or make it perfect. Instead of perfecting the world, they usually wanted to ameliorate some of society's worst conditions, particularly to ensure that people's standard of living was sufficient to make family and religious life fulfilling. The Irish poet John Boyle O'Reilly condemned poverty and class differences in his writings; journalist Patrick Ford bitterly described urban poverty and unemployment in the pages of the Irish World; Henry George, author of *Progress and Poverty* (1879), proposed a "single tax" on all profits from the sale or rental of land; and Irish political machines freely distributed food, fuel, and jobs to poor people in the cities.

The evangelical Protestants, however, felt an intense need to purify the world of sin, to change people's minds and behavior. While the ritualists turned to the parish and parochial school to preserve their values, the evangelicals ultimately tried to legislate their morality. Because Catholics and conservative Lutherans would not abandon their saloons and parochial schools voluntarily, the evangelicals sought to force them to do so. To achieve their objectives, they turned to the Republican party, which in the middle of the nineteenth century had promoted strong government, free land, and abolition. Carrie Nation's crusade against alcohol and in favor of prohibition was just one example of cultural politics in the nineteenth century. Ritualists turned to the Democratic party for just the opposite reasons, because it opposed a strong central state and respected the prerogatives of local communities.

Throughout the nineteenth century evangelical Republicans advocated change while ritualistic Democrats supported tradition and stability. The Protestants opposed parochial schools as preserving Old World traditions and Catholic values, so they promoted public schools. The Catholics saw the public schools as "Protestant" schools: Protestant ministers served on school boards, Protestant prayers were repeated each morning, and the King James Bible was used for instruction. The Protestants supported prohibition as a means of purifying the world, but the ritualists viewed liquor as a harmless diversion and opposed the temperance movement. The Protestants supported Sabbath laws to close stores and taverns on Sunday, and the Catholics opposed such laws as unnecessary invasions of their privacy. So while Protestants in the Republican party worked to create a homogeneous America free of sin, Catholics and high-church Lutherans in the Democratic party tried to create a stable world where family and religious values could flourish. After 1900, as industrialization continued its inexorable transformation of the social structure, economic issues would become more important; but in 1890, culture still shaped political loyalties and group relations in the United States.

Part II
ETHNIC AMERICA IN TRANSITION, 1890–1945

Between 1890 and 1945 the United States changed so much that all previous upheavals in American history seemed mild in comparison. Despite the Civil War, the westward movement, and ten million immigrants, the United States in 1877 was still an isolated society of small farmers and small towns. Independent and relatively self-sufficient, most Americans lived in a world of "island communities," small clusters of people insulated in networks of personal relationships. They still looked out on the world through an individualistic lens and confidently believed that God viewed white Protestant America with special affection.

Seventy years later—after industrialization, the flight to the cities, the new immigration, two world wars, and the Great Depression—doubts had tarnished that confidence. America had become an even more ethnically complex society of white- and blue-collar workers living in crowded cities, and few people viewed reality through a single prism of individuality. Industrialization had created a vast national market of impersonal economic relationships, while the rise of the cities had brought a social anonymity. Individualism was giving way to organization and bureaucratic routine.

But some threads of history were intact, for Americans were still trying to make the ideals of 1776 succeed. Between 1890 and 1945, American pluralism became more intricate as new immigrants from eastern and southern Europe and Asia settled in the cities, and as native Americans, African Americans, and Mexicans began demanding their place in the sun. Once again Americans would have to decide whether egalitarianism applied to everyone regardless of race, religion, or national origins. Time and time again, from the rise of Jim Crow laws in the 1880s to the incarceration of Japanese Americans in the 1940s, white America would fail the test, but the ideological commitment survived. Most Americans tried to work out their dream amidst the traumas of war, economic collapse, and social change—to discover "America" and interpret its mission. Pluralism, equality, and nationalism, the ideological pantheon of the American Revolution, remained the vision of 1945.

The most fundamental transformation was economic, and changes in the production of goods brought monumental changes in social life. Ever since 1607 the American economy had been "exceptional," marked by a virgin continent, seemingly limitless resources, a labor shortage, and an entrepreneurial zeal unmatched in the Western world. The result was the greatest economic machine in history. As expanding networks of turnpikes, canals, and railroads created a national market, farmers mechanized commercial agriculture, and large corporations shipped goods everywhere. Just as the rise of factories was drawing workers into the cities, the mechanization of agriculture was driving farmers off the land. Between 1877 and 1945 the United States ceased to be a country of farms and villages and became a nation of cities and factories, complete with an industrial proletariat and a bureaucratic middle class working for large corporations.

Public policy changed with industrialization. In the past Americans had viewed government as the greatest threat to individual liberty, and the Bill of Rights and the laissez-faire philosophy were originally designed to limit government interference in people's lives. But with the rise of giant corporations, people began to see private interests as the real threat to liberty. Once considered the enemy of freedom, the federal government now became the only force capable of dealing with corporate power. The Populist movement of the 1890s and the Progressive movement of the early 1900s worked to preserve competition and regulate the corporations, and in the 1930s the New Deal went on to underwrite economic investment, provide jobs, and supply social welfare. To offset corporate power, others organized countervailing interest groups. Doctors, dentists, lawyers, professors, and engineers formed professional associations. Skilled workers joined the Knights of Labor and the American Federation of Labor, and later on skilled and unskilled workers joined the Congress of Industrial Organizations. Farmers set up marketing cooperatives, federations, shipping associations, and trade groups. The reign of economic individualism was over, and only through interest groups could people hope to protect themselves.

The New Immigrants

If industrialization threatened individualism, the "new immigration" challenged cultural pluralism. Late in the nineteenth century, countries in southern and eastern Europe were integrated into the Atlantic economy just as industrialization was creating millions of jobs in the United States. Peasant life in Europe had remained unchanged for centuries. People yearned for stability and tradition, not for profit and change. At the center of their world was the family and the land. Land was the source of survival, status, and independence, and families possessed a temporary stewardship over it. Marriages were negotiated between families; spouses and children were expected to contribute to the family and the land and to remain all their lives within reach of home and loved ones. Several families made up a village, and beyond that microcosm of family, farm, parish, and village lay an alien world of strangers. Life and destiny were local affairs, and governments, foreigners, and aristocracies were either malignant or irrelevant.

Economic changes upset that tranquillity, threatening land ownership and family security. Enormous population increases in Poland, Russia, Italy, Austria-Hungary, and the Balkans fragmented landholdings until it was difficult for peasants to support their families. Large landowners functioned as a social and political elite; and although serfdom was rapidly disappearing, most peasants were still tied to the large estates as tenants or owned tiny plots. In 1880, of the 1.7 million Polish peasants in Galicia, the average farmer owned fewer than six acres. Eighty percent of the Magyars in Hungary lived off agriculture, but half the peasant farmers owned fewer than five acres. Another 1.5 million were farm laborers or tenants. In some parts of Croatia and Serbia the average peasant holding was fewer than three acres.

Population increases were devastating. Serbia's population, for example, grew from 1.7 to 2.9 million between 1878 and 1910, and Russia's was expanding by a million people each year. Although population density was often lower than in western Europe, the number of people per acre of tilled land was much higher. In the Like-Krbava district of Croatia in 1880, nearly 270,000 people were trying to make a living on only 225,000 acres of arable land. Not only did peasants have difficulty supporting their families, but it was almost impossible for younger people to acquire land. One Polish peasant wrote to the Emigrants' Protective Association in Warsaw, asking it

> to advise me how I could migrate to America with my family . . . I intend to go also and buy there some land, for in Wolyn it is very dear—a desiatina costs as much as 500 roubles. What can I buy, when I have 5 boys and only 2,000 roubles? I could perhaps buy in Russia, but what is the use of it since there are no Catholic churches and my faith would get lost. *

Nineteenth-century Croatia was an agrarian society organized into *zadrugas*, communal villages where land was owned by kinship systems rather than by private individuals. Class distinctions blurred in the zadrugas, and the order and tempo of daily life were predictable. But population increases destroyed zadruga life; the village could not support all the people. Similar conditions developed throughout eastern Europe.

Technology also changed peasant life. Early in the nineteenth century, cereal culture had spread throughout Bohemia, Moravia, Slovakia, out to the Pannonian Plain of Hungary, and into Poland, Lithuania, the Ukraine, Slovenia, and Croatia. But late in the century, American wheat began depressing grain prices in eastern Europe. In some areas peasant income fell to only fifteen dollars a year. To compete with American producers, the larger commercial farms of eastern Europe converted to capital-intensive agriculture, increasing production and further depressing prices. With frightening consistency, peasant society deteriorated.

At the same time, alternative sources of income were being eliminated. For centuries, industrial production had been a household affair. Peasants could supplement their incomes as artisans, and sons could remain close to home by apprenticing out as blacksmiths, coopers, cobblers, and carpenters. Industrialization changed all that by concentrating production in urban factories. Unable to compete with cheap, mass-produced factory goods, peasant craftsmen went on the road looking for work. Slovak and Russian peasants (from the Transcarpathia region of modern Slovakia) moved to the wheat fields of the Pannonian Plain in Hungary; Sicilians migrated seasonally into the northern provinces; Slovenes and Croatians moved to the factories of Trieste and Fiume; Magyar, Bohemian, Moravian, and Slovakian craftsmen traveled to Prague, Budapest, Vienna, and Graz. German Poles went to the coal mines, iron mills, and leather tanneries of Upper Silesia, while Austrian Poles drifted into the mines and mills of

---

*W.I. Thomas and Florian Znaniecki, *The Polish Peasant in Europe and America* (Boston, 1918), p. 27.

Bohemia and Silesia. Russian Poles, Ruthenians, and Ukrainians took up jobs in the coal basins of Dabrowa, the textile mills of Lodz and Czestochowa, and the steel mills of Sosnowiec, Zgierz, and Tomaszow. Forced to stay away from home for months to make a living, peasants saw an opportunity to improve their lot in the United States.

Immigrants came not only from the regions characterized by large estates and landless peasants, but also from areas with a wide distribution of property or long leases on the land. Most peasant immigrants were independent people who were accustomed to working land of their own and found the discrepancy between need and income too great.

TABLE 2
AMERICAN IMMIGRATION, 1890–1940

	1890s	1900s	1910s	1920s	1930s	Total
Austria-Hungary[1]	592,707	2,145,266	900,656	214,806	31,652	3,885,087
Denmark	50,231	65,285	41,983	32,430	2,559	192,488
Finland[2]			756	16,691	2,146	19,593
France	30,770	73,379	61,897	49,610	12,623	228,279
Germany	505,152	341,498	143,945	412,202	114,058	1,516,855
England	216,726	388,017	249,944	157,420	21,756	1,033,863
Scotland	44,188	120,469	78,357	159,781	6,887	409,682
Wales	10,557	17,464	13,107	13,012	735	54,875
Greece	15,979	167,519	184,201	51,084	9,119	427,902
Ireland	388,416	339,065	146,181	220,591	13,167	1,107,420
Italy	651,893	2,045,877	1,109,524	455,315	68,028	4,330,637
Netherlands	26,758	48,262	43,718	26,948	7,150	152,836
Norway	95,015	190,505	66,395	68,531	4,740	425,186
Poland[3]	96,720		4,813	227,734	17,026	346,293
Portugal	27,508	69,149	89,732	29,994	3,329	219,712
Rumania	12,750	53,008	13,311	67,646	3,871	150,586
Spain	8,731	27,935	68,611	28,958	3,258	137,493
Sweden	226,266	249,534	95,074	97,249	3,960	672,083
Switzerland	31,179	34,922	23,091	29,676	5,512	124,380
Russia	505,290	1,597,306	921,201	61,742	1,356	3,086,895
China	14,799	20,605	21,278	29,907	4,928	91,517
Japan	25,942	129,797	83,837	33,462	1,948	275,166
Turkey	30,425	157,369	134,066	33,824	1,065	356,749
Canada	3,311	179,226	742,185	924,515	108,527	1,957,764
Mexico		49,642	219,004	459,287	22,319	750,257
TOTAL	3,611,313	8,511,098	5,456,867	3,902,415	471,719	21,953,412

[1]Austria-Hungary includes Austrians, Hungarians, Galician Poles, Czechs, Slovaks, Rusins, Ukrainians, Slovenes, Croatians, and Serbians.
[2]Finland was part of Russia until after World War I.
[3]Poland was not really independent until after World War I, and Polish-speaking people were scattered throughout Austria-Hungary, Russia, and Germany.

Years of poverty and the search for work made immigration palatable. Several young men from a village would usually set out together for America. Unencumbered with wives and children, and usually unskilled, they found work in the same mill, factory, or mine and lived in a boardinghouse with relatives or friends who had preceded them. A few came as contract laborers, and thousands of Italian, Greek, and Syrian workers were recruited or kidnapped by padrone labor bosses. Most came on their own however, and intended to live in America only long enough to save money and then return home to buy land or redeem the family mortgage. More than half the Italian immigrants returned home in the 1890s, and more than 500,000 Polish immigrants returned between 1900 and 1915. But gradually the peasants began staying longer and sending money back home to bring their families.

Immigration patterns changed dramatically. Between 1850 and 1860, when approximately 2.6 million people came to the United States, about 951,000 were from Germany, 914,000 from Ireland, 292,000 from Britain, and nearly 36,000 from the Netherlands and Scandinavia. But between 1900 and 1910, when nearly 8.8 million immigrated, approximately 2.2 million were from Austria-Hungary, 2.1 million from Italy, 1.6 million from Russia, and almost 308,000 from China, Japan, and Turkey. Only about 553,000 arrived from Holland and Scandinavia, 341,000 from Germany, 526,000 from Britain, and 340,000 from Ireland. Once a movement of white Protestants, the Great Migration had become a mass movement of Eastern Orthodox, Roman Catholics, and Jews from eastern and southern Europe. This was the new immigration.

Most immigrants left Europe as steerage passengers in transatlantic steamships. Walking, riding in wagons, or traveling in emigrant trains, they moved to coastal cities and lived in temporary steamship-sponsored villages until the vessels were ready to depart. The Jews, Poles, Czechs, Slovaks, and Lithuanians went to Bremen and Hamburg in Germany or to Antwerp and Le Havre; Scandinavians still left from Christiania and Goteborg for England, and then traveled with the British immigrants from Liverpool; the South Slavs and Greeks left from the Adriatic ports of Trieste and Fiume; and the Italians departed from Naples. All along the way, as they passed from district to district and country to country, they were checked, fumigated, and overcharged for food, drink, and passports. Short of money, confused, and wary of strangers, they boarded the ships and headed for America.

Steamships made the voyages safer than before, even though the immigrants were not much more comfortable. The old six-to-eight-week voyage of the colonial period had been reduced to only twelve days from Liverpool and twenty days from Trieste. The mortality rate fell dramatically. In 1907, when 1.2 million immigrants came to America, less than 250 died en route, as compared to the figures in 1847— admittedly the worst year—when Canadian officials discovered that 17,000 people of the 100,000 setting out for Canada had died at sea, in port cities, or in local hospitals. The voyage was also cheaper. At one point in 1911 an Italian laborer could sail from Naples to New York for fifteen dollars.

For most of the nineteenth century, immigrant ships stopped at Staten Island, in New York Harbor, where state officials inspected people and quarantined the sick and insane. The ships would then dock on the Hudson or East river, the passengers would go through customs, and barges would carry them to Castle Garden, where a small hospital treated the sick and where the immigrants collected mail, bought rail or steamship tickets to the interior, exchanged money, and talked to employment agents. After 1892, when the federal government took control of immigration, the immigrants arrived at the new installation at Ellis Island. At Boston, Philadelphia, Baltimore, New Orleans, and San Francisco the receiving facilities were more primitive.

Most Jews and Italians stayed in New York City, while the Slavic Catholics and other eastern Europeans moved throughout the urban Northeast, taking unskilled jobs in mines, mills, and factories. Relatively few went into rural areas, because the best land was already taken and they would have been cut off from churches and compatriots.

After the Civil War white farmers began a trek to the cities that continues today; poor blacks began leaving the South during World War I for jobs in northern factories; and millions of European peasants filled the cities after 1880. Urban America teemed with ethnic ghettos, jobs, and vitality. Eighty-five percent of Americans had lived in rural areas in 1877, but in 1945 more than 70 percent lived in the cities.

Chapter Five

The New Immigrants

For the first 250 years of American history, the vast majority of the immigrants came from northern and western Europe. They were primarily English-, German-, and Scandinavian-speaking Protestants who were either skilled workers or took up farms in rural areas. The great exception were the Irish, who were Roman Catholics and settled in urban areas where demand existed for unskilled labor. But after the Civil War, the phenomena that had affected northern and western Europe in the early nineteenth century—industrialization, population growth, and commercialization of agriculture—made their way into eastern and southern Europe, upsetting traditional lifestyles and creating a large pool of people ready to find a new life in the United States. Called the "new immigrants" by historians, they were Roman Catholics and Eastern Orthodox who settled in cities and found jobs in factories, mines, and urban construction.

Southern Europeans and Italians

The Portuguese and Spaniards

About 230,000 Portuguese came to America during the Great Migration, most settling in New England, where they worked in the fishing and cotton textile industries, and in northern California, where they became farmers and fishermen. By 1910, Portuguese communities could be found in Boston, Cambridge, Fall River, and Lowell, Massachusetts; Providence, Rhode Island; Hartford, Connecticut; New York City; and Oakland, California. Welcomed at first as hard workers, the Portuguese soon fell victim to the anti-Catholic spirit of the 1890s, and their inclination to join labor unions angered many businesspeople. Irish workers resented them because of job competition and declining wages. And the African Portuguese who came from the Cape Verde Islands were the object of racial animosity.

During the same period nearly 140,000 Spaniards left Iberia for America. Impoverished financially, plagued by an arid climate, and burdened with much infertile soil, Spain declined economically, and thousands of peasants headed to the United States. Many were Basques, a northern ethnic group that had long enjoyed its own language and cultural independence. The Basques settled in Utah, Idaho, Oregon, Nevada, and California, and herded sheep where the Utes and Shoshones had once roamed. Northern Nevada and southwestern Idaho are still the home of thousands of Basque ranchers and herdsmen; summer Basque festivals are still popular; and Boise, Idaho, is still the center of Basque culture.

The Italians

Between 1880 and 1924, 4.5 million Italians came to America, and if the arrival of thousands of Iberians worried older Americans, millions of Italians from the Mezzogiorno (the six provinces of Abruzzi, Campania, Apulia, Basilicata, Calabria, and Sicily) generated a sense of shock. Until the 1880s Italians had immigrated quietly, but their numbers were few and most were artisans, businessmen, professionals, artists, and missionaries. With skills and money so desperately needed in the early American economy, they were considered assets. Perhaps 10,000 Italian merchants, plasterers, carpenters, glassblowers, cabinetmakers, and stonecutters lived in America in 1860. Between 1850 and 1880 about 80,000 people emigrated from northern Italy. Northern Italy was more prosperous than the south, and lighter-skinned northerners looked down on darker Sicilians. They left Italy to earn higher wages in the United States. By 1870 there were northern Italian colonies in Boston, New York, and Philadelphia. They slowly merged into the American mainstream and were largely forgotten when southern Italians came in the 1890s.

From the Mezzogiorno to America In the late nineteenth century southern Italy was undergoing a series of social traumas. In the 1870s, Italian

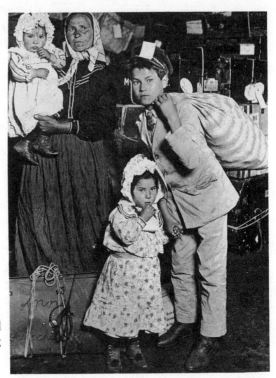

An Italian mother and her
three children upon arrival
at Ellis Island after making
the voyage in steerage.
(The Bettmann Archive)

padrone labor bosses had recruited teenage Sicilians to come to work in
America; then, as life became more difficult between 1880 and 1910,
immigration achieved a momentum of its own, sustained by the letters
and cash sent home to Italy from the first immigrants. Between 1890
and 1924, Italian immigrants sent more than $1 billion home to their
families. American propaganda, emigration, and returning cash inspired the hardpressed *contadini* (peasants), of southern Italy to come to
the United States.

Until the 1860s, Italy was divided into a number of small principalities and city states. Although Sardinia, the Papal States, and Sicily
were independent of foreign control in 1850, Austria controlled
Lombardy and Venetia, while the Hapsburgs ruled Parma, Tuscany,
and Modena. Inspired by the nationalism sweeping through Europe at
mid-century, Italian patriots like Giuseppe Mazzini and Giuseppe
Garibaldi knew the resurrection of Italian greatness depended on political unification. Modern Italy was finally born in 1870. Unity did little
to improve the lot of southern Italians. Everything south of Rome was

neglected. The government financed land-development programs and schools only in the north, and promises of land reform—particularly division of the great *latifundia* (landed estates)—were quickly forgotten. Northern politicians taxed everything the contadini produced.

Life had always been desperately hard for the contadini, and even a short drought or death of a farm animal spelled disaster. When economic change swept Europe in the nineteenth century, hundreds of thousands were pushed to the brink of starvation. Bumper citrus crops in California and Florida in the 1880s dealt a severe blow to Italian exports of lemons and oranges. The wine industry suffered a double blow between 1870 and 1900 when the plant disease phylloxera attacked the vineyards and France imposed heavy tariffs on Italian wines. Finally, cholera epidemics killed tens of thousands between 1870 and 1910; volcanic eruptions from Vesuvius in 1906 and Etna in 1910 buried whole towns; and earthquakes rocked the peninsula every year. In 1908, more than 100,000 people died when a tidal wave swept through Messina on the Sicilian coast.

Threatened by economic change, many Italians went to America not so much to abandon traditional ways as to preserve them. In the 1880s and 1890s, in fact, most southern Italian immigrants returned to Italy after a short stay in America. Their only intention had been to find temporary work in the United States, save money, and return home with the financial resources to buy land or redeem debts. Not until the early 1900s, when they saw that opportunities in America exceeded those in Italy, did they typically migrate with their families and stay in the United States.

Most Italians settled in urban centers from Boston to Norfolk; perhaps 15 percent located in cities along the Great Lakes out to Chicago. Invariably they chose to live close to one another. If relatives were living in Lowell, Massachusetts, the immigrant would try to find them, live with them for a while, and take a job in a local textile mill where other family members worked. If an immigrant was the first of his family to come to America, he would usually seek out companions from his own region of Italy. This was the spirit of *campanilismo*, an extreme loyalty to the native village. In New York, for example, Mott Street between East Houston and Prince held Neapolitans, as did Mulberry Street. On the opposite side of Mott Street were the Basilicati. Calabrians settled Mott Street between Broome and Grand, Sicilians lived on Prince Street, and the Genoese were on Baxter Street. Italians even settled along village lines. In Chicago western Sicilians congregated together: the immigrants from Altavilla lived on Larrabee Street, the people from Alimena and Shiusa Sclafani on Cambridge Street, those from Bagheria on Townsend Street, and the people from Sambuca-Zabut on Milton Street. When neither family nor neighbors could be found, the new immigrant settled with other southern Italians.

Whether it was on Mott and Mulberry streets in New York City, Chicago's West Side, San Francisco's North Beach, Boston's North End, or North Broadway in Los Angeles, the southern Italians settled together. By 1900 there were Italian communities in every American city in the Northeast, with restaurants selling hard bread, wine, cheese, salami, and pasta. There were pushcarts and organ grinders, Columbus Day parades and religious *festas*, newspapers like *L'Italia* in Chicago or *L'Eco d'Italia* in New York, and tomatoes and garlic drying in back yards everywhere. At first Italians filled the menial, unskilled jobs vacated by upwardly mobile northern and western Europeans. Italians worked in factories, mines, quarries, wharves, mills, and smelters, and they toiled as farm laborers in the West. Many established small shops, grocery and confectionery stores, restaurants, and pharmacies; others were coal dealers, ice cream and fruit vendors, or ragpickers. Many skilled craftsmen found jobs in the construction industry and became carpenters, plasterers, masons, cement workers, electricians, roofers, plumbers, and cabinetmakers. Little Italys sprouted around America.

Italian-American ethnicity In the ancient values of the Mezzogiorno, justice and the legal system were often contradictory, the law often an instrument of oppression. True security rested only in the family, *la famiglia*, and in the fellowship of friends and neighbors, the spirit of *campanilismo*. Italian Americans were proud, independent, self-reliant people, committed to one another by blood and history. An extended clan of relatives, the family was the purpose of existence, the marrow of the social system. All other institutions—political, economic, and religious—were of minor importance. Patriotism meant love for the family, and abiding by the law meant obedience to the rules of the family. Centuries of invasions, of discrimination by northern Italians, and of exploitation by rich landlords had made southern Italians suspicious of strangers and the upper classes—the *signori*—and reinforced their commitment to family and the spirit of campanilismo.

Even the Catholic church was suspect. In Sicily the church had been a major landowner, and after years of collecting tithes and rents from the contadini, the church had become part of the signori. Although the Italians were profoundly religious, their suspicions about the church prevented them from making the same institutional commitment the Irish, French Canadians, and eastern Europeans made. Indeed, because of hostility from Irish Catholics, the church in the United States strengthened the Italian sense of distance from the larger culture.

While many Protestants criticized the Italians for being Roman Catholic, many Catholics criticized them for being superstitious. Italian Catholicism bore traces of Greek, Moslem, and Byzantine culture well into the twentieth century. For Italian peasants, life was not a series of random events. All events, blessings as well as catastrophes, had their origins in the world of spirits, and religion was a means of appeasing those spirits through rituals, prayers, and charms. Church doctrine and authority were not important to the peasants. Usually they considered the celibate, cassocked priests effeminate, an attribute hardly admired in a society placing so much emphasis on masculine virility. As the one person who could preside over baptisms, confirmations, marriages, burials, and exorcisms, the priest was essential to peasant religion; but as a moral leader who urged weekly attendance at mass, confession, and communion, he was often disregarded, especially by the men.

Peasant religion also reflected that view of the world. Italian Catholics believed strongly in *clientelismo*, the use of saints as intermediaries to God. Since God was a distant figure who could not concern himself with mundane affairs of the village or family, the peasants relied on saints—San Rocco, Santa Lucia, San Michele, San Gennaro, Santa Rita, San Biagio, and San Francesco di Paolo, to name a few—to intervene on behalf of the petitioner. Theirs was a cultist faith that raised the Virgin Mary to the level of a deity. The sense of cosmic magic even transcended the power of the church, for most Italians believed in *malocchio*, the evil eye, as the source of disaster and unhappiness. Malevolent spirits caused all sorts of problems, and could be warded off only through incantations, charms, and potions. Many southern Italians kept lucky charms and amulets to drive off evil spirits and purchased wax statues of heads, hands, and feet to give to their favorite saints to cure physical ailments. Once a year the Italians celebrated a *festa*, the day of their village patron saint. A party atmosphere imbued the entire community, and attendance at a high mass was exceptionally large. Money, candles, grain, or prizes were given to the church; elaborate afternoon processionals complete with brass bands, marching confraternities, and statues of the patron saint raised the festive mood and induced charismatic moods of weeping, tranced solemnity, and excited laughter; and feasts, dances, and fireworks were held in the evening.

The church could not compete with la famiglia or the village for the loyalties of the Italian immigrants. Only the family could be trusted; only the family deserved allegiance; and only the family guaranteed security. Even Italian-American mutual aid societies had a Mezzogiorno flavor, for most of them provided employment, health, and death benefits for particular families and villagers. Italians rarely established community or national organizations. By 1924 every major American city had hundreds of Italian mutual aid societies, each governed by one or a few families from a village group. Despite their poverty, Italian immigrants rarely turned to Protestant philanthropies or social welfare agencies for assistance. Dependence on strangers brought dishonor to the family, exposing an inability or, worse, an unwillingness to care for one another. Honor, family, independence—these were the values of the Mezzogiorno.

If reverence for the family and the village translated into self-reliance, the Italian work ethic accounted for economic independence. Work, not necessarily prosperity, was the gauge of respectability. The indolent poor as well as the idle rich were despised in the Mezzogiorno and in the ghettos of America. Hard work, whether that of a common laborer or a famous surgeon, dignified people by sustaining the family. It trained people, disciplined them, prepared them for the vicissitudes of life. Idleness was a depravity, a sign of moral decay, because it made life difficult for the family and that was unpardonable. It was not surprising that the Great Depression of the 1930s was as much a moral crisis as an economic one in the Italian community. Many Italian immigrants remained in blue-collar occupations even when opportunities for professional or corporate success began to materialize. First-generation contadini suspected higher education because it introduced young people to the outside world, created new allegiances, and might keep them from contributing economically to the family.

Since education was a prerequisite to bureaucratic and professional success, many Italian Americans cut themselves off from those livelihoods. The contadini also avoided administrative work in corporations and bureaucracies because success there was a group rather than an individual matter, and daily contact with *stranieri*, or strangers, was too common. They did take jobs with police and fire departments in the cities, but those local organizations had a Mezzogiorno flavor because so many Italians worked there. The corporate world offered no such compensations, however, and for most Italians its demands were excessive. Success required a realignment of loyalties from the family to the business, a step Italians were often unwilling to take. Nor did the contadini come to America with the compulsion to succeed. Life in the Mezzogiorno had too often destroyed their dreams, and stoicism permeated their view of life. For emotional stability they had often limited their ambitions. Finally, many Italians stayed in blue-collar jobs because work was synonymous with production. When the mason finished the wall, when the tailor finished the suit, they felt pleasure and satisfaction. Pride came from seeing the results of one's labor.

The overpowering loyalty to the family had a dramatic impact on Italian-American women. Unlike most other poor immigrant women living in the cities, Italian-American women usually did not work outside their own homes, and rarely did they take jobs as domestics in other homes, since the idea of serving someone else's family was unthinkable. They quit school early as well, and rarely went to college, because schools often created different loyalties in the minds of young women. The opportunities available to women in America produced a tension in Italian-American culture, because as third- and fourth-generation women decided to take advantage of those opportunities, traditionalists viewed it as a threat to la famiglia.

Second- and third-generation Italian Americans in general were torn between the old and new. Urban life, public education, and geographic mobility placed great pressures on the old way, but their loyalty to the family and the patterns of Italian life was powerful. In the second generation more than 80 percent of Italian men and nearly all Italian women married Italians, and even today Italian remains one of the strongest second languages in the United States. In the 1940s, when some Italians joined the exodus to the suburbs, they moved with the family in the spirit of campanilismo. Little Italys appeared on Long Island and in Westchester, New York, and in Wheaton and Silver Spring, Maryland. *La via vecchia* commanded an extraordinary loyalty.

Eastern European Catholics

Millions of Roman Catholics left Poland, Lithuania, Bohemia, Moravia, Slovakia, Hungary, Croatia, Slovenia, and Ukraine for the United States. Because of political rivalries and frequently changing national boundaries in eastern Europe, it is difficult to measure the exact number of immigrants who came from that part of the world. The Poles were scattered through eastern Germany, western Russia, and northern Austria, and immigration officials often counted them as Germans, Austrians, or Russians. Still, perhaps three million Poles arrived between 1877 and 1924. More than 200,000 Lithuanians left the northern Baltic coast and 400,000 Ukrainians moved from Ukraine, but they too were often counted in the larger Russian migration. And from the Austro-Hungarian Empire came approximately 750,000 Magyars (Hungarians), 500,000 Czechs, 600,000 Slovaks, 225,000 Slovenes, 300,000 Croatians, and 600,000 Rusins.

The Migration

While a small number of eastern Europeans came to the United States during the colonial and early national periods, no substantial immigration occurred. Thousands, however, came after the revolutions of 1848

and formed an elite group of politically aware intellectuals. Between the creation of the Dual Monarchy in 1867 and the disintegration of Austria-Hungary during World War I, more than six million eastern European Catholics settled in the United States. After the invasion of Hungary in 1848, four thousand Hungarian political refugees fled to America. When he visited the United States, the revolutionary leader Louis Kossuth was the recipient of awards, banquets, salutes, parades, and audiences with famous Americans. After 1860, Russian officials began persecuting Lithuanian nationalists, suppressing the Lithuanian language, and outlawing the use of the Latin alphabet. They also harassed Catholic priests. The Russians imposed similar controls in Poland and began confiscating church property. Bismarck pressured the Prussian and Posen Poles in the 1870s by outlawing the Polish language, taking control of parochial schools, and forcing Polish nobles to sell their estates to Germans. Thousands of these political refugees headed for the United States. Usually well-educated and intensely conscious of their nationalities, they settled in the Northeast and formed the nucleus of the eastern European urban communities.

After them came millions of peasants. Acquainted with industrial labor because of their wanderings in Europe, most of the peasants went to work in the mines, mills, and factories of the urban Northeast and

Midwest. By 1920, substantial numbers of eastern Europeans were living in Massachusetts, New York, Ohio, Pennsylvania, Indiana, Illinois, Michigan, Wisconsin, and Minnesota. Although there were more than a thousand separate Polish and Lithuanian settlements in 1900, more than half the immigrants lived in Detroit, Milwaukee, Buffalo, Cleveland, and Pittsburgh, and the largest colonies were in Chicago. Chicago was also the center of Bohemian and Croatian culture. More than half the Slovaks, Rusins, and Ukrainians settled in Pennsylvania, and the major Slovenian colony was in Cleveland. "Little Hungary" could be found in every major northeastern city. Fewer than 20 percent settled in rural areas.

Because the Czechs were the first Slavic group to immigrate in large numbers, they established an agricultural base that set them apart from other Slavic immigrants. By 1877 there were eight thousand Czechs farming in Iowa, Nebraska, Wisconsin, and central Texas. The first Slovenes settled as homesteaders in Michigan, Minnesota, the Dakotas, and California and founded their own town in Minnesota— Kraintown—named after Carniola, or Krain, a province of Austria. Polish farming communities appeared in Wisconsin, Minnesota, North Dakota, South Dakota, Nebraska, and Texas. But farming did not become the main livelihood of the Slavic and Magyar immigrants because the best land was either taken or too expensive. Nor did they want to be cut off from their Roman Catholic parishes.

They put up with menial, often dirty industrial jobs and tolerated life in crowded tenements at first because their migration was transitory. Like the earliest immigrants from southern Italy, many eastern Europeans had no intention of staying in America. One Pole wrote to the Emigrants' Protective Association in Warsaw that three

> of us have decided to go [to America]. We will leave our wives and children at home and perhaps we shall be able to earn some money and come back to our country. Many people among us go to America . . . they come back and everybody brings some money with him. Here it is very difficult to advance. I want to live, though poorly, yet decently, and to give my children some education at least . . .*

Living in a bachelor society without wives and children, and often traveling in groups and staying in the same boardinghouses, they suffered poverty and discrimination, but most of them tolerated the abuse. Perhaps 500,000 Polish immigrants returned home between 1890 and 1924. Ultimately, eastern European immigrants decided that job and

*Quoted in W. I. Thomas and Florian Znaniecki, *The Polish Peasant in Europe and America* (Boston, 1918), p. 24.

income opportunities were too good in America and too dismal at home, and they began bringing their wives and children with them. But they still lived in the cities, where they could hear Old World languages spoken, read of news from Europe, and worship in their churches. With their families here, they planted roots in America.

Ethnicity in America

The closeness that eastern Europeans felt for one another revolved around nationalism, land, family, and religion. Although peasants had little sense of nationalism, the educated, middle-class political refugees preceding them had well-developed national loyalties. Since the partition of Poland in 1795, for example, Polish liberals had yearned for independence; and in 1831, 1846, 1848, and 1863 they had rebelled unsuccessfully against Prussia, Austria, and Russia. After each rebellion small streams of Polish exiles came to the United States and formed the nucleus of an American Polonia. They formed the Polish Committee and the American Committee for Polish Welfare in 1834, the Democratic Society of Polish Exiles in 1852, and the Polish National Alliance in 1880.

During the 1850s the Magyar refugees founded the mutual aid societies and ethnic newspapers so common to immigrant America. The Hungarian Sick Benefit Society, the New York Hungarian Association, and the Verhonay Fraternal Insurance Association were already in existence when the new immigrants arrived, as were such newspapers as the *Hungarian Exiles Journal, Hungarian America*, and the *American National Guard*. Few peasant immigrants had ever read newspapers before, but in the United States the ethnic press was a vital link with the Old World. The Czech Slavic Benevolent Society was formed in 1854 by nationalistic refugees of the Bohemian uprising in 1848. If ethnic politics based on an independent Poland or Bohemia or Hungary seemed remote to the peasant majority, it was real and immediate to the literate, politically conscious minority.

While the immigrant elites carried their history to America and eventually imbued the peasant immigrants with an awareness of Old World politics, nationalism was only one dimension of eastern European ethnicity. Visions of land, family, religion, and community were more important. To Slavs in Europe the land was life and fertility, and they worked it not just to make a living but to define their place in the universe. The ownership of land brought social status and prestige. People farmed the land during the day and returned at night to compact villages where friends, family, and priests lived. Theirs was a life of mutual dependence and community support. Only when economic

Immigrants from eastern
Europe learn English in
New York public schools.
(Culver Pictures, Inc.)

changes took the land, destroyed dreams of acquiring more, and undermined community life did Slavs look to America for new beginnings.

In America their love of property became a desire for home ownership. Despite low-paying jobs they saved money diligently, even while
sending some back to their families in Europe. To concentrate capital
and finance home construction, they established ethnic building and
loan associations, such as the Pulaski Building and Loan Association of
Chicago, and funneled money into them. After years of scrimping and
saving to finance a home loan or purchase, eventually most eastern
European immigrants owned their own homes in immigrant neighborhoods. Their yearning for property was fulfilled, and, more important,
they were able to enjoy the village atmosphere of the Old World.

Within the New World communities, the cement of the society was
the peasant family. Status and reputation in the Old World were local
affairs, confined to a village or at most an area containing several
villages. Culturally and emotionally the Slavs lived in an isolated

world. Individual independence was impossible because family networks were prerequisites to success. Daily life was public, society personal, and family reputations the standard gauges of respectability. Deviations from the norms compromised the family's good name. The Slavic family was a magnet that attracted the loyalty of generation after generation of children to the community.

Just before the migration, there occurred changes in family life that prepared the immigrants for conditions in urban America. For centuries the nuclear family had been highly independent, and the rituals of baptism, confirmation, marriage, funeral, and name day had confirmed its central role. Such ritual occasions as Holy Week and Christmas provided symbolic links between the immediate family and the larger community. The social order was ceremonial and predictable. But the nineteenth-century consolidation of small estates and destruction of household industry placed peasants under the influence of impersonal economic forces and undermined family independence. People began to feel insecure and vulnerable, and they turned to new institutions outside the family to sustain them. Slowly, kinship relations became more formal through marriage, dowries, foster parents, and godparents that bound several households together and increased the number of people on whom families could rely. They also formed mutual aid associations to insure against sickness and death, support schools, organize trades, and promote political activity. Religious associations—to support feast days, shrines, and patron saints—multiplied, as did religious confraternities and sodalities. All these arrangements helped restore stability to family life and would continue to do so when the Slavs immigrated to America.

Roman Catholicism was central to peasant ethnicity. Caught between the Eastern Orthodoxy of the Russians, the Islamic faith of the Turks, and European Protestantism, eastern European Catholicism was sharply defined and generated a spiritual as well as an institutional commitment to the church. Catholicism explained the mysteries of life, gave peasants a place in the universe, and served as the center of social and family life. Unlike Italian Catholics, who were suspicious of the organized church, the eastern Europeans cherished the church as an institution.

The first eastern European immigrants worshiped in Irish or German Catholic parishes, but religion in an alien tongue hardly seemed religion to them. The village church and priest, the festivals, and the saints' days were too important, as the institutions through which peasants came to terms with their lives and deaths. In America they wanted to celebrate the same festivals, exalt the same patron saints, join the same confraternities and sodalities, and listen to the same priests, especially during confession, that they had had in the Old World. Only Czech or Slovak or Polish parishes with Czech or Slovak or Polish priests gave them ceremonial links to the past and spiritual continuity in the present. Polish parishes began appearing in the 1870s, and the largest, St. Stanislaus in Chicago, was founded in 1893. Eventually hundreds of Polish parishes emerged across the country. St. George's parish in Chicago became the largest Lithuanian congregation. The first Czech Catholic chapel, St. John Nepomuk, was dedicated in St. Louis in 1854, and by 1917 there were 270 Czech-speaking priests in 320 parishes and missions.

Beginning in 1890 with the arrival of Father Karoly Boehn in Cleveland, the first Hungarian Catholic parish in the United States was established; soon hundreds of others appeared in other Magyar communities. Relatively few Croatian priests made the migration, and although there were many Croatian parishes across the country, including St. Jerome's in Chicago, the immigrants from Croatia did not pursue ethnic-language churches with the passion of the Poles, Magyars, Lithuanians, Slovenes, Czechs, or Slovaks. By 1920, in every major city and many smaller cities in the Northeast, each nationality had its own Roman Catholic parish. All these eastern Europeans, but especially the Poles, would ecstatically celebrate the election of Karol Wojtyla, Cardinal Archbishop of Cracow, as Pope John Paul II in 1978.

The struggle to establish those parishes sharpened peasant ethnic identity. In Europe parish and priest had been facts of life in every village; in America the immigrants had to take the initiative in petitioning for an ethnic parish and making financial sacrifices to build it. In the process they became even more involved in religious affairs. They were irritated by the Irish control of the Roman Catholic hierarchy in the United States. The ethnic Catholics struggled for their own parishes, appointment of ethnic priests, and selection of ethnic bishops, and the religious controversies imbued them with a strong sense of group identity. Ethnic associations, which eastern Europeans had started in the Old World to broaden family networks, reflected their commitment to a Roman Catholic village perspective and acted to protect their values from the outside world. Church newspapers, parish societies, and parochial schools reconstructed the stable environment of preindustrial villages. More than 80 percent of these immigrants' children attended parish schools where Old World languages were used; and although the immigrants might move within the city or from one city to another, the need to attend the ethnic parish church, send children to parish schools, and participate in parish societies was overpowering. Cultural continuity and religious stability—promoted through the parish, parochial school, and parish society—supported the eastern European community in America.

Eastern Orthodoxy

Between 1880 and 1924 many people from eastern Europe, the Balkans, and the Near East decided for economic and religious reasons to come to America. More than 500,000 Russian and Belorusian Slavs came from Russia; over 400,000 people came from Greece; about 200,000 from Serbia; 150,000 from Romania; 125,000 from Armenia; and 75,000 from Bulgaria. Although the Russians, Greeks, Serbs, Bulgarians, Romanians, and Armenians were separate peoples, they were all loyal to the patriarch of Constantinople, the leader of Eastern Orthodox Christianity. The church was the religious arm of the Byzantine Empire. It was the state religion: the emperor selected the patriarch, and the church was part of the political bureaucracy. Unlike the pope, who was expected to be independent of nationalism, the patriarch of Constantinople was subordinate to the emperor. Church and state were one, and the state was supreme.

The schism between eastern and western Christianity began in the fourth century, when the popes began to call Rome the apostolic center of the church. All other bishoprics were secondary, as juridical authority flowed from the papacy through the priesthood; sovereignty resided in Rome. Emperor Theodosius of Constantinople, accustomed to controlling church and state, was unwilling to share power with anyone. In 381, he rejected papal claims and declared that there were two centers of Christianity; Roman Catholicism and Eastern Orthodoxy both represented God on earth. Political relations between the two centers slowly deteriorated, and the split deepened during the iconoclastic controversy of the eighth century. Emperor Leo III of Constantinople removed icons (painted or mosaic representations of Christ or a saint) from churches throughout the empire. Riots erupted, troops crushed the rebellion, and Pope Gregory II bitterly condemned the decision. Not until 843 were the images restored, and by then the ill will between the two churches had become permanent. In 1054, the pope and the patriarch excommunicated each other, and the Fourth Crusade of 1204, when Catholic crusaders sacked Constantinople, completed the split.

Eastern Orthodoxy evolved into several independent churches. The reigning patriarch remained in Constantinople, but others appeared in Alexandria, Antioch, and Jerusalem. After the fall of Constantinople to the Ottomans in 1453, the patriarch of the Russian Orthodox church assumed actual leadership, and several other independent exarchates emerged in Serbia, Bulgaria, Greece, Romania, Syria, and Armenia, all with the power to consecrate priests. This was Orthodoxy—an autonomous association of the eastern patriarchies that recognized the patriarch of Constantinople as honorary leader.

Beyond the major controversy over power, other differences divided them. Rome insisted on a celibate priesthood, whereas the eastern churches permitted priests to marry. They also argued about the procession of the Holy Spirit; Catholics believed it went from the Father and the Son to man, while Orthodoxy claimed it came only from the Father. Other differences were cultural and demographic. Catholicism was comparatively homogeneous—the pope was the acknowledged head of the church, and Latin was the liturgical language everywhere. But in the East, where ethnic groups were more isolated, religious pluralism developed, and in each region the church had its own liturgies, usually in the local language. In the West religion and nationality were distinct, but in the East the church was part of nationhood and the nation an expression of the church. The western dualism between church and state gave rise to the idea that all power did not rest in the state and that other segments of the society could criticize and even transcend the political establishment.

But in the East a more authoritarian tradition developed; since the patriarch was an agent of the state, the church could play no role in criticizing national politics. When the Slavic invasions weakened Byzantine control over the Balkans in the sixth century, missionaries from Rome and Constantinople proselytized there, converting the Slavic tribes; but as the Christian division became more pronounced, the churches competed for control of southeastern Europe. Much to the chagrin of the Catholics, Orthodox missionaries converted Serbs, Bulgarians, Greeks, and Romanians. Each group formed its own national church reflecting the union of church and state, religion and nationality. After the Turkish invasions in the fifteenth and sixteenth centuries, the church became their sole expression of nationality. Orthodoxy was the only means of expressing ethnicity, nationalism, and religious loyalties.

The Russians and Belorussians

During the course of the eighteenth century, several thousand ethnic Russians settled in Alaska and the coast of the Pacific Northwest. Three diplomatic agreements formally brought the Russian settlers into the United States. The Treaty of 1846 with England placed Oregon and Washington in American hands; the Treaty of Guadalupe Hidalgo of

1848 did the same for California; and in 1867, the United States purchased Alaska from Russia for $7,200,000. Several thousand Russians then became Russian Americans.

Later in the century the main migration of 500,000 Russians and Belorussians to the United States began. More did not come because there was so much unoccupied land on the vast plains east of the Ural Mountains. While American farmers migrated west, Russian peasants were carrying out an eastward movement of their own. Russians and Belorussians settled in the industrial centers of Pennsylvania, Ohio, Indiana, and Illinois. Slavic customs seemed alien. The Russian immigrants were often stereotyped as lazy and ignorant, even though they worked ten or more hours a day at their jobs, seven days a week, for perhaps two dollars a day. Although their poverty was only to be expected at first, some Americans held them personally responsible for it, as if it were due to a flaw in the Slavic character. Cultural perspectives also set them apart. While Western values exalted the individual, Russian values had always subordinated individual interests to group concerns. Even the Russian communism of the twentieth century was to be fitted into the same cultural scheme. Moreover, from the thirteenth to the fifteenth century the catastrophe of the Golden Horde— the Mongol invaders—had left Russia with a fear of outsiders and an atmosphere of national emergency. Subsequent menacing threats by the Swedes and Lithuanians, by the French during the Napoleonic Wars, and in the twentieth century by the Germans during the two world wars reinforced those feelings. Russians were insular and trusted only other Russians.

Religion strengthened their sense of unity. For a thousand years the Russian Orthodox church had been the essence of Russian culture, the alter ego of Russian nationalism. For religion to survive institutionally in the United States, the Russian Slavs had to band together and form their own congregations; otherwise the patriarch in Moscow would not have sent priests or authorized the construction of chapels. It was not until 1792 that the first Russian Orthodox church was built on Kodiak Island, and not until 1872 that the headquarters of the church was established and a bishop placed in San Francisco. In a reinforcing cycle, ghetto settlements made possible the transplantation of the church, and the presence of the church strengthened the cohesiveness of the Russian community.

The Serbs and Bulgarians

Two empires and two religions divided the Balkans. Slovenes and Croatians became part of the Holy Roman Empire and the Serbs and Bulgarians fell under Byzantine and then Turkish influence. Slovenes and Croatians were Roman Catholics, while the Serbs and Bulgarians were Eastern Orthodox. Serbia had been part of the Ottoman Empire since the fourteenth century, but Turkish rule was relatively even-handed. The peasants paid modest taxes and the Serbian Orthodox church functioned as a government, with the Turks appointing the patriarch but the church exercising sovereign legal and administrative powers.

As the Ottoman Empire disintegrated between 1804 and 1830, the Serbs became independent. Bulgaria too had been under Turkish rule since 1396, and the Bulgarian Orthodox church, though independent since 1767, was controlled by Greece. Greeks monopolized church offices; Greek liturgies were introduced into the mass; and Greek be-came the official language of the parochial schools. Bulgarian national-ism became in part a religious discontent at Greek domination of the church. Throughout the 1800s the Bulgarians insisted on the appoint-ment of people from their own church to head all dioceses, and in 1870 the Turks created a separate Bulgarian exarchate, despite bitter protests from Greek authorities. Part of Bulgaria finally won independence in 1878, and the rest of the country in 1908.

Serbs and Bulgarians immigrated to America in significant numbers beginning in the 1880s. Political instability was partly responsible. After the Bulgarian uprising of 1876, the Turks slaughtered fifteen thousand Bulgarians in reprisal, and between 1885 and 1918—the later Bulgar-ian rebellions, the Balkan wars, and World War I—more Serbs and Bulgarians fled the political instability of the Old World. But even more important were the economic problems of overpopulation, declining farm prices, and artisan unemployment. Most of the Serbs and Bulgar-ians passed through New York City and settled in the industrial towns and cities of Pennsylvania, Ohio, western New York, Indiana, and Illinois, where they worked in mines, factories, and food-processing plants. A large Serbian settlement rose in Pittsburgh; the headquarters of the Serbian Orthodox church was in Libertyville, Illinois; and Gran-ite City and Chicago, Illinois, along with Pittsburgh, Pennsylvania, became home for thousands of Bulgarian Americans.

Most of them tried to reconstruct the environment of their Old World villages where they could attend their own church and speak their own language. Father Sebastian Daboric set up several Serbian Orthodox churches in the United States: the largest was St. Sara Cathe-dral in Milwaukee. Serbs and Bulgarians worked and saved to buy their own homes; newspapers such as *Unity* and *United Serbdom* kept them in touch with other immigrant communities and the Old World; and ethnic associations like the Serbian Orthodox Federation provided mutual aid and social outlets. Still, an identity crisis profoundly trou-bled Serbian and Bulgarian immigrants, as it did most of the Orthodox people in America.

The Romanians

The non-Slavic Romanians were descended from the Dacian tribes, and despite repeated conquests by Slavs, Hungarians, and Turks, their language retained its Latin vocabulary, syntax, and morphology. When the Roman Empire crumbled, Byzantine culture filled the vacuum. Except for some Uniate Catholics in Transylvania, most people were Orthodox. Romania fell to the Turks in the sixteenth century but eventually achieved independence in 1859. Romanian immigrants took blue-collar jobs in the northeastern cities. Because they came in small migrations, they were geographically mobile, seldom remaining in their first city of settlement. While the Italian and Syrian immigrants transplanted their village loyalties to the United States, the Romanians were committed to broader religious and national objectives, even though they still tried to recreate the social and ethnic atmosphere of the Old World.

They began organizing Romanian Orthodox parishes and parochial schools in 1902; Carpathian mutual benefit societies appeared shortly thereafter, as did Romanian clubs, the union of Romanian Societies, and the Romanian American Association. They were successful economically. They moved more readily than other new immigrants, not only from place to place but from job to job. Most of the first generation went from unskilled to semiskilled and skilled jobs; the second generation retained that status and frequently moved into white-collar and professional positions. Like other immigrants, Romanians were hardworking and acquired homes with a passion; but unlike many others, they limited family size. While most immigrant families were large and parents urged their children to quit school early and go to work, Romanian immigrants had fewer children, urged them to obtain good educations, and built a foundation for the success of the second generation. Nearly half their children finished high school and went on to some type of further education. Sixty-five percent of the second generation and ninety percent of the third generation married non-Orthodox partners, usually Roman Catholics, and that too gave Romanians membership in a broader community. By fostering education and by keeping their families small, they pushed their children toward middle-class status in America.

The Armenians

The Turks overran Constantinople in 1453, and the Ottoman Empire rose on the ruins of Byzantine civilization. South of the Black Sea and extending from the eastern Mediterranean to the Caspian Sea, Armenia had for a thousand years suffered repeated invasions by Persians, Russians, and Turks. Armenian Christians began feeling a religious nationalism in the nineteenth century, and Moslem rulers in Turkey worried about a possible secession from the empire. To discourage such a spirit, Abdul Hamid II slaughtered a million Armenian Christians between 1894 and 1915. Economic life was totally disrupted. During World War I, when Turkey sided with Germany, Armenian Christians allied with the Russians, and in retaliation the Turks murdered another million Christians. Nationalistic but not independent, the Armenians expressed their ethnicity through the Armenian Orthodox church, and their patriarch in Echmiadzin was a spiritual and patriotic leader.

Searching for religious and political freedom as well as economic security, more than 120,000 Armenians came to the United States after the massacres. They settled in New England, the mid-Atlantic states, and the Far West—especially Fresno, California. They worked in mines, smelters, and small trade shops; in textile, shoe, and wire factories; and were especially adept at rug weaving. The Armenian Orthodox church moved with them to the United States; the Armenian General Benevolent Union helped new immigrants; the Armenian National Union campaigned for the liberation of Armenia from Turkey; the Armenian Educational Association promoted vocational and professional education; and such newspapers as the *Hairenik* in New York City and the *Arekag* in Jersey City provided news of both the Old World and the New World settlements.

The Greeks

More than 400,000 Greeks came to America during the Great Migration; given the fact that the population of Greece was only 2 million in 1800, this represented a major social upheaval. Greek immigrants arrived in three stages. During the 1820s and 1830s several hundred Greeks came to study in the United States at the urging of Protestant missionaries. In the 1850s, several Greek import-export firms opened in American cities, and a few employees brought their families with them. The major wave of Greek immigration, however, did not begin until the 1880s, when economic changes disrupted traditional ways of life. Many of the new Greek immigrants went to work in the textile factories of New England; thousands of teenagers, recruited by labor bosses, worked as shoeshine boys; others worked on railroad construction gangs. Those with entrepreneurial skills established restaurants, candy stores, flower shops, grocery stores, and ice cream parlors in Greek-American communities. Greek fishermen went after lobster in New England and sponges in Florida, and Greek peddlers sold their wares across the country. By 1924 there were more than a hundred separate Greek communities in cities throughout the United States.

The Greek immigrants may have abandoned Greece, but they did not turn their backs on Greek culture. Ethnocentrism, familialism, and religion were the three bases of Greek ethnicity and explain the rise of a ghetto culture in America. More so than most immigrants, educated Greeks were proud of their heritage, of Plato and Aristotle, the birth of democracy in the Greek city-states, and the courage and tenacity of the Spartans. They saw Greece as the cradle of Western civilization, and their repeated struggles for freedom against the Turks had reinforced national pride. During World War I more than 45,000 Greek Americans returned to fight with Greece against the Turks. Family ties also kept them together. As in so many peasant societies, the extended family had for years been the mainstay of the social structure; and although kinship relations were disrupted by the migration, the need to continue them by mail or to persuade relatives to come to America helped sustain ethnic identity.

Greek Orthodoxy was a final link to the Old World. Although most Greeks were more loyal to the spirit than the organization of Greek Orthodoxy, the church nevertheless helped support immigrant ethnicity. Beginning in 1922, with the establishment of the first archdiocese, the church eventually established more than 425 parishes in the United States. Greek immigrants established formal and informal organizations to govern life in the local communities. The *kinotitos*, community councils, supervised local churches and Greek-language schools, paid the salaries of priests and teachers, and resolved local disputes. More than a hundred Greek-language newspapers reported news from Greece. The Greeks also established *topikas*—societies based on regional origins and dedicated to debate, education, and health and life insurance programs. Founded in 1907, the Panhellenic Union recruited Greek Americans to fight for Greece in case of another war with Turkey; the American Hellenic Educational Progressive association asked Greek immigrants to take up American citizenship while preserving the Greek language, Orthodox church, and Hellenic culture.

At the most informal level, Greeks established coffeehouses as recreational centers for drinking and card playing; employment offices where job information was exchanged; and political forums where Greek patriots, labor organizers, and priests could present their views. Because of their cultural heritage, the Greeks became one of the most visible groups in America, even though their numbers were comparatively small. And because more than 450,000 Greeks have immigrated to the United States since 1924—300,000 of them since 1950—Greek culture has been continually replenished from the Old World. Even today first- and second-generation Greek Americans account for a large segment of the Greco-American population.

Old World Loyalties, New World Lives

For the first and even second generations in the United States, the new immigrants became even more aware of their ethnic identity than they had been in the Old World. Urban life in America made them more aware of their individual heritages. Except for the Italian and Jewish neighborhoods of New York City, ethnic ghettos were not enclaves dominated by a single group. Instead, immigrants found themselves living with people from other backgrounds. Magyars, for example, had traditionally been the dominant group in Hungary and had always felt superior to the Slovaks, Romanians, and Serbs living there as minorities; when they found ethnic Slavs near them in America, those feelings of superiority came to the surface immediately. Life in the Old World had also been rather homogeneous. Because peasants usually lived and worked only with people like themselves, they were hardly conscious of an ethnic identity. But in the urban ghettos of the United States, the existence of dozens of other ethnic groups reinforced more particular feelings of community.

More conscious of politics and ethnicity than ever before, the eastern European immigrants gradually acquired a strong sense of ethnic nationalism. By 1914 they were deeply concerned with events in Europe. The Polish National Alliance campaigned vigorously with the Wilson Administration during World War I to use American power at the peace conference to create a free Poland. When Poland was reconstructed in 1918, American Poles celebrated; when German and Russian troops overran Poland in 1939, they protested vehemently. Similarly, Magyar Americans demanded a Hungary free from Austria in 1918. Czech and Slovak Americans, through their national organizations, played a critical role in persuading President Wilson to insist on the creation of an independent Czechoslovakia in 1918. Croatian, Serbian, and Slovenian patriots in the United States wanted to see an independent Slovenia and Croatia and Serbia carved out of the Austro-Hungarian Empire and accepted the establishment of Yugoslavia in 1918 as an effective compromise. Ukrainians campaigned in 1918 for national autonomy in Europe. Tired of a thousand years of Magyar domination of Transcarpathia, the Greek Catholic Union asked Wilson to place a clause in the Treaty of Versailles including Transcarpathia in Czechoslovakia. Although they failed in their goal of creating an independent Ukraine, this campaign too forged stronger community bonds in the

United States. The Greeks, Romanians, Bulgars, Armenians, and Russians also kept a close watch on events in the Old World. Once bound to parochial villages, the eastern European peasants in America rediscovered their links to the fortunes of the Old World.

For all these immigrants the Old World values of land, village, and parish were translated into home, neighborhood, parish, and political nationalism in America. Social and geographic mobility seemed irrelevant to many of them;, indeed, mobility was often the antithesis of order and continuity because it meant community disintegration. Corporate or professional success often implied movement out of the neighborhoods and parishes that meant so much to first-generation immigrants. Many peasants were also suspicious of intellectualism and discouraged higher education. As a result, the eastern and southern European immigrants tended to remain in blue-collar occupations. More than 50 percent of first-generation Czechs and Slovaks moved into skilled jobs before their deaths, as did 80 percent of their children. This was typical of peasant immigrants from eastern Europe, who aspired to skilled, propertied, working-class status.

Their goals stood in contrast to prevailing Protestant values. For two centuries Americans had defined success in terms of social and geographic mobility and income. People who left their families and roots for new opportunities, new places, and new money were admired; those satisfied with their first homes and first jobs seemed to lack ambition and drive. But most eastern and southern Europeans had large families, acquired property in their original neighborhoods, and often maintained extended kinship ties. The local parish and parochial school filled all their social, religious, and educational needs. Being a school dropout and a blue-collar laborer carried no stigma as long as one worked and was independent, and staying in the same neighborhood among the same people was expected. Stable families, stable neighborhoods, religious loyalty, and hard work were the immigrant Catholic alternatives to the Protestant ethic in America.

Chapter Six

The Jews of America

The Jewish experience had unique elements. No other group possessed the Jews' historical consciousness. For three thousand years Jews had looked on themselves as children of Abraham, the chosen people of God. They were enslaved in Egypt and later suffered at the hands of Christians and Moslems; persecutions and pogroms had molded a collective Jewish ego. Only the Jews left ghettos in Europe for ghettos in America. Only the Jewish ethnicity involved no territory. Polish-American ethnicity emerged out of Roman Catholicism and Poland; Greek identity out of Greek Orthodoxy and Hellenic Greece; and Russian ethnicity out of Russian Orthodoxy and the motherland. Jewish ethnicity rested solely on Judaism and Jewish history; political nationalism hardly existed among the first immigrants. But their theological, prophetic hopes for the ultimate gathering of Judah carried a dormant nationalism that would reach fruition in the creation of Israel after World War II.

The Sephardic and Ashkenazic Migrations, 1654–1776

The first Jewish immigrants came to America during the colonial period. They were Sephardim, Jews of Spanish and Portuguese origins, and Ashkenazim, Jews from central and eastern Europe. Both groups were fleeing persecution. Ever since Moslems conquered Spain in 711, Arabs and Jews there had accommodated each other as blood relatives (the Arabs as descendants of Ishmael and the Jews of Jacob, both descendants of Abraham). Between 900 and 1492, however, the Christian *Reconquista* (Reconquest) gradually drove the Moors back to Africa. After six centuries of war with "Islamic infidels," Spanish Catholics ruled with a vengeance. Holding Jews responsible for the death of Jesus, they persecuted them unmercifully, slaughtering three hundred Jews at Seville in 1391 and hundreds more at Toledo in 1449. Thousands of individual pogroms took place. After the expulsion of the Moors in 1492, Jews who refused to renounce Judaism were exiled. Many escaped exile by "confessing Christianity" but remained practicing Jews in secret. Of those who left, most went to North Africa and others scattered to Italy, Russia, Brazil, and the Dutch West Indies. But when Portugal conquered several of the Dutch colonies in 1654, the Jews fled, some to New Netherland. These Sephardic Jews spoke *Ladino* (Judeo-Spanish) rather than Spanish, generally had Spanish or Portuguese surnames, and, because of years of successful accommodations to the Moslems, were interested in success and even assimilation. Other Sephardic Jews followed in the 1700s.

Toward the end of the seventeenth century, groups of Ashkenazic Jews came from central and eastern Europe. During the Crusades religious zeal led to intense persecution of European Jews. Pogroms continued during the Reformation and Counter-Reformation. Jews were expelled from Lithuania in 1496; Pope Paul IV required all Jews to wear identifying symbols after 1555; thousands were slaughtered in Poland and Ukraine in the 1640s and 1650s; and in 1648, Jews had to leave Hamburg and Vienna. Some came to America, and by 1776 there were nearly three thousand Jews in the colonies, half Sephardic and half Ashkenazic. Compared to Europe, America was free and prosperous. An inconspicuous minority in a population of nearly three million people, the Jews inspired few fears. And in a society where more than 95 percent of the people lived in rural areas, the Jews settled in Boston, Newport, New York, Philadelphia, Baltimore, and Charleston. Few Americans even knew they were there.

Jews also benefited from religious toleration. Calvinists had set the cultural tone in America, and they were fascinated with the "Hebrews"—the people of the Old Testament. Though frustrated that more Jews did not convert, the Puritans deflected anti-Semitic attitudes. Both groups believed in decentralized congregations, despised Roman Catholicism, and dreamed of material success. The early Jewish immigrants flourished in America. Often prohibited from owning land in Europe, they came from urban, commercial backgrounds and went into business as merchants, salespeople, peddlers, teamsters, and shippers helping transfer goods between eastern cities and the farms in the hinterland. In the labor-starved markets of colonial America, Jewish artisans commanded high wages and often built their skills into small manufacturing concerns. As the economy matured after 1776, Jewish businesses began specializing in banking, commerce, insurance, securities, textiles, footwear, mining, warehousing, real estate, and construction. America was indeed the promised land.

The German Jews, 1830–1890

American Jewry changed with the immigration of German Jews. As late as 1830 there were still only 6,000 Jews in the United States, but the rapid influx of the Germans increased the number to 22,000 in 1850 and more than 250,000 in 1880. A wave of anti-Semitism swept through central Europe in the mid-1800s. Hundreds of Jews died in pogroms at Würzburg, Bamberg, Frankfurt, Darmstadt, Hamburg, and Danzig, and the homes and businesses of thousands were destroyed. To limit Jewish population, Germans established quotas on marriage licenses to Jews; and although industrialization was creating new jobs, Jews were forbidden to become apprentice trainees. Curfews, special taxes, and housing segregation were common. With little to lose, the German Jews joined the migration.

They settled in the cities with other Jews, even though they differed markedly from the Sephardic community. In addition to distinct dialects and rituals, the German Jews came from a Teutonic tradition and the Sephardic Jews from an Iberian, Mediterranean culture. Because the Sephardic Jews were already established and financially secure, class distinctions also divided the two groups. Still, assimilation soon occurred; sharing ethnicity as well as religion, they had much in common and slowly came together in the nineteenth century, the Sephardic Jews often disappearing into the much larger German-Jewish community.

German Jews also went into commerce and business. Industrialization and the westward movement were creating unprecedented opportunities in merchandising and finance. A large, scattered population gave rise to enormous marketing problems. There was also a tremendous demand for investment capital. Some German Jews became skilled artisans and specialty farmers, but more than any other immigrant group the German Jews entered business and finance. Jewish peddlers trekked all over the country selling goods to housewives in the hinterland; eventually many of them established their own stores. Julius Rosenwald, a German Jew who started out as a peddler, purchased a small watchmaking company named Sears, Roebuck and transformed it into the most successful mail-order house in the world. Most of the famous department stores in the United States—including Saks Fifth Avenue, Bloomingdale's, Joske's, Sakowitz, Gimbel's, Abraham & Straus, Macy's, Goldblatt, Bamberger's, Neiman-Marcus, and B. Altman's—began with those poor German-Jewish peddlers. From this commercial elite came the great Jewish bankers. With excess capital from Jewish merchants and loans from Jewish financiers in Europe, Jewish bankers financed industrial projects throughout the country. Such famous banking houses as Kuhn Loeb and Company, Goldman Sachs and Company, Lehman Brothers, Rothschild and Company, Bache and Company, and Guggenheim and Company all had Jewish roots. With commercial skills finely honed in the past and living in an environment blessed with opportunity and freedom, German Jews succeeded far beyond their expectations.

In the eighteenth century, German-Jewish intellectuals such as Moses Mendelssohn introduced Western rationalism into traditional Judaism to prepare upwardly mobile Jews for life outside the ghetto. Some Jewish intellectuals had grown impatient with traditional religion, and as free-thinking rationalists they drifted toward agnosticism, finding Judaism an inadequate tool for interpreting the world. In Europe even the most agnostic Jew remained close to the the the ghetto, by law if not by choice, but in America that social dimension of Judaism seemed less important. Middle-class Jews also yearned for social acceptance in America, not just toleration. Embarrassed by the customs and traditions of Orthodox Judaism, they wanted to make the faith more relevant to life in nineteenth-century America.

Reform Judaism made changes in both the style and substance of Orthodox traditions. Instead of sexual segregation in synagogues, repeated Hebrew prayers, passionate recitations, and cantillation (chantings of scripture), the Reformers used a Protestant model, with hymns, instrumental music, sedate prayers, pews, choirs, sermons, and a subdued reverence. The Torah (scriptures) and Talmud (Jewish law) were translated into German and English. Reform Jews regarded the Torah and Talmud not as literal explanations of reality but as historical literature and religious symbols, and as a result they found strict Jewish law—such as multiple daily prayers, regular synagogue attendance, dietary rules, and complete cessation of weekday activities on the Sabbath—too restrictive. They discarded much of the law and emphasized the ethical values of Judaism. In some instances they changed their Sabbath observance, which extended from sundown Friday to sundown Saturday, to the Christian Sunday. Reform Jews also reinterpreted the whole concept of Zionism, the idea of setting up a Jewish national homeland in Palestine. While Orthodox Jews saw the exile from

Palestine as a temporary condition awaiting messianic redemption, the Reformers saw it as a blessing, an opportunity to carry Judaism throughout the world. Instead of waiting for a literal, personal Messiah who would create a Jewish nation in Palestine, they yearned for a great leader who would bring peace and justice to all people. For them, America was Zion.

Led by Issac Wise, Reform Judaism received its institutional base in 1889 with the creation of the Central Conference of American Rabbis. But the Reform movement threatened Jewish ethnicity. Because of the relaxed social code, the attack on older ways, and the move toward liberal rationalism, the synagogue lost its rationale as a cultural foundation of the Jewish community. Resolution of congregational disputes was difficult because rabbis had neither the political nor the theological power to impose their will; congregations divided and subdivided until they became small autonomous units. Reform synagogues gradually resembled Protestant chapels in form as well as purpose—houses of weekly worship without the social, economic, and personal welfare functions so important to European Judaism. New Jewish organizations, which had never existed in Europe because the rabbi and synagogue assumed temporal responsibilities, appeared in the United States. Jewish hospitals and orphanages were built in the 1860s; *Bikur Cholim* societies cared for the sick and indigent; *Gemilath Chasodim* served as mutual savings and loan banks; and *B'nai B'rith* functioned as a fraternal society. The synagogue was no longer central to Jewish life, and religious apathy eroded the commitment many German Jews felt to the faith of their fathers. Although rationalism seemed a more realistic way of interpreting the modern world, it separated Jews from their history. Only the arrival of the eastern European Jews would expose the weaknesses of Reform Judaism.

The Eastern European Jews, 1881–1945

For centuries Ashkenazic Judaism survived in eastern Europe as a communal people tied together by spiritual bonds, the Yiddish language, and a special sense of time and history. God and heaven were not myths or distant realities but part of everyday life. The Ashkenazim were intimate with God, sometimes even critical, because their conviction that they were the chosen people made them feel that God was bound to them in a holy covenant. All 613 of their elaborate commandments on how to slaughter ritual animals, what food to eat, how the Talmud was to be read, how to shatter the glass in a marriage ceremony, and so on reflected God's expectations of men, a divine arrangement for the chosen people. For eastern European Jews, the secular and spiritual worlds were one.

Although Hebrew was the language of prayer and the scriptures, Yiddish was the language of everyday affairs and reflected the scattering of Jews throughout much of central Europe and the Near East during the Middle Ages. Originally a Middle High German dialect written in Hebrew, Yiddish emerged between the ninth and twelfth centuries in Europe. Hebrew words peculiar to Jewish religion were added, and as most European Jews moved east out of Germany, a Slavic vocabulary was added as well. Traces of other European languages also found their way into Yiddish. Rich in idiomatic expressions, Yiddish was especially able to convey subtle nuances of personality and emotion. It was also an assimilative language for Jews. From the Pale of Settlement (an area of 386,000 square miles in Russia extending from the Baltic to the Black Sea where Jews were legally permitted to settle) and Ukraine to Hungary, Poland, and Rumania, Yiddish united eastern European Jews into a single community.

Finally, eastern European Jews were caught up in a singular vision of time and history. Because they believed that the coming of the Messiah and their own redemption was imminent, they viewed themselves as the central characters in the human drama. And having been so threatened for so long, they had an almost fanatical concern for the survival of Judaism. The extension of the Jewish faith into that future—through ceremonial marriages, religious family life, and loyal communalism—was an ethnic compulsion. Survival of the group, of Judaism, was the marrow of social and cultural life. Out of this world came millions of Jewish immigrants.

Like the eastern European immigrants in general, the Jews suffered from the decline of the peasant economy, either directly or because people could no longer buy the goods and services they were selling. There were also population pressures: the Jewish population of the Pale increased from less than one million in 1800 to nearly five million in 1890. When Tsar Alexander II was assassinated in 1881, anti-Semitic fears ignited into vicious pogroms. It became the official policy of the Russian government and the Russian Orthodox church to rid the country of Jews, through conversion if possible or extermination if necessary. Pogroms erupted in Kiev, Odessa, Warsaw, and in countless smaller cities. Government-sponsored propaganda increased; quotas on Jewish admissions to universities were imposed; and the May Laws of 1882 forbade Jews to purchase property, secure mortgages, conduct business on Sunday, or travel from town to town. When Russia lost the Pacific war to Japan in 1905, more pogroms broke out in Odessa, Bialystok, and Zhitomir. Similar persecutions occurred in Romania and Austria-

Hungary. Between 1881 and 1924 approximately 2,750,000 Jews left eastern Europe for the United States: nearly 2 million from Poland, Lithuania, and Russia; about 600,000 from Austria-Hungary; and perhaps 150,000 from Romania.

Unlike other new immigrants, they had no intention of ever returning; theirs was a communal, family migration, a collective movement of people ready to begin a new life in America. Just as important, they came from diverse backgrounds, from cities as well as from farming villages, while most of the other new immigrants were peasants. Only 20 percent of the other new immigrants had occupational skills compared with nearly 70 percent the Jews. They were suited for urban life, and only a tiny minority, like the Am Olam (Eternal People) group who tried to establish rural communes, settled outside the cities. During the centuries of their dispersion Jews had come to believe that "life is with people," that Jews had obligations to one another. They felt obliged to help other Jews, and as Jews moved into business other Jews were pulled along economically. Finally, they were more attuned than some groups to the idea of success, and had a long history of respect for learning. Many interpreted their own status according to the achievements of their children (as did many other immigrants).

The largest eastern European Jewish communities were in the northeastern cities, especially New York. By 1910 there were more than 500,000 Jews living in the Lower East Side of Manhattan, and smaller communities in Harlem, the East Bronx, Brownsville, Borough Park, and Brooklyn. Extreme poverty characterized life in the *shtetl* at first. Manhattan's Lower East Side was controlled by Irish and German immigrants who had arrived earlier; German and Irish youth gangs harassed the new Jewish immigrants at every opportunity. Housing was inadequate, and in tenements like "Big Flat" it was not uncommon to have a thousand people living on one acre. Congestion was intense, the noise unbearable, sanitation nonexistent, and the death rate well above the national average. Tens of thousands accepted the only work available—the crushing labor of garment-district sweatshops. Whole families slaved at sewing and cutting machines in dingy tenement apartments yet barely eked out an existence. Indeed, because the industry was so competitive, wages actually declined in the 1880s from $12 to $7 a week. Those not in the sweatshops but without skills were out in the streets with peddlers' pushcarts. Economic success would soon come to many of these immigrants, but in the 1880s and 1890s they were suffering.

The first Jewish immigrants from eastern Europe experienced severe emotional problems in leaving the Old World, surviving the crowded steerage, and settling into the tenements of the Lower East Side. Unlike the Old World, America was a secular society. No longer could Judaism alone direct the political affairs of the Jewish community. In Europe, where Jews had suffered persecution, the suffering itself had been a communal experience transcending class lines, and no stigma followed the sufferers. But in the United States the suffering was an economic matter, and as such was an individual rather than a collective experience. Some Jews consequently found themselves cut off from traditional sources of psychological comfort. And out of the poverty and cultural chaos came previously unheard of problems, such as juvenile delinquency, prostitution, gambling, and crime. Arnold Rothstein became notorious as a gambler and fixer; Isaac Zucker as an arsonist; Harry Joblinski as a trainer of pickpockets; and Marm Mandelbaum as a fence. Family life was also troubled. It became common to hear of despondent fathers, emasculated by the poverty of ghetto life, who had abandoned their families; of people who had committed suicide; of children who refused to listen to their parents. It seemed impossible to transfer Old World stabilities to America.

But after 1900, conditions slowly began to improve. Crowding, noise, and unsanitary conditions still prevailed, but there was a new energy as well. By the turn of the century the Jewish population on the Lower East Side had grown enormously, and Irish and German control of the area declined. Jewish organizations were more active on behalf of the immigrants. Such German-Jewish philanthropies as the United Hebrew Charities and the settlement houses of Lillian Wald and Jacob Schiff helped with housing, medical, and employment problems, while the Hebrew Immigrant Aid Society helped new settlers adjust to the United States. Between 1903 and 1910 thousands of *landsmanshaften* were formed. A lodge association of people from the same village or region in Europe, the landsmanshaft provided a secular but non-ideological outlet for the east European Jewish immigrants. Ordinary people found it a home away from home that provided health and death benefits, news of the Old World, and social association with peers.

After 1900, more Jewish intellectuals began arriving from Europe, and the cultural life of the community, especially through the Yiddish press and theater, quickened. Wages rose after the depression of 1893, and a small middle class of independent businesspeople and store-keepers appeared. Synagogues had been established on a firm footing, and although not all the immigrants observed the daily attendance of the Old World, they celebrated Rosh Hashanah and Yom Kippur as periodic rituals to confirm their self-images as Jews. Streets were being paved; local housing codes were requiring improvements in the tenements; water and sewage systems were becoming more reliable; and small parks, libraries, and theaters were being constructed. Life was slowly becoming more meaningful in the New World shtetl.

Jewish youth of the early 1900s wearing a *tallis* (prayer shawl), which is given to a Jewish boy when he is *bar mitzvah* at age thirteen. (Shames Family Archives/Black Star)

But in good times and bad, the Jews never lost faith in the future, and that faith was buttressed by ambition. Throughout history Jews had venerated learning, particularly Talmudic learning, for scholarship—just as much as service, worship, and righteousness—was the pathway to God. Those with learning enjoyed high status in the community and the right to sit along the eastern wall of the *shul* (synagogue) near the holy ark. For thousands of years the primary method of serving God had been studying the Torah. In America the Jews quickly perceived education as the key to economic achievement, and the quest for secular knowledge became a passion. Samuel Gompers remembered immigrant cigarmakers working extra hard so one of their associates could read law, literature, and politics to them during the day; the Educational Alliance and People's Institute sponsored lectures attended by thousands each week; cafes throughout the Lower East Side bristled each day with debate and intellectual controversy; and people flocked to night schools sponsored by the Board of Education, the settlement houses, and the labor unions. Jews filled a disproportionate number of seats in the City College of New York; in less than a generation the shtetl was sprinkled with accountants, dentists, physicians, lawyers, and pharmacists. Although fear and resentment undoubtedly exaggerated his opinion, one civil official remarked in 1912:

> Nearly all of the 6,500 positions in the city government are awarded on the basis of competitive civil service examinations. As a result, the Jews are rapidly driving out the Irish, the Germans, and the native Americans. . . . The Jews study long and hard, and their examination papers are so immeasurably superior to the average offered by representatives of other races that they invariably secure preferred places . . .*

Similar observations were made by Yankee and German teachers in the public elementary and high schools of New York, Boston, and Philadelphia, where Jewish children consistently achieved at higher levels than other groups. Jews became one of the most upwardly mobile groups in America.

American Jews Divided

Despite the bonds that held Jews together, profound differences existed in the community. After 1880 a split developed between the German and eastern European Jews in America. As anti-Semitism increased, German jews became concerned about discrimination in a nation that until then had been remarkably tolerant. On the premise that Americans discriminated against east European Jews only because of their numbers, poverty, and Old World ways, German Jews set out to change the east Europeans. In ghetto settlement houses they tried to Americanize the new immigrants, but their plan was hopelessly naive. When they found that the new immigrants would not readily change their ways, German Jews then tried to separate themselves from their new associates. One Jewish writer recalled:

> We quit the Franklin Street [in Philadelphia] house in 1902. In that year almost every old family in the block moved away . . . A blight had hit the street in the form of a diaspora from the ghetto. With the arrival of the first few families, we . . . smiled tolerantly at their *scheitels* [ritual wigs worn by married women], their matted beards, and their Talmudized customs. We treated them distantly and with condescension, and a few of us hoped we might be able to freeze them out.**

The two communities grew apart, seriously divided by culture, class, religious practices, and Zionism. Interested in rapidly assimilating, the

*Quoted in Irving Howe, *World of Our Fathers* (New York, 1976), p. 166.
**Phillip Goodman, *Franklin Street* (New York, 1942), *pp.* 3–4.

German Jews had quickly adopted English as their main language, so the Yiddish-speaking eastern European Jews seemed strange and incomprehensible to them. To many German Jews, Yiddish culture was the problem, so elimination of Yiddish became an important goal, one way of Americanizing their eastern European brethren. In 1902, to speed that process, some famous German-Jewish families—the Marshalls, the Guggenheims, the Seligmans, and the Bloomingdales—sponsored *Yidishe Velt* (Jewish World), a Yiddish-language newspaper that advocated good citizenship, support for the Republican party, the virtues of Reform Judaism, use of the English language, Americanization, and gratitude to German Jewish philanthropies. Eastern European Jews hated such condescending patronization and cultural imperialism and the newspaper failed, but it did provide an odd paradox—German Jews using Yiddish to support the destruction of Yiddish culture. German Jews were advocating Anglo conformity, and their efforts to "reform" eastern European Jews were just as offensive as Protestant attempts to convert them.

Class differences existed as well. Most eastern European Jews had been skilled craftspeople in the Old World and once in America they took factory jobs in sweatshops or piecework in their homes. More than 40 percent went to work making clothes; by 1900, Jewish workers made more than 90 percent of the clothes produced in America. Conditions in the sweatshops were crowded, hot, and dangerous. In the spring of 1911, at the Triangle Shirtwaist Company on the Lower East Side of Manhattan, a fire broke out and in less than twenty minutes killed 146 Jewish and Italian women workers. The working-class community was outraged. That German Jews often owned the sweatshops and let out the contracts only exacerbated class tensions. To overcome low wages and degrading working conditions, Jewish workers began organizing labor unions. The United Hebrew Trades Union was founded in 1890, and by 1914 the International Ladies Garment Workers Union and the Amalgamated Clothing Workers dominated the clothing industry. Jewish workers controlled them. Strikes became common and desperate.

The Rise of Jewish Socialism

Jewish socialism reinforced class differences between eastern European and German Jews. Given the blue-collar character of the early eastern European Jewish community, ideas of class struggle and economic democracy appealed to some Jewish intellectuals. Such men as Morris Hillquit, who had immigrated from Russia in 1886 and taken a law degree at New York University, accepted Marxist views of capital and

The Triangle Shirtwaist
Company fire kills 146 and
draws national attention.
(The Bettman Archive)

labor and decided that government ownership and worker control of
production were the only means of redistributing wealth in the United
States. Through their newspaper, *The Forward*, and such groups as the
Workmen's Circle, they supported socialist politicians throughout the
country, especially in New York City. German Jews hated socialism;
they had too much to lose. Together, Jewish labor and Jewish socialism
magnified class differences and precipitated more conflict between German and eastern European Jews.

A number of Jewish women rose to prominence in the labor union
movement and in radical politics. In the eastern European shtetls,
Jewish tradition had kept women from positions of power in the synagogues and excluded them from Talmudic schools, but they had nevertheless developed an equally powerful tradition of expressing their
opinions about temporal matters. In America, with so many Jewish
women working outside the home in sweatshops, it was only natural

that Jewish women protest their exploitation. Like Rose Schneider-
man, some worked diligently to organize workers into mass production
unions; while others, like Emma Goldman, took the radical option,
seeing in socialism and even communism the only way to really change
the social order.

But at the same time, some Jews doubted the efficacy of Jewish
politics, and many of the early socialists wanted Jews to abandon tradition for modern culture, to trade an ethnic perspective for an international working-class vision. They were so impolitic as to expect
Jewish immigrants to give up religion for revolution. Not until the
arrival of men like David Dubinsky and Sidney Hillman, people committed to Jewish culture and the Yiddish language as well as to economic democracy, did Jewish labor unions and socialist movements
gain momentum and define political debate in the New World shtetl.
Even then the seeds of radical demise already existed; for while Jewish
immigrants debated revolution, the vast majority of them also harbored
deep middle-class yearnings for material comfort and security. Jewish socialism was a lively but temporary phenomenon, a movement
doomed to failure but one that politicized eastern European Jews and
gave them the secular, worldly outlook needed to demand justice in the
United States.

From Religious Factionalism to Zionism

Religious controversies also continued. After two generations in America the German Jews had accommodated themselves to the New World
culture and in the Reform tradition had rejected older customs and
theology. Eastern European Jews found Reform Judaism repulsive, a
denial of the faith and a rejection of their fathers, and they clung to the
old Orthodox ways. But both sides were losing ground. Because Reform
Judaism was so "Protestant," demanded so little of its communicants,
and possessed no real commitment to Judaism, the children and grandchildren of German Jews found it meaningless. A minority already,
Reform Jews were destined to have even less influence in the future. At
the other extreme were millions of eastern European Jews trying to
preserve Orthodoxy in secular America. What had been a key to survival in the hostile environment of eastern Europe was becoming a
curious anachronism in the United States, as the children of the immigrants discarded the most visible dimensions of Orthodoxy. That faith
too was threatened in America.

Out of the chasm between Orthodoxy and Reform, and the class
divisions of German and eastern European jews, came a cultural

compromise known as Conservative Judaism. The moving forces behind it were Sabato Morais, founder of the Jewish Theological Seminary in 1886, and Solomon Schechter, head of the seminary after 1902, who tried to accommodate tradition with change and Jewish history with American reality. Conservatism preserved the vision of a chosen people, the direct relevance of the scriptures, the keeping of the Sabbath Day, and the observance of dietary laws, but it also adopted the quiet services of the Reformers as well as the mixed seating of women and men, congregational scripture readings, and the wearing of ordinary clothes. Loyal to tradition and Jewish ethnicity, the Conservatives accepted cosmetic changes in worship services, appealing both to the middle-class mentality of the German Jews and to the more secular perspective of second-generation Orthodox children. The compromise worked. By 1920 Conservative Judaism had more active congregations than the Reform movement, and by 1945 more than the Orthodox branch.

The debate over Zionism also exposed differences between German and eastern European Jews. German Reform Jews had long since discarded the notion of any final gathering of "Israel" in the Holy Land. Assimilation in the United States, not the gathering of Israel, was their goal. But for eastern European Jews raised in the shtetl atmosphere of Yiddish culture and Orthodoxy, assimilation was unthinkable. Judaism was their world, their reason for being. For the Orthodox Jew the scattering of Israel was a curse that would soon be remedied when the Messiah gathered them to Palestine. German Jews feared Zionism would retard the Americanization of the east Europeans, who supported it for precisely that reason—because it was the major thread in the fabric of Jewish identity. Zionism was the antithesis of assimilation because it predicted the indefinite survival of Jewish ethnicity.

Despite German misgivings, Zionism steadily gained ground in the United States. Zionist organizations appeared in the 1890s and won more followers between 1900 and 1945. Much of that success was due to the efforts of such German Jews as Louis Brandeis, Julian Mack, Felix Frankfurter, and other members of the American Jewish Committee. Just as Conservatism was a religious compromise between Orthodoxy and Reform, American Zionism became a middle ground between the cultural Zionism of eastern European Jews and the assimilationist spirit of German Jews. At first, Zionism aimed to resurrect Jewish culture as well as colonize Palestine, but the German Jews transformed Zionism into "Palestinianism." They supported Jewish settlement in Palestine but not the cultural demands that all Jews must settle there and resurrect Orthodoxy.

World War II had a dramatic impact on American Zionism and American Judaism. American Jews emerged from World War II with a vision of the Holocaust, Hitler's extermination of six million European Jews in such death camps as Auschwitz, Treblinka, and Maidanek. The Nazi onslaught represented anti-Semitism carried to the extreme of genocide. By 1942, American policymakers and Jewish organizations knew something horrible was happening to European Jewry, but the magnitude of the Holocaust was beyond belief to most American officials at the time. When President Franklin Roosevelt finally established the War Refugee Board in an attempt to rescue European Jews from Nazi persecution, it was already too late.

In 1945, with the liberation of the concentration camps, the enormity of the Holocaust became apparent. Hitler's Germany had practically annihilated European Jewry, leaving American Jews the dominant branch of the faith. In the wake of Nazi atrocities, the establishment of a Jewish state in Palestine seemed imperative to many Jews. Once a point of contention in the American Jewish community, Zionism became more important than ever to Jewish identity. The Holocaust was the central experience in modern Jewish history, a tragedy that raised the consciousness of Jews everywhere. American Jews would enter the postwar era still divided by class and religious differences, still concerned about the secularizing effects of American life, but they were all committed to two ideals: the viability of the state of Israel and the notion, "Never again."

Chapter Seven

Asian America, 1882–1945

The Chinese Exclusion Act of 1882 satisfied the most racist of California voters, as well as those white workers worried about competing with Chinese laborers, but it posed a problem for employers who needed workers. Demand for cheap labor still existed in California, and in the late nineteenth century it only intensified. Because the Chinese Exclusion Act greatly restricted new Chinese immigration to the United States, the Chinese population began a steady decline in the 1880s and 1890s as immigrant workers either died in America or returned home. From its peak population of approximately 325,000 people in 1880, the Chinese American population declined to less than 200,000 people by 1945. California employers needed a new source of cheap labor to replace the Chinese, and once again they looked to Asia—the Philippines and Japan.

The Filipinos

After the Spanish-American War of 1898, the Philippines became United States territory, and immigration restriction laws did not apply to Filipinos. They began coming to Hawaii and California in 1900. By 1935, when the act granting the Philippines commonwealth status subjected them to the National Origins Act, nearly 125,000 Filipinos had arrived in Hawaii and perhaps 75,000 in California. They worked migrant farm laborers, bellboys, house servants, porters, and waiters. Between 1935 and 1946, when the Philippines became an independent republic, Filipino immigration was gradually prohibited. Like the Japanese and Chinese, the Filipinos lived and worked in the large commercial farms of Hawaii and California. Carlos Bulosan, an immigrant and writer, described his life in the 1920s:

> My first sight of the . . . land was . . . exhilarating. . . . I knew that I must find a home in this new land . . . we were sold for five dollars each to work in the fish canneries of Alaska. . . . We were forced to sign a paper which stated that each of us owed the contractor twenty dollars for bedding and another twenty for luxuries. What these luxuries were, I never found out. It was the beginning of my life in America, the beginning of a long flight that carried me down the years fighting desperately to find peace in some corner of life . . . *

Compared to the Japanese and Chinese, the Filipinos had a much more difficult time lifting themselves out of poverty. Discrimination and lack of capital prevented them from establishing a business foothold, and racist attitudes in many unions sealed off access to skilled jobs. Equally important, the Filipino community was heterogeneous; while trying to adjust to America they also had to cope with their own differences. Immigrants from the Visaya Islands spoke Visayan; those from Manila spoke Tagalog; and those from the northern provinces of Luzon, Ilocos Norte and Ilocos Sur, spoke Ilocan. Divided internally and disliked by many Americans, they struggled for security, but most Filipinos remained unskilled workers with median incomes among the lowest in the nation.

The Japanese

The second wave of Asian migration began in 1868, when Japanese workers crossed the Pacific for Hawaii and the North American mainland. By 1924 there were more than 275,000 Japanese in the United States. Although they came in the wake of the anti-Chinese agitation, most Americans welcomed them at first. Japan was becoming a major industrial power; and American politicians, aware of Japan's new strength in the Pacific, were concerned about the treatment given the Japanese immigrants. Equally important, the Japanese-American community seemed less sexually threatening than the Chinese: Chinese men had outnumbered women by nearly twenty to one, but the ratio

Quoted in Cecyle S. Neidle, *The New Americans* (New York, 1967), pp. 303–304.

was much smaller for the Japanese. Finally, most of the Japanese immigrants were literate, and that impressed Americans. Unfortunately, their toleration would be short-lived.

The Island Kingdom

On July 8, 1853, Commodore Matthew C. Perry of the United States Navy sailed four ships into Tokyo Harbor, ending the self-imposed isolation that had marked Japanese history since the 1600s. Japan was a rural, agrarian nation of about 150,000 square miles. When the reign of the Tokugawa *shoguns* (military rulers) began in 1603, Japan was a feudal society of eighteen million people. It had had considerable contact with the West, and the Japanese were concerned about European aggressiveness. In 1638, the shoguns turned the Island Kingdom into a cocoon, expelling foreigners, prohibiting emigration, and calling all overseas Japanese home. During the two centuries the Tokugawas ruled Japan, the standard of living rose modestly and the population increased to about thirty million. Tokugawa Japan seemed cut off from time, a feudal nation still living in the Middle Ages.

Concepts of place and conformity were strong in Japan because the Japanese believed power flowed from above. Peasants eked out a living on less than an acre of land but rarely protested their fate. Precise codes of social conformity governed individual behavior, and spontaneous deviance was unthinkable. The Japanese strongly discouraged aggressive behavior and contentiousness. The ability to compromise and resolve disputes privately was an intimate part of social morality. While American society would produce hundreds of thousands of lawyers trained to solve disputes through political agencies, Japan had little need for so many attorneys. Criminal behavior was limited by social conformity, and civil lawsuits were rare because of a widespread desire to avoid controversy and conflict.

Religion reinforced the social order. Although Shinto, Buddhism, and Confucianism were the three main religions of Japan, history had witnessed a great divergence in theology and ritual between various sects of each faith, and all three religions had at one time or another borrowed from one another. Shinto, the oldest religion in Japan, combined a pantheistic worship of nature with deification of the emperor. The emperor was the living *kami*, the eternal authority who guarded the temporal fortunes of ordinary people, and Shintoism demanded duty to the nation and devotion to the interests of the community. The basic unity of all people with all of nature was similarly essential to the Shinto faith. So while Shintoism underwrote Japanese nationalism, it reinforced the prevailing social code by emphasizing duty, honor, and suppression of individual needs to community interests.

Buddhism, which came to Japan from Korea and China in the sixth century, filled a void in Shinto by furnishing a vision of eternal life. While the Shinto kami governed earthly affairs, the Buddhist deities controlled the world of the dead. Consistent with Japanese values, Buddhism offered not a conscious individual immortality but a promise that through self-denial and personal righteousness the soul would merge after death with Nirvana, a divine freedom from pain and sorrow. Still, Buddhism was less concerned with morality than with existence, less worried about good and evil or innocence and guilt than about the cosmic nature of human life.

It was Confucianism, also introduced from China in the sixth century, which supplied the Japanese with their vision of morality. Confucianism emphasized worship of the family and ancestors and imposed on all people the obligation of accepting their station in life. Personal honor depended on social complacency; one had to behave in accordance with the expectations of society, and the essence of personal behavior was obedience, submissiveness, and peaceful acquiescence in the social hierarchy. Filial piety and acceptance of authority were central tenets of Confucianism. Thus all three Japanese religions sustained the prevailing social code. Duty, obedience, and personal subordination—these were the standards of society.

Veneration of the family was deeply embedded in the culture. Property ownership resided in the clan, and when branch families were begun, they still owed deference and service to the stem family. Nuclear families were looked upon as economic devices, means of transferring property from one generation to another. An economic bond between two clans, marriage was carefully arranged to serve both families. The Japanese honored family name, and each individual was duty bound to respect the *ie* (house). Indeed, absolute obedience was the norm for all adults. The internal bonds of the Japanese family had little to do with romantic love, which the Japanese found to be temporary and unpredictable, but with the eternal social and economic interests of the clan. The pull of family values was so strong that other political and corporate institutions in the society reflected similar attitudes. Rebellion only shamed the family, so loyalty and discipline ran through the fabric of Japanese society.

Emigration commenced only after Japanese leaders decided to open the country up to international economic activity. The merchant princes of Osaka and Kyoto strongly opposed restrictions on foreign travel and international commerce. Fortunes were to be made in foreign trade, and they insisted on reopening Japan to the world. Perry's visit exacerbated tensions already existing, and in 1854 Japan joined the world economy. But foreign manufactured goods soon brought trade deficits, inflation, and political instability. The subsequent rebellion deposed the rulers of Japan—the shogun—and restored the emperor to at least symbolic power. This was the Meiji Restoration.

During the next fifty years Japan changed from a feudal kingdom to a modern power. The new government began assessing taxes on the value of land rather than on the size of the harvest. In the past peasants had been liable only for a percentage of profits, but after 1873 they paid a fixed tax regardless of income. Between 1873 and 1900, hundreds of thousands of Japanese farmers lost their land because of tax delinquency. Recognizing the need for some relief, the Meiji government legalized emigration, and thousands of rural peasants began leaving their homeland, first for Hawaii and then for the American mainland.

First Stop: Hawaii

Although historians still debate Polynesian origins, it now seems clear that Polynesia was occupied early in the Christian era, and from Samoa or Tonga to Fiji, and then to Tahiti, the Polynesians sailed to Hawaii around 750 C.E. Governed by a royal family, worshiping the gods of ancestors, animals, and the elements, the Hawaiian population grew to more than 250,000 by 1750. The English explorer and naval captain James Cook ended their isolation in 1778, and throughout the nineteenth century Europeans and Americans colonized the islands. Christian missionaries, intent on ending idolatry and sin, poured in. American settlers also came, seized land from the natives, and created vast sugarcane plantations. In 1893, the planter-missionary elite deposed Queen Liliuokalani and established the Republic of Hawaii. Five years later the United States annexed the islands. While liberal reformers, unscrupulous speculators, and well-meaning settlers were destroying native Hawaiian society, the conquest of the islands continued. Unable to resist European diseases, the Hawaiian population declined to 100,000 people in 1840 and 35,000 in 1890.

As the native population declined, the need for labor increased; in 1850, sugar planters began importing workers from China. By 1890 there were 12,000 Chinese in Hawaii. Japanese workers also immigrated and eventually became Hawaii's largest ethnic group. Although racial and ethnic tolerance developed in the nineteenth century, cultural life in Hawaii remained pluralistic and intermarriage was relatively rare. In 1941 there were approximately 80,000 Europeans, 160,000 Japanese, 70,000 Filipinos, 30,000 Chinese, and 25,000

Hawaiians, with a mixed population of only 20,000 Hawaiian-Europeans and 18,000 Asian-Hawaiians.

The *Issei*, first-generation Japanese immigrants, who settled in Hawaii were a blend of the old and the new. Because Japan had modernized so recently, feudal remnants survived in a reverence for the past, for roots, for tradition, and for family. But the Issei also had the desire for financial betterment so characteristic of industrial societies. Memories of the past and visions of the future provided them with the ambition to succeed in an industrial economy and the cohesiveness to survive in a racially mixed society. Maintaining a unique interest in the fate of its people, Japan contracted with Hawaii to send workers only as long as Hawaii paid full passage for them and their families, helped settle them, and guaranteed free housing, medical care, a minimum wage, and a maximum ten-hour work day. Between 1886 and 1894, nearly 30,000 Japanese workers settled there. When the United States annexed Hawaii in 1898, the Issei became Japanese Americans.

From Japan and Hawaii to the Mainland

The first Japanese settlement on the mainland was the Wakamatsu Colony, near Sacramento, California. Arriving in 1869, the immigrants planned to produce silk and raise tangerines, grapes, and tea, but in a few years drought, poverty, and internal bickering destroyed the settlement. Except for a few hundred students attending American universities in the 1870s, these were the only Japanese immigrants before 1882. But after Congress passed the Chinese Exclusion Act, demand for farm laborers increased, and Japan's decision to permit emigration helped fill the demand. More than 25,000 Japanese farmers immigrated in the 1890s, and thousands more came from Hawaii. In the next decade 129,000 Issei immigrated, as did another 125,000 between 1910 and 1924.

Most Issei went into farming, and by 1910 nearly 35,000 were working on commercial citrus, grape, vegetable, hops, and sugar-beet farms. At first they were poor, seasonal field hands moving from farm to farm, but they were ambitious, and through contract labor succeeded in raising their wages and improving their standard of living. By underbidding competitors, Japanese labor gangs monopolized the farm labor market in California, but as harvest approached they often threatened to strike. Rather than worry about the labor supply, many growers chose to lease their land to Issei tenants. Avoiding the commodities whites raised—wheat, citrus, walnuts, and livestock—the Issei concentrated on beans, celery, peppers, cauliflower, strawberries, tomatoes, lettuce, onions, watermelons, carrots, spinach, and flowers. Soon they dominated the truck-crop industry. They saved money, bought land, and became independent farmers. In 1900, there were only thirty-nine Issei farms, totaling 4,700 acres, but by 1920 there were five thousand Issei farms with more than 460,000 acres. In Japan the average farm had been only one acre, but in America a typical farm was forty acres, and by any standard of the Old World that meant success.

Aside from farming, employment opportunities were limited. The skilled trades were not open because of union hostility; discrimination by colleges eliminated professional careers; and federal laws against Issei citizenship closed the civil service. The Japanese had to rely on un-skilled jobs and their own resources. More than 10,000 worked as section hands on the Southern Pacific, Central Pacific, and Great Northern railroads; 3,000 labored in the lumber mills of northern California, Oregon, and Washington; perhaps 2,500 worked in the coal mines and smelting plants of Utah, Nevada, and Colorado; nearly 5,000 had jobs in fish canneries and food-processing plants along the Pacific coast; nearly 10,000 were domestic servants by 1940; and 5,000 Japanese went into gardening, landscaping, and horticulture, and came to dominate the industry. The Issei ran cafes, restaurants, laundries, cleaners, produce stands, grocery stores, dry goods shops, barber shops, and newsstands.

The Anti-Japanese Crusade, 1900–1940

In the American environment Japanese culture underwent several changes that were natural consequences of acculturation. Most Issei were Buddhists, and they brought with them the Tendai, Zen, Shingon, Nichiren, Jodo, and Shin denominations. But rather than confining themselves exclusively to religious activities, the Buddhist temples in America set up English-language schools, sponsored scout troops, and organized self-help groups. Buddhist priests in America often became preachers too, offering sermons every Sunday. Buddhist Sunday Schools were complete with hymn books, blackboards, pictures, magazines, and school and national flags. Buddhist temples often took on the ex-ternal trappings of American Protestantism. Conversion was another form of acculturation. While the vast majority of Issei were Buddhists, nearly half of the Nisei (second generation, American-born Japanese) were Christians and most Sansei (third generation) and Yonsei (fourth generation) were Christian. However, all Japanese in the United States continued to honor the Buddhist-Confucian ethics of filial piety, obedi-ence, and reverence for authority.

But the acculturation was not extensive enough to prevent the devel-opment of a virulent, anti-Japanese nativism along the West Coast.

Issei immigration went relatively unnoticed during the 1890s. Too many people were worrying about Catholics and Jews to be concerned about a few thousand Japanese. But as the pace of Issei immigration quickened, many Americans began lumping the Japanese and the Chinese together. Since Japan was a rising military power, some saw the Issei as agents preparing an invasion of America. An exclusion movement gathered force, led by California and its labor unions. After Japan defeated Russia in the war of 1904–1905, immigration increased; and the Japanese Exclusion League, a group of prominent California politicians and labor leaders, along with the American Federation of Labor, called for an end to Japanese immigration.

A diplomatic crisis developed after the San Francisco earthquake of 1906 destroyed school buildings. To guarantee a place for white children, the board of education ruled that Asian students would have to attend makeshift, segregated schools. The Japanese government protested, demanding equal treatment for its emigrants, and rumors of war flashed on both sides of the Pacific. President Theodore Roosevelt wanted to defuse the controversy but knew he had no authority to interfere in California affairs. Realizing that the school crisis was only a symptom of a deeper problem, he worked out the "Gentlemen's Agreement" with Japan in 1907 and 1908. Japan promised to restrict future emigration to nonworkers and the wives of Issei already in the United States if the federal government would work for the equal treatment of Japanese in America. Roosevelt then persuaded the San Francisco board of education to permit English-speaking Nisei to attend public schools with white children. The crisis was over—for the moment.

Immigration from Japan slowed after the Gentlemen's Agreement but never ceased completely. Yearning for a normal family life, the Issei began writing home asking single women to immigrate. To get around the Gentlemen's Agreement, they exchanged pictures and married these women by correspondence; the "picture brides" received passports and came to America. California nativism revived, and some towns began refusing to license Japanese businesses. Calls for total exclusion became more intense.

As more and more Issei bought their own land, white farmers began worrying about filling their labor needs. The California State Grange and the California Farm Bureau Federation campaigned for laws to restrict independent Japanese farms, and in 1913 the state legislature passed the Alien Land Act prohibiting those ineligible for citizenship from purchasing land. Since federal law prevented Asians from becoming naturalized citizens, the Issei could no longer buy land. Six other states passed similar laws between 1917 and 1923, and the Supreme

Court upheld their constitutionality in 1923. Japanese agricultural holdings declined to 300,000 acres in 1925 and 221,000 acres in 1940.

After World War I the exclusionists succeeded. Immigrants founded such organizations as the Japanese Association of America and the American Loyalty League to promote their interests, but they had no political strength since Issei could not vote and Nisei citizens were too young to vote in the 1920s. White politicians had nothing to lose by ignoring them and everything to gain by supporting nativists. The American Legion, the Japanese Exclusion League, and the Native Sons of the Golden West all joined the clamor, and the National Origins Act of 1924 ended immigration from Japan.

External hostility bound the Japanese together, but group cohesiveness had existed long before they arrived in the United States. Most Japanese immigrants came from eleven prefectures in southern Japan, where they had belonged to *kenjinkai* associations based on prefectural origins. Each prefecture had its own dialect and personality, and the members of each kenjinkai felt a sense of obligation to one another and a need to marry within the group. They brought the kenjinkai to America, and the ken sponsored social activities, published newspapers, offered legal assistance, and served as employment agencies. When ten thousand Japanese were left homeless after the San Francisco earthquake, the kenjinkai took over and few Issei had to accept public welfare. The ken looked after their people the same way during the Great Depression. In rural areas the Issei settled in small villages or *buraku*, and members of each buraku met to conduct Buddhist or Shinto ceremonies and discuss community problems.

Because skilled jobs were closed to them and California farmers were pushing them off the land, the Issei began to move to towns and cities. White banks would not make loans to the Issei, so the kenjinkai sponsored *ko, tanomishi*, and *mujin*—rotating credit associations providing investment capital to members. The kenjinkai also directed the economic and demographic development of the Issei community. Since employed Issei were socially and morally obligated to locate jobs for others in their ken, ken members congregated in the same occupations and same areas. The Issei of San Francisco and Oakland, for example, were from the Hiroshima ken, and in Seattle most of the restaurateurs were from the Ehine ken. Competition arose, so the Issei founded trade guilds to set prices, regulate markets, and sustain one another during times of sickness or recession. By 1940 the Japanese-American economy was self-contained; nearly 40 percent of all Issei were self-employed, and the majority were independent of the larger economy.

The Issei also founded the Japanese Association of America. A coalition of kenjinkai, the association provided English-language instruction, translation services, legal aid, employment advice, and maternal and child care. It also campaigned for Issei citizenship. Because the Meiji government had promoted education, most Issei were literate; they encouraged their children to learn English and established part-time Japanese-language schools to preserve their cultural heritage. Buddhist and Shinto temples bound Japanese Americans together as well. Amidst widespread discrimination the buraku, tanomishi, kenjinkai, trade guilds, Japanese Association, and religious temples provided strength and security to the immigrants and their families. Loyalty to family and ken, the great social ethos of Japan, became the lifeblood of the Issei in America.

The Internment Camps, 1941–1945

Immigration restriction in 1924 eased nativist suspicions. The Nisei-based Japanese American Citizens League campaigned against alien land laws and for Issei citizenship in the 1920s without raising nativist ire, but after 1930 the old fears revived. When Japan invaded Manchuria in 1931, and four months later attacked Shanghai, white antagonism immediately reignited. The Committee of One Thousand, a group of prominent southern California citizens, boycotted Japanese-American businesses, and the American Legion warned about war with Japan. Rumors circulated that Issei farmers were poisoning their products and that thousands of Issei and Nisei engaged in secret military training. By 1937, after Japanese aircraft destroyed the United States gunboat *Panay* on the Yangstze River in China, the American mood turned even angrier. Hollywood discontinued the once popular "Mr. Moto" films, and many Americans came to believe that Issei and Nisei wanted to destroy the United States. The stage was set for a social and constitutional nightmare.

The nightmare began on December 7, 1941, when Japan bombed Pearl Harbor. Americans were shocked, and Californians felt especially vulnerable, not only because of their geographical proximity to Hawaii and Japan but because more than 90 percent of the 125,000 Japanese on the mainland lived there. Japanese victories at Guam, Wake Island, Hong Kong, Singapore, Sumatra, Borneo, Bataan, and Corregidor in the first few months of the war aggravated those fears. Rumors of an imminent invasion appeared in the press, and stories of Issei and Nisei sabotage circulated freely. The Chamber of Commerce, the American Legion, the Veterans of Foreign Wars, and the remnants of the Japanese Exclusion League demanded the arrest of all Japanese aliens.

Hoping to expose sabotage, the Federal Bureau of Investigation began investigating Japanese Americans and in a few months arrested nearly two thousand people of Japanese descent, including Issei and Nisei businessmen, leaders of the Japanese Association and the Japanese Citizens League, Shinto and Buddhist priests, editors of Japanese publications, and teachers in Japanese-language schools. Only one man was convicted, and his crime was forgetting to register an importing firm as a business agent for the Japanese government. The others were released, much to the distress of the general population, and calls for incarceration of all Japanese Americans became more intense.

Tensions mounted early in 1942, and many people blindly concluded that all Japanese Americans were threats to the national security. General John DeWitt, army commander of the western defense area, called for the evacuation of the Japanese from the coast. State and federal officials worked out the details, and on February 19, 1942, President Franklin D. Roosevelt signed an executive order calling for the relocation of 40,000 Issei and 70,000 Nisei living in California, Oregon, Washington, and southern Arizona. Because the 15,000 other Japanese Americans on the mainland were widely scattered, they were not affected. The 157,000 Japanese in Hawaii were vital to the local economy, and even though there were demands for their removal, they were never relocated.

Although thousands of German and Italian aliens were arrested by the FBI, no general evacuation occurred, for while the Japanese were Asians, the Germans and Italians were white. They were also Christian and European, whereas the Japanese were Shintoists and Buddhists from a totally different culture. Nor were the German and Italian populations densely concentrated as the Japanese were. Besides, most Americans in 1942 looked upon the war in Europe as a distant threat; the Germans and Italians had not attacked American territory. The war with Japan seemed closer and more ominous on the West Coast.

Late in March 1942, army troops took the first group of Japanese Americans from their homes in Los Angeles and moved them to an assembly center in Owen Valley, California. By May more than 100,000 Japanese Americans were living in sixteen temporary assembly centers. They lost their homes, farms, and businesses in the evacuation. Federal officials offered to help them in protecting their property, but only if the evacuees agreed to sign documents waiving any government liability if monetary losses occurred. Most Japanese Americans were understandably suspicious and tried to store their valuables or sell them immediately. Because of the time factor, tremendous financial losses were incurred as homes, farms, and businesses were liquidated on short notice. Contemporary historians estimate that more than $400 million in property losses occurred among Japanese Americans during World War II. After the war, a series of unfavorable federal court decisions as well as complicated legal procedures made it extremely difficult for Japanese Americans to recover more than 10 percent of their losses.

The War Relocation Authority (WRA) administered the detention program, and between March and October, 1942, it constructed ten concentration camps in California, Arkansas, Idaho, Wyoming, Colorado, Utah, and Arizona. By November all 110,000 Japanese Americans had left the assembly centers for permanent homes in the camps. They had no idea how long they would be confined there nor what the circumstances of their incarceration would be.

Respectful of authority, most Japanese Americans accepted their fate quietly, going peacefully to the assembly centers and the camps. Rebelliousness was out of character. Still, some did resist. At the Santa Anita assembly center in California a riot broke out after the Japanese heard rumors that WRA authorities were confiscating Japanese property for personal use. At the Manzanar assembly center and the Poston relocation camp, mass protest demonstrations against crowded, dehumanizing conditions occurred late in 1942. The most militant Japanese were sent to the camp at Tule Lake, California, where security and discipline were strict. But in general the evacuation process was an orderly, if humiliating and frustrating, experience for Japanese Americans.

The relocation centers resembled minimum-security prisons where the bare necessities of life were provided. At each center hundreds of wood-frame tar-paper barracks housed the evacuees. Divided into four 20 × 25 foot rooms, each barrack housed four families or thirty people. Community mess halls and latrines met basic physical needs, and schools and hospitals were added later. Barbed-wire fences surrounded each center, and military police patrolled the perimeter. Within each center the evacuees were permitted some self-government. Several barracks had a block leader and an elected block council responsible to a WRA administrator. They maintained records, kept count of evacuees, planned cultural events, and carried grievances to the WRA. Buddhist and Christian churches flourished at each camp, but Shinto was suppressed because of its emperor worship. Camp authorities permitted inmates to publish newspapers in both English and Japanese.

Still, life was difficult. Most of the camps were in barren desert areas; the poorly insulated buildings were stifling in summer and cold and drafty in winter. Family life, because of the barracks and community mess halls, was strained and privacy severely limited. Problems erupted between Christians and Buddhists; Shintoists felt frustrated; rural and urban Japanese competed for influence; and geographic divisions between people from various western states emerged. The most serious rift was between the Issei and the Nisei. Issei parents felt deprived of

Japanese Americans, victims of war hysteria, arrive at an internment camp.
(The Bettmann Archive)

authority, especially after the WRA gave the most responsible positions
in camp authority to Nisei citizens. Financially ruined and politically
powerless, the Issei experienced identity crises and the old family structures weakened. During the loyalty-oath controversy in 1943, when
men of draft age were asked to declare allegiance to the United States,
most Nisei agreed but many Issei refused. The debate intensified the
generation gap.

Despite the penal atmosphere of the camps, some resettlement began
even before the last evacuees had reached the centers. Sponsored by
denominational colleges, four thousand Nisei left the camps to attend
school in the East and Midwest. Agricultural laborers worked seasonally in the fields, and after receiving security clearances some moved to
the East. Nearly eighteen thousand Nisei served in the army, a few in
nonsegregated units but most with the 100th Infantry Battalion and the
442d Regimental Combat Team, which fought in Europe but were not
trusted to fight in the Pacific. In Italy and France the 442d sustained
nearly ten thousand casualties and—with 3,600 Purple Hearts, 810
Bronze Stars, 550 Oak Leaf Clusters, 342 Silver Stars, 123 divisional
citations, 47 Distinguished Service Crosses, 17 Legions of Merit, 7

Presidential Unit citations, and 1 Congressional Medal of Honor— became the most decorated military unit in World War II. In one of the most painful scenes in American history, Issei parents, still in the relocation camps, were awarded posthumous Purple Hearts for their dead sons.

As victory over Japan became more certain in 1944, Japanese Americans seemed less threatening. In July 1942, Mitsuye Endo, a Nisei from Sacramento, filed a writ of habeas corpus, arguing that the WRA had no right to detain her. On December 18, 1944, after nearly two and a half years of litigation, the court unanimously decided that as a civilian agency the WRA had no constitutional authority to incarcerate loyal, law-abiding citizens. Two weeks later General Henry C. Pratt of the western defense area ordered the camps closed, and by December 1945, except for some pro-Japan sympathizers awaiting deportation, the Japanese Americans were released. The ordeal was finally over.

Chapter Eight

The Nativist Reaction

Although the Chinese and Japanese were the first immigrant groups to experience outright bans on their entrance into the United States, nativist fears eventually expanded to a much broader variety of immigrants as well. Unlike the immigrants of the seventeenth and eighteenth centuries, who had been overwhelmingly English-speaking Protestants, an increasing number of nineteenth- and early twentieth-century immigrants were Roman Catholics, Eastern Orthodox, and Jews. Unlike earlier generations of immigrants who had settled in rural areas and took up farming, the new immigrants got jobs in mines, factories, and wharves and lived in large urban concentrations, where they were highly visible. It had taken American Protestants more than two centuries to learn to tolerate one another, and just when it seemed that freedom of religion was finally becoming a reality, the influx of millions of new people precipitated a new debate about the meaning of cultural pluralism.

Anti-Catholicism

Anti-Catholicism became a dominant social theme midway through the nineteenth century. Newspapers, books, and pamphlets ridiculing Catholics became best-sellers, and frightened Protestants avidly consumed the most sensational propaganda. *The Awful Disclosures of Maria Monk* (1836)—allegedly the confessions of a former nun, who described depraved priests, licentious nuns, and monastic orgies—was a piece of religious pornography that sold more than 300,000 copies before the Civil War. Many Americans were convinced that Irish Catholics were sexually irresponsible alcoholics subject to the dictates of Rome. Occasionally the anti-Catholicism turned violent. On Christmas Day 1806, mobs in New York City disrupted Catholic religious services; and in August 1834, arsonists set fire to the Ursuline convent in Charlestown, Massachusetts. During the 1840s, when Catholics protested sectarian instruction in public schools and requested tax support for church schools, the parochial school issue caused considerable debate and exploded into the Philadelphia Riots of 1844, when priests and nuns were attacked, homes burned, and Catholic churches vandalized. In 1854, a mob destroyed the Irish ghetto in Lawrence, Massachusetts.

American Protestants also worried about Irish community organizations and the distinct ethnic culture represented in such newspapers as the *Gaelic-American*, the *Irish World*, and the *Irish Nation*. To assist incoming immigrants, the Irish formed the Irish Emigrant Society; and in every eastern city a number of volunteer firemen's groups, militia companies, and benevolent associations served the Irish community. The Irish also made enormous financial sacrifices to build Catholic parishes and parochial schools in their neighborhoods. With their devotion to the liberation of the old country, their religion, and their communities, they defied Anglo-American conformity. Many Americans resented such pride.

Poverty, crime, and unemployment in the Irish ghettos convinced some Americans that the Irish were an illiterate, brutish people incapable of improving themselves. Except for the most menial, low-paying jobs, many Americans preferred not to hire Irish workers at all. As always, much of the social prejudice had economic roots: the newest immigrants would work for the lowest pay and were seen as a threat by other workers as well as by middle-class businesspeople. Newspaper advertisements in New York and Boston during the 1840s and 1850s commonly asked for Protestant workers or stated flatly that "Irish need not apply." Irish children were mistreated in public schools; but when their parents established parochial schools, some Americans were enraged. The Irish were poor but they could not get good jobs; they were illiterate but Americans did not want them educated in church schools.

Many Anglo-Americans also targeted the German immigrants for nativist abuse. Their exclusiveness and cultural peculiarities worried many Americans, who considered the Germans less frightening than the Irish but far more threatening than English or Scandinavian immigrants. Many Germans were Catholics, and some Americans conjured up sinister German conspiracies to transform America into a papal outpost. Others worried about the German attachment to Old World values. Many cities outlawed German militia companies, gymnasiums, and shooting clubs, while others refused to charter German social and mutual aid societies. The Irish bore the brunt of Know-Nothing venom, but Germans and particularly German Catholics suffered as well. Anti-German disturbances erupted in St. Louis, New Orleans, Philadelphia, Cincinnati, Columbus, and Louisville in the 1850s, and in some cases homes, churches, schools, and businesses were vandalized. This anti-German paranoia would rise again during World War I. All this helped create a sense of unity among German immigrants.

French Canadians were also targeted. Many Americans welcomed artisans and professionals from France but worried about the French Canadians. Poor and unskilled, ignorant of English, and concentrated into "Little Canadas," the French Canadians were a conspicuous and growing minority in the nineteenth century. Their loyalty to Roman Catholicism and suspicion of public schools generated even more uneasiness. The nineteenth-century immigrants from France were often worldly and even rather secular about religion. But this was not true of the French Canadians, and they encountered the wrath of Know-Nothing activists in the 1850s and the Yankee sensitivities of other antiforeign groups in the 1890s.

The establishment of parochial schools by Irish, German, and French-Canadian Catholics became a major focus of American nativists in the nineteenth century. To Anglo Protestants, the parochial schools were a slap in the face, a bald, callous admission that Irish Catholics had no intention of accepting American values and assimilating into the society. Through the public schools, native Americans hoped to "smooth the edges" of the immigrants, transforming them into law-abiding, hardworking, Protestant citizens. The appearance of the parochial schools undermined those hopes and enraged many American Protestants who had not accepted Roman Catholicism as a permanent fixture of life in the United States. In 1841, the New York legislature specifically prohibited the use of any public funds in private schools. During the 1850s, the Know-Nothing movement attacked the notion of parochial schools. After the Civil War, several states—Illinois in 1870, Pennsylvania in 1873, and Colorado in 1875—followed New York's earlier lead in outlawing the use of state funds for religious institutions. The public school movement—with its promotion of universal, compulsory, tax-supported education—was the most cherished of Anglo-Protestant reforms, Yankee society's way of preserving its own dominance and preventing the cultural balkanization that mass immigration threatened to create. Catholic opposition to the public school movement, especially its requests for public financing of parochial education, seemed to undermine American culture.

Language was another battleground in the public schools. In areas where non-English-speaking immigrants were the majority group— such as the French-Canadian communities in upper New England or the German-American regions in the upper Midwest— public school classes were often conducted in the immigrant language. But anti-Catholic nativism in the 1880s and 1890s was creating new concerns about the use and abuse of foreign language instruction in public schools. Since the early nineteenth century, German immigrants in some states had enjoyed enough political influence to legislate German as the language of instruction in public schools. By the 1880s, however, many native Americans were concerned about the status of English in these schools. It was not uncommon for all subjects to be taught in German without English even presented as a second language. Those concerns led to new education laws in several states, including the Edwards law in Illinois (1887) and the Bennett law in Wisconsin (1889), requiring English instruction in all the schools of the state, parochial as well as public.

The New Immigration

Beginning in the 1890s, the large-scale immigration from eastern and southern Europe only intensified nativist concerns. America in the 1890s was in the grip of self-doubt and fear, with people worrying about the depression of 1893, labor violence, and the Populist revolt. Some looking for scapegoats turned to the Jews. While Jews made up less than .5 percent of the American population in 1877, they would reach nearly 4 percent by 1920. Some people saw their increasing numbers as a dangerous omen for the future, especially in face of the migration of "bizarre" Orthodox Jews from eastern Europe. People were bewildered by women wearing ritual wigs, by bearded, earlocked men wearing praying garments, by ritual slaughterhouses and Yiddish-speaking ped-dlers. Anti-Semitism increased in the 1890s and early 1900s. In 1915, a Jewish businessman named Leo Frank was lynched in Georgia for the murder of a small girl even though there were serious doubts about his guilt. And throughout the country Jews were excluded from private clubs and schools, hotels, college fraternities, private universities, and certain residential neighborhoods.

But the most violent nativist crusades were aimed at the Italians. Calling them "black dagos" and "wops," many Americans considered Italians ignorant, inferior, and superstitious, lacking ambition and social taste. The size of the Italian migration alarmed them, as did Italian Catholicism and concentration in urban ghettos. Italian immigrants often became scapegoats for the problems of crime, slums, and poverty.

Rumors of organized crime circulated wherever Italians settled. In the 1890s the Black Hand conspiracy, imported from Italy, was supposedly responsible for the increase of crime in America. Some people blamed the Mafia for social problems in the 1920s and 1930s, and as late as the 1950s and 1960s people were worrying about the Cosa Nostra. The relationship between crime and Italian immigration was complex, an outgrowth of life in America and the Mezzogiorno. For centuries Sicily and southern Italy had been overrun by Spanish, French, Italian, Austrian, and Turkish invaders, and disrespect for law, authority, and governments became central to Sicilian culture. Peasants lived in a hostile environment where personal security was the responsibility of the family. In western Sicily armed *mafiosi*, originally local strongmen hired to protect estates and collect rents from peasants, became a private government of small groups controlling crime in different towns, villages, and cities. Few mafiosi migrated to the United States, but suspicion of authority and a tendency to resolve disputes outside the law accompanied many of the Italian immigrants.

There is a relationship between ethnicity and crime, since crime was one route out of the slums. The Irish first dominated racketeering in the United States. Following its Calvinist impulses, Protestant America prohibited certain goods and services that they considered vices but that many people wanted. What legitimate businesses could not supply, illegitimate businesses did supply, and gambling, liquor, and prostitution rackets—run largely by the Irish—came into being. But as the Irish created the Democratic machines, power and status came through politics and control of construction, public utilities, and the waterfront. For a time in the early twentieth century such Jews as Arnold Rothstein, Louis "Lepke" Buchalter, and Jacob Shapiro controlled gambling and labor racketeering in New York City. Some Italian immigrants turned to crime, but it was more difficult in the United States than in Sicily. Except in densely populated New York City, extortion practices were not as lucrative. In other cities the concentration of Italian immigrants was not high enough; residential dispersion as well as the constant flow of new immigrants into the city and the flight of older immigrants to better neighborhoods prevented the stable colony life that made extortion threats meaningful. Still, some Italian displaced the Irish and used gambling, narcotics, liquor, and prostitution as avenues to success. During the 1920s they found in prohibition an unprecedented opportunity to market an illegal commodity. Later,

Italian racketeers branched out into loan-sharking, fencing stolen goods, and peddling narcotics. But there was never a nationwide crime conspiracy to take over America. When crime did exist in Italian America, it was family-oriented, decentralized, and involved only a tiny segment of the population. Today, African and Hispanic Americans control some of the ghetto rackets in only the latest instance of what has become a tradition in American history.

Violence against Italian immigrants began as early as the 1870s. In 1874, four Italian strikebreakers were killed by union mine workers in Buena Vista, Pennsylvania; and in 1886, a mob in Vicksburg, Mississippi, lynched an Italian American. When an Italian immigrant was murdered in Buffalo in 1888, the police summarily arrested 325 other Italians as suspects. The worst incident occurred in 1891. Since the mid-1880s, New Orleans newspapers had speculated on the existence of a Black Hand conspiracy, and the Irish police chief of New Orleans, David Hennessey, had built a political reputation investigating Sicilian crime. In 1891, he was murdered, and an outraged public decided the Mafia was responsible. Nine Italians were arrested, but a jury acquitted six of them and declared mistrials for the others. An outraged mob entered the parish jail and lynched eleven Italian inmates, three of whom were Italian nationals. In 1899, a mob in Tallulah, Louisiana, murdered five Italian storekeepers because they had given black and white employees equal pay. In 1914, after Italian miners had gone on strike in Colorado, the governor called in state troops, and in the ensuing melee three miners were shot and eight women and children burned to death. Other lynchings occurred in West Virginia in 1891 and 1906; Altoona, Pennsylvania, in 1894; Erwin, Massachusetts, in 1901; Marion, North Carolina, in 1906; Tampa, Florida, in 1910; Wilksville, Illinois, in 1914; and Johnson City, Illinois, in 1915. And in 1920, marauding people invaded the Italian neighborhood of West Frankfurt, Illinois, and systematically burned the community to the ground.

Anti-Italian sentiment reached its height in the Sacco and Vanzetti case of the 1920s. On April 15, 1920, a shoe company in South Braintree, Massachusetts, was robbed of $15,000 and two employees were killed. Two Italian immigrants, Nicola Sacco and Bartolomeo Vanzetti, were arrested and charged with the crime. A hostile judge instructed the jury to disregard eyewitness testimony that neither was anywhere near the scene of the crime. When the prosecution revealed that both men were under investigation by the Department of Justice for political radicalism, their fate was sealed. Both were convicted, and in 1927, despite serious doubt about their guilt, they died in the electric chair.

Sacco and Vanzetti on their way to trial. (UPI/Bettman)

Immigration Restriction

Industrialization, the rise of the cities, and the new immigration had precipitated a series of cultural crises. By the 1890s the old faith in a political and economic system blessed by God no longer seemed so certain. In 1890, the Department of the Interior announced the closing of the frontier, and many Americans wondered where discontented people could go to release pent-up frustrations. The depression of 1893 left millions hungry and out of work; Jacob Coxey's army of the unemployed was marching on Washington; Eugene Debs and the American Railway Union had struck the Pullman Company; the Populists were up in arms in the South and West; and all this came in the wake of the Homestead Strike at the Carnegie Steel Works and the Haymarket Riot in Chicago. People feared revolution. And the cities—full of Catholics and Jews, strange languages, exotic foods, and crowded tenements—seemed breeding grounds for political and social unrest. An atmosphere of crisis—first in the 1890s and again during World War I, the 1920s, the Great Depression, and World War II—precipitated nativist fears throughout the country.

These tensions first appeared just when racist theories were becoming popular. Many whites accepted implicitly the inferiority of African

Americans, native Americans, and Mexican Americans, and late in the 1800s these theories reached fruition in Jim Crow laws, the native American reservation system and the Dawes Act, the acquisition of Mexican-American land, and even the decision of the McKinley Administration to take possession of the Philippine Islands in 1898. Racism was a fact of life. But it gained new intellectual adherents in the 1870s, and some argued that there were fixed racial differences among white Europeans.

After Charles Darwin published his *Origin of Species* in 1859, social scientists such as Herbert Spencer in England and William Graham Sumner in the United States began applying the theory of natural selection to human society. This was Social Darwinism, the belief that certain people were genetically more "fit" than others and destined for success. At the same time, historians George Bancroft and Herbert Baxter Adams, political scientists Francis Lieber and John W. Burgess, biologist Robert Knox, and classicist William F. Allen began promoting the theory of Teutonic origins, arguing that the Anglo-Saxon, Nordic, and Germanic peoples were the superior race, responsible for free-enterprise capitalism, technology, and political liberty. They also claimed that Jews, Slavs, Italians, and Greeks, though racially "above" black and brown people, were markedly inferior to Germans, English, and Scandinavians in intellectual capacity, ambition, and social organization. A eugenics movement urging Anglo-Saxon, Nordic, and Germanic Protestants to marry among themselves and perpetuate their gene pool accompanied the racist propaganda. Written in 1916, Madison Grant's *The Passing of the Great Race* popularized those feelings:

> The cross between a white man and an Indian is an Indian; the cross between a white man and a Negro is a Negro; . . . and the cross between a . . . European and a Jew is a Jew. . . . The man of the old stock is being . . . driven off the streets of New York City by the swarms of Polish Jews. These immigrants adopt the language of the native American, they wear his clothes, they steal his name and they are beginning to take his women, but they seldom adopt his religion or understand his ideals. . . .
>
> The Nordics are, all over the world, a race of soldiers, sailors, adventurers and explorers, but above all, of rulers, organizers and aristocrats in sharp contrast to . . . the Alpines. The Nordics are domineering, individualistic, self-reliant and jealous of their personal freedom both in political and religious systems, and as a result they are usually Protestants.

Because of the new immigration, the white Protestants among the earlier immigrants now seemed much less ominous to most Americans. Except for the Norwegians, the "old immigration" had peaked in the

1880s, and second-generation British, German, Dutch, and Scandinavian Americans became more dominant in their communities. While their parents struggled to keep the old ways, the children were culturally assimilating at a rapid rate. As the public school movement permeated education after 1890, the children of the immigrants learned American history and spoke English fluently. Indeed, they preferred English, often to their parents' dismay. Some Anglicized their names or gave their children first names more traditional in American society. The ethnic-language press for these white Protestants peaked around 1910 and then entered a long period of decline. And with each generation, intermarriage became more common. Although British Protestants were by far the largest group in New England, they were intermarrying nearly half the time by 1910. Scandinavians were still marrying Scandinavians nearly 70 percent of the time in the upper Midwest, but in New Haven, Connecticut, for example, their in-marriage rate declined from more than 80 percent in 1900 to only 30 percent in 1930. In the German triangle, Germans usually married among themselves, but in New York their in-marriage rate dropped from nearly 70 percent in 1900 to only 40 percent in 1939. When these people did intermarry, they selected white Protestants more than 90 percent of the time. All these changes reassured older Americans about the future of their culture. It was the "new" immigrants who now seemed a threat.

Congress investigated the new immigration, and in 1907 issued the 41-volume report of the Dillingham Commission. Claiming the new immigrants were unskilled, illiterate, and transient males traveling without their families, the report confirmed some of the worst fears. To be sure, there were differences between the "old" and "new" immigrants. Most of the old immigrants were northern and western European Protestants, while the new immigrants were largely southern and eastern European Jews and Catholics. Other distinctions were not so clear. Although the Italians and Slavs were frequently illiterate men immigrating on a temporary basis, the Jews, Syrians, and Armenians were usually skilled, literate workers migrating with their families—indeed, less likely to return home than the English, German, and Scandinavian immigrants were. Moreover, the Dillingham Commission unfairly compared the immigrants of 1907 from eastern and southern Europe, where the Industrial Revolution had only just taken hold, with the 1907 immigrants from Britain, Germany, and Scandinavia, where industrialization had matured. Naturally, the two groups would differ in their level of skills. Back in the 1840s and 1850s, most of the so-called old immigrants had also been unskilled peasant farmers. However, people tended to accept the findings of the Dillingham Commission at face value.

As crisis after crisis struck between 1890 and 1945, nativist fears waxed and waned, erupting often enough to remind everyone that pluralism still challenged American ideals. In the 1890s, rumors of international conspiracies of Jewish bankers or of the pope to take over America were spread by such groups as the American Protective Association, the American Super-Race Foundation, and the Daughters of the American Revolution. Discrimination against Jews and Catholics became common. Two months after the 1915 lynching of Leo Frank, the Ku Klux Klan began to grow again. It persecuted Jews and Catholics, as well as African Americans, burning crosses at cathedrals and synagogues, and attacking priests, nuns, and rabbis. Klan membership rose to nearly five million by 1926. D. W. Griffith produced the epic film *Birth of a Nation*, which condemned Black Reconstruction and extolled the virtues of the Klan. When Al Smith, an Irish Catholic, ran for president in 1928 against the Republican Herbert Hoover, he stood no chance because of rural anti-Catholicism.

During World War I, German Americans experienced a variety of indignities, sometimes so severe that they lost their jobs or had to give them up and become recluses. Antiblack race riots broke out in dozens of cities during and after the war, the worst ones occurring in East St. Louis in 1917 and Chicago in 1919. After the war, nativism intensified and led to the famous Red Scare, in which left-wing immigrants were harassed and deported, and to such injustices as the Sacco and Vanzetti case. Lynchings of African Americans in the South were common before World War II. And during World War II, in addition to the Japanese-American relocation, more race riots against African Americans and Mexican Americans broke out; the most severe were in Detroit and Los Angeles in 1943.

The apparent crises, the periodic violence, and the vast changes occurring in the society worried many Americans, and they saw two solutions to the problem of cultural conflict. To eliminate it in the future, such groups as the Immigration Restriction League and the American Protective Association (both directed primarily by Yankee Protestants), along with allies in the Knights of Labor and the American Federation of Labor, began pressing Congress for immigration restriction. Despite the lobbying of German and Irish immigrant associations and such business groups as the National Association of Manufacturers and the Chamber of Commerce (which hoped to keep wages low by increasing the supply of labor), Congress passed a long series of restrictive immigration laws, beginning in 1882 with the Chinese Exclusion Act and a law prohibiting the entry of convicts and the insane. Although contract labor had never been a major problem, Congress soothed labor interests by outlawing it in 1885. Polygamists, indigents, and people with contagious diseases were banned in 1891; epileptics, prostitutes, and anarchists in 1903; and the mentally retarded in 1907. Congress approved a literacy test for new immigrants in 1917. Finally, there was the National Origins Act in 1924. At first assigning each country an annual quota of 2 percent of its representation in the American population of 1890, the law after 1929 permitted each country a quota established according to its representation in the 1920 American population. Immigrants from the Western Hemisphere were exempted. After 1929, except for those from the Western Hemisphere, only 150,000 immigrants could enter the United States each year. The Great Migration was over.

But securing the future was not enough. Nativists also worried about the present, about "Americanizing" the immigrants. In a spirit of sympathy and tolerance such groups as the Young Men's Christian Association and the urban settlement houses (such as Hull House in Chicago) helped immigrants adjust to American life, but the nativist groups were more heavy-handed. While the Dawes Act and the federal government tried to turn the Indians into small-scale Christian farmers, nativist groups like the Daughters of the American Revolution and the American Legion demanded that immigrants adopt "American ways." After World War I, the Americanization movement became a national crusade involving schools, churches, patriotic societies, civil groups, and chambers of commerce, all coordinated by the National Americanization Committee. They pressured immigrants to forget Old World languages, shed Old World customs, abandon parochial schools, and discard Old World political loyalties. Naive as such campaigns were, they were still the dominant themes of the transitional decades. The American commitment to pluralism, equality, and nationalism would still survive in 1945, but only after being tested again.

Chapter Nine

Native Americans: The Assault on Tribalism

In 1876, the major crises of the previous century seemed over. The disruptive question of political sovereignty was resolved when the Civil War defeated the states' rights philosophy, and—at least on the surface—the Fourteenth and Fifteenth amendments had established racial equality as the natural right of all people. The melting-pot theory was gaining popularity. Mines were producing vast quantities of raw materials, and factories were transforming them into a glut of consumer and capital goods. Agricultural surpluses were flooding domestic markets, and western land was filling with settlers just as the railroads were creating a national market. The future seemed bright.

But one shadow still lurked from the past. It was "the Indian problem." Thousands of years of tribal autonomy, freedom of movement, and environmental harmony were coming to a tragic end. Native Americans were on the brink of annihilation—their land taken, their game gone, and their population dwindling rapidly. White people and their machines were everywhere. Between 1877 and 1890, the last vestiges of native American resistance—the flight of the Nez Percé in Montana, the guerrilla wars of the Apaches in the Southwest, and the battles of the Plains Indians—were wiped out. It was a terrible story, the stuff of which thousands of western novels and films have been made. Arapaho dancers by the 1880s were singing a plaintive refrain:

My Father, have pity on me!
I have nothing to eat,
I am dying of thirst—
Everything is gone.*

And it was gone. European civilization—with its large fenced farms, towns and cities, railroads, and diseases—ultimately defeated native Americans. One scholar estimates that between 1789 and 1890, "only" four thousand Indians died by the sword; the rest succumbed to changes brought by white society. As the buffalo disappeared, Indian men were deprived of their economic importance; and elders on the reservations lost their decision-making authority to white agents. Restricted in their movements, without independence or means of resistance, native Americans were no longer able to struggle, violently at least, against white society. Life was different on the reservations. Instead of deferring to tribal leaders, native Americans found themselves subject to the authority of Interior Department agents. Traditional attitudes toward power, authority, and responsibility were expected to change completely. Reservation Indians had to surrender the hunter-warrior ideal and accept passive roles as wards of the state. They also had to accept the constant presence of white idealists and missionaries bent on converting them to Christian civilization.

With their independence lost, their cosmic rationale gone, and their culture under siege, thousands of native Americans turned to alcoholism and peyotism. Local agents often supplied liquor as a pacifier, and native Americans readily accepted it as an escape from reality. Others turned to peyote. A derivative of the cactus plant, peyote found a ready clientele among the hopeless hunters of the Indian Territory because it gave its users spectacular dreams and a heightened sense of personal value. The peyote cult had come from Mexico to the Mescalero Apaches, who passed it on to the Kiowas, Caddos, and Comanches. Quanah Parker, who was a mixed-blood child of a Comanche chief and a white mother and had resisted white settlement until his surrender in 1875, became a leader of the peyote cult and gained great influence over reservation Indians. By the 1880s peyotism had spread to the Cheyennes, Shawnees, and Arapahos; and by 1900 to the Pawnees, Delawares, Osages, and Winnebagoes. In the early 1900s peyotism reached the Omahas, Utes, Crows, Menominees, Iowas, Sioux, and Shoshones; and in the 1920s and 1930s it spread to the Gosiutes, Paiutes, Blackfoot, Creeks, Cherokees, Seminoles, and Chippewas. Eventually peyotism was institutionalized into the Native American Church, which was designed to bring peace to people living a life over which they had no control.

*Quoted in Ralph K. Andrist, *The Long Death* (New York: Macmillan, 1961), p. 338.

Reservation life also produced a burst of supernaturalism. Sometime between 1869 and 1872 a Paiute prophet named Wovoka claimed to have received a special revelation from the Great Spirit, and his vision soon evolved into the Ghost Dance religion, which spread throughout the plateau, the Great Basin, and on to the Great Plains. The ceremony consisted of four straight nights of physically exhausting dances, and the religion offered a spiritual explanation for the native American dilemma. According to this theology, God had punished the Indians for their sins by sending whites to rape the land and slaughter the people. Soon, however, with Indian repentance complete and sins atoned for, God would destroy whites, resurrect the Indian dead, and restore the buffalo herds. Although details varied from tribe to tribe, the Ghost Dance looked for the day when the promises would come true, and in the meantime believers wore sacred undergarments to protect themselves from danger. Not until 1890, when the slaughter at Wounded Knee proved the Ghost Dance did not protect from soldiers' bullets, did the religion begin to decline.

Finally, a new version of an old native American religion called the Sun Dance appeared. Before the conquest several nations had used the Sun Dance to bring successful hunts, shore up personal courage, and guarantee victory over enemies. Days of dancing, fasting, and self-mutilation—men slicing open the skin of their chests, passing rawhide skewers through the cuts, tying the rawhide to poles, and stepping back forcefully until the skewers ripped through the skin—were supposed to bring peace with the Great Spirit and prosperity in the world. On the reservations the Sun Dance became extremely popular with the Utes, Shoshones, and Gosiutes of the Great Basin and changed fundamentally in character to a redemptive, individual religion. By participating in the Sun Dance, avoiding alcohol and sexual infidelity, and living a thoughtful, considerate life, believers felt they could transform their personalities. Where the Ghost Dance promised changes in reality, the Sun Dance promised only the possibility of individual virility and understanding of reality, a oneness with the universe that white people could never achieve. Alcoholism, peyotism, the Ghost Dance, and the Sun Dance were hardly the conversion that white idealists were after.

Anglo-Conformity

As the Indian wars ended in the 1880s, and as "cultural aberrations" appeared on the reservations, a major reassessment of federal policy got under way. Ever since 1607 the British and American governments had treated the tribes as independent nations, sovereign on their own land, and Congress had negotiated diplomatic treaties to resolve disputes. Some whites also believed in the ability of reservations to protect the natives from white racism and to free surplus land for development by whites. Virginia had established the first formal reservations in 1646, when the House of Burgesses set aside portions of York County for the Pamunkey and Chickahominy nations. Two hundred years later, after President Jackson had pushed the wood-lands Indians across the Mississippi River, reservations seemed the only answer to "the Indian problem." Sovereignty and reserva-tions were the twin ideas governing Indian policy before 1870. Thou-sands of Americans, however, were concerned about the plight of native Americans in 1877. The native American population had fallen from 600,000 in 1776 to less than 250,000, and smallpox, measles, mumps, cholera, and syphilis were ravaging the reserva-tions. Unaccustomed to sedentary life, most native Americans vege-tated in their state of humiliating dependency. The catastrophe was apparent to even the most casual observers. Although the federal gov-ernment still recognized tribal autonomy, reservation life lacked the economic purpose so essential to social stability. Native Americans were wards of the state, dependent on food shipments from the govern-ment for survival.

In the 1870s and 1880s prominent whites, disturbed by the eco-nomic decline of native Americans and their turn toward alcoholism, Sun Dance, Ghost Dance, and peyotism, questioned the wisdom of both sovereignty and reservations. In 1858, Bishop Henry Whipple of the Episcopal church had written *A Plea for the Indian*, which con-demned the reservation system because of repeated white encroach-ments on the land. The Sand Creek massacre of 1864 exposed the tragedy of military confrontation, and subsequent congressional hear-ings revealed the horrible conditions on most reservations. In 1868, Lydia Child wrote her *Appeal for the Indian*, and Peter Cooper founded the United States Indian Commission to bring an end to the frontier wars. The American Anti-Slavery Society changed its name to the Reform League in 1870 and took on the plight of native Americans as its new crusade. In 1881, Helen Hunt Jackson wrote her famous indictment of American Indian policy, *A Century of Dishonor*. Three years later her novel *Ramona* portrayed the tragic extinction of the California Indians. And in 1881, the Indian Rights Association came into existence to force changes in government policy. White liberals, even though paternalistic, were gaining influence.

But old approaches survived. Reformers still wanted to divest Indi-ans of their cultural heritage, introduce them to Christianity, teach them English, and prepare them to function in a white economy. White hostility toward them, liberals confidently believed, would then

Geronimo (1829–1900)
Apache chieftain.
(UPI/Bettmann)

rapidly disappear. This was Anglo-conformity in its purest, most naive form, particularly since whites still coveted Indian land. Before American society would even begin to accept them as anything but obstacles to progress, native Americans would have to yield all the land whites wanted. Even then, regardless of how they acted or what they believed, they would not be accepted as equals. Most liberals, however, were not conscious of the obstacles in their path; working through the federal government and Christian churches, they set about changing native Americans.

Congress began appropriating money for Indian education after the Civil War, and money also flowed in from white philanthropists and Christian churches. Enthusiastic missionaries descended on the reservations ready to teach and preach the gospel. Nonreservation boarding schools such as the Carlisle School in Pennsylvania, designed to remove native American children from the tribal environment, sprouted across the country, and there missionaries taught Christianity, English, and various skills. Urging native Americans to become commercial farmers, the Department of the Interior sent agriculture teachers, farm implements, and instruction books to the reservations. But the transformation never occurred. Native Americans remained doggedly loyal to tribal ways. They preferred their own religious ceremonies to

Teachers and pupils at the government school on the Swinomish Reservation, La Conner, Washington, in 1907. Education was seen as a means of promoting Anglo conformity. (Culver Pictures, Inc.)

Christianity, and the once proud hunters viewed farming as demeaning "woman's work." Native American children, after graduating from the boarding schools, showed a marked propensity for returning to the reservations, even though they had learned valuable skills. Expecting eradication of native American society in a single generation, not through violence but through conversion, reformers were astonished at its tenacity.

Frustrated missionaries and government agents tried to prohibit the expression of native American culture. In a nation where religious freedom was sacred, Congress authorized government agents on the reservations in 1884 to cooperate with local missionaries in suppressing native American religions. They outlawed the Ghost Dance on the Sioux reservations and the Sun Dance on the Ute and Shoshone reservations. In New Mexico the Pueblos could not continue initiation rites for the young, and the Arapahos in Wyoming had to give up their funeral ceremonies. Federal narcotics officers zealously tried to destroy the peyote culture. On reservations everywhere, government agents punished native American children for speaking native dialects and prohibited tribal dances, drumming, and body painting. Since the federal government was at this time trying to stamp out polygamy among Utah Mormons, reservation agents also dissolved plural marriages among native Americans, giving little thought to the plight of women deprived of their husbands. Some Indian agents even insisted that former warriors cut their hair short.

The reformers sincerely believed that cultural change would help native Americans. Trying to explain the continuing vitality of the culture, white reformers focused on government policy. Tribal sovereignty and reservation life, they decided, reinforced Indian culture. The real solution was to break up the tribes, distribute reservation land to individual families, and turn the people into yeoman farmers. Only in the absence of a tribal community could native Americans be reasonably expected to shed their culture for white ways. What the reformers did not take into account was that although the reservation policy had been a failure, its original rationale had at least implied the existence of legal boundaries, acres of land confining native Americans but also restricting the access of whites. Even that legal implication was about to end. Once content to try to change the native American outlook on heaven and hell, white reformers now wanted to destroy the native American tribal culture to save its members.

The Allotment Program

The idea of dissolving tribal lands and allotting small farms to individuals had had its advocates in the colonial period, but the first real allotment program came in 1839, when the federal government divided the lands of the Brotherton nation in Wisconsin. Similar programs were later tried out on the Chippewas, Shawnees, Wyandots, Omahas, Ottawas, and Potawatomies. In each case the law provided that once the allotment process was complete, the affected individuals would become citizens of the United States. Convinced that allotment would protect native Americans from further white encroachments, white liberals in such groups as the Indian Rights Association and the Conference of the Friends of the Indians supported a national allotment program. Congress began moving on proposals to end tribal sovereignty in the 1870s, and in the 1880s the allotment programs finally triumphed.

In 1871, Congress stopped recognizing native American tribes as independent nations; and instead of negotiating, the federal government began legislating for them. Congress then directed its attention to the economy of native America. Thousands of native Americans had tilled the land before the white conquest, but they had been communal farmers, producing just enough to meet their own needs. Commercial production of surpluses was alien to them, and for the nomadic hunters of the Great Plains, farming of any kind was degrading. Furthermore, on the dry windy plains of the Midwest and in the semideserts of the Great Basin and deserts of the Southwest, agricultural success depended on capital and technology. As native Americans had neither, most of their efforts at farming would be doomed. Nevertheless, in 1875 Congress passed the Indian Homestead Act, permitting native Americans to take ownership of up to 160 acres each.

Liberal reformers realized that few native Americans would voluntarily leave their tribes for rural life. Benign, paternalistic coercion, they decided, would have to be employed. Carl Schurz, the German Forty-Eighter and Secretary of the Interior under President Grant, remarked in 1881:

> Stubborn maintenance of . . . large Indian reservations must eventually result in the destruction of the redmen . . . [it is necessary to] fit the Indians . . . for the habits and occupations of civilized life by work and education; to individualize them in the possession and appreciation of property by . . . giving them a fee simple title individually to the parcels of land they cultivate . . . and to obtain their consent . . . for a fair compensation, in such a manner that they no longer stand in the way of the development of the country as an obstacle, but form part of it and are benefited by it. *

An ominous note then sounded; land-hungry speculators began supporting the reform movement. If the reservations were broken up into individual holdings, it would be easier to purchase land from the native Americans. The reservations totaled 138 million acres and were controlled by only 250,000 people. Even the most generous arithmetic showed that if every individual received 160 acres, it would amount only to about 40 million acres. What was to become of the other 100 million? Greedy land lobbyists saw a windfall in the making. Senator Henry L. Dawes, a well-meaning but misguided reformer, introduced an allotment bill to Congress in 1879, and the ensuing debate raged for eight years. A few reformers realized that the bill might lead to native Americans' loss of even more land, but minority fears eventually succumbed to majority demands, and on February 8, 1887, the Dawes Severalty Act became law.

Under the law the president could allot tribal lands on the following basis: each adult native American head of family received 160 acres; single adults and orphans got 80 acres; and single, unattached youths received 40 acres. Native Americans could choose their land, but if they failed to do so, the Department of the Interior would do it for them. To prevent them from selling their individual holdings, title to

---

*Quoted in Robert Kelley, *The Shaping of the American Past* (Englewood Cliffs, NJ: Prentice Hall, 1976), p. 500.

the property was placed in trust for twenty-five years. Those accepting allotments and leaving their tribes were to be awarded American citizenship, subject thereafter to the laws of the states in which they lived. Finally, the act provided that surplus lands not allotted could be sold by the government to white settlers.

The prophets of doom proved correct; predictions that native Americans would lose their land were tragically fulfilled. The most valuable land was first to go. Whites went after the rich grasslands of Kansas, Nebraska, and the Dakotas; the dense, black soil forests of Minnesota and Wisconsin; and the wealthy oil and natural-gas lands in Texas and Oklahoma. In 1887, for example, the Sisseton Sioux of South Dakota owned 918,000 acres of rich virgin farmland on their reservation. But because there were only two thousand of them, allotment left more than 600,000 acres. In short order the Department of the Interior opened the surplus land to white farmers, who subsequently moved in among the native Americans, thus wrecking any vestiges of tribal culture.

Similar events occurred all across the country. The Chippewas of Minnesota lost their rich timber lands; once all members had claimed their land, the government leased the rest to lumber corporations for exploitation. The Colvilles of northeastern Washington lost their lands to cattlemen who fraudulently claimed mineral rights there. In Montana and Wyoming the Crows lost more than 2 million acres, and the Nez Percés had to cede communal grazing ranges in Idaho. In the Indian Territory the Cheyenne, Arapahos, and Kickapoos all had their lands allotted, and in the case of the Kickapoos, 200,000 surplus acres were sold for less than thirty cents an acre. In all, the native American tribes lost more than 60 million "surplus" acres under the allotment law.

The Five Civilized Tribes were initially exempt from the Dawes Act, but in 1898 Congress passed the Curtis Act subjecting them to allotment. In their bitterness toward the federal government after the removals of the 1830s and 1840s, many members of the Five Civilized Tribes had sided with the Confederacy during the Civil War, and in retaliation the government opened their land to white homesteaders in 1889. The subsequent discovery of oil in Oklahoma unleashed new pressures on the land as excited wildcatters and large oil corporations, supported by corrupt county politicians, systematically took much of the remaining land from the Creeks, Cherokees, Choctaws, Chickasaws, and Seminoles. Between 1887 and 1924 the land of the Five Civilized Tribes declined from approximately 30 million to less than 2 million acres.

Still the land hunger continued. In 1902, the federal government began voiding the twenty-five-year trust period originally designed to prevent the sale of allotted lands. The Dead Indian Land Act of 1902 permitted native Americans to sell land they had inherited from deceased relatives, and the Burke Act of 1906 authorized the secretary of the interior to declare native American adults competent to manage their own affairs and sell their allotted lands. Between 1906 and 1917 the secretary cautiously issued competency patents to only 9,984 native Americans, but then the pace quickened, and more than 20,000 received patents between 1919 and 1924. Greedy real estate salesmen, corrupt government agents, land speculators, and white merchants all began buying allotted land from Indians, usually at greatly deflated prices. The Sisseton Sioux lost another 200,000 acres, leaving them with little more than 100,000 of the 918,000 acres they had owned in 1887. Under the Burke Act more than 27 million acres were sold to whites by native American farmers, and by 1924 native Americans held only 48 million of the 138 million acres they had owned in 1887, half of it arid and of marginal value.

White Atonement: The Indian Reorganization Act of 1934

In 1924, Congress passed the Indian Citizenship Act, conferring citizenship on Indians born in the United States. In one sense the law represented the final assault on tribalism. Assimilationists yearning to transform native American culture hoped the law would distract Indians from their tribal loyalties. But in another sense the act inaugurated a new era. Conscious of what had happened to native Americans in the previous century, some whites believed citizenship was a first step in rectifying past wrongs, an admission that native Americans had every right to expect equal treatment under the law. And despite three hundred years of mistreatment, native Americans had enlisted by the thousands during World War I to fight for the United States. Sympathetic whites demanded citizenship in recognition of that military service.

Conditions on the reservations inspired sympathy. Thousands of native Americans had discovered that 160 acres in the arid West was insufficient to make a living, and as older native Americans died the inheritance of their children was even smaller. Four children, for example, received only forty acres each, and many nearly starved to death on such miserable holdings. Life was even more difficult for those who had sold land under the Burke Act. In a few months most had spent the cash; left with neither money nor land, they drifted back to the reservations, destitute and again dependent on government welfare. By 1920, life on the reservations was scandalous, and the native American death rate—because of malnutrition, tuberculosis, trachoma, and dysentery—was more than twice the national average.

During the 1920s the entire allotment program and its Anglo-conformity ideology collapsed under pressure from muckraking journalists, native American lobbyists, and white liberals. A new respect for tribalism and native American religions appeared. Eager to expose corruption, muckraking journalists turned their attention to the plight of native Americans. Article after article in newspapers and magazines, and program after program on the radio and lecture circuits, described how the Dawes Act had plundered Indian land and destroyed Indian culture. Descriptions of the demise of Indian culture were premature, but the muckrackers did arouse public opinion.

Native Americans were also organizing to fight government policies, and young white liberals were joining them. Organized in 1911, the Society of American Indians—led by such educated native Americans as Arthur Parker (Seneca), Sherman Coolidge (Arapaho), Charles Eastman (Santee Sioux), and Carlos Montezuma (Apache)—campaigned for Indian citizenship and denounced the Bureau of Indian Affairs. In 1923, white liberals formed the American Indian Defense Association to oppose all future attempts to steal native American land. Such resistance was timely, for the federal government was preparing its final assault on that land.

In the election of 1920, Republican Warren G. Harding of Ohio became president; in 1921, he appointed Albert Fall secretary of the interior. Sympathetic to land and timber interests, Fall selected none other than Charles H. Burke, author of the Burke Act, to be commissioner of Indian affairs. They quickly ruled that native Americans did not possess mineral rights on reservation land, and that oil and gas companies could petition the federal government for leasing options. At the same time they submitted the Omnibus Indian Act to Congress to pay native Americans cash for their remaining land. The government could then resell it and retire completely from Indian affairs. Finally, Senator Holm O. Bursum of New Mexico submitted a bill recognizing the land titles of white settlers who had illegally squatted on the Pueblo reservation. Had all three measures passed Congress, they would have taken most of the 48 million acres that native Americans still owned.

Native Americans rallied immediately against the measures. Looking back to 1680, when they had revolted against Spanish oppression, the Pueblos formed the All Pueblo Indian Council, enlisted the support of muckraking journalists, and carried their case to Congress and the American public, demanding rejection of the Bursum bill. A national uproar followed, and nervous congressmen realized that a momentous shift in public opinion was under way. The results were immediate. The Osage Guardianship Act of 1925 reversed Fall's oil and gas leasing program and protected Osage land in Oklahoma. At the same time, Congress refused to act on the Omnibus Indian Act, thereby guaranteeing native Americans control of their remaining assets. In 1927, the Department of the Interior stopped issuing fee-simple patents altogether, ending the Burke Act of 1906. And Senator Bursum's bill to take Pueblo land gave way to the Pueblo Lands Board Act of 1924, which established a government commission to mediate the dispute between Indians and whites in New Mexico. Whites retained title to the land, but not before Congress paid the Pueblos more than $1 million in compensation. It was a paltry sum compared to the value of the land, but it was the beginning of the end for allotment.

Other reformers concluded that only a return to tribal authority could save native Americans from extinction, and in 1926 such groups as the Committee of 100 and the Indian Rights Association persuaded the new secretary of the interior, Hubert Work, to investigate federal Indian policy. To make sure the Bureau of Indian Affairs did not prejudice the findings, Indian rights advocates asked the Brookings Institution to direct the investigation. Issued in 1928 and known as the Meriam Report, the study shocked the nation, confirming rumors of poverty and disease on the reservations and detailing the murders, physical intimidations, robberies, and legal chicaneries used to take native American land under the Dawes Act. Although the Meriam Report held out hope for the eventual assimilation of Indians into American society, it argued that the process would have to be voluntary—on their terms and at their pace. Until native Americans abandoned their own culture for white values, they would have to be able to enjoy community control through tribal authority, economic reconstruction, and freedom of religion.

In 1929, President Herbert Hoover appointed Ray Lyman Wilbur, the socially liberal president of Stanford University, secretary of the interior. Wilbur identified closely with native American problems, and he named Charles Rhoads, head of the American Indian Defense Association, commissioner of Indian affairs. Rejecting the policy of placing native American children in boarding schools far from home, Rhoads supported day schools near the reservations where children could learn useful vocations while remaining close to their families. It was a major change in the direction of federal Indian policy.

The Great Depression of the 1930s aggravated conditions on the reservations and made the findings of the Meriam Report even more urgent. Support for tribalism received strong encouragement when Franklin D. Roosevelt became president in 1933 and appointed John

Collier commissioner of Indian affairs. A founder of the American Indian Defense Association, Collier opposed allotment and had argued for years that Indian culture must be preserved if native Americans were to survive. Despite protests from missionary groups, Collier set out to revive native American culture by introducing bilingual education in the schools; ending requirements that children living at federal boarding schools attend Protestant church services; encouraging traditional dances, crafts, and drumming; and diverting federal funds used for suppressing peyotism to other purposes. Finally, he campaigned for the Indian Reorganization Act, which Congress passed in 1934. Allotment was dead.

The Indian Reorganization Act restored tribal authority. Under the law each tribe could draft its own constitution and assume ownership of all reservation lands; all unallotted surplus land reverted automatically to the tribe, as did Department of the Interior land withdrawn from Indian control for homesteading but never taken. The act encouraged the tribes to organize themselves into business corporations to manage reservation resources, and the federal government established a $10 million revolving fund to help Indians move toward self-sufficiency. Finally, the act appropriated $2 million each year for the secretary of the interior to buy new land for the tribes. Fifty-eight tribes composed of 146,194 native Americans approved the law, and thirteen tribes consisting of 15,213 native Americans opposed it. With such overwhelming support, the Indian Reorganization Act became the new bible for native American affairs.

If not completely successful, the act was encouraging. By 1945 ninety-five tribes had drafted constitutions and taken control of surplus reservation lands. More than seventy tribes had incorporated themselves and were developing reservation resources. The Department of the Interior spent more than $5 million purchasing 400,000 new acres of land, and several pieces of congressional legislation added another 900,000 acres. The department returned more than a million acres that had never been homesteaded and surrendered a million acres of public-domain grazing land. With their own funds native Americans managed to buy 400,000 new acres, so that in all they recovered nearly 4 million acres of land they had lost under the Dawes Act. Most encouraging, the native American population decline, which had been unabated ever since the seventeenth century, reversed itself. After World War I a sustained period of growth began, and from its low of 220,000 people in 1910, the Indian population had grown to nearly 550,000 by 1945.

Tribal structures had been repaired, and the service of thousands of native Americans in World War II had impressed the public, but serious problems remained. Although the Indians had recovered 4 million acres, they had lost 90 million acres since 1887, and much of what they recovered was land that whites had not wanted. Economic dependence on the federal government remained a fact of life on the reservations despite the lofty goals of the Indian Reorganization Act. Poverty, disease, and unemployment were far higher there than among other Americans. Compared with life in 1600, the conditions of 1945 were not good; but compared with 1920, times had changed, and the future was brighter for native Americans than it had been for many years.

Chapter Ten

Jim Crow and Ghettos: African Americans

The Civil War and Reconstruction had raised the hopes of African Americans, but dreams and even laws cannot immediately change the economic and social structure of a country. The economy of southern society had rested on slavery, and by themselves the Emancipation Proclamation and the Thirteenth, Fourteenth, and Fifteenth amendments could not alter that reality. White Southerners rapidly regained the power to enforce the roles they had assigned their former slaves, and the imperatives of slavery, if not the institution itself, persisted. Late in the nineteenth century, whites tried to turn blacks once again into a controlled, exploited minority.

African-American voting was the first target; so long as blacks voted, white politicians would have to treat them as a constituency, and such appeals would inevitably give the former slaves some power. Since the Fifteenth Amendment prohibited voting discrimination on the basis of race, whites had to use other methods to deprive African Americans of the right to vote. Physical intimidation was common during the 1880s, as were threats by white employers to fire blacks who tried to vote. Between 1877 and 1900 the South also adopted the poll tax, which required people to pay a fee before voting. The tax laws did not mention race and technically circumvented the Fourteenth and Fifteenth amendments. The same was true of the literacy tests, which disfranchised citizens unable to read or answer complex legal questions. Because poll taxes and literacy tests discriminated against poor illiterate whites as well as African Americans, southern legislatures passed "grandfather clauses" declaring that those unable to pay poll taxes or pass literacy tests could vote if their grandfathers had been eligible to vote in 1860. Whites were thus exempt from the restrictions. And to keep educated, solvent African Americans from the polls, the South created "white primaries." In primary elections to select candidates for office, Democratic party workers would not permit blacks to vote, and since the Republican party hardly existed in the South, the exclusion amounted to disfranchisement. Political parties rather than the state governments controlled primary elections, so the exclusion was not technically unconstitutional.

Disfranchisement was only a first step. For two hundred years the southern economy had relied on African-American labor, and after the Civil War whites still needed that labor. If blacks managed to gain economic self-sufficiency, they would be free of white control. So whites made sure African Americans stayed poor. Threats of physical injury kept them from applying for skilled jobs, joining trade unions, or buying their own farms. Some states passed laws prohibiting African Americans from buying land or leasing it on a long-term basis. Most African-American workers ended up as tenant farmers, migratory laborers, sharecroppers, or domestic servants. Some whites demanded that black labor be replaced by white immigrants, and in the late nineteenth century thousands of white workers displaced African-American artisans, especially in such skilled, urban occupations as carpenters, iron workers, railroad workers, coopers, blacksmiths, tailors, and construction workers. Few whites replaced blacks in agriculture and heavy industry. It amounted to economic disfranchisement.

Debt peonage also appeared. Former slaves signed yearly labor contracts and borrowed food and commodities from local white merchants, planning to pay back the loans with the proceeds of the next harvest. But when settlement time came in the fall, they usually discovered their share of the crop would not pay the debt. They would borrow again to make it through the winter and spring, only to have the cycle repeat itself. Since they could never get ahead of the debt, and since farmers with debts could not leave the county, they were practically slaves again.

Finally, many whites felt socially vulnerable after emancipation. To restore the control they had once exercised over blacks, whites began enacting "Jim Crow" laws late in the 1880s, segregating blacks in theaters, buses, trains, streetcars, waiting rooms, schools, housing, hospitals, prisons, parks, amusements, toilets, restaurants, and at drinking fountains. The Supreme Court ratified the Jim Crow philosophy in the *Plessy v. Ferguson* decision of 1896, deciding that "separate but equal" public facilities were constitutional. Social ostracism now joined political oppression and economic discrimination.

African Americans and Freedom

Active black resistance to white oppression began after the Civil War. During Reconstruction, African Americans in New Orleans, Charleston, and Louisville launched boycotts of city transportation lines when segregated horsecars were introduced; and after 1900, black transportation companies appeared in Norfolk, Chattanooga, and Nashville to meet the needs of African Americans refusing to ride segregated city lines. In 1899, black parents in East Orange, New Jersey, kept their children home from school after local officials began separating white and black students. Similar boycotts occurred in many Ohio schools in the 1920s. Even though most outlets for protest were closed to them, African Americans tried to realize the freedom that the Civil War had promised. Ultimately they decided that political and economic organization would help them achieve the equality they so desperately wanted.

Fresh waves of antiblack violence made the need for organization even clearer. Between 1900 and 1917 more than eleven hundred blacks were lynched, and even then federal antilynching laws failed in Congress. After three companies of African American soldiers were accused of rioting in Brownsville, Texas, in 1906, President Theodore Roosevelt discharged them without conducting a formal investigation. Between 1904 and 1908, race riots erupted in Statesboro and Atlanta, Georgia; Springfield, Illinois; Greensburg, Indiana; and Springfield, Ohio. During and after World War I there were more race riots, the worst in East St. Louis in 1917 and Chicago in 1919. Many African Americans began realizing that their only hope lay in becoming economically and politically powerful in their own right. The idea of "black power" began to take form.

The rise of an educated African-American middle class reinforced the desire for equality. In the antebellum period southern blacks had relied on African-American culture to define values and supply emotional security. They had few alternatives: whites determined all their occupational and economic choices. Slaves yearned after the freedom, prosperity, and power whites enjoyed, but African-American culture still commanded their loyalty. Once they were freed, their opportunities had broadened. The Freedmen's Bureau set up more than four hundred elementary and secondary schools for African-American children in the South, and private philanthropists established Howard University, Hampton Institute, St. Augustine's College, Johnson C.

Jazz musician George Bohannon and his family make music together. (Spencer Grant/The Picture Cube)

Smith University, Atlanta University, Storer College, and Fisk University for black students. More than five thousand northern teachers descended on the South after the Civil War and taught ex-slaves that they were free, equal, and entitled to everything American democracy offered. Initially freedom had been the elusive goal of African Americans, but contact with northern teachers made equality the new priority. Over the years, as business people, journalists, ministers, lawyers, teachers, physicians, nurses, and social workers came out of the black colleges, a self-conscious middle class appeared in the African-American community. Enjoying relative economic security, they constantly compared their segregation and discrimination with the egalitarian values of American culture.

All these changes came at a difficult time in American history. Early in the 1900s the Progressive movement was trying to solve the problems created by industrialization. Dedicated to political democracy and an end to corporate privilege, Progressives called for antitrust laws, railroad regulation, the use of the secret ballot in local as well as national elections, primary elections, women's rights, and conservation of natural resources. Most of them were not very sympathetic to African-American rights. President Woodrow Wilson, for example, acquiesced in the segregation of federal employees, and white primaries came to the South during the Progressive period.

Still, some white liberals felt that Progressive ideals of social justice applied to blacks, just as during the Revolution some northerners had seen the contradiction between slavery and the natural rights philosophy. Oswald Garrison Villard, grandson of the abolitionist William Lloyd Garrison, called for black civil rights; writers William Walling and William Dean Howells condemned racism; philosopher John Dewey protested Jim Crow laws; and social workers Jane Addams and Mary White Ovington demanded political and economic equality. These influential white liberals gave the civil rights movement respectability, convincing some whites that African-American equality was a compelling need instead of a revolutionary notion.

More important than white liberalism was the northern migration of southern blacks after 1914. Between 1870 and 1890 some 80,000 had moved out of the South, and 200,000 more left between 1890 and 1910. Compared to the influx of European immigrants, the African-American migration was inconsequential; they were still only a tiny minority in the cities. But that changed when the South was hit by an economic recession in 1914 and by the cotton-destroying boll weevil attacks in 1915. Thousands of jobs disappeared just as northern and midwestern industries were booming during World War I. African Americans headed north by the thousands. Between 1910 and 1920 the black population of the North increased from 850,000 to 1.4 million people, and by 1930 it numbered more than 2.3 million. Two million more left the South during the Great Depression and World War II, and African-American ghettos appeared in cities throughout the Northeast and Midwest.

The cities provided a new experience for African Americans. During the years of slavery, blacks had developed horizontal networks of associations to meet the needs of transitory children. Children who were sold from one plantation to another were immediately adopted by a black family in their new home. Also, since most African-American slave women worked in the fields every day, they had to designate one among them to care for small children during the day. African-American women maintained those support networks in the northern cities to make sure that someone was able to take care of their children when they and their husbands went to work every day.

Whites were frightened by the large African-American influx, and frequent race riots were malignant responses to those fears. But despite white hostility, African Americans now lived in their own communities without constant white intervention, and slowly but surely they developed into a force to be reckoned with by white politicians.

During the Great Depression urban blacks shifted from the Republican to the Democratic party. Most African Americans voted for Franklin D. Roosevelt, and many northern Democrats began to support legislation they wanted. African Americans had a new, if reluctant, ally.

The northern migrations produced a black renaissance that represented cultural separatism. Northern ghettos—with their African-American lawyers, teachers, ministers, doctors, nurses, social workers, and businesspeople—also produced African-American musicians, writers, and artists, all of them with a new determination. Their movement was centered in the "Harlem Renaissance." People such as James Weldon Johnson, Claude McKay, Jean Turner, Countee Cullen, Langston Hughes, Richard Wright, Irving Miller, and Anne Spencer graphically portrayed the plight and promise of black people and protested discrimination. They revitalized African pride and treated black culture neither as a mirror of white culture nor as a pathological reaction to racism, but as a fulfilling if sometimes frustrating way of life. They became the moral spokespeople for the African-American community.

Both world wars also contributed to raising African-American consciousness. During World War I nearly 400,000 African-American men served in the armed forces, as did more than 1 million in World War II. Segregated though they generally were, they served with distinction; and when they returned home, they were less willing than before to accept second-class status. Hundreds of thousands had been overseas in less racist societies, where they had experienced a tolerance unknown in the United States. Their return to Jim Crow societies was a shock. And because both wars had stimulated black migration out of rural areas and the acquisition of good jobs and better pay, African Americans expected more. Raised expectations inevitably created more impatience with inequality.

Four African-American Leaders

Several African-American leaders emerged in the late nineteenth and early twentieth centuries. Four men in particular—Booker T. Washington, W. E. B. Du Bois, Marcus Garvey, and A. Philip Randolph—symbolized the hopes of 10 million African Americans. They took different approaches to the "American dilemma," but all four sought the same goal: the end of poverty and discrimination.

In the 1890s, Booker T. Washington became the premier advocate of "black power," though he did not use the term. Born a slave in 1856, he went to Hampton Institute in 1872 and learned his lifelong philosophy: through hard work and industrial education, African Americans

The educator Booker T.
Washington serves as a
voice for a seen but unheard
part of American society.
(The Bettmann Archive)

could end the poverty of tenant farming and sharecropping. Washington believed that as long as southern blacks remained tied to someone else's land, they would always be poor and powerless, and only when they gained real economic skills would they become truly free. He assumed the presidency of Tuskegee Institute, in Alabama, in 1881 and built the school into a major center of vocational education. Washington came to national attention when he spoke at the Atlanta Exposition in 1895. Apparently uninterested in civil rights, he told African Americans to forget about social equality, accept segregation, and concentrate on material advancement and economic independence. White people, he insisted, could be allies as long as they did not feel threatened by social amalgamation:

> We shall prosper in proportion as we learn to dignify and glorify common labour and put brains and skill into the common occupations of life. . . . It is at the bottom of life we must begin, and not at the top. . . . In all things that are purely social we can be as separate as the fingers, yet one as the hand in all things essential to mutual progress . . . agitation of questions of social equality is . . . folly . . . progress must be the result of severe and constant struggle rather than of artificial forcing . . . *

Privately, Washington believed in civil rights, but he considered them subordinate to economics. His constituency was the poorest African

*Quoted in Robert C. Twombly, ed., *Blacks in White America Since 1865* (New York, 1971), pp. 79–81.

Americans of all, people locked into the rural poverty of the South, and he believed that for them economic survival took precedence over civil rights. Washington appealed to wealthy whites for funds to build African-American vocational schools and concentrated on elevating the living standards of millions of poor people in the South. White people hailed him, presidents sought his advice on racial matters, and when he died in 1915 he was the most beloved African American in the United States.

But Washington was not universally popular among blacks. If for no other reason, antiblack violence had convinced many of them that whites would never willingly permit real black progress. William Edward Burghardt Du Bois became the spokesman for those who believed that African Americans must work for their own civil as well as economic rights. Born in Massachusetts in 1868, Du Bois attended Fisk University and received a Ph.D. from Harvard in 1895. Later he taught history at the University of Pennsylvania. Calling for racial pride and group solidarity, Du Bois chastised Booker T. Washington for advocating a program that would forever keep blacks in an inferior social and political position. Instead of accepting discrimination, African Americans should openly demand equality. Instead of confining themselves to vocational education, the "talented tenth" of African Americans should study law, medicine, and public administration. Only then could they end racism and discrimination. Separation meant subordination, and Du Bois wanted no part of it.

To implement his philosophy, Du Bois invited a group of northern blacks to Niagara Falls, Canada, in 1905; there they formed the Niagara Movement to fight discrimination and urge young African Americans to enter the professions. Five years later a group of white liberals led by Oswald Garrison Villard gave him its support, and Du Bois joined Villard's group and other African-American activists in forming the National Association for the Advancement of Colored People. Through legal action in state and federal courts, the NAACP hoped to overturn Jim Crow and enfranchise black people. Much of the misunderstanding between Washington and Du Bois can be traced to their different constituencies. Washington represented the rural southern poor, for whom higher education seemed infinitely remote, and Du Bois represented in part a more economically secure middle class able to take action to achieve equality.

The third major African-American figure of the early twentieth century was Marcus Garvey, a West Indian immigrant. Garvey based his theories on pan-Africanism. A Jamaican, he came to the United States, settled in Harlem, and founded the Universal Negro Improvement Association (UNIA) in 1916. Protesting white imperialism in Africa and discrimination in America, he asked black people to look to Africa for strength, telling them that the world could not ignore 400 million people. Garvey exalted everything black, urging his followers to be proud of their color, physical characteristics, and heritage. By 1920 there were branch offices of the UNIA in Boston, Philadelphia, Pittsburgh, Cleveland, and Chicago claiming a total membership of more than a million people. Garvey had become a national figure.

For Garvey, the ultimate salvation of African America depended upon resurrecting the African background and creating a broad base of economic power. The UNIA established a network of businesses to implement his ideas, including the Black Star Shipping Line, the Black Cross Navigation and Trading Company, the Negro Factories Corporation, the African Legion, and the Black Cross Nurses. As far as Garvey was concerned, whites would always be prejudiced, and blacks would have to build their own economic civilization. Convicted in 1923 of using the federal mails fraudulently, he was imprisoned at the federal correctional facility in Atlanta for two years and then deported to Jamaica. Deprived of his leadership, the UNIA slowly disappeared, but its record of black pride and pan-Africanism remained a powerful element in black social thought.

The last great pre–World War II African-American leader was A. Philip Randolph. Publisher of the radical New York *Messenger* in the 1920s, Randolph questioned the theories of Washington, Du Bois, and Garvey. He criticized Washington for acquiescing in segregation, yet accused Du Bois of being too concerned with the African-American upper class, oblivious to the economic suffering of the masses and too willing to court white liberals. Garvey, he thought, was a curious oddity who would do little to improve the lives of most African Americans. Randolph was also suspicious of social movements composed of blacks and whites because he feared the coalitions offered only subordinate positions to blacks. He concentrated on African-American workers and argued that only through labor unions would they exert any real power. He organized the National Association for the Promotion of Labor Unions Among Negroes in 1920, and in 1925 created the American Negro Labor Congress. That year he also formed the Brotherhood of Sleeping Car Porters and Maids, and after twelve years of struggle the railroads finally recognized the union.

When World War II broke out in Europe, Randolph was enraged over job discrimination in American defense plants. He demanded equality in defense industries; and when the Roosevelt administration ignored him, he turned to mass action and threatened to lead a hundred thousand African-American workers in a march on Washington to promote his demands. In response Roosevelt issued Executive Order 8802 on June 25, 1941, creating the Fair Employment Practices Commission

(FEPC) and outlawing discrimination in defense industries. Compliance with the order was mixed, and the FEPC went out of existence at the end of World War II, but the commission was an important victory in African-American history.

Despite the efforts of Washington, Du Bois, Garvey, and Randolph, racial equality was still a distant goal in 1945. There had, however, been some notable accomplishments. In 1925, the New York Citizens' League for Fair Play boycotted white-owned businesses in Harlem until African-American workers were hired. In 1928, Oscar DePriest of Illinois became the first African American to enter Congress since Reconstruction, and Arthur Mitchell followed him in 1936. In 1930, after Republican President Herbert Hoover nominated the racist John J. Parker to the Supreme Court, the NAACP lobbied so powerfully against the nomination that the Senate refused to confirm him. And throughout the 1930s, the NAACP blocked the executions of the "Scottsboro boys," nine black youths falsely accused of raping two white prostitutes in Alabama. The Congress of Industrial Organizations—which included such unions as the United Mine Workers, Amalgamated Clothing Workers, and International Ladies Garment Workers—accepted African-American workers as full, equal members during the 1930s, and the NAACP worked closely with the CIO in strikes against the steel, automobile, rubber, and packinghouse industries. A. Philip Randolph had been right: African-American workers in the CIO unions benefited from their union membership, eventually enjoying higher wages, shorter hours, and better working conditions because of it.

To increase African-American support in the Democratic party, Franklin D. Roosevelt appointed several black leaders to advisory positions in his administration. Edgar Brown and Mary McLeod Bethune worked as advisers on black affairs for the National Youth Administration and the Civilian Conservation Corps. Robert C. Weaver was a racial advisor in the Department of the Interior, and Robert L. Vann served as assistant to the attorney general. During World War II the government integrated army officer candidate schools and hundreds of infantry units in Europe.

African-American Culture in the United States

Beneath this increasingly visible world of African-American organizations was the cultural world of black people as a whole. Some historians concluded that because there was so little resistance to slavery and discrimination, African Americans must have internalized white descriptions of African-American inferiority, that they had no group consciousness and were an "infantilized" people who passively accepted a subordinate role in America. Black society was pictured as docile, obsequious, and immature. But African-American culture after slavery was much as it had been during slavery—positive, fulfilling, and spontaneous—and African Americans were well equipped to deal with nineteenth-century society.

The desire to acculturate to white values had never taken root during slavery because the advantages of white society were so out of reach. Freedom, however, had quickly given birth to visions of equality, and some African Americans assumed that by conforming to white expectations they might be able to achieve their dreams immediately. The Jim Crow system intensified those attitudes, making it seem even more imperative to adapt to white culture. The northern white teachers in the South after the Civil War confirmed those hopes and told African Americans that by discarding black English for standard English, emotional religion for a more subdued Protestantism, and traditional games, dances, and stories for white activities, they would accelerate their acceptance into white society.

Some African Americans, especially those who were educated, became embarrassed by black English and adopted white phrases, accents, and grammatical constructions. In some churches the old slave spirituals gave way to standard Protestant hymns, and shouting, dancing, and handclapping became less common. Even the traditional slave story of the "trickster" declined. Trickster tales in West Africa had often involved "Anansi the spider," but in America it was frequently "Brer Rabbit" who outwitted the aggressive foxes and bears and wolves, won contests and games, escaped from one tight situation after another, and constantly came out on top at the expense of the rich, the powerful, or the aristocratic. After emancipation, although trickster tales continued to serve as vicarious experiences in success and power for poor African Americans, they were not as common as they were before the Civil War and essentially died out among the African-American middle class. Some blacks even began using skin-bleaching cream, hair dye, and hair-straightening lotions to appear more "white."

But like native Americans, African Americans let acculturation proceed only to a certain point and eventually developed a dualistic way of dealing with reality. Many African Americans were essentially bilingual, able to speak two languages. When they were with whites, they spoke a standard English, but when they were with family, friends, and neighbors, they reverted to black English. Although slave spirituals had declined, they were gradually replaced by the gospel sounds of singers such as Mahalia Jackson. To be sure, gospel singing was different from the spirituals. The gospel hymns were usually performed by a soloist for a church audience, rather than sung by the congregation; and while the spirituals had been spontaneously created and passed from generation to generation, the gospels were professionally composed and produced. Still, the gospels were links with the African-American past: performances had a communal flavor and were always accompanied by shouts of "Hallelujah" and "Amen"; gospel singers were physically active and rhythmic, their bodies swaying with music.

The same dualism was reflected in the rise of blues music. Promoted by such performers as Big Bill Broonzy and Jelly Roll Morton, the blues tradition reflected the individualistic ethos of modern America; each song was little more than the experiences, fears, and hopes of the individual performer. And yet, with its emphasis on improvisation, polyrhythmic routines, and calls and responses, the blues retained communal ties to antebellum African America and West Africa. Even the instrumental jazz music of Louis Armstrong, which emerged early in the twentieth century, confirmed the black sense of freedom, spontaneity, and communal power. Black music was clearly different from the more standardized white music of the time.

Finally, African Americans still had their own heroes. Although the black middle class attending Presbyterian or Episcopal churches may have been ill at ease about black English, folk religion, gospel songs, the blues, and jazz, and may have held up prominent whites as role models, most African Americans still looked to other blacks as psychological surrogates. The most common heroes—one of whom was portrayed in Alex Haley's book *Roots* and film about his ancestor, Kunta Kinte—were slaves or Reconstruction blacks who had escaped; who had resisted or outwitted masters, overseers, or the Ku Klux Klan; or who had helped others beat or resist the system. African Americans in the twentieth century also had their bandit heroes, people like Aaron Harris or Staggerlee, whose violence and aggressive independence of all standards pained and outraged white society. Joe Louis's defeat of James J. Braddock for the heavyweight championship on June 22, 1937, made him a hero in the black community because he had overwhelmed the white world playing by white rules. His quiet, well-mannered domination of heavyweight boxing sustained that heroic status through the 1940s. Decades earlier, Jack Johnson had also become an African-American hero after defeating Tommy Burns for the heavyweight championship in 1908, but his status in the black community had been raised even more by his willingness to flout the conventions of white society by living flamboyantly and ridiculing white values. Joe Louis and Jack Johnson had different styles, one aimed at cooperative success and the other at rebellious success, but both thrilled the African-American masses with their victories. African America, if somewhat more attuned to white society under freedom than it had been under slavery, was still a distinct society in the United States.

The great irony of African-American history, of course, was that African Americans were in many ways the most "American" of any people in the United States. Their families had lived here as long as those of any other immigrant group; their labor had helped build the American economy since colonial times; and their yearnings for freedom and equality had been prolonged and intense. Yet they had encountered the worst discrimination of all; the color line was carefully drawn, hindering their progress and keeping them from assimilation.

Chapter Eleven

The Mexican Americans

With the stroke of a pen the United States acquired more than a million square miles of land and 78,000 new citizens in 1848. Manifest Destiny and the lightning victories of the Mexican War led most Americans to see it all as the will of God, but it was a different story in Mexico. The proud young nation lost nearly half its territory, for which it received only $15 million, and saw the war as a humiliation by the "colossus of the North." As for Mexican Americans, they became a "colored," Spanish-speaking, Catholic minority in a white, English-speaking, Protestant society.

California

Except for 3,000 whites, California in 1848 was a social pyramid of more than 110,000 people. At the top was the Mexican (*californio*) elite, a small aristocracy of 1,000 people who controlled more than 15 million acres of land and the best positions in the government. In the middle was a *cholo* class of 10,000 mestizo artisans, soldiers, *vaqueros* (ranch hands), and small farmers. At the bottom were 100,000 California Indians. Even before the discovery of gold, people had considered California a bonanza of lumber-filled forests, rich soil, mineral wealth, good rivers, excellent harbors, and one of the world's most temperate climates. The Mexican residents of California owned fifteen million acres of land.

All that changed, however, when the gold rush raised the Anglo population to more than 80,000 people, most of whom settled in northern California. The californios became an instant minority, and although a few entered the territorial assembly and constitutional convention of 1849, they were hard pressed by the American influx. Despite their protests the assembly passed the Foreign Miners' Tax law prohibiting Chinese and californios from the mine fields. At the same time, white vigilantes attacked californio miners and drove them from the goldfields. Terrorists lynched twenty *californio* miners in Sonora in 1849 and burned the homes of hundreds of others. As the goldfields played out and prospecting gave way to corporate mining, the forty-niners who had not struck it rich turned to farming. But the best acreage was already in the hands of the californios, especially the wealthiest two hundred families, and their titles were guaranteed by the Treaty of Guadalupe Hidalgo. Poor whites began squatting on californio land to support themselves and protested to Congress and the state legislature when the californios tried to remove them. Congress then passed the Land Act of 1851.

The Land Act created the Board of Land Commissioners to resolve confusing land titles, but it was hopelessly biased in favor of the squatters. White Americans controlled the board, hearings were conducted in English, and the obligation to prove title rested on californio owners rather than on the squatters. That alone encouraged thousands of whites to invade the ranchos. Between 1852 and 1856 the board received 813 title cases and rejected 175 californio claims, freeing more than three million acres for white homesteading. If the squatters appealed the decisions upholding californio titles, the cases entered federal courts, where litigation averaged seventeen years. Court costs and attorney fees imposed enormous financial burdens on hundreds of californio landowners. Salvador Vallejo, a rancher in Napa, spent a decade and nearly $100,000 clearing his title; in the process he had to mortgage his land and sell much of his livestock to meet legal expenses. Hundreds of other californios had similar experiences, and even after clearing title many were short of capital and had to sell anyway.

Mobs of armed squatters often completed the process. After rioters burned his crops and slaughtered his herds, Salvador Vallejo finally sold his Napa ranch; another rancher, Domingo Peralta, was held hostage by a vigilante army until he sold out. Dishonest lawyers defrauded Spanish-speaking clients into signing English-language documents that forfeited title to their land. Economic changes also hurt californio landowners. Heavily in debt to banks for loans used to pay court costs, many californios went under economically when the Sonora and Texas cattle drives of the 1850s glutted beef markets and depressed cattle prices to less than a dollar a head. Severe droughts in the 1860s ruined hundreds of other landowners who had survived everything else. By 1880, Mexican Americans had lost their land, and during the 1850s and 1860s people with Spanish surnames gradually disappeared from the state legislature.

Many protested, none more vocally than Francisco Ramírez, editor of *El Clamor Público* in Los Angeles. He denounced the Board of Land Commissioners in editorial after editorial, proclaiming that "we are Native California Americans born on the soil and we can exclaim with the Poet, this is 'OUR OWN, OUR NATIVE LAND.'" Other forms of protest were more violent. Bandit-heroes emerged as social prototypes of revolution in California. Juan Flores escaped from San Quentin prison in 1851 and led fifty Mexican Americans in a minor rebellion. Joaquin Murieta terrorized Anglos in Calaveras County in the early 1850s. Tiburcio Vasquez also escaped from San Quentin and attacked Anglo settlements in the 1860s and 1870s. All three men became folk heroes to californios. Stereotypes of Mexican Americans quickly moved beyond paternalistic images of "lazy Latins" to pictures of criminally irresponsible people with no respect for law.

In southern California the ethnic accommodation was more peaceful. Because of the absence of gold and lack of water, southern California attracted few white settlers, and immigration from Mexico provided californios with a majority until 1880. Although whites controlled business in Los Angeles and San Diego as well as most state government offices, californios participated in local politics. Juan Sepulveda served as Los Angeles *alcalde* (mayor), and Antonio Coronel was superintendent of schools there. But that participation ended in 1876, when the Southern Pacific Railroad finally linked Los Angeles with the rest of the United States. Thousands of white settlers poured into southern California and by 1890 outnumbered Mexican Americans by ten to one. The cycle of land litigation, fraud, and forced sales repeated itself.

New Mexico

Ethnic relations in New Mexico had relatively tranquil beginnings. According to most historians, the conquest of New Mexico in 1846 was a bloodless affair; *nuevos mexicanos* welcomed American soldiers. Nuevo mexicano society rested on a small group of wealthy businessmen and landowners (*ricos*) living in Santa Fe and Albuquerque and a larger class of perhaps 50,000 peon workers. When General Stephen Kearny's troops arrived, the ricos welcomed them because they were desperate to keep their property. Aware of American prejudice against "greasers" (Mexicans), the ricos defined themselves as "Spanish Americans," European descendants of the original conquistadores rather than the mestizo progeny of Spaniards and Indians. It was, of course, a fantasy; most ricos as well as peons were of mestizo descent, but the *ricos* nurtured the myth of "pure" origins and hoped whites would distinguish between them and the others. Fear, not enthusiasm, inspired cooperation.

Hispanic culture remained dominant in New Mexico for twenty-five years. Since Juan de Oñate established Chamita in 1598, the nuevo mexicano elite had functioned in a stable, well-organized society; and the lack of major mineral discoveries until the 1880s saved them from the massive American immigration that overwhelmed californios in the 1850s. The nuevos mexicanos outnumbered whites and would continue to do so until well into the twentieth century. And between 1850 and 1890 there was little conflict over land titles because transfers were based on legal sales. Individuals with Spanish surnames functioned in the territorial legislature; and when New Mexico became a state in 1912, the nuevos mexicanos obtained constitutional guarantees of their right to vote and hold public office. State law also required sessions of the state legislature to be conducted in English and Spanish.

But troubles had begun for the nuevos mexicanos in the 1870s. Completion of the southern transcontinental railroads linked New Mexico with the national market and stimulated booms in mining, cattle, cotton, and timber. Pacification of the Apaches in the 1880s brought the political stability necessary for economic investment. White settlers began immigrating. The silver, coal, and copper mines of southeastern New Mexico expanded, as did the gold mines near Taos; ranchers moved cattle to the eastern grasslands; timber interests bought property and leases in northwestern New Mexico; and on the northeastern plains bordering the Texas Panhandle, southern farmers transplanted cotton culture. The new settlers wanted exclusive control of the land they were using, and schemes to get it led to a repetition of the California experience. Pressures on the land increased in 1891, when Congress created several national forests in New Mexico. Millions of acres of land formerly used as communal grazing property were suddenly closed to nuevo mexicano sheep and cattle herds.

Led by the Santa Fe Ring, whites gradually took control of much nuevo mexicano land. A small political clique of white bankers, merchants, and lawyers allied to twenty wealthy nuevo mexicano families, the ring controlled the territorial legislature and courts. It manipulated the law and imposed heavy property taxes on nuevo mexicano land. When Mexican Americans could not pay the taxes, their land was auctioned, and ring members purchased it at bargain prices. And by charging nuevo mexicano landowners exorbitantly high interest rates, ring bankers forced defaults and foreclosures. As owners of railroad stock, ring members indirectly gained control of still more land when Congress and the territorial legislature made land grants to the railroads. In all, the Santa Fe Ring acquired several million acres of land from the original nuevo mexicano owners.

White immigration and vigorous lobbying in Washington produced more land fraud when Congress created the Court of Private Land Claims for New Mexico, Colorado, and Arizona in 1891. Like the Board of Land Commissioners in California, the Court of Private Land Claims put the burden of proof on the nuevo mexicano owners. But land titles were extremely difficult to prove in New Mexico. The Pueblo uprising of 1680 had destroyed records of the earliest land grants; retreating Mexican soldiers had carried other records away in 1846; and the state archives burned in 1892. With little evidence to support their claims, the nuevo mexicano landowners were helpless, and in thirteen years of hearings the Court of Private Land Claims upheld their titles in only 75 of 301 cases. Whites took the uncleared grants. Most land fell into the hands of white Americans.

As white authority increased, so did the hostility between the two communities. Just after the arrival of American troops in 1846, Diego Archuleta and Father Antonio José Martínez conspired unsuccessfully with the Taos Indians to expel the invaders. One month later several nuevos mexicanos assassinated territorial governor Charles Bent and killed twenty other white landowners. As in California, the bandit-hero emerged in New Mexico; Sostenes L'Archeveque, in retaliation for the murder of his father in Santa Fe, killed twenty-three whites and became a folk hero. Vigilante organizations such as *Las Gorras Blancas* (The White Caps) and *La Mano Negra* (The Black Hand) raided white settlements often in the 1880s and 1890s, cutting fences, slaughtering cattle, and destroying railroad property.

Still, the situation in New Mexico was not as severe as the one in California, where Mexican Americans were virtually powerless in state affairs. Because of three conditions—the large numbers of nuevos mexicanos and their population majority throughout the nineteenth century, the generally peaceful transition to American rule in 1846, and the survival of the elite nuevo mexicano families in the Santa Fe Ring—ethnic relations in New Mexico were more relaxed than those in Texas or California. Throughout the twentieth century, people with Spanish surnames—for example, Dennis Chavez, Joseph Montoya, Jerry Apodaca—have been influential in New Mexican politics. Racism and discrimination occurred, to be sure, but not on the same scale as in Texas and California.

Texas

Race relations were most violent in Texas. Ethnic relations there grew out of the 1836 revolt, when Texans seceded from Mexico. Conflict was common along the border for ten years before the Mexican War. Most Texans were southern Protestants, intensely prejudiced against "colored" *tejanos*. As early as 1840 they outnumbered tejanos by ten to one and twenty years later by sixteen to one. Tejano political activity was discouraged at all levels, and the Texas Rangers (state police) enforced the unwritten rule.

In the Rio Grande Valley, where the tejano population was most heavily concentrated, conflict was widespread. Unlike California and New Mexico, where the Spanish government had made vague land grants during the colonial period, Texas had well-defined deeds. There was no need for a public land commission to clear titles. Improving standards of living in the industrialized nations, as well as the rise of railroads and steamships, greatly increased world demand for beef in the 1870s and 1880s; sheep raising increased too, fed by the textile revolution and railroad links with eastern markets. Cotton production came in the 1880s. The white desire for grazing and farming land increased enormously.

A mad scramble ensued. The state legislature and local townships imposed heavy taxes on tejano land, and banks charged high interest rates, forcing many Mexican Americans to default. Foreclosures followed. In Hidalgo County, land was auctioned at a penny an acre after tejano owners failed to pay their taxes. Judicial fraud also occurred. After dozens of poor white settlers illegally squatted on the land of Francisco Cavazos in Brownsville, Charles Stillman, a white settler, purchased their claims. When Cavazos appealed in court, Stillman offered him $33,000 for the land, perhaps 15 percent of its real value. Fearful of mounting court costs, Cavazos agreed to sell and the deeds were signed. But Stillman then refused to pay, and Cavazos lost his land.

Some whites used intimidation to acquire land. Historians believe that the Texas Rangers may have killed nearly five thousand Mexican Americans during the 1800s. To be sure, the Texas frontier was a violent place and criminals abounded, but in hundreds of cases the Rangers simply helped whites "dislodge" tejanos from the land. Richard King was one of the Texas robber barons who used the Rangers to enforce his often fraudulent land claims. The son of poor Irish immigrants, he moved to south Texas and founded the King Ranch. In 1852, he bought the 15,000-acre Santa Gertrudis Grant for two cents an acre, and as president of the Stock Raisers Association of Western Texas he increased his holdings to more than 600,000 acres. Similar events

occurred throughout south Texas, and by 1880 only two of the wealthiest three hundred landowners in the state were tejanos. The transfer of
land was complete.

Tejanos resisted. The Cart War of 1857 broke out when white teamsters began ambushing Mexican-American freight trains and murdering
drivers. The tejanos responded in kind. Twenty years later the El Paso
Salt War erupted over access to the Guadalupe salt mines. Hoping to
corner the supply, a few whites killed some tejanos who were trying to
get to the salt, and the war went on for six months. Once again the
bandit-hero, this time in the person of Juan Cortina, emerged. During
the 1850s Cortina raided several towns and killed whites who had
mistreated tejanos. After federal troops drove him across the border,
Cortina became a hero to Mexicans on both sides of the Rio Grande.
Eventually he became governor of the state of Tamaulipas. Cortina,
however, was more of a revolutionary than a bandit. From Cameron
County in south Texas he said in 1859:

> Mexicans! My part is taken; the voice of revelation whispers to me that to me
> is entrusted the work of breaking the chains of your slavery, and that the Lord
> will enable me, with powerful arm, to fight against our enemies . . . to the
> improvement of the unhappy condition of those Mexican residents . . . exter-
> minating their tyrants, to which end those which compose it are ready to shed
> their blood and suffer the death of martyrs. *

The Mexican-American Community in 1900

By 1900, Mexican Americans were becoming almost a colonial people.
The appearance of huge commercial farms with heavy investment in
machinery, fertilizers, and irrigation systems gradually priced Mexican-
American farmers out of business. Unable to compete, they had to sell
their land and became laborers. Whites dominated politics throughout
the region, and in some areas, especially south Texas, Mexican Americans faced the poll taxes and literacy tests that had already disfranchised
African Americans in the South. Whites segregated Mexican-American
children in schools and discouraged the use of Spanish. The Treaty of
Guadalupe Hidalgo was being turned upside down.

The Mexican-American family encountered serious challenges. Traditional family life had revolved around extended kinship ties wherein
children and young adults, even after marriage, deferred to the discipline and leadership of their parents. Respect for elders and family

*U.S. Congress, House of Representatives, House Executive Document No. 52, *Difficulties
on the Southwestern* Frontier, 36th Cong., 1st Sess., 1861, p. 81.

solidarity were highly valued, and the authority of the father was unquestioned. But the demise of the old rancho system undermined the agrarian values that had sustained the paternalistic extended family. Between 1850 and 1880 in Los Angeles, for example, the number of californio families headed by women rose dramatically until more than one-third were matriarchal. The number of common-law marriages and consensual unions similarly increased. Both phenomena played central roles in the transition from extended to nuclear family life, but in the process the family became less able to cope with economic modernization. Now a suppressed ethnic minority in a secular, indus-trializing society, Mexican Americans saw an erosion of parental authority, discipline, and the financial resources that extended families could muster. The Mexican-American community was ill-prepared for the American vision of progress and modernization.

North from Mexico, 1900–1945

Before 1900, the Mexican-American population never exceeded 300,000, but between 1900 and 1930 more than 1.5 million people left Mexico for the United States. Porfirio Díaz took over the Mexican government in 1876 and ruled with an iron hand for thirty-four years. Openly sympathetic with large landowners, foreign investors, and the upper class, he encouraged investment, helped the rich acquire more land, and discriminated against mestizos and Indians. As hacienda owners and foreigners grew richer, the masses became poorer. Their standard of living further declined as the population grew from 9 mil-lion to 15 million.

A revolutionary upheaval destroyed the Díaz government in 1910, and until 1920 Mexico suffered from widespread instability and eco-nomic disruption. Francisco Madero assumed power in 1911, but his refusal to return hacienda lands to the Indians led Emiliano Zapata and his guerrilla warriors to begin assassinating hacienda owners and attack-ing the Madero government. Madero was killed in 1913, and Victori-ano Huerta took over; but after two years of fighting with Venustiano Carranza, Pancho Villa, Emiliano Zapata, and Alvaro Obregón, Huerta went into exile and was replaced by Carranza. When Carranza was assassinated in 1920, Obregón took over and the bloodshed dimin-ished, but during the chaos more than a million Mexicans had died.

At the same time, economic growth in the United States was attract-ing immigrant workers. Because of irrigation and fertilizers, farm acreage in the West increased threefold and irrigated land from 60,000 to nearly 1.5 million acres between 1870 and 1900. Cotton production in western Texas, the Salt River Valley of Arizona, and the San Joaquin Valley of California boomed; so did sugar-beet production in Utah, Idaho, and Colorado; and vegetable and citrus production in southern Texas and the Imperial Valley of California. Meanwhile, the Chinese Exclusion Act of 1882 and the so-called Gentlemen's Agreement in 1907 limited immigration from Asia. Demand for farm laborers was rising just as the pool of workers was shrinking, and American growers sent labor bosses to Baja California, Sonora, and Tamaulipas to recruit Mexican workers.

Industrial development also stimulated demand for workers. The Southern Pacific and Santa Fe railroads recruited Mexicans to complete trunk lines in the Southwest. When World War I broke out in Europe, the international demand for United States foodstuffs soared, and tens of thousands of new acres were brought into production. More Mexicans immigrated. And when the United States entered the war in 1917, thousands of Mexican Americans took industrial jobs in the North. There were Mexican-American *barrios* (ghettos) in Denver, Detroit, St. Louis, Chicago, and Pittsburgh, as well as in El Paso, San Antonio, Albuquerque, Tucson, Phoenix, San Diego, and Los Angeles. As Mexican Americans left their jobs in the Southwest, new Mexican immigrants moved in to fill them. The trend continued in the 1920s, especially after Congress passed the National Origins Act in 1924, limiting immigration from Asia and Europe. Immigration fell off drastically during the Great Depression but picked up again when World War II improved the domestic economy.

Most immigrants left northern Mexico for southern Texas and California. Many came from a hacienda background as peons, people with no land or power who labored for the hacendado. But they also lived within an emotionally secure world of extended families where all daily acquaintances were familiar. Consequently, they highly valued personalism, even to the point of applying human attributes to animals and nature. And finally, they were not inclined to make fine distinctions between the sacred and secular worlds, but instead viewed the two as one—religion, magic, folk medicine, work, life, and death were all part of one holistic existence. It is not surprising that when they were suddenly thrust into the American world of urban anonymity, rapid social and technological change, democratic mobility, and secular competitiveness, they experienced a long period of confusion and alienation.

The barrios of the Southwest became internal colonies for the Mexican immigrants, the place where they lived out their lives and made their accommodation to white society. Very rapidly they adopted the utilitarian items of American culture such as wooden and metal toilets, metal kitchen utensils, sewing and washing machines, automobiles,

Political turmoil at home and employment opportunities in the United States caused large numbers of Mexicans to cross the border after 1900. (Culver Pictures, Inc.)

radios, bathtubs, sinks, metal stoves, and refrigerators. Language in the barrio reflected the acculturation process as well. Although public schools were dedicated to the elimination of Spanish, several hybrid English-Spanish border languages developed—for example, *Calo* in California and *Texmex* in southern Texas. English words were adapted to Spanish syntax, and the result was a vocabulary containing such terms as *el troque* (truck), *la ganga* (gang), *loncherias* (lunch counters), *huachale* (watch it), *pushele* (push it), and *parquiarse* (park the car). In the barrios the immigrants could relax amidst the smells of corn tortillas, beans, fried rice, and peppers; the sounds of traditional folksongs like "La Cautiva Marcelina" or "El Vaquero Nicolas"; and the noise of children playing *la pelota* (ball) or el *coyotito* (little coyote). Like the first Little Italys, shtetls, Chinatowns, and Paddy's villages, the barrios were a unique combination of economic poverty and emotional comfort, one more cultural island in ethnic America.

Whites tried desperately to Americanize the Mexican immigrants. Viewing Mexican culture as an anachronism unsuited for industrial society, business, educational, and social groups attempted to acculturate them. Individual employers, trade associations, and chambers of commerce tried to convince Mexican laborers to work gratefully at low wages without complaint, to come to work on religious holidays, to show up on time every day, and to remain on the same job for as long as possible. Public schools forced Mexican children to abandon Spanish for English, inculcated consumer culture and American patriotism, and urged young men into vocational rather than academic studies. Through homemaking classes they encouraged young women to discard Mexican foods and clothing for those of America. And Protestant missionary societies proselytized the immigrants, hoping to divest them of their Catholicism, extended family life, use of alcohol, and folk culture.

Mexican Americans had always faced discrimination in American society, but it was not until the middle of the twentieth century that organized Mexican-American groups began demanding equality. Although the tejano, californio, and nuevo mexicano natives had worked for change, Mexican immigrants arriving after 1900 seemed more apathetic, partly because they had little inclination to conform to American society. Like the French Canadians, they were close to the mother country, returned home frequently to visit friends and relatives, and repeatedly renewed their cultural roots. Many viewed their sojourn in the United States as a temporary means of supporting their families back in Mexico.

At the same time they were a mestizo people who for centuries had encountered poverty and discrimination at the hands of the Spanish upper class. Lower-class status was all they had ever known, and unlike the californios, nuevos mexicanos, and tejanos, who had known prosperity and hated losing it, they had never enjoyed comfort and security. The treatment they received from white growers in the Southwest was not much different from the treatment meted out on the Mexican haciendas. By 1945, only one in ten Mexican Americans of immigrant heritage was a descendant of a tejano, nuevo mexicano, or californio. For all the poverty and discrimination immigrants found, life in the United States was better than the chaos they had left behind. Not until their children and grandchildren reached adulthood after 1945 would *Chicanismo*, a movement for cultural pride and political activism, really begin.

The Beginnings of a Mexican-American Political Movement

In the late 1930s and early 1940s the *pachuco* culture emerged in the barrios of the Southwest. Caught in a cultural squeeze between Mexico and America, Mexican-American teenagers formed gang clubs in their blocks and neighborhoods. Carrying such neighborhood names as the White Fence Gang and the Happy Valley Gang, the clubs served as outlets for the frustration and social needs of young people. Members tattooed emblems on their left hands, spent their time together, wore flamboyantly styled zoot suits, spoke Calo or Texmex, and asserted territorial rights in their neighborhoods. Wars between rival gangs were common. Through their clothing, tattoos, barrio language, and attitude of sullen rebellion, they flaunted their cultural differences with the larger society. Indeed, they were different. Unlike their immigrant parents, the pachucos had attended public schools and had been exposed to white values. But instead of assimilating, they insisted on maintaining their own values; pachuco culture was an instinctive rebellion, a stubborn assertion of personal and ethnic identity. *Pachuquismo* was exaggerated and aggressive, and by flaunting the values of American society, the pachucos established contact with a culture that was rejecting them. Notoriety established them as antiheroes.

By representing pure liberty and disorder, rebellion and the forbidden, pachuquismo seemed exotic and dangerous to those Americans conditioned to expect smiling obsequiousness from Mexican Americans. That fear erupted into the so-called zoot-suit riots in June 1943, when hundreds of white sailors entered Los Angeles barrios and assaulted Mexican-American youths wearing zoot suits. Police ignored the attackers, and the local press treated the incident as if Mexican-American gangs had precipitated it. The fracas went on for several days, until military police sent the sailors back to their ships and canceled all shore leave.

Middle-class Mexican Americans faced special problems of their own, for while a relative prosperity separated them from lower-class immigrants, Mexican culture isolated them from the surrounding white society. Like middle-class blacks or German Jews, they wanted to be accepted in American society, even to the point, for some, of assimilation. Worried about white attitudes, many of them still adhered to the idea of being "Spanish-American," denying their origins in a mestizo culture. They hated pachuquismo for fear it would invite the wrath of Anglo-conformists and make life difficult for all Mexican Americans. Border languages such as Calo and Texmex embarrassed them as being culturally inferior, poor English as well as poor Spanish. And cloistered in neat homes and apartments, they were alienated by the sights and sounds of the barrios, by the poverty and folk culture.

Politically, the middle class concentrated on civil rights problems. More secure economically, they saw discrimination rather than poverty as the immediate problem, and in the 1920s they organized to deal with it. Established in 1927, the League of United Latin American Citizens (LULAC) advocated higher education as the "way out of the barrio" and called for an end to discrimination. In the 1930s the Congress of Spanish Speaking Peoples also emphasized education and denounced discrimination. Then, in the 1940s, these civil rights groups rallied to the support of the defendants in the Díaz murder trial. In 1942, José Díaz was found dead in the Sleepy Lagoon barrio of Los Angeles. Police arrested twenty-two members of a pachuco gang, and a grand jury indicted them for assault and murder. At trial the prosecutor and judge repeatedly declared that Mexican Americans were cruel and violent, were communist inspired, and had probably murdered the boy. In January 1943, three of the young men were convicted of first-degree murder, nine of second-degree murder, and five of assault, while five were acquitted. Mexican-American organizations formed the Sleepy Lagoon Defense Committee and campaigned against the convictions. Nearly twenty months later a federal appeals court reversed the convictions on the grounds that the judge had been biased and that there had been no evidence linking the boys to the crime. It was an important victory for Mexican-American civil rights groups.

Unlike members of the middle class, Mexican-American workers found their economic plight more compelling than discrimination, arguing that the right to enter a restaurant was meaningless without the money to pay the bill. Union organization seemed especially promising. Such agribusinesses as the Newhall-Saugus Land Company and the DiGiorgio Fruit Corporation were powerful, but perishable crops made them vulnerable to labor disruptions. Even a brief strike could be disastrous. For just these reasons growers fought to keep the farm labor force as large and mobile as possible in order to keep wages down, overcome work stoppages, and prevent the growth of unions. American unions lobbied to restrict Mexican immigration, while the farm bloc, sugar companies, mining concerns, and southwestern railroads lobbied for open borders. Before World War II, business prevailed over labor in the national debate, and Mexico was exempted from the National Origins Act of 1924.

As difficult as union activity was, some workers organized. Sugar-beet workers in California struck in 1903 and won the right to deal with growers directly rather than through labor contractors. Mexican-American railroad and factory workers in Los Angeles struck for higher wages several times. In 1915, copper workers walked out in Arizona to protest higher wages paid to whites. The cantaloupe workers struck in the Imperial Valley in 1928, as did the pecan workers in San Antonio in 1938. The Confederation of Mexican Workers Unions was established in 1927, and the Cannery and Agricultural Workers Union followed in 1931. Before their strike in 1938 San Antonio workers established the Pecan Shelling Workers Union to represent them. Most of these unions failed, but foreshadowed the 1960s, when Cesar Chavez would succeed.

By 1945, the Mexican-American community had changed. Those eighty thousand californios, nuevos mexicanos, and tejanos of 1848 had become more than 3 million people of mestizo descent. Most of the original inhabitants had lost their land, and along with millions of immigrants from Mexico they found themselves without much power or respect in American society. Poverty and discrimination were serious problems, and there were differences in the community based on class and generation values. But at the same time powerful bonds of language, religion, culture, and family united Mexican Americans. Resentment about past discrimination was accumulating across class and generation lines, and Mexican Americans were beginning to organize cultural, political, and economic interest groups. Like so many other groups in American society, they too would soon be demanding equality.

Part II Conclusion

Ethnic America
in 1945

By 1945, Americans were looking back on the 1800s with nostalgia, as if those years had been especially stable. Industrialization and urbanization, the fluctuations of the business cycle and the Great Depression, two devastating world wars, and immigration had transformed America from an isolated agrarian society to an industrial world power. Of more than 150 million people, perhaps 110 million consciously sensed membership in an ethnic community as either foreign-born immigrants or their descendants. Although each ethnic group was represented in virtually every social class and in a wide variety of jobs, occupational patterns had emerged.

Seven million African Americans living in the rural South of 1877 had become more than 16 million in the South and in the cities of the North and West. Most of them worked as small or tenant farmers, farm laborers, sharecroppers, factory operatives, or domestics. The Mexican-American community, especially after the Revolution of 1911, had expanded from 300,000 to 3 million people, still living in the rural Southwest and urban barrios. After the Indian Reorganization Act of 1934, nearly 550,000 native Americans were living on government reservations—economically dependent on, but culturally free of, white society. Finally, more than 550,000 Asian Americans were located primarily on the West Coast and in Hawaii: 200,000 Chinese and 240,000 Japanese worked as farmers, service employees, or independent entrepreneurs, while approximately 125,000 Filipinos worked on large commercial farms.

The world of the "old immigrants" had also changed by 1945. More than 25 million people still claimed a British heritage as English, Scots, Welsh, or Scots-Irish, and they were scattered throughout the country as skilled workers, successful farmers, white-collar employees in government and business, corporate managers, and educated professionals. With an urban and rural base still centered in the German triangle, the German-American community numbered nearly 20 million people. Throughout urban America but especially in the Northeast and Midwest, more than 13 million Irish Catholics worked in skilled blue-collar jobs or as civil servants in state and city government. In the mill towns of New England, the rural villages of southwestern Louisiana, and in some well-to-do neighborhoods in New Orleans, perhaps 4 million people still looked to France or French Canada for their cultural roots. In the upper Midwest more than 6 million Scandinavians worked as skilled laborers, business people, farmers, and white-collar workers. And in New York, Michigan, and Wisconsin, approximately 750,000 people of Dutch descent retained their group identity.

The most drastic change since 1890 had been the arrival of the southern and eastern Europeans. Numbering only 250,000 Germans in 1877, the Jewish community consisted of nearly 5 million people in 1945. They lived in the Northeast, especially in New York City, and worked in the needle trades and as entrepreneurs, educated professionals, entertainers, and intellectuals. More than 9 million Slavic immigrants and their descendants—Poles, Czechs, Slovaks, Rusins, Ukrainians, Croatians, Serbians, Slovenes, Russians, Belorussians, Bulgarians, and Lithuanians—lived in the industrial cities and worked in mines, mills, factories, and railroads. By 1945 they had purchased homes in their own neighborhoods, established Catholic and Orthodox parishes, and moved into skilled trades. More than 500,000 Greeks took pride in their heritage and worked in small businesses and skilled crafts, while more than 200,000 Romanians had become skilled and educated white-collar workers. Approximately 6 million Italian Americans, largely a working-class community, lived in the urban North and East, as did nearly 1 million Magyars. These were the "new immigrants."

The Security of the Ghettos

American cities were collections of communities inhabited by European and Asian immigrants, African Americans, and Mexican Americans. The ghettos had two dimensions, cultural and residential, and what had characterized the Irish and German settlements in 1877 became norms for the Italians, Poles, Africans, Rusins, Ukrainians, Czechs, Slovaks, Croatians, Serbians, Slovenes, Magyars, Chinese, Japanese, Greeks, Mexicans, and Russians by 1945. The ghettos were neither pathological expressions of fear nor walled, escape-proof communities. Ethnic groups lived there in part because of the emotional security they offered. Havens rather than prisons, the ghettos eased the adjustment to American life.

In the Polonias, Paddy's Villages, Chinatowns, Little Tokyos, Little Syrias, or Little Italys, immigrants could hear their own language and live near friends and relatives. On New York's Lower East Side, the Italians were divided into Genoese, Calabrians, Abruzzians, and Sicilians, for example, while the Jews clustered along Galician, Romanian, Hungarian, Russian, or German lines. Germans had divided themselves according to their origins in Prussia, the Palatinate, Bavaria, Württemberg, Swabia, Darmstadt, Schleswig-Holstein, or the Weser Valley. After several years the regional clusters within national groups broke down, but they were comforting in the beginning.

Informal institutions of all kinds also reassured them. The buildings and shops of the ghettos had the flavor of home. In Milwaukee the hotels served ethnic clienteles: the Cross Keys (English), the Caledonian (Scottish), the Lakes of Killarney (Irish), and the *Zum Deutschen Haus* (German). Italians on Mulberry Street in New York noticed the cheeses and sausages and pasta in the stores, the opera posters, and the ubiquitous pictures of the Madonna; Greeks, Syrians, and Armenians frequented such coffeehouses as the Acropolis, the Parthenon, and the Beirut House; Jews sat in cafes along Hester Street and talked business or debated religion and politics; Germans in St. Louis or Cincinnati had their beer gardens, bowling alleys, and shooting galleries; Japanese and Chinese purchased fish and vegetables in the shops of Little Tokyo in Los Angeles or Chinatown in San Francisco; Irish and Slavic Catholics used local taverns as gathering places; and young Mexican Americans in the barrios walked the streets in their zoot suits. Boardinghouses sheltered new immigrants from the same country; neighborhood youth gangs—the Irish Bowery Boys in New York, the Mexican pachuco gangs in Los Angeles, the Italian Forty-Two gang in Chicago, the Chinese tong societies in San Francisco—taught young people how to survive in urban America; and baseball and football teams organized along ethnic lines competed for neighborhood and city championships.

The ghettos celebrated ethnic holidays: St. Patrick's Day for the Irish; *Cinco de Mayo* for Mexican Americans; *Volks und Schutzenfest* for the Germans; Passover for the Jews; New Year or the Festival of the Dead for the Chinese; Mardi Gras for the Cajuns; Independence Day or St. Basil's Day for the Greeks; Midsummer for the Scandinavians; St. Ignatius Day for the Basques. Ethnic theaters produced plays depicting immigrant life or the great classics of Shakespeare, Goethe, and Schiller. Uptown Jews as well as the poorest sweatshop workers crowded each night into the Yiddish theaters of New York's Lower East Side; Chinese workers sat through six-hour segments presented over several weeks until a single long play was completed; Italians by the thousands laughed and cried at the experiences of the comedy character Farfariello. These neighborhoods, hotels, stores, cafes, coffeehouses, bowling alleys, boardinghouses, gangs, holidays, and theaters were the emotional fabric of the ghettos.

More formal ethnic institutions met community needs as well. Fraternal lodges, among the most common, provided a peaceful setting for social activities as well as health, life, and burial insurance. Some of the lodges—Norwegian bydelag societies, Jewish landsmanschaften, Japanese kenjinkai, Chinese hui kuan, and Greek topikas —were based on regional origins in the Old World. Other groups, such as the Sons of Norway, the Vasa Order, the Knights of Kaleva, or the Sons of St. George, were simply based on national origins. Thousands of mutual aid societies were established, including such groups as the Six Companies of Chinatown, the Ukrainian National Association, the Sons of Italy, and the Hungarian Sick Benefit Association. For economic assistance to start a business or purchase a home, the immigrants founded various financial institutions; here again we find the Chinese hui kuan, Japanese tanomishi, Finnish food cooperatives, and Jewish, Polish, German, Irish, Hungarian, Czech, and Slovakian building and loan associations. Ethnic ghettos sustained the churches so important to immigrant ethnicity: Presbyterian, Episcopal, Methodist, and Baptist; English, Dutch, Congregational, Belgian, and German Reformed; German, Swedish, Norwegian, Danish, and Finnish Lutheran; Irish, German, Czech, Slovak, Croatian, Slovenian, Polish and Lithuanian Catholic; Melkite, Maronite, Rusin, and Ukrainian Uniates; Reformed, Conservative, and Orthodox Jew; Russian, Greek, Serb, Romanian, Bulgarian, Armenian, and Syrian Orthodox; and Buddhist, Shinto, and Confucian. Parochial schools, parish societies, and denominational colleges completed the institutional framework of immigrant religion.

The ethnic press further helped immigrants adjust to America. Most had been illiterate peasants in the Old World, but they took up reading with a passion to keep in touch with distant friends and relatives, and to get news of the old country, and to protect themselves from exploitation in America. Because many European languages had traditionally been suppressed—Finnish by the Swedes and Russians, Polish by the Germans, Ukrainian by the Russians, and Bulgarian by the Greeks—the ethnic press offered a perfect medium for pent-up literary energies. In

1920 there were more than a thousand ethnic newspapers offering news of Old World politics and harvests, ghetto events, editorials, advice columns, and advertisements. The most prominent ethnic newspapers were the *Pittsburgh Courier* and *Chicago Defender* for African Americans; *Y Drych* for the Welsh; *Scottish American Journal, Irish World,* and *Gaelic American;* the *Dakota Freie Presse* for Russian Germans; *Staats-Zeitung* for Germans; *Skandinaven* for Swedes; *Nordlyset* for Norwegians; *Amerikan Uutiset* for Finns; the *Japanese American News; Desteaptate Romane* for Romanians; the *Daily Forward* and *Freiheit* for the Jews; *Il Progresso Italo Americano; Zenske Listy* for Czechs; *Russkoye Slovo* for Russians; *Svoboda* for Ukrainians; *Franco Americaine* for the French; *L'Independent* for French Canadians; *Hungarian America; Narod Polski* for Poles; *New World* for Lithuanians; the *Greek Catholic Messenger* for Rusins; *Napredek* for Croatians; *United Serbdom;* and *Hairenik* for Armenians. Some ethnic newspapers had circulations in the hundreds of thousands and others in the dozens, but all promoted ethnicity and aided adjustment to the New World.

Ethnic nationalisms and Old World events bound the immigrants into self-conscious communities. Many organized gymnastic and athletic groups to promote physical training, love for America, and a patriotic concern for the Old World. The German *turnvereine,* the Scandinavian *turners,* the Czech *sokols,* and the Polish *falcons* stimulated ethnic nationalism. More formal organizations promoted national unification or liberation—or both—abroad: such as the Fenian Society for the Irish, the Nordmanns-Forbundet for Norwegians, l'Union Saint-Jean-Baptiste d'Amerique for French Canadians, the Polish National Alliance, the Lithuanian Alliance of America, the National Slovak Society, the Czech-Slavonic Benevolent Society, and the National Croatian Society. Dutch Americans assisted the Boers in their war with the English in 1899, and the Irish repeatedly tried to influence American foreign policy against the English. During World War I Polish Americans lobbied with the Wilson administration for the creation of an independent Poland; Czechs and Slovaks for Czechoslovakia; Serbs, Croats, and Slovenes for Yugoslavia; the Rusins for incorporation of Transcarpathia into Czechoslovakia; Ukrainians for an independent Ukraine; and Magyars for the separation of Hungary and Austria. Irish Americans campaigned to keep America out of World War I, and some hoped for a German victory that would liberate Ireland; many German Americans were also isolationist at that time. Nazi aggression in the 1930s and 1940s raised the political consciousness of those descended from Poles, Lithuanians, Czechs, Slovaks, Croats, Serbs, Slovenes, Greeks, Russians, Norwegians, Danes, Dutch, Belgians, French, Jews, and the British, for they worried about the survival of ancestral homelands. Old World politics in 1945 was still contributing to ethnicity in America.

Finally, the fact that the residential ghetto was not a fixed, static, and closed neighborhood reinforced ethnicity. Except for a few massive concentrations of immigrants—the Jews and Italians of New York, the Irish of Boston and New York, the Poles of Chicago, and the Chinese of San Francisco—the ghettos were mixed neighborhoods. In most cities the "stranger next door" was very real. In the mill towns of New England the Irish, Italians, Portuguese, and French Canadians worked together in the factories and lived within a few blocks of one another; the same was true of the Slavs, Italians, and Irish in the Pennsylvania mines; of the Italians, Slovaks, and Romanians in the Cleveland steel mills; of the Jews, Syrians, and Italians in the New York needle trades; and of the Poles, Irish, Lithuanians, Germans, Czechs, and Italians in Chicago. Churches, synagogues, businesses, public schools, parochial schools, and ethnic societies were concentrated spatially, and people were able to see clearly the differences between their own and other ethnic communities. Not until World War II, with the continued migration of African Americans to northern cities, did large, ethnically homogeneous ghettos appear throughout the country.

Ethnic Mobility

Just as ghetto boundaries were diverse and vague, ghetto populations were fluid. The idea of a stable population, with the same people spending their whole lives trapped in urban ghettos, inadequately explains urban life in America. Poor urban immigrants were just as mobile as earlier nineteenth-century farmers, but instead of moving from farm to farm they moved from city to city or neighborhood to neighborhood. In preindustrial pedestrian cities the rich had lived downtown, close to the seats of political, religious, and economic power, while the poor were near the warehouses and railroad terminals where they worked. But as factories appeared downtown and streetcars, subways, and elevated trains crisscrossed the city and reached outside its limits, the rich relocated in the suburbs. The poor filled the vacuum, often turning the large single-family homes of the rich into multifamily tenements. But as soon as they could save enough money, the immigrants purchased homes in the outskirts of the city or in the suburbs and traveled downtown to work. Although the Irish, Italian, German, Slavic, and Jewish neighborhoods survived in the cities, they were rarely occupied by the same people for more than a few years. New immigrants from Europe would crowd into the same tenements while older immigrants and their children moved to nicer neighborhoods. English, German, Scandinavian, Romanian, and Jewish (except those in New York City) immigrants moved most quickly out of the original settlements, while the Italians, Slavs, Hungarians, and Greeks followed them at a slower pace.

By 1945, African Americans were filling up the old immigrant neighborhoods as the most recent arrivals to the cities. Surrounding the black ghettos were rings of housing districts based on income. Except perhaps in New York, where ghetto populations were more stable, the pattern of mixed ethnic neighborhoods was repeating itself. Depending on their incomes, the immigrants and their children lived near people with different backgrounds, "strangers next door," as they had done in the urban ghettos. Because of their high incomes, the British, Scandinavians, Germans, and Jews lived in the most distant suburbs; the Italians, Irish, Hungarians, and Slavs occupied the newer housing districts in the cities; and the African Americans and remaining immigrant poor came into the urban core. The ethnic ghettos between 1890 and 1945 were transit stations from which people moved to more permanent neighborhoods.

The Shaping of New Identities

By 1945, ethnic America was more complex than ever before, the melting pot still an elusive dream. Acculturation, however, was rapidly increasing. Because of restrictions imposed by the National Origins Act of 1924 as well as the Great Depression, which dimmed the attraction of America, immigration had dropped drastically between 1931 and 1940. During those ten years 3,563 people came from Austria; 7,861 from Hungary; 4,817 from Belgium; 938 from Bulgaria; 14,393 from Czechoslovakia; 2,559 from Denmark; 2,146 from Finland; 12,643 from France; 114,058 from Germany; 21,756 from England; 6,887 from Scotland; 735 from Wales; 9,119 from Greece; 13,167 from Ireland; 68,028 from Italy; 2,201 from Lithuania; 7,150 from the Netherlands; 4,740 from Norway; 17,026 from Poland; 3,329 from Portugal; 3,871 from Romania; 3,258 from Spain; 3,960 from Sweden; 5,512 from Switzerland; 1,356 from Russia; 5,835 from Yugoslavia; 4,928 from China; and 1,948 from Japan. Compared with the more than 4 million immigrants of the 1920s, the decline was dramatic.

As immigration waned, so did ethnic institutions. The foreign-language press lost ground: between 1920 and 1945 the number of German-language publications dropped from three hundred to seventy; *Skandinaven*, the oldest Scandinavian newspaper, stopped publication in 1940; and between 1940 and 1945 more than two hundred other ethnic-language newspapers failed. Active membership in the ethnic associations declined as well. In the German Catholic Central Verein, membership dropped from 125,000 in 1917 to 85,000 in 1935 to less than 40,000 in 1945, and the Norwegian Nordmanns-Furbundet suffered severe losses in membership. The whole range of ethnic theaters, language schools, political organizations, and lodges began to serve an older clientele, as the second generation accustomed themselves to American values.

Some of the changes were deceptive. For the Germans, Hungarians, Czechs, and Poles arriving after 1890, the presence of tiny colonies of German, Magyar, Czech, and Polish refugees of 1848 raised their political consciousness and helped make them more aware of ethnicity. Also, many peasant immigrants exchanged their parochial perspectives of the past for broader, national outlooks. At first, for example, the German, Galician, Romanian, Hungarian, and Russian Jews had settled into separate neighborhoods, but by 1945 they were intermarrying. Similar mergers affected other groups. Slowly but surely German, Austrian, and Russian Poles melded together, as did Neapolitan, Abruzzian, Calabrian, and Sicilian Italians; Banatan and Bukowinian Romanians; Bohemian and Moravian Czechs; Prussian, Bavarian, and Palatinate Germans; and Alleppian, Zahleh, and Beirut Syrians. In the process, organizations based on regional origins declined: the Jewish landsmanschaften, Japanese kenjinkai, Norwegian bydelags, Chinese hui kuan, and Greek topikas. The process occurred at different rates among different groups, with the Italians retaining regional loyalties for the longest period of time, but for everyone the parochial mentality of the Old World gradually died out. Although on the surface national identities seemed to intensify, immigrants were actually developing a broader sense of community and settling into the larger society.

The immigrants were also acquiring new identities based on occupation and political affiliation. When Syrian, Jewish, and Italian workers in the needle trades suffered from poverty and inhumane working conditions, they were drawn together by an esprit de corps that transcended ethnic lines. In the International Ladies Garment Workers Union or the Amalgamated Clothing Workers Union, immigrant members sensed a kinship based on class. The same was true of the Irish, Italian, and Slavic immigrants of Pennsylvania and Ohio who joined the United Mine Workers and the Steel Workers Union, and of the Syrians, Greeks, Italians, and Slavs in the United Automobile Workers Union. By urging members to learn English, become citizens, organize economically, and vote, the unions stimulated the transition from purely cultural to economic interests.

American politics was another acculturating force. Political divisions had often been cultural, between the western European pietists—Norwegian, Swedish, Dutch, Welsh, and German sectarians and British Baptists and Methodists—who usually voted Republican, and the ritualists of the conservative churches—Irish and German Catholics and liturgical German Lutherans—who usually voted Democratic. The great exception was the South, which had become solidly Democratic despite the Protestant loyalties of its white population. Between 1877 and 1945 anti-Catholicism, anti-Semitism, nativism, prohibition, and parochial schools had reinforced the prevailing cultural bias. Except for the South, the Republican party still reflected the interests of native Protestants and the Democratic party those of newer immigrants and Catholics.

But industrialization introduced an economic cleavage to American politics, with people from upper-income, business backgrounds usually voting Republican and lower-income, working-class people supporting the Democrats. The Great Depression of the 1930s widened the economic cleavage. Working-class people—whether Welsh miners, Polish steel workers, Swedish butchers, or Italian construction workers—came into the Democratic party. African Americans and Mexican Americans also voted Democratic. All these working-class people, including African Americans by 1936, became part of the New Deal coalition that elected Franklin D. Roosevelt (1932, 1936, 1940, 1944), Harry S. Truman (1948), John F. Kennedy (1960), Lyndon B. Johnson (1964), Jimmy Carter (1976), and Bill Clinton (1992) to the White House and kept Congress a Democratic club for years. In 1928, Chicago Democrats sent Oscar DePriest, an African American, to Congress, and the voters of Harlem sent Adam Clayton Powell in 1944. Dennis Chavez, a Mexican American, became the United States senator from New Mexico in 1935; Lucien J. Maciora, a Ukrainian, became a congressman from Connecticut in 1941; John Blatnik, president of the Minnesota American-Yugoslav Association, was elected to Congress in 1946; Frank Lausche, a Slovenian American, became governor of Ohio in 1944; Anton Cermak, a Czech, was mayor of Chicago in 1931; and John Pastore, an Italian American, was elected governor of Rhode Island in 1945. The ethnic communities were acquiring political identities.

In addition to being of English descent, an Anglo-American living in Worcester, Massachusetts, in 1945 might have looked on himself as a physician, a Yankee, a Republican, and a member of the upper class. A Roman Catholic nun teaching at a parochial school in Detroit at that time might also view herself as an Irish American and an educated woman. A Chicago Polish American might have also identified himself as a butcher, a Democrat, a member of the Packinghouse Workers

Organizing Committee, and a worker. A Lebanese woman working at the Ford Motor Company plant in River Rouge during World War II would also identify herself as a member of the United Automobile Workers and an Arab American. A German American in Milwaukee could consider his job as a machinist, his membership in the AFL, or his Democratic loyalties more important badges of personal identity than the fact that his great-great-grandfather had immigrated from the Rhineland in 1844. Social and economic developments accelerated acculturation. World War I and World War II both generated American loyalty crusades; unquestioning allegiance and service in the armed forces helped blur surviving Old World loyalties. The two world wars also stimulated unprecedented movement across the country. A young Polish marine, stationed at Camp Pendleton near Oceanside, California, might not be able to locate a Polish Catholic parish or a Polish chaplain and would have to be satisfied with a nonethnic parish. The same would be true of a Minnesota Swede in Seattle. Cut off from the traditional centers of ethnic culture, people became more acculturated to other values. This process was helped along by the rise of mass culture. Radio, movies, and the syndicated press undermined ethnic culture and acclimated Americans to similar tastes and styles. Jewish entertainers such as Al Jolson, Eddie Cantor, Ethel Merman, Jack Benny, George Burns, and Groucho Marx began to reach broader audiences, as did such Irish performers as James Cagney, Bing Crosby, Martha Raye, and George M. Cohan and Italians Frank Sinatra, Perry Como, Anne Bancroft, and Tony Bennett. Under the impact of mass culture, English became the language of the entire society and dialects began to disappear. Finally the Great Depression exacerbated class tensions and intensified feelings of community based on occupation and income.

The pace of acculturation varied from group to group and place to place. Among French Canadians and Mexican Americans, the use of the old language survived because of the proximity of the mother country, but for Serbs or Slovenes the Old World was gone forever and English the only language for survival in the United States. German Jews rapidly acculturated because they wanted so much to assimilate, while Orthodox Jews resisted acculturation and accepted Conservative Judaism only as a compromise with American reality. Polish Catholic ethnicity survived because of the Poles' ability to create ethnic institutions in the large urban ghettos, but the Orthodox ethnicity of the Romanians and Bulgarians weakened because they were so dispersed.

If acculturation was well advanced, full assimilation was still a long way off. True, more than 40 million Americans, primarily the descendants of the colonial and early-nineteenth-century immigrants, possessed such diverse, multiethnic backgrounds and complex social and economic roles that they no longer identified themselves as members of a particular ethnic community. After five generations of intermarriage—among the Norwegians, Finns, Danes, Swedes, Germans, Dutch, and British in the Midwest; or among the the English, Scots, Scots-Irish, and Germans of New England, the mid-Atlantic states, and the South—many had lost touch with their roots. Indeed, one primary American identity was that of being white and Protestant. Another was that of being white and Catholic, for when the Poles, Czechs, Lithuanians, or Irish married into other ethnic groups, they chose Catholics nearly 90 percent of the time in the first and even the second generation. These perspectives, however, were in the minority in 1945. Most whites still had a distinctly ethnic outlook.

The racial minorities, of course, had not even begun to assimilate. They had acculturated to some extent—opting for the clothes or cars or homes of other Americans when opportunity permitted—but for all intents and purposes, the African, Asian, Mexican, and native American communities were sealed off from the larger society. Native Americans were still confined to reservations and many retained the cultural integrity they had possessed in 1607. Japanese and Chinese Americans were edgy in 1945 because of the relocation camps. Although the Chinese had escaped them, they realized only too clearly that anti-Asian racism could hurt them at any time. Filipino and Mexican Americans still lived in extreme poverty as migrant workers and factory laborers and continued to face racial hostility. And African Americans, now split into a rural base in the South and an urban one in the North, still maintained a structural and cultural separation from the larger society. These 20 million people were nowhere near being absorbed into America's legendary melting pot.

Part III
CHANGE AND CONTINUITY IN ETHNIC AMERICA, 1945–PRESENT

The texture of American life has changed dramatically since the seventeenth century. Industrialization, urbanization, the rise of big government, and the triumph of business values and a consumer culture created the wealthiest, most powerful nation on earth. But beneath the surface old questions are still unanswered, old values still unfulfilled. Tensions among cultural pluralism, individual rights, and political nationalisms, the dominant themes in the eighteenth and nineteenth centuries, still pull at the social fabric, testing the American experiment. After World War II such tensions became severe. No longer satisfied with the rhetoric of equality, racial minorities began insisting that the society and its values come together. Afraid of losing cloistered security, many whites responded by demanding the preservation of their own exclusivities. The consequence was a political debate over culture and ethnicity that would set the tone for modern American history.

Postwar America seemed an unlikely place for conflict. Social and economic changes were blurring old cultures and mass education was producing an educated people freer of prejudice than ever before. The image of Adolf Hitler still reminded people of racism's potential destructiveness. Anti-Catholicism, a consistent theme of American history since the 1840s, was waning, enough that Americans elected a Catholic president in 1960 and gave Pope Paul VI a tumultuous welcome to New York City in 1965. Anti-Semitism eased as housing and resorts became equally available to Jews, and colleges eliminated quotas on Jewish admissions. Mass production, a national market, and the mass media had integrated the country into an economic community of consumers; and as always, geographical mobility continued to shape the American experience. In the new growth areas of the South and West, and in the suburbs, whites lived in small homes and apartments and were isolated from the urban centers of the East and Midwest. The prosperity of the 1940s, 1950s, and early 1960s eased ethnic conflict and produced a more tranquil social climate. Changing immigration patterns helped to ease nativism. Once about 10 percent of the total population each decade, immigration declined to less than 2 percent in the 1970s.

For a time, Americans felt more generous toward new immigrants. In December 1945, President Harry Truman admitted 40,000 World War II refugees, and the War Bride Act of 1946 permitted 120,000 foreign-born wives and children of American GIs to enter the United States. The Displaced Persons Act of 1948, though discriminating against Jewish refugees until its amendment in 1950, admitted more homeless Europeans, as did the Refugee Relief Act of 1953. Germans came throughout the 1950s, Chinese after the Maoist revolution of 1949, Magyars after the Hungarian rebellion of 1956, Cubans after the victory of Fidel Castro in 1959, and Vietnamese after the fall of the Saigon government in 1975.

The McCarran-Walter Act of 1952 retained the quota system but ended the prohibition on Asian immigration. The Immigration and Nationality Act of 1965 ended the forty-year-old system of ethnic quotas based on national origins. The United States would permit a total of 170,000 people from the Eastern Hemisphere to immigrate each year on a first-come, first-served basis, except that no more than 20,000 people could come from any one country. Preferences went to refugees, those with family members already in the United States, and professional and skilled workers. The act also, for the first time in United States history, limited immigration from the Western Hemisphere to 120,000 people per year, and they were allowed to enter on a first-come, first-served basis without categorical preference or limits from any given country. The 1976 amendment to the act extended the preference system and 20,000 limit to immigrants from the Western Hemisphere, and it exempted Cuban refugees from the annual Western Hemisphere quota. Under all these laws, more than 11 million people legally immigrated between 1945 and 1979.

But if one set of forces was obliterating cultural differences, other forces were strongly affecting the racial minorities. When Rosa Parks refused to step to the back of a bus in Montgomery, Alabama, in 1955, she unleashed the hopes of African Americans and precipitated a major political controversy. World War II had already tested American values. Setting themselves up as the standard for equality, Americans had made the war against Nazi Germany a holy crusade to cleanse the world of racism and spread the gospel of pluralism and freedom. From the beginning of the cold war to President Bill Clinton's controversial commitment to international human rights, the United States promoted individual liberty and tried to make America an ensign to the world.

But standard-bearers invite scrutiny, and just as politicians were broadcasting American virtues abroad, African, Indian, Asian, and Hispanic Americans were taking a closer look at reality. Just out of the relocation camps or back home from the war in Europe, Nisei and Sansei Americans were especially familiar with discrimination, as were poor African Americans in the rural South and urban North, native Americans on the reservations, and Mexican Americans in the barrios. Poverty and discrimination were still very real to them, and after 1945 these minority groups felt that it was time for all Americans to enjoy the equality their citizenship promised. The civil rights movement reflected a broad consensus about American values. It called not for the destruction of the society but for political action to achieve the American promise. To be sure, times were better for most people than ever before, but progress is relative, and minority groups wanted the ideal and the real to be closer still.

Because of their numbers, dispersion across the country, and power in the Democratic party, African Americans were on the cutting edge in the civil rights movement. Beginning with the Montgomery bus boycott of Martin Luther King, Jr., in 1955, African Americans built on a foundation laid earlier by W. E. B. Du Bois and the NAACP. Through civil disobedience and the direct political action, they sought to end the discrimination that had plagued them since 1619. Joined by politically conscious Mexicans, native Americans, Puerto Ricans, and Asian Americans, as well as white liberals, the movement achieved the Civil Rights acts of 1964 and 1968 and the Voting Rights Act of 1965.

Federal laws, however, do not necessarily change reality, and millions of poor people still suffered from poverty. Urban rebellions erupted in African-American, Puerto Rican, and Mexican-American communities throughout the 1960s. Political activitists decided to move beyond civil rights to the economic sphere. They succeeded in getting the Johnson administration to declare the War on Poverty in 1965, and having conquered *de jure* (by law) racism, they turned to the *de facto* (in fact, real) institutional racism permeating the society. Tired of poverty and unemployment, they demanded economic equality and equal access to labor unions, law and medical schools, political parties, government agencies, and corporations, insisting that America guarantee equality in the present and compensate for injustices in the past. Changes in the society and the economy are often more disruptive than changes in the law. In the 1970s, when economic problems in the United States became more intense, many Americans became increasingly concerned about the volume of illegal immigration. While 11 million people immigrated legally between 1945 and 1979, perhaps another 20 million had come illegally. Totaling more than 30 million people, that migration appeared to be among the largest in American history. Older fears of job competition, declining wages, and unemployment reasserted themselves, and resentment toward foreigners, especially Mexican laborers, became more severe. People accused them of taking jobs from other Americans, filling the welfare rolls, and burdening the schools with children.

Federal attempts to institutionalize equality further exacerbated people's feelings. When the federal courts and the Department of Health, Education, and Welfare ordered school districts to integrate—which sometimes required busing children to city schools—graduate schools to admit minority students, and labor unions and corporations to accept members of all races into the same seniority lines, a backlash set in. The 1970s was the decade of "Roots," of the search for ancestral origins, and whites too were reaching back for their origins as a means of identifying themselves in a mass, secular society. More important, the revolution in demands by the racial minorities threatened the position of whites in the society. Many whites objected to the busing of African-American children into suburban schools, but even more were upset about having their children bused into distant ghetto schools. With few positions available in medical, dental, and law schools, white students resented quota systems reserving several openings for minorities. And white workers feared the loss of seniority to minority workers employed by government mandate. By the late 1970s not only were African Americans, Chicanos, native Americans, Asians, and Puerto Ricans pressing the struggle for pluralism and equality, but white people were showing themselves quite unwilling to let that movement undermine their own security.

The ethnic controversies of the 1960s and 1970s were played out against a background of war, dissent, and economic stress. Ever since John Winthrop and the Puritans had settled in Boston, Americans had possessed a special sense of mission. In the beginning that mission had been to build the Kingdom of God on earth; in the nineteenth century it had been to conquer the continent; and in the twentieth century it became a mission to export American values abroad. But the underlying philosophy in all three periods contained the same basic assumptions: that American democracy was the best political system; that free-enterprise capitalism was the most effective economic system; and that God had destined both to govern the world some day.

The traumas of the 1970s revolved in part around the demise of these assumptions. The corruption of the Nixon Administration showed the world that the American government was less than perfect, while inflation and recession exposed weaknesses in the economy. Forty million "colored" Americans were decrying poverty and discrimination. And finally, the war in Vietnam, the most unpopular war in United States history, had soured domestic and world opinion about the virtues of American democracy and capitalism. Americans were frightened in the 1970s, riddled with misgivings about the future, and social debates were infected with that malaise.

Not much changed in the 1980s, at least in terms of those doubts and fears, but the pattern of immigration underwent a radical alteration. Between 1900 and 1910, a total of 8.8 million immigrants entered the United States, and of that total more than 90 percent were Europeans. During the ten-year period from 1955 to 1964, the percentage of Europeans was down to 50 percent, and in the 1980s it fell to only 10 percent. In the 1980s, 56 percent of the immigrants came from Canada, Mexico, Central America, and the Caribbean, while 29 percent were from Asia. They brought with them a bewildering kaleidescope of languages, religions, and cultural traditions. In addition to those legal immigrants, there were approximately 3 million illegal immigrants living in the United States in 1992, and that number was annually increasing by 250,000 people.

Congress tried to deal with the changing immigration patterns through two major pieces of legislation. The Immigration Reform and Control Act of 1986 tried to address the problem of illegal immigration. It dramatically escalated the penalties on employers hiring undocumented workers and increased the resources of the Immigration and Naturalization Service so that the law could be enforced. Since the legislation was guaranteed to make it more difficult for undocumented workers to find jobs, Congress decided to ease the burden on those aliens who had been in the United States for an extended period of time. The law offered resident alien status to any individual who proved that he or she had been living in the United States continually since 1982. During the late 1980s, more than 3 million workers, most of them from Mexico and Central America, took advantage of the law. For a few years, the new law seemed to stem the tide of illegal immigration, but the global recession of the early 1990s, as well as political instability around the world, made the United States a seeming haven for the poor and oppressed even if finding work was difficult. By 1993 the number of people illegally entering the country was as high as ever.

Congress also tried to deal with the occupational profiles of the immigrant millions by passing the Immigration Act of 1990. More and more economists argued in the 1980s that increased immigration could actually be an advantage to the United States, especially since younger immigrant workers could help sustain America's increasingly aged population. In what some critics called the "give me your rich and well-to-do elites law," Congress tried to attract rich and well-educated people from around the world. The law promised permanent residence status to up to 10,000 people annually who would invest at least $1 million each in an American business employing a minimum of ten people. For years American companies had been able to sponsor an annual total of 54,000 skilled and professional immigrants, and the law increased that quota to 140,000 people. The number of people allowed to enter the United States each year was increased from 500,000 to 750,000, with preference given to individuals with job skills and/or family members in the country.

Chapter Twelve

Black Power:
The African Americans

When World War II ended, African Americans joined the rest of the country in celebrating peace. After four years of sacrifice and death the country was anxious for tranquillity and the more mundane pursuits of life. But although African Americans were escaping the more overt racism of the South for better jobs in northern factories, life there was hardly carefree; they had traded de jure for de facto segregation. In housing, schools, jobs, and public facilities they found themselves separated from the white community, still victims of prejudice and discrimination. By 1945, race riots had become common, the worst ones in Philadelphia and East St. Louis in 1917; Chicago and Washington, D.C., in 1919; and Detroit and Los Angeles in 1943. Slum housing, unemployment, crime, poor schools, inadequate city services, and poverty characterized ghetto life. Concentrated in urban islands rather than rural villages, African Americans were more visible than ever before.

But ghetto life had also strengthened them. For the first time African Americans were functioning in an environment largely free of whites. The Harlem Renaissance of the 1920s had fueled the new confidence, and the words of author and educator James Weldon Johnson, W. E. B. Du Bois, writer Claude McKay, poet Countee Cullen, and novelist and poet Langston Hughes built an ideological foundation on which Martin Luther King, Jr., Elijah Muhammad, Malcolm X, Stokely Carmichael, Whitney Young, and Jesse Jackson would later construct the civil rights movement. Urban life had also provided blacks with political power they had not enjoyed since Reconstruction. The urban machines of the Democratic party needed their votes, and the mass production unions of the CIO needed their support. African Americans were becoming the most loyal Democrats in the country. A black professional and white-collar class had emerged to serve the economic, medical, legal, and educational needs of the community. West Indian immigrants especially helped this middle class accumulate property, status, and power. Just as inexorably, African Americans became less patient with social segregation and began demanding access to government jobs, professional schools, transportation facilities, theaters, parks, restaurants, and recreational facilities, wanting nothing less than the end of both de facto and de jure discrimination.

The Supreme Court and the End of Jim Crow

In 1945, as never before, African Americans were ready for changes. Of all the approaches of the past, the NAACP had been the most successful. Thurgood Marshall, leader of the NAACP Legal Defense Fund, had always argued in the federal courts that racial discrimination was unconstitutional, a violation of the First, Fifth, Fourteenth, and Fifteenth amendments. And under chief justices Harlan Stone (1941–1946), Fred M. Vinson (1946–1953), and Earl Warren (1953–1969), the Supreme Court proved surprisingly consistent in condemning segregation. Between 1941 and 1964 the court invalidated virtually every form of de jure segregation.

The *Plessy v. Ferguson* decision of 1896 had upheld "separate but equal" facilities, but after 1940 the whole constitutional edifice of Jim Crow collapsed. In *Mitchell v. United States* (1941) the court declared that the denial of a Pullman berth to an African-American traveler violated the Interstate Commerce Act, and in *Morgan v. Virginia* (1946) the court prohibited segregation in public buses crossing state lines. Subsequent decisions invalidated racial segregation in other interstate transportation as well. With *Shelley v. Kraemer* and *Hard v. Hodge* in 1948, the court also prohibited restrictive covenants excluding blacks from housing developments. Other court orders integrated parks, theaters, and private businesses operating on public property, and in 1964, in *McLaughlin v. Florida*, the court outlawed a Florida statute prohibiting interracial sexual relations. Finally, in an assault on political discrimination, the court declared that white primaries (*Smith v. Allwright*, 1944) and literacy tests (*Schnell v. Davis*, 1949) were violations of the Fifteenth Amendment.

But if these court decisions irritated white Southerners, desegregation of the schools enraged them and led to "massive resistance" in the 1950s and 1960s. Arguing that "separate but equal" was inherently discriminatory and unconstitutional, the Supreme Court dismantled the central institution of Jim Crow. The outline of the future had appeared in 1938 when the court declared, in *Missouri rel. Gaines v. Canada*, that by refusing to admit an African-American student to the state law school, Missouri had violated the equal protection clause of the Fourteenth Amendment. After World War II the NAACP continued to set its sights on higher education, and in *Sweatt v. Painter* (1950) the Supreme Court decided that a separate law school for Texas African Americans was unconstitutional. Shortly thereafter, in *McLaurin v. Oklahoma State Regents* (1950), the court outlawed University of Oklahoma regulations segregating an African-American graduate student to special desks and tables. Then, in *Brown v. Board of Education* (1954), the court unanimously declared that by imposing inferior status on African-American children, de jure segregation of schools denied them equal protection of the law. In one stroke the court destroyed the legal foundation of de jure segregation.

While the Supreme Court was taking on Jim Crow, urban blacks were flexing their new political muscle in the Democratic party. In such cities as Chicago, Detroit, New York, Cleveland, and Philadelphia, they often held the balance of power. Their demands for equality received firm support from sympathetic Jews and ethnic Catholics, who had so often been the victims of discrimination themselves. Franklin Roosevelt and the New Deal had periodically expressed concern for the economic condition of African Americans, and the first fruits of black power had appeared in 1941 when Roosevelt created the Fair Employment Practices Commission (FEPC) to stop discrimination in defense industries. Facing a close election in 1948, President Harry Truman appointed a commission on civil rights and called for a permanent federal civil rights commission, a federal antilynching law, prohibition of the poll tax, and a comprehensive civil rights bill. By executive order he integrated the armed forces between 1948 and 1950. At the Democratic National Convention in 1948 Truman won the nomination, but his civil rights measures had exposed an Achilles heel in the Democratic party: the split between southern whites and northern blacks erupted when Strom Thurmond of South Carolina led a "Dixiecrat" rebellion from the convention. Truman surprised everyone by defeating Thurmond as well as the Republican Thomas Dewey of New York, and African voters provided him the margin of victory, as they would later do for John Kennedy in 1960, Jimmy Carter in 1976, and Bill Clinton in 1992.

Mrs. Nettie Hunt explains to her daughter, Nikie, what the court ruling means. (UPI/Bettmann Newsphotos)

But white resistance threatened all the achievements. After the *Brown v. Board of Education* decision, when resistance to integration spread throughout the South, the desegregation movement stalled. At first whites tried an outdated constitutional ploy, interposition, which supposedly nullified federal court decisions in individual states. The Civil War had long since resolved that question, and the Supreme Court quickly overturned all interposition laws. Southerners then tried to gerrymander school districts, offer tuition support of private white schools, and cut funding to integrated public schools. Finally, when all else failed, a number of southern governors tried to block integration. After federal courts had ordered Little Rock, Arkansas, to integrate its all-white high school in 1957, Governor Orval Faubus called out the Arkansas National Guard to prevent African-American students from entering the school. President Eisenhower had to send United States troops to enforce the court order. Governor Ross Barnett of Mississippi used state police to keep James Meredith out of the state university in 1962, and white mobs rampaged through the campus until President Kennedy sent in federal troops. A year later Governor George Wallace blocked the registrar's door at the University of Alabama to keep two African Americans from registering, but he too yielded at President Kennedy's insistence.

For African Americans, massive resistance was terribly frustrating, especially after the exhilaration they had felt when Truman integrated the armed services and the Supreme Court destroyed Jim Crow. By 1960, less than 1 percent of southern schools were integrated, and segregation was still widespread in other areas because court orders were not being enforced. In Congress, Southerners were filibustering civil rights measures; and when civil rights acts did emerge in 1957 and 1960, they were very weak, giving the federal government authority to condemn segregation and investigate voter fraud but little else. African Americans had expected much more. Southern life had changed little despite the laws and court decisions.

Tired of delays and impatient for change, some African Americans began considering more direct action. They even resented traditional black organizations. Upper-class in its values and closely allied with white liberals, the NAACP and National Urban League were beginning to seem timid and conservative, too willing to accept a glacial pace of change.

The Civil Disobedience Movement

The shift in African-American attitudes had already begun, modestly enough, in the most unlikely of places: a commuter bus in Montgomery, Alabama. One day in 1955 Rosa Parks, tired after a long day of work, sat down on a city bus and refused to move to the back, where blacks were traditionally confined. Her decision set off a chain reaction in which African Americans boycotted Montgomery city buses and pushed the system toward bankruptcy, demanding integration and more black bus drivers. The leader of the boycott, a young minister named Martin Luther King, Jr., rocketed to national prominence as the boycotts spread to other southern cities. In retaliation, white groups such as the Ku Klux Klan, the National Association for the Advancement of White People, and White Citizens' Councils tried to boycott African Americans and, in some cases, even assaulted them in their homes. Several African Americans were murdered in Mississippi, South Carolina, Alabama, and Georgia.

On February 1, 1960, African-American students from the Negro Agricultural and Technical College at Greensboro, North Carolina, entered several department stores and demanded service at lunch counters. When denied service because they were black, they refused to leave and the "sit-in" movement began. It quickly spread across the country; white and black students "sat in" in designated white sections of restaurants, theaters, bars, libraries, parks, beaches, and rest rooms,

In 1955 Rosa Parks refused to move to the back of a Montgomery, Alabama bus. Her refusal triggered the modern civil rights movement. (UPI/Bettmann)

all in defiance of segregation statutes. Martin Luther King, Jr., became the unofficial leader of the movement, using nonviolent civil disobedience to startle whites into accepting social change. For King,

> nonviolence . . . does not seek to defeat or humiliate the opponent, but to win his friendship and understanding. The nonviolent resister must often express his protest through noncooperation or boycotts, but he realizes that these are not ends themselves; they are merely means to awaken a sense of moral shame in the opponent. The end is . . . the creation of the beloved community . . .*

Jailed in Atlanta for a department store sit-in in 1960, King was released after John Kennedy, then the Democratic nominee for president, intervened with local authorities. The significance of the event was not lost on African Americans; they turned out in record numbers and helped to elect Kennedy.

In May 1961, the Congress of Racial Equality organized African-American and white "freedom riders" to go into the South to see if interstate transportation facilities had been integrated; white mobs attacked the demonstrators and federal troops had to be called in. The

---

*Quoted in Robert C. Twombly, ed., *Blacks in White America since 1865* (New York, 1971), p. 387.

Southern Christian Leadership Conference (SCLC) and the Student Nonviolent Coordinating Committee (SNCC) sent thousands of freedom riders into the South until the Interstate Commerce Commission ruled that all terminals serving interstate carriers had to be integrated.

The pressure mounted in 1962 and 1963, especially after Martin Luther King, Jr., took his crusade to Birmingham, Alabama. Celebrating the centennial of the Emancipation Proclamation, his SCLC marched in favor of equal employment opportunities, integration of public facilities, and enforcement of court-ordered desegregation formulas. Birmingham police used tear gas and guard dogs against the demonstrators while millions of Americans watched on television. When Medgar Evers, director of the Mississippi NAACP, was assassinated in June 1963, civil rights demonstrations erupted all over the South. Most Americans were convinced that African Americans had rarely been afforded the freedom and equality guaranteed by the Constitution. Sensitive to that problem and looking to the election of 1964, when he would again need the African-American vote, President Kennedy submitted a civil rights bill to Congress in 1963 calling for integration of all public facilities, even those privately owned, and the withholding of federal money from segregated institutions.

Southern opposition was fierce, but a string of events, tragic and ennobling, brought history and black demands together. In August 1963, nearly 250,000 people—led by the NAACP, SNCC, SCLC, American Jewish Congress, National Council of Churches, American Friends Service Committee, and the AFL-CIO—gathered at the Lincoln Memorial to support the bill, and Martin Luther King, Jr., gave his famous "I Have a Dream" speech. One month later, when an African-American church in Birmingham was bombed on Sunday morning and four children died, white sympathies were touched and support for the civil rights bill grew stronger. Finally, in November 1963, John Kennedy was murdered in Dallas, Texas, and his successor, Lyndon Johnson, pushed the civil rights bill as a legacy to the fallen leader, a sign of his own liberalism, and a redemption of his home state. After a Senate cloture ended the filibuster in June 1964, the Civil Rights Act became law. It outlawed discrimination in voting, education, and public accommodations; established the Equal Employment Opportunity Commission; permitted the federal government to freeze funds to state and local agencies not complying with the law; and provided funds to the Department of Health, Education, and Welfare to speed desegregation of the schools.

The rhetoric over the Civil Rights Act of 1964, the pain and struggle to see it through Congress, and the rejoicing over its passage raised people's expectations. Some African Americans expected the act to

Civil rights movement continues as African-American students accompany whites to school. (UPI/Bettmann)

make a difference right away, and when life did not change, they became frustrated. Some decided, as others had done when "massive resistance" began in the South, that more vigorous steps would have to be taken to reshape America.

The Civil Rights Act of 1964 did not put an end to segregation, but even had it done so, it had little to offer the black ghettos. As whites fled to the suburbs, businesses were relocating outside the city, making it more difficult for African Americans to find work. At the same time the whole American economy was shifting from a manufacturing to a service base; blue-collar jobs were steadily decreasing as white-collar ones became more plentiful. But white-collar jobs required educational and technical skills, and large numbers of underprivileged African Americans were unable to qualify. While earlier immigrants had used unskilled urban jobs as the bootstrap out of the ghettos, African Americans no longer had those choices. They were trapped in a changing economy and a deteriorating physical environment, and their poverty became endemic and permanent, passing from one generation to the next. In 1970 more than one in three African-American families functioned below the poverty line, and the median black income was only about 60 percent that of whites. Unemployment was twice as high as for white workers, and joblessness for African-American teenagers reached more than 40 percent in some cities during the 1970s. A terribly poor African-American underclass emerged, made up of people who had never had jobs or lived in decent homes. In the face of such debilitating economic problems, the end of formal segregation no longer took first place. For people worrying about how to pay their rent, utility, and food bills, whether or not their community was integrated was less important than how to support themselves.

In addition to focusing on economic problems, African American activists began looking at the de facto segregation of the North. For years many Americans had assumed racism was a southern problem, but in terms of housing, jobs, and schools, African Americans were just as segregated in the North, even if the law had nothing to do with it. Combined with ghetto poverty, de facto segregation seemed even more insidious than de jure segregation, for by 1970 most African Americans in the United States were in segregated communities often deprived of normal city services, living in dilapidated slum housing, attending poorly financed schools, and looking fruitlessly for jobs. Many African-American leaders decided that de facto segregation would have to go the way of de jure segregation.

African-American leaders also worried about unconscious, institutional racism. To many people it became increasingly clear that as long as blacks were trapped in poor neighborhoods and deficient schools, they would be unable to compete successfully with middle-class whites for jobs and status. Corporations, government agencies, and universities all based admission and promotion on competitive examinations which underprivileged people or those from different cultural backgrounds had more difficulty in passing. Some attempt to reverse such subtle but insidious forms of discrimination had to be made.

In the South, despite the Civil Rights Act of 1964, whites were still resisting federal mandates, harassing African Americans and making it difficult for them to vote. After the assassination of John Kennedy in 1963, an atmosphere of violence began to grip the nation. Other assassinations would follow: Malcolm X in 1965, Martin Luther King, Jr., and Robert Kennedy in 1968. Meanwhile, the Ku Klux Klan was gaining members, and as the SNCC and the SCLC escalated voter-registration drives, abrasive confrontations were inevitable. In July 1964, a month after the Civil Rights Act was passed, an African-American teacher on duty with the army reserve in Georgia was murdered, and a few weeks later three civil rights workers in Mississippi were killed while under arrest for an alleged traffic violation. During the summer of 1964 more than fifty African-American homes were bombed and burned, and early in 1965 two more civil rights workers

Martin Luther King, Jr., leading the 1965 Selma-Montgomery civil rights march. (Dan Budnik/Woodfin Camp)

were murdered in Selma, Alabama. One month later Martin Luther King, Jr., and fifty thousand civil rights demonstrators marched in Selma to protest the violence, and that evening angry whites shot and killed another civil rights worker. President Lyndon Johnson and Congress responded to the violence by passing the Voting Rights Act of 1965, permitting representatives of the Department of Justice to register voters in the South.

The Black Power Movement

The shift to "black power" appeared in two guises, one spontaneous and emotional, the other deliberate and ideological. In August 1965, the Watts ghetto of Los Angeles exploded when thousands of African Americans rioted after a young black was arrested for reckless driving. White businesses were looted, snipers fired at police, and before it was over, thirty-four people were dead, more than a thousand wounded, and over $40 million worth of property destroyed. Another racial rebellion erupted in Newark, New Jersey, in 1967, and that summer Detroit was engulfed in a major conflagration, with angry African Americans turning on police and white-owned businesses. The assassination of Martin Luther King, Jr., in April 1968 caused racial uprisings in many cities; and nine years later, when an electrical failure darkened New York City for a night, thousands of unemployed African Americans and Puerto Ricans engaged in an orgy of looting. In every instance the eruptions were unpremeditated rebellions, illegal to be sure, against the frustrations of ghetto life. White America was outraged and frightened by the insurgency; but as they condemned the violence, whites also scrutinized the racial crisis as never before.

The ideological rise of black power came to the surface in 1966, even though signs of the philosophy had appeared earlier. After a lifetime of scholarly writing and support of black political activism, W. E. B. Du Bois finally despaired of changing America and joined the Communist party. The Black Muslims, founded by Elijah Muhammad in 1930, rose to national prominence in the 1960s. Preaching the ultimate doom of "devil" whites and the triumph of blacks, the Muslims took up where Marcus Garvey had left off, calling for black pride, black enterprise, and a separate black state. They also called on African Americans to think less about being nonviolent and more about returning violence for violence. In 1959, Robert Williams, an NAACP leader in North Carolina, was dismissed from the NAACP for advocating violence in self-defense; escaping to Cuba after allegedly kidnaping an elderly white couple, he became leader of the Revolutionary Action Movement (RAM).

But all these groups were relatively obscure until James Meredith, an African American, decided to prove in 1966 that he could march to Jackson, Mississippi, during voter registration week without harassment. One day into the march, he was wounded by a shotgun blast, and civil rights leaders from all over the country descended on Mississippi to complete the "freedom march." But while Martin Luther King, Jr., still spoke of nonviolent civil disobedience, Stokely Carmichael, the young leader of SNCC, startled the nation by ridiculing nonviolence and crying out for black power. On the other side of the country, Eldridge Cleaver and Bobby Seale established the Black Panthers in Oakland, California, and called for African-American control of the urban ghettos.

Despite the rhetoric of black power and the fear it sent through white America, it meant different things to different people. To whites, the slogan was incendiary, somehow implying that the social order was about to undergo revolutionary change. To the Congress of Racial Equality (CORE), black power meant direct political action through the Democratic party, the mobilization of African American votes in the South. The Black Panthers and the SNCC viewed it as community control; they demanded African American police and African-

American firefighters in African-American neighborhoods, African-American teachers and principals in African-American schools, and African-American-owned businesses to serve the African-American market. And to some radical groups—including the Black Panthers, RAM, The Republic of New Africa, and the SNCC—black power implied the use of retaliatory violence to end poverty and discrimination.

Although the rhetoric of black power alienated many moderate African Americans, the new movement inspired a more open spirit among all black people. In May 1968, Ralph Abernathy led the SCLC in a march on Washington, D.C., and at their "Resurrection City," between the Lincoln Memorial and the Washington Monument, they dramatized poverty in America. The Reverend Jesse Jackson, working out of Chicago in the 1970s, carried his People United to Save Humanity program throughout the country demanding African-American control of the ghettos. Whitney Young and then Vernon Jordan of the National Urban League turned from mild, solicitous attitudes toward white businesspeople to more heated demands for funds and federal job assistance. The Black Economic Development Conference in 1969 demanded "reparations" from white churches to atone for past sins against African Americans. Black moderates may have rejected the militant rhetoric of black power, but they could not help being affected by its spirit. Led by the NAACP, the African-American community set its sights on the end of de facto discrimination. The Civil Rights Act of 1968 had eliminated many forms of housing discrimination, but African-American leaders concluded that if school integration were to wait for integrated neighborhoods, it would probably never happen. They believed that busing children was the only way to overcome segregation in schools and second-class education for African-American children. And to deal with black economic problems, the NMCP, CORE, National Urban League, SCLC, SNCC, and other African-American organizations demanded economic assistance and job training for educationally disadvantaged and low-income blacks and "affirmative action" admissions, hirings, and promotions of African Americans by business, government, and universities. Congress passed the antipoverty program in 1965 to assist lower-class blacks and other poor people, and in the 1970s the Equal Employment Opportunity Commission ordered government agencies, corporations, and universities to establish hiring, promotion, and admission policies favoring African Americans until the racial mix in American institutions, from the lowest service positions through the administrative hierarchy, reflected the racial composition of the whole society.

Black Pride: The Common Denominator

By the late 1970s there were several African-American worlds in the United States. For the black lower class in the ghettos there was poverty, crime, and unemployment, but there was also a subculture of energy and survival, a world with its own sights, sounds, and values. From Harlem to Watts, the ghettos abounded with the smells of barbecued and deep-fried food, soul music from bars and pool halls, the swagger of teenagers, the talk of groups on street corners, and the sounds of black English. African Americans felt comfortable there. Among the ghetto underclass, abject poverty and hopelessness encouraged gambling, alcoholism, narcotics addiction, sexual promiscuity, and pathological violence. But for the rest of the lower class there was the fulfilling world of the church and lodge, the status given to deacons, ushers, Sunday School teachers, gospel singers, preachers, and fraternal officers. These African Americans respected stability and family values, yearned for economic advancement, and felt emotionally secure among other blacks.

The African-American middle class, people who had good jobs and lived in the "gilded" ghettos, looked down on the emotional religions and ghetto English of lower-class blacks. They desperately wanted civil rights and decent schools for their children, and were torn between their desire for acceptance by whites and their pride in being African American. At the same time that they favored de facto integration, they worried about the dilution of African-American values. Finally, there was the African-American upper class, well-to-do businesspeople and professionals who lived in a world of Greek fraternities and sororities, alumni associations, professional groups, and civic, social, and business clubs. No longer tainted with feelings of inferiority, they resented the fact that upper-class white society remained unprepared to accept them. Despite class differences, the African-American community was still united by race in the 1970s, if only on an emotional level. The career of Muhammad Ali serves to illustrate those feelings. When he took the world heavyweight championship from Sonny Liston in 1964, Ali at once electrified African-American audiences and became a folk hero. At first his appeal was much like that of Joe Louis or Floyd Patterson; by defeating white people at their own game, he brought status to the black community. But shortly after the Liston fight, Ali announced his conversion to the Black Muslim faith of Elijah Muhammad, implicitly suggesting that American whites were depraved and doomed. In that instant he took upon himself the mantle of Jack Johnson, the earlier black champion who had flouted the conventions of white society. In 1967 Ali refused induction into the U.S. Army on religious grounds; denied conscientious objector status, he was indicted, convicted, and sentenced to five years in prison. Stripped of his title, he still defied militarism and white values. After the Supreme Court overturned his conviction, Ali fought again, this time taunting such African-American opponents as Joe Frazier, Floyd Patterson, and George Foreman as "Uncle Toms." Ali defeated Foreman and regained the title, which he both lost to and regained from Leon Spinks in 1978. Proud and rebellious, yet successful and generous, Muhammad Ali symbolized for many people the hopes of African Americans in the 1970s.

Echoes from the Past

During the 1980s and early 1990s, a new sense of pessimism about race relations surfaced throughout the country. There were, of course, some symbols of progress. When the 103d Congress of the United States took its oath of office in January 1993, more than forty African Americans were in the House of Representatives and the Senate. Clarence Thomas was sitting on the United States Supreme Court, Ronald Brown had been named Secretary of Commerce, Douglas Wilder was governor of Virginia, and Carol Braun of Illinois was the first African-American woman in United States history to serve in the United States Senate. Thousands of African Americans were holding public office at state and local levels throughout the country.

The 1991 hearings of the Senate Judiciary Committee, painful as they had been in terms of gender issues, had performed one service to the African-American community. Tens of millions of Americans spent hours watching two well-educated, highly articulate African Americans engage in a vigorous debate. Clarence Thomas, with his Yale law degree and years on the federal bench, had defended himself with power and dignity, while Anita Hill, professor of law at the University of Oklahoma, had just as resolutely and articulately accused him of sexual harassment. Thomas was eventually confirmed by a narrow vote, Hill became a heroine to the women's movement, and white America had witnessed a powerful testament to the potential of African Americans if society would only provide them the opportunities.

But those successful African American voices were more than drowned out by sounds of anger, frustration, and poverty in the 1980s and 1990s. The economic condition of the African-American community deteriorated during the Reagan years, even while the politicians were applauding themselves for almost a decade of economic growth. The economic base of urban areas eroded during the 1980s, with jobs and tax revenues continuing their flight to the white suburbs. Because of the decline of manufacturing jobs in the American economy, labor unions steadily lost membership and power, and in the process African Americans lost a faithful ally in their struggle for economic progress. The African-American unemployment rate remained at twice the national average, and joblessness among African-American young people approached 50 percent in the early 1990s.

Changing public policies also had an economic impact on African Americans. The affirmative-action programs of the 1960s and 1970s helped ease the effects of institutional racism and de facto discrimination, but beginning with the Supreme Court's 1978 decision in *Regents of the University of California v. Baake,* which outlawed rigid special-preference admission programs for minorities, those federal mandates lost their punch. A series of decisions during the years of the Reagan administration gutted affirmative-action programs further. Severe budget cuts in federal programs for health care, job training, public education, housing, and infrastructure improvements in the 1980s pulled money out of the cities and damaged the economic environment where most African Americans lived.

In addition to these economic problems, a new climate of fear and misunderstanding seemed to affect race relations in the late 1980s and early 1990s. Although Clarence Thomas claimed that he was undergoing a "high-tech lynching" at the hands of the Senate Judiciary Committee, other African Americans experienced real lynchings. Hate crimes were on the rise in the late 1980s and early 1990s, and the Ku Klux Klan was on the move again, holding public demonstrations and burning its crosses as in years past. White audiences were frightened by the angry lyrics in the rap music of African-American performers like 2 Live Crew, Ice T, Ice Cube, and Sister Soulja. When Ice T released a record entitled "Cop Killer" in 1992, a police-led nationwide boycott of Time Warner, which produced the record, forced the company to pull the song from circulation. In the spring of 1993, President Bill Clinton nominated Professor Lani Guinier of the University of Pennsylvania to head the civil rights division at the Justice Department. Her academic writings speculated on the need to consider election outcomes, not just election procedures, as evidence of racial discrimination. White critics charged her with advocating election outcome quotas, in which certain racial, ethnic, or gender groups are entitled to political offices regardless of election results. The political controversy over her nomination was so intense that President Clinton was forced to withdraw it before the Senate Judiciary Committee even considered it.

But no event more clearly symbolized the rise of racial tension than the Los Angeles riots of 1992. On March 3, 1991, several Los Angeles police officers, after a high-speed car chase, repeatedly beat Rodney King with a night stick while, unknown to them, a bystander videotaped the attack on a camcorder. Records of the police transmissions before, during, and after the attack bristled with antiblack racial epithets. Four police officers eventually went to trial on assault charges, but the defense attorneys managed to secure a change of venue and moved the trial to Simi Valley, California, a comfortable white suburb. During the previous year television news stations around the country had broadcast and rebroadcast the videotape of the beatings, and conviction of the officers seemed a foregone conclusion.

But on April 29, 1992, an all-white jury essentially acquitted the officers. The African-American community of Los Angeles exploded in rage. Whites were randomly beaten, including a truck driver whose near-fatal assault was videotaped by newsmen in a helicopter hovering overhead. Only the intervention of several African-American bystanders saved the truck driver from death. Rioters then began an orgy of looting and burning, especially targeting small retail businesses owned by Korean Americans. Governor Pete Wilson of California was forced to call out the National Guard to quell the rioting, but not before fifty-eight people were dead and more than $1 billion worth of property destroyed. Maxine Waters, the African-American woman serving in Congress from the 29th district in California, came to national attention in her condemnations of the police acquittals and the violence, but her most telling remarks reminded America of how little progress had been made in the twenty-seven years between the Watts riots of 1965 and the Los Angeles riots of 1992.

Chapter Thirteen

The Hispanic Mosaic

From 78,000 people in 1848, the Hispanic-American community has grown to more than 23 million people today, and Mexicans, Cubans, Puerto Ricans, Central Americans, South Americans, and people from the Caribbean continue to immigrate. Including illegal aliens, there may be 18 million people of Mexican descent living in the United States, most of them in California, Arizona, New Mexico, Colorado, and Texas. The Puerto Rican population is expanding because Puerto Rico, a commonwealth partner of the United States, is exempt from immigration laws. There are more than 2.2 million Puerto Ricans in America, most of them in northeastern ghettos, especially New York City. Cuba has sent a stream of refugees until today there are more than 1.3 million Cubans in America. In addition, since 1960, more than 500,000 people have come from the Dominican Republic, 45,000 from Costa Rica, 210,000 from El Salvador, 105,000 from Guatemala, 70,000 from Honduras, 60,000 from Nicaragua, 70,000 from Panama, 90,000 from Argentina, 60,000 from Brazil, 50,000 from Chile, 270,000 from Colombia, 135,000 from Ecuador, 100,000 from Peru, and 35,000 from Venezuela.

Despite major differences in customs and history, the Hispanic immigrants share a common perception of life. Although the Caribbean immigrants claim a more racially diverse heritage, all the groups have some cultural fusion of Spanish and native American values, a "Hispanic" heritage. From the voyages of Columbus to the Spanish-American

War of 1898, most of Latin America consisted of Spanish colonies. From the Spanish the Hispanics inherited a spiritual individualism that saw the soul as the most important ingredient of character, and a romantic individualism that, in the tradition of Don Quixote, emphasized honor, self-respect, integrity, and personal self-expression. From native Americans they acquired a trust for one another, a spiritual communalism, a comfort with the rhythms of nature. In the United States individualism was a matter of competing for social and economic power, of fulfilling oneself, but Latin individualism rested more on pride in the uniqueness of each human spirit, attended by an implicit trust of one's *compadres*.

Because the people embraced these values, organizations and groups and bureaucracies and systems were suspect and commanded no loyalty in Hispanic-American society. Puerto Ricans in New York City, for example, often preferred shopping at a local *bodega*, a small grocery shop, even though bodega prices were considerably higher than those at supermarkets. Out of that personalism and spiritual individualism came *machismo*, or personal courage and masculine confidence, fortitude in the presence of crisis. While many Americans were primarily interested in success in the material world, the Hispanics were equally concerned with defining the spiritual world and their place in it. Finally, the Hispanics shared a Roman Catholic heritage, one quite different from the Catholicism of the Irish, Germans, Slavs, or French Canadians. Hispanics viewed religion more as a community than a church. Their faith was another form of personal individualism and community membership, not an obedience to specific ordinances. Like the Italians, they perceived religion in this world and the next as a set of personal relationships to the saints, the Virgin, and the Lord. And with or without the church, Latin spirituality thrived. Indeed, Latinos could be bitterly hostile to the church without feeling disloyal to the faith.

The Cuban Immigrants

Ever since the Spanish-American War of 1898, Americans had felt close to Cuba. The U.S. government recognized the dictatorship of Fulgencio Batista, who came to power in 1934, only because he was anticommunist and protected American investments. But there were two Cubas under his reign, the glittering gaiety of Havana and the grinding poverty of the American-owned sugar plantations. Batista's oppressive policies disturbed many Americans. Then Fidel Castro led a guerrilla uprising, and in 1958 the Eisenhower administration embargoed arms shipments to Batista. Castro's popularity became hero worship in Cuba, and Batista's government collapsed in 1959. Castro assumed power.

He soon shocked everyone by announcing he was a Communist. Nationalizing American property, executing or imprisoning major Batista supporters, and redistributing land among the peasants, he enraged the United States and exhilarated most of the Cuban masses. Hoping to force Castro into submission by economic action, Washington stopped the importation of Cuban sugar and embargoed exports to the island. The Soviet Union then began to fill the vacuum. Although the peasants continued to revere Castro, discontent spread among independent farmers, small businesspeople, and corporate employers frightened by socialism. Immigration to the United States increased dramatically. Some came on authorized refugee airlifts from Havana and others sailed the ninety miles to Florida in motorboats and dinghies. By 1979 more than 700,000 Cubans had settled in the United States, and the Cuban-American population had reached more than a million. Those numbers surged again with the Mariel boatlift in 1980, when more than 100,000 new Cubans came to the United States to escape economic collapse and political oppression on the island. During the 1980s, more than 250,000 Cubans settled here.

Most Americans admired the Cuban immigrants. They seemed bright, hardworking, and refugees of Communist aggression. During the 1980s, however, there was a subtle shift in attitude, especially after the Mariel boatlift. Although there was no truth to the rumor, many Americans believed that large numbers of the Mariel refugees were criminals and mentally deranged. Most of them were blue-collar working-class people, not the middle and upper classes of the earlier migration, and approximately one percent of them had serious criminal records. For a few years in the early 1980s, some politicians called for limits on Cuban immigration, but those demands had largely dissipated by the early 1990s.

Today more than one-third of the city of Miami is Cuban, and "Little Havanas" have sprouted all over Florida. The Cuban Refugee Emergency Center on Biscayne Boulevard in Miami greets new immigrants and helps settle them, while the English Center of the Cuban Refugee Program helps them overcome language problems. Along West Flagler and Southwest Eighth Street, block after block of cafeterias, *farmacías, panaderías* (bakeries), *mueblerías* (furniture stores), and bodegas serve Cuban consumers. The first waves of immigrants came from middle-class backgrounds, so a strong entrepreneurial spirit imbued the Cuban-American community. In Miami alone there are more than twenty thousand independent Cuban businessowners and perhaps forty thousand throughout Florida. There is a Latin Chamber

Hispanic residents in Miami take the oath of citizenship at a naturalization ceremony. Despite its problems, America remains a beacon of hope and light. (The Bettmann Archive)

of Commerce, a Cuban Rotary Club, a Cuban Lions Club, and a Cuban Kiwanis Club. Most construction in Miami now involves Cuban contractors; service workers in tourist businesses are largely Cuban; and the Miami garment district depends on Cuban seamstresses. Four Cuban-owned radio stations broadcast to the Cuban community; dozens of Spanish-language newspapers, including *Diario Las Americas* of Miami, circulate throughout Florida; and Cuban bars, theaters, schools, and clubs thrive in the Little Havanas.

Most Cubans immigrated for political reasons and have been successful economically. They are unashamedly patriotic, grateful to the United States for their freedom, and politically conservative. Cubans are cut off from the island by political barriers, and their love for the island is a deep, nostalgic yearning fired by hatred of Fidel Castro. Cuban-American ethnicity, therefore, is a function of political nationalism as well as language and personalism. Fiercely anticommunist and pro-American, Cuban activism revolves around foreign-policy issues. Since the first refugees filtered into the United States in 1959, Cuban groups have worked to overthrow Castro, and during the cold war of the 1960s the United States government supported them. Soon after Castro announced that he was a Communist, the Central Intelligence Agency began training a Cuban refugee army in Guatemala. In 1961 the CIA-trained forces landed at the Bay of Pigs, but Castro's soldiers, joined by civilians, crushed them on the beaches. The "invasion" was a fiasco. World opinion condemned the United States, but Cuban Americans were still determined to overthrow the Castro regime. Throughout the 1970s amd 1980s, radical groups such as Alpha 66 ran guns to Cuba, launched hit-and-run attacks on the island, and engineered repeated acts of sabotage against Castro. Their love for "their" Cuba still strong, and their commitment to what they consider its liberation undimmed, Cuban Americans are today a united, self-conscious ethnic community bound by blood and birth to the mother country and by recent history to the United States. In the early 1990s, the prospects of the collapse of the Castro regime in Cuba exhilarated the Cuban-American community.

Puerto Rican Americans

After the Spanish-American War, Puerto Rico became an American possession. There were about 1,500 Puerto Ricans in the continental United States by 1910 and more than 50,000 by 1930, but after World War II the migration became much larger. There were approximately 900,000 Puerto Ricans on the mainland in 1960, nearly 1.4 million in 1970, and about 2.2 million by 1990. With only 3,400 square miles of territory, a population of more than 3 million by 1977, and most capital controlled by United States corporations, Puerto Rico had severe economic problems. Because the economy revolved around sugar, tobacco, and coffee production, much employment was only seasonal. With jobs available on the mainland, air fare to New York City less than $50, and no immigration restrictions, the United States seemed the answer. Thousands went first as contract laborers working commercial farms from Florida to Massachusetts, but nearly all the Puerto Ricans ultimately settled in the cities, especially New York's urban ghettos in the Bronx, the South Bronx, the Lower East Side, Spanish Harlem, and the Williamsburg section of Brooklyn. By 1970 many school districts in New York City had sizable Puerto Rican populations, and there were other colonies throughout major northeastern cities.

The immigrants brought a uniquely syncretic heritage with them. Because of their Hispanic culture, they placed great value on the uniqueness of human nature, seeing a special quality to life regardless of race, religion, or class. Compassion and empathy, for them, were the most important parts of human character. But after more than sixty years of United States rule in Puerto Rico, they had acquired some Anglo-American attitudes about politics—an emphasis on political equality, individual freedom, and the rule of law. This view of society, to be sure, was still in its infancy in the Puerto Rican value system, but it had appeared nevertheless. Theirs was a dual heritage, at once a love of compassionate emotionalism and a growing respect for utilitarian pragmatism.

Still, the immigrants had problems. Especially troubling was their lack of a firm ethnic identity. The United States granted Puerto Ricans citizenship in 1917 and the right to elect their own governor in 1947, but Puerto Rican politics always revolved around the question of independence versus commonwealth status (granted in 1952) or statehood. The political debate retarded nationalism. The immigrants' displacement from an agrarian society into North American cities and the disruption of family and kinship networks so important to Hispanic society further eroded their sense of identity. Color also challenged Puerto Rican ethnicity and divided the community. At home, race had hardly been an issue; for centuries whites, blacks, mestizos, and mulattoes had mingled socially. But on the mainland a racial wedge split the community for the first time, with white Puerto Ricans aligning themselves with white Americans rather than with black Puerto Ricans, and black Puerto Ricans emphasizing their Spanish language to distinguish themselves from African Americans. In the 1960s and 1970s, when the civil rights movement gained momentum, white Puerto Ricans could not sympathize with calls for integration and cared little about de facto segregation.

The more educated Puerto Ricans opened bodegas, *botánicas* (stores selling herbs and spiritual medicines), cafes, restaurants, bars, and travel agencies, but these ethnic businesses could not maintain the community economically. Well into the 1980s nearly half the Puerto Rican families in the continental United States had poverty-level incomes, and nearly 40 percent were receiving welfare assistance. Less than 15 percent in 1990 were employed in professional, technical, and management positions.

Several problems explain Puerto Rican poverty on the mainland. Discrimination was real, but there were other reasons. One was the welfare system. Although it helped the Puerto Ricans at first by providing a minimal level of assistance, it also prevented them from developing the mutual aid spirit of earlier immigrants. There was no Puerto Rican equivalent of the Chinese hui kuan, the Japanese kenjinkai, the Finnish cooperatives, or ethnic building and loan associations. Open housing laws and welfare housing assistance dispersed the population throughout the cities, weakening the immigrants' potential political strength. Their Hispanic bias against bureaucracies further retarded efforts to form ethnic institutions to fight poverty. And because the Irish controlled the Catholic church and with other ethnic groups dominated the labor unions in New York City, Puerto Ricans had little access to the institutions that affected their lives.

Their language and cultural values also hurt them economically. Most Puerto Ricans did not speak English, but because of their Hispanic pride they chose not to speak English at all rather than speak it poorly. Reading levels and educational attainments were far below the national average. The American emphasis on personal achievement and competition in an impersonal economic world was alien to Puerto Ricans; they had little desire to embark on such a struggle, and American society judged them accordingly. The Puerto Rican love of children and large families, a fact of life on the island, became an economic handicap on the mainland, exacerbated by the lack of extended kinship networks to help them out. And to cope with life on the mainland, people had to be able to deal with large organizations and bureaucracies—social service agencies, health clinics, government bureaus, educational institutions, and the like—but the Puerto Rican suspicion of impersonal relationships made them shy away from such encounters. Finally, most Puerto Ricans entered the cities just as job opportunities were shifting to the suburbs and employment required education and technical skills; they found only minimum-wage service jobs that would never lift them above the poverty line. Most Puerto Ricans joined the "working poor," people with jobs that do not generate enough income for a minimum standard of living. Not until the 1960s did Puerto Ricans begin organizing in their own interests. Many joined the Democratic party, and New York labor unions and Democratic politicians mounted campaigns to register Puerto Rican voters, but because of population dispersal and the Hispanic alienation from organizations, getting out the vote continued to be a major challenge.

Some Puerto Rican groups concentrated on education as the way out of the ghetto. In 1961 the Puerto Rican Forum established Aspira to help young Puerto Ricans go to college. Aware that young people needed positive images, the Forum, Aspira, and the Conference on Puerto Rican Education became the most active groups in the Puerto Rican community. The Puerto Rican Legal Defense and Education Fund, a largely middle-class organization, promoted higher education and fought discrimination. Other Puerto Rican leaders promoted bilingualism and demanded bilingual teachers in schools, special programs to preserve the Spanish language, courses in Puerto Rican history and culture, and community participation in education. Arguing that the school system was top-heavy with Anglos and Jews, groups like the

United Bronx Parents called for community control of schools, Puerto Rican administrators and teachers in predominantly Puerto Rican schools, and Puerto Rican paraprofessionals. Jewish and Anglo educators felt threatened, fearing the loss of their jobs or lack of promotions in favor of Puerto Ricans, and decentralization met bitter opposition from the New York United Federation of Teachers.

Other Puerto Ricans opted for economic action. The Puerto Rican Merchants Association encouraged small businesses, and the Puerto Rican Civil Service Employees Association promoted the interests of Puerto Rican government workers. Under the War on Poverty program begun in 1965, the federal government funded a Puerto Rican Community Development Project that sponsored drug treatment, summer jobs, job training, and school tutoring programs. Puerto Rican workers joined labor unions and eventually constituted a major segment of the International Ladies Garment Workers Union. A number of welfare rights groups demanded greater funding, fairer treatment of recipients, and more advertisements of benefits. The East Harlem Tenants Council organized for lower rents, safer apartments, and better maintenance from landlords. Puerto Rican social workers formed the Puerto Rican Family Institute to assist families coming to the mainland, and after securing funds from the Council Against Poverty in 1965, the institute began marriage, employment, and family counseling. Some Puerto Ricans turned to militancy. The Free Puerto Rico Now group and the National Committee for the Freedom of Puerto Rican Nationalist Prisoners advocated the use of violence to achieve Puerto Rican independence and "occupied" the Statue of Liberty in 1977 to dramatize their demands. During the 1960s the National Committee for Puerto Rican Civil Rights demonstrated for civil rights, affirmative action in the hiring of Puerto Rican teachers, police officers and firefighters and Puerto Rican studies programs in schools. They also protested the City University of New York's decision in 1975 to charge tuition. Young Lords, a militant group of Puerto Rican students formed in the 1960s, demanded Puerto Rican studies programs in the city colleges, community control of community institutions, and an end to police brutality.

Mexican Americans

In 1990, Mexican Americans were the largest foreign-language group in the United States; because of their ability to visit their homeland and the constant flow of new immigrants, group identity remained strong. The need for farm workers in the United States grew dramatically after the end of European immigration, the flight to the cities, and

World War II job opportunities. To meet that demand, the United States established the *bracero* (work hands) program in 1942, and by 1964 more than five million Mexican braceros had worked seasonally in the Southwest, most of them on commercial farms and railroads. By American standards they were poorly paid, but they welcomed the chance to send money home to their families.

After more than twenty years of lobbying between commercial farmers and labor unions, Congress finally gave in to the unions and terminated the bracero program in 1965. Abolition only increased the flow of undocumented Mexican aliens because Mexican workers formerly admitted under the bracero program contacted their previous employers and went to work illegally. Since 1945, Mexicans not included in the bracero program had crossed the border anyway, only to become the most exploited workers of all. Afraid of immigration authorities, they could not complain about job conditions; and employers, free of government-mandated wage, housing, and transportation standards, actually preferred them. When the Immigration and Nationality Act of 1965 imposed a quota of 120,000 immigrants from the Western Hemisphere each year, the number of illegal aliens increased again. And the amendment to the law in 1976 gave Mexico a quota of only 20,000 immigrants per year. Under these laws the number of legal Mexican aliens declined, and illegal immigration increased.

But federal legislation was only a minor factor influencing the flow of undocumented aliens; traditional push-pull forces were responsible for the Mexican migration. Population growth in Mexico has been staggering, rising from an annual rate of 2.1 percent in 1940 to more than 3.5 percent in 1990. With a total population of more than 70 million today, more than 2 million people are added to the workforce each year. But the labor market has been unable to absorb them. Industrial development and agricultural mechanization are breaking up the traditional hacienda society, and millions of farm laborers have been displaced from the land. In 1940, more than 65 percent of the Mexican workforce was engaged in agriculture, but that declined to less than 50 percent in 1984. Unemployment rates climbed above 30 percent in the 1980s. In the meantime, more than 15 million new acres of irrigated land were put into production in the American Southwest, and along with industrialization there, the need for unskilled laborers increased greatly. With wages in the United States three to four times as much as Mexican wages for equivalent jobs, millions of farm laborers crossed the border.

The undocumented aliens constituted a rather homogeneous social group once in the United States. Most of them came from either Baja California or the densely populated, economically depressed western mesas of central Mexico, and they usually left behind rural villages rather than urban centers. They were generally working-class mestizos, for Indians and upper or middle classes rarely emigrated. And for the most part, they came to the United States in search of low-skill labor occupations as a means of supporting family members back home. Until the 1970s the illegal migrations did not create a sense of national crisis; labor unions in the 1950s protested the presence of undocumented Mexican aliens, but the general prosperity of the 1950s and 1960s, as well as the full economy of the Vietnam War years, produced a labor shortage and an unemployment rate, by 1966, of only 4 percent. But in the 1970s, as both unemployment and inflation rates reached frightening proportions, the national sense of alarm over the aliens was magnified. Many Americans argued that illegal aliens exacerbated unemployment and underemployment problems, depressed wage levels, and overburdened the welfare and educational systems. From Operation Wetback in 1954, when the Immigration and Naturalization Service deported more than a million undocumented workers, to the Immigration Reform and Control Act of 1986, the federal government grappled unsuccessfully with the issue. The 1986 law imposed severe penalties on businesses that employed undocumented workers, while allowing residency to those workers who could prove that they had been living continuously in the United States since 1982. Many Mexican-American civil rights activists protested the law, arguing that frightened employers would not give jobs even to Mexican Americans who were citizens.

Between 1945 and 1990 border patrols apprehended more than 21 million undocumented Mexican aliens, but perhaps that many more made the crossing successfully. Although the Immigration Reform and Control Act temporarily stemmed the tide in the late 1980s, it had completely resumed by the early 1990s because of economic conditions in Mexico. The Mexican government generally ignores the problem because the migration serves as a safety valve to lower-class frustration in Mexico and as a source of hard currency to offset trade deficits with the United States. And when the Immigration and Naturalization Service decided to construct a six-mile fence along the border between El Paso, Texas, and Juarez, Mexico, the illegal migration became a cultural issue as well because Mexican-American activists termed the proposal a "racist measure."

But the illegal migrants infused Mexican-American culture with old traditions, perpetuated ethnic characteristics, and retarded acculturation. By the late 1980s, Mexican Americans were one of the most self-conscious, visible ethnic communities in the United States. More than 90 percent of Mexican Americans—citizens, legal alien residents, and undocumented aliens—still lived in the Southwest, and 85 percent of them were in California and Texas. And most Mexican Americans in California lived in the Los Angeles area while those in Texas resided in the lower Rio Grande Valley. In Colorado and New Mexico perhaps one-third of the Mexican Americans lived in rural areas, but in California more than 90 percent were urbanized.

Until recent years, several subcommunities existed in the Southwest. The Hispanic people of New Mexico gradually came to refer to themselves as "Spanish Americans," and although they too were a mestizo rather than European group, they had retained a good deal of Spanish folk culture. When the United States took over in 1848, most of the Spanish-speaking people of the Southwest lived in New Mexico, and because twentieth-century migration from Mexico to New Mexico was minimal, they did retain certain archaic speech patterns, folk songs, and religious art forms that were Iberian in nature. By "Spanish American" they meant a native-born person of Spanish (European) descent, free of mixed or Indian parentage; they also maintained feelings of superiority toward other Mexican Americans, whom they considered to be poor, uneducated, and "Mexican." In California and Texas, where so many millions of twentieth-century Mexican immigrants settled, the forms of self-identity were different. The violence and siege mentality prevailing for so long in Texas between the white majority and tejano minority made for a tenser situation. Throughout the nineteenth century the latter referred to themselves as "tejanos" or "Mexicans"; but after the massive immigration from Mexico began in 1910, the term "Latin Americans" became more common as a means of distinguishing themselves from the immigrants. In California also there was a division between the californio natives and the Mexican immigrants. Hoping to avoid white discrimination, the californios separated themselves from the new immigrants and began using the term "Spanish" in the early twentieth century. Thus for reasons of nativity and class, the following subcommunities had appeared in the Southwest by the 1950s: the more prosperous and established Spanish Americans of New Mexico, Latin Americans of Texas, and Spanish of California; the pachuco culture of the urban barrios, where native-born Mexican Americans found themselves caught between American and Hispanic value systems; the rural society of native-born Mexican Americans in parts of New Mexico and southern Colorado; and the lower-class Mexican culture of the legal and illegal immigrants living in Texas and California.

But other factors united them and helped build a sense of Mexican-American identity, especially after World War II. As a mestizo people despised for generations by white Mexicans of European descent, they felt a community spirit when faced with similar treatment by whites in the United States. At the same time, many Mexican Americans held similar prejudices against African Americans and were caught in the unique position of being a lower class separated from black Americans by race and culture and from white Americans by race, culture, and income. The color line in America served to isolate Mexican Americans from whites while uniting them to one another.

Religion also bound them together, though not so much in an institutional sense. Allied with the white elite, the Catholic church had been a conservative force in Mexico, controlling vast amounts of land while peasants starved. Many mestizo farmers had come to view the institutional church as an adversary, and since the 1830s they had periodically attacked church property and driven priests into the cities. The Mexican immigrants came from that part of Mexico where parochial schools were few, finances weak, religious instruction sporadic, and attendance at mass irregular. In the United States they still viewed the church suspiciously, not only because of past hostilities but because of the legalistic, organizational stamp of the Irish hierarchy. By insisting on English instruction and citizenship training, the church in the early twentieth century became an Americanizing force, and Mexican parishioners maintained their polite distance. Though Roman Catholic in a village and cultural sense, Mexican Americans attended church infrequently, disagreed openly with church doctrines on birth control and sexual conservatism, contributed little financially to church programs, and supplied few priests and nuns to the hierarchy. What the immigrants did support and share was a folk and cultural Catholicism, one based on mixtures of Indian and European religion and nurtured by a personalistic communalism. Every village had a patron saint and every individual his own saint's day. So whether it was the festival of the Virgin of Guadalupe or a personal saint's day, Mexicans felt constantly in touch with the spirit of Catholicism.

A family ethos also held Mexican Americans together. In Mexico peasants had lived in clustered villages where networks of extended families assisted one another. And in the United States, as long as families moved together as migrant laborers, family unity and parental authority were maintained. Wives were expected to be obedient and sexually loyal to their husbands; children were supposed to be subservient; and husbands were expected to be sexually free but economically loyal. Even in the cities, when extended kinship ties were weakened, the family ethos survived, and all members of the family subordinated individual demands to family needs.

Finally, Mexican Americans were bound by language and culture. Whether the border language of Calo or Texmex, the purer Spanish of the educated elites, or the Spanish of the foreign-born, language separated them from American society and provided a special way of interpreting life and expressing personal reactions. They shared memories or hero worship of Pancho Villa or Emiliano Zapata, foods, *folklórico* dances, and distinctive types of dress and hairstyles. And they shared the generally Hispanic respect for machismo and personalism. In the American world of mass consumer goods and anonymous bureaucracies, these values clearly distinguish Mexican Americans.

After 1945, Mexican-American society changed somewhat, and those changes cleared the way for the *chicanismo* spirit of the 1960s, 1970s, and 1980s. Mexican-American barrios were worlds unto themselves, islands bound by language and culture. Ethnicity survived there, but so did problems. Mexican Americans suffered from chronic poverty. If not in the fields, they usually found work only in unskilled capacities, as cooks in restaurants, porters in large buildings, maids in hotels, or laborers. By 1990 nearly two-thirds of Mexican-American families had incomes below the poverty line; few Mexican-American adults had educations above the ninth grade; and large numbers of Mexican-American high school students were functionally illiterate. And they too were caught in cities losing jobs and a national economy making the transition from a manufacturing to a service base requiring education and technical skill. Urban poverty also changed family relationships, primarily because unemployed fathers were unable to fulfill their roles as breadwinners.

Despite economic problems and ethnicity, signs of acculturation became more and more evident. Second and third-generation Mexican Americans were increasingly bilingual; Mexican-American wives, rather than acquiescing in the sexual infidelity or authoritarianism of their husbands, began to demand sexual loyalty and the sharing of child-rearing responsibilities; and young people were more independent. More important, Mexican Americans began overcoming their cultural bias and building an institutional base to improve their status. Middle-class Mexican Americans still relied on the League of United Latin American Citizens (LULAC) to fight discrimination, but new organizations also appeared. Nearly 350,000 Mexican Americans served in the armed forces during World War II; but after the war, when they were denied membership in the American Legion and the Veterans of Foreign Wars, and when authorities in Three Rivers, Texas, refused to hold memorial services or bury Felix Longoria, a GI killed in the Philippines, Mexican-American soldiers formed the American GI Forum to work for equality through legal action. The Unity Leagues of Texas and California campaigned against segregated schools, and in the 1950s Fred Ross established the Community Service Organizations in California to help Mexican Americans meet citizenship requirements, adjust to American customs, obtain pension benefits, and enjoy full civil rights.

They soon realized that legal action was ineffective without political power, and in 1958 formed the Mexican-American Political Association (MAPA) in California, the Political Association of Spanish-Speaking Organizations (PASO) in Texas, and the American Coordinating Council on Political Education (ACCPE) in Arizona. MAPA worked for only Mexican support and the others for a coalition with white liberals, black activists, and labor unions, but all three tried to mobilize Mexican-American political power. John Kennedy's campaign in 1960 worked through MAPA, PASO, and ACCPE to form Viva Kennedy clubs, and in 1962 MAPA and PASO ran successful candidates in the Crystal City, Texas, elections. José Gutiérrez rose out of those elections and in 1970 formed *La Raza Unida*, a political party dedicated to community control of Mexican-American counties in southern Texas. Corky Gonzalez founded the Crusade for Justice in 1965. Schooled in local politics and Denver antipoverty programs, Gonzalez demanded reform of the criminal justice system, an end to police brutality, and good housing, schools, and jobs for Mexican Americans. Culturally nationalistic, Gonzalez also sponsored Chicanismo, a pride in being Mexican American and in mestizo roots, and a consciousness of ethnic origins that reflected an earlier pachuco culture. A host of Chicano writers and artists—including novelists Raymond Barrio and Richard Vásquez, short-story writer Daniel Garza, playwright Luis Valdez, and painter Raul Espinoza—evoked the Chicano spirit, and Chicano studies programs swept through the schools of the Southwest in the 1970s and 1980s.

Reies Tijerina was another Mexican-American activist of the 1960s and 1970s. After traveling widely in Spain and the United States, he formed the *Alianza Federal de Mercedes* (Federal Alliance of Land Grants) in 1963 and demanded the return of land taken from tejanos, californios, and nuevos mexicanos. Militant and articulate, Tijerina was a charismatic leader who denounced racism and called for ethnic solidarity. In 1966, claiming millions of acres in New Mexico and urging secession, he "occupied" Kit Carson National Forest and assaulted several forest rangers. On June 5, 1967, Tijerina and some of his supporters raided the courthouse at Tierra Amarillo, New Mexico, shot two deputies, released eleven Alianza members, and fled the town with several hostages. Sentenced to prison, Tijerina was paroled in 1971 on the condition that he dissociate himself from the Alianza, and without his leadership the movement died.

No Mexican-American leader rivaled Cesar Chavez in influence. A counterpart in time and philosophy to Martin Luther King, Jr., he too

Cesar Chavez and farm laborers demonstrate during a strike against California grape growers. (George Ballis/Black Star)

believed in nonviolence but was more committed to economic action than to civil rights. Born in 1927 in Yuma, Arizona, Chavez worked as a migrant laborer after his parents lost their farm in a tax auction. Early in the 1950s, as a worker in the Community Service Organization, he saw the potential of mass action. He moved to Delano, California, in 1962 and shortly thereafter organized the National Farm Workers (later the United Farm Workers). For two years he built the union; then he struck the Delano grape growers, demanding better pay. The growers refused and Chavez turned the strike into a moral crusade, an appeal to the conscience of America. The growers used violence, strikebreakers, and anticommunist rhetoric; Chavez appealed to white liberals including Robert Kennedy and Hubert Humphrey, labor unions such as the AFL-CIO, Martin Luther King, Jr., and other black leaders, and white students on college campuses. For five years Chavez led a national boycott of California grapes; he fought the growers as well as the Teamsters, which tried to organize a rival union, and finally, in 1970, succeeded in winning a long-term contract with the growers. Chavez had been the most successful Chicano of all.

These are the Mexican Americans. No longer subservient and quiet, they want what American society promised to all; and fed by the continuing waves of undocumented aliens, they are the fastest-growing ethnic group in the United States. And yet they are proud of their language and culture—their roots in the Old World and the New—and hope to preserve the familialism and personalism so central to their identity.

The New Hispanic Kaleidoscope

Throughout much of the twentieth century, Mexican Americans, Cuban Americans, and Puerto Ricans constituted the Hispanic community in the United States. But late in the 1960s, a host of new immigrant groups from Spanish-speaking countries in the Caribbean, Central America, and South America began arriving in the United States, and they gave the Hispanic community a complexity it had not had before.

The largest of the new Hispanic groups in the United States were immigrants from the Dominican Republic. Comprising the eastern two-thirds of the island of Haiti, or Hispaniola as it was known earlier, the Dominican Republic experienced a series of economic and political problems after World War II. Throughout the 1950s and early 1960s, the country suffered from an endemic political instability that did not end until the rise to power of Joaquín Balaguer in 1966. Nearly 100,000 people left the Dominican Republic during the 1960s, and most of them settled in the New York City area. Although Balaguer worked hard at improving the country's economic infrastructure, poverty levels were high. Urbanization increased dramatically in the 1970s, and those Dominicans moving to the cities became more aware of economic opportunities in the United States. The global depression of the 1980s severely depressed the price of sugar, the Dominican Republic's main export, and intensified the country's economic problems. During the 1970s nearly 150,000 people emigrated, and during the 1980s that number increased to 210,000 people. By the early 1990s, more than 10 percent of the population of the Dominican Republic was living in the United States.

Although there are Dominican communities in places such as Miami and Philadelphia, more than 90 percent of the Dominican immigrants live in New York City—in upper Manhattan and in the Corona-Jackson Heights area of Queens. A racially mixed people, the immigrants mostly originated in the Cibao region of the island, an area known for its relatively high incomes. The Dominicans' two-parent families remained intact in the United States, and the immigrants proved to be ambitious and resourceful. Most of them took jobs in service industries or started small businesses, and by the late 1980s their incomes exceeded those of Puerto Ricans. They tend to be quite loyal to the Roman Catholic church and to the Democratic party.

Central America also sent a large contingent of immigrants to the United States in the 1960s, 1970s, and 1980s—more than 600,000 people. There the migrations were inspired by violent civil wars and economic suffering. Except for Costa Rica, which enjoyed a remarkable political stability, the other countries of the region faced guerrilla wars between Marxist-backed left-wing guerrillas and U.S.-backed right-wing governments. In 1979, the Marxist-backed Sandinistas triumphed in Nicaragua and imposed a repressive police state. They soon exported revolution to El Salvador and then to Honduras. The United States supported the right-wing governments in those countries, and the resulting civil wars created untold misery for peasant farmers and workers. The immigrants became known as "feet people" because they basically walked to the United States, making their way north through Guatemala and Mexico to the border. The immigrants from Guatemala preferred settling in Los Angeles, while many of the Hondurans and El Salvadorans preferred Texas and the Gulf Coast. Other Hondurans settled in New York City, as did large numbers of Panamanians. By the early 1990s, there were also large settlements of Central Americans in Los Angeles, Chicago, Miami, San Jose, and San Francisco.

The largest group of South American immigrants came from Colombia—70,000 in the 1960s, 78,000 in the 1970s, and more than 100,000 in the 1980s. After World War II a small Colombian community appeared in the Jackson Heights area of New York City. Most of the immigrants were middle-class professionals—nurses, pharmacists, technicians. In the 1960s and 1970s, however, the migration accelerated because of political instability—the era of *La Violencia*—and because industrialization and the mechanization of agriculture displaced tens of thousands of peasants and workers. All this happened amidst rapid population growth and declining air fares to the United States. By 1970 there were nearly 30,000 Colombians living in "Chaperino," their neighborhood in Jackson Heights. Most of them were from central Colombia and they were primarily of European or mestizo descent. The Colombians settling in Chicago were known as *costeños*, or people from the coast, and were more likely to be of mixed African, Indian, and European descent. They tended to be very well educated and often had professional backgrounds.

The arrival of the new immigrants diversified the Hispanic community, even though many Americans simply lumped them together. The immigrants often resented that process, viewing it as insensitive and ignorant. They came from different countries, and they had cultures that were region specific. Some did not even speak Spanish: tens of thousands of Mayan Indians—Kekchis, Cakchiquels, Mopans, Quiches, and others—were part of the migration, and they spoke their Indian dialect as their first language. Although the vast majority of the immigrants did speak Spanish, a great variety of dialects existed among them, and those dialects helped dictate ethnic identity. Significant racial differences existed also. Although most of the early waves of Cuban immigrants were primarily of European descent, the immigrants of the 1980s included a large African-Cuban component. Thousands of *Garifunas*—people descended from escaped African slaves who had intermarried with Karib Indians on the island of Dominica before England relocated them to the Atlantic coast of Central America—came to the United States. Many Indians emigrated from Central America, Venezuela, Ecuador, and Colombia. By the early 1990s, the so-called Hispanic community of the United States was hardly a single community at all.

Chapter Fourteen

Asian Americans in the Modern World

The Immigration and Nationality Act of 1965, which finally eliminated the ethnic quotas from the National Origins Act of 1924 and the McCarran-Walter Act of 1952, provided new opportunities for Asian immigration. Preferences for family members and highly educated people allowed many Asian professionals to settle here. Each Asian country now had a quota of up to 20,000 immigrants per year, and the legislation almost immediately led to dramatic increases in immigration from China, the Philippines, and Korea.

The political and cultural perspectives of Asian Americans changed after World War II, and soon most Americans no longer thought of them disparagingly as Chinks or Japs. Out of the rubble of the war Japan became a leading economic power, and the entrepreneurial and educational success of Japanese Americans was just as striking. The internal cohesiveness of the Chinese-American community, as well as its economic success, won Americans' respect, and the fact that many post-1945 Chinese immigrants were refugees from communism increased the admiration. Some discrimination continued. Asian Americans were still absent from most social clubs and the corporate elite, but as never before in their history, they were enjoying access to political and educational opportunity. It was a mixed blessing, however, for acceptance increased the cultural tensions already inherent in the Asian-American community. For both Chinese and Japanese, the institutional relationships that governed them before World War II

271

began to deteriorate after 1945. Hui kuan and tong societies no longer commanded blind loyalty, and even the family associations were losing some power. Also, the postwar Chinese community was divided between native-born Chinese Americans and new immigrants from China, Hong Kong, and Taiwan. More than 850,000 Chinese came to the United States after 1960, and because the 1960 Chinese-American population numbered only about 250,000 people, the new immigrants had an enormous impact on Chinatowns. By the early 1990s, nearly 1.6 million people in the United States were Chinese Americans, and they constituted the largest of the Asian communities here.

Japanese Americans saw a similar breakdown in the prefectural associations. Although the Issei had found the kenjinkai valuable tools for cultural survival, the Nisei, Sansei, and *Yonsei* (fourth generation) considered prefectural ancestry irrelevant. And by 1990, with the Japanese-American community totaling more than 800,000 people, the native-born dwarfed the Issei in numbers and influence. Both Chinese and Japanese Americans had identity problems: how to move freely in American society while still feeling the pull of traditional loyalties.

In addition to the Chinese and Japanese immigrants, there were several other East Asian and Southeast Asian minorities: the immigrants from the Philippines, Korea, and Indochina. By 1990, the number of Filipinos living in the United States had increased to more than 1.4 million. The Korean-American community had grown to more than 750,000, and the Indochinese immigrants numbered more than one million people.

The Chinese

More than any other ethnic group, the Chinese lived in America without becoming part of the larger society. Segregated in ghettos and overwhelmingly male, early Chinese communities had been self-governing societies with their own systems of justice and social welfare. The Chinese Six Companies spoke for the whole community and were the main source of employment, housing, and loans for new immigrants. Suspicious about nativism, the Six Companies and family associations urged the Chinese to work hard, save money, avoid publicity, and stay away from white America. Because the Six Companies and family associations monopolized economic opportunity, and because the immigrants felt strong loyalties to family and regional associates and distrust for the host society, the Six Companies and clans served as a conservative private government.

Social and personal goals reinforced the isolation. Because so many immigrants returned to China, the foreign-born outnumbered the native-born until 1940. Residential segregation was natural. Nearly three out of four Chinese Americans lived in California, Hawaii, or New York in 1945, most of them in three cities—San Francisco, New York City, and Honolulu. A century after the trek to the "Golden Mountain," Chinese America was still a transient, closed society.

That changed after 1945. Chinese Americans had opposed immigration restriction since the time of the Chinese Exclusion Act of 1882, but the size of the community had decreased from nearly 300,000 in 1882 to 90,000 in 1900 to only 80,000 in 1930. Exclusion also made it difficult to establish nuclear families because Chinese men outnumbered women and new immigration was difficult. The Chinese-American Citizens Alliance campaigned to end exclusion as the only way to achieve a normal family life, and in 1924 the Citizens Committee to Repeal Chinese Exclusion joined the campaign. Chinese Americans were no longer willing to accept discrimination quietly.

The campaign was hopeless until World War II, because labor unions, patriotic groups, and nativist organizations were still preaching about the "yellow peril." The bombing of Pearl Harbor, however, made the United States and China allies, and to counter Japanese propaganda, Congress repealed the exclusion in 1943, assigned China a quota of 105 immigrants a year, permitted foreign-born Chinese to apply for citizenship, and made special provisions for the immigration of war refugees and families of Chinese American citizens. More than 25,000 Chinese immigrated between 1943 and 1950, most of them women and children. By 1950 there were nearly 120,000 Chinese in the United States, more than half of whom were native born. When Mao Zedong and the Communists took power in mainland China in 1949, the Chinese-American community, cut off from its homeland, finally acquired a sense of permanence in America.

Chinese Americans continued to oppose quotas because the yearly allowance of 105 immigrants would never create a sexual balance, and when Congress eliminated quotas in 1965, Chinese immigration increased dramatically. Between 1966 and 1990 the Chinese community grew from 250,000 to 1.6 million people. Chinese-American life began to break out of traditional boundaries. New immigrants came from all over China, not just from Kwangtung and Fukien. They looked down on Cantonese traditions and felt no loyalties to the hui kuan. And because so many were poor workers employed by Chinese businessmen, they were hostile toward the well-to-do. For the first time the integrated, morally united Chinese community began to feel the centrifugal forces of American life.

Chinese Americans began taking advantage of new opportunities. For centuries the Chinese had valued education, but in America colleges had been closed to them. After World War II, however, they went to college in record numbers. In 1940, less than 3 percent of Chinese Americans were professional workers, but by 1960 that number had increased to 18 percent and by 1990 to more than 33 percent. In 1960, while 16 percent of white high school graduates went on to college, nearly 30 percent of the Chinese did. As housing discrimination eased after 1960 and many college-educated Chinese moved to integrated neighborhoods, Chinatown became a place to visit on Sunday afternoons to stock up on food or visit friends and relatives. The political, social, and economic authority of the hui kuan oligarchy was waning, just at the time new immigrants were refusing to take them seriously.

Intergenerational conflicts also contributed to the decline of hui kuan authority. Unlike their immigrant parents, the native born had little affection for the villages and provinces of China and found their parents' territorial loyalties archaic. They felt closer to other native-born Chinese, regardless of ancestry, than to the foreign born. And while the foreign born always looked to the day when they would return to China—at least until 1949—the native born were American citizens expecting to live out their lives in the United States. Instead of relying on the Six Companies or family associations for jobs or wives, they turned to American social and political institutions or simply to friends. One Chinese American expressed those feelings:

> All the family associations, the Six Companies, any young person who wants to make some changes, they call him a communist. . . . I think the reason is, a lot of these people have a little business, they're doing pretty well, they have no ideas about how the society might change. They hold on to everything the way it was in China, in Kwangtung. Even though we're in a different society, a different era.*

As long as the native born were a minority, the power of the traditional hierarchy had gone unchallenged; but after 1945, because of the numbers of native-born and non-Cantonese immigrants, the Six Companies ceased to be the only voice representing the Chinese in the United States.

The native born supported the Chinese-American Citizens Alliance in its campaign for citizenship, an end to exclusion, and federal laws against discrimination. While the Six Companies called for isolation, submission, and a low profile, the native born were more outspoken more demanding in their quest for justice and equality. Through

---

*Quoted in Victor Nee and Brett DeBary, *Longtime Californin'* (New York, 1973), p. 190.

hard work, entrepreneurial skills, and education, native-born Chinese Americans had achieved middle-class status by the 1970s and wanted political recognition and social respect for themselves as well as economic opportunity for new Chinese immigrants. They protested images of the Chinese that appeared in such TV programs as "Hawaii Five-O" and "Mission Impossible," and in such films as *The Good Earth* (1937), *The World of Suzie Wong* (1961), and *The Manchurian Candidate* (1962). The Chinese-American Citizens Alliance, the Chinese-American Democratic Clubs, the Chinese-American Chamber of Commerce, and a host of voluntary professional, business, and youth groups extolled their ethnic origins.

Chinese Americans became more politically active. Wing F. Ong became an Arizona state legislator in 1946; Hiram Fong of Hawaii entered the United States Senate in 1959; and Wing Luke was elected to the Seattle City Council in 1962. Some Chinese Americans were actively protesting against poverty. By 1973 Chinatown had become divided along class lines between a professional and entrepreneurial elite and the poor immigrants from China, Hong Kong, and Taiwan. The poor lived in slum housing and worked at subsistence wages. Like young leaders in the African-American and Chicano movements, Chinese-American youths began to demand federal action.

Still, Chinese Americans remained outside the melting pot in the late 1980s. More visible and politically active than ever before, they maintained an ethnic perspective although some acculturation had occurred. In public schools they spoke English and behaved like other Americans; they celebrated major American holidays and joined the Boy Scouts and Girl Scouts. They watched programs on American television, drove American cars, and wore American clothes. On the other hand, most Chinese Americans were still fluent in or at least familiar with a native language—Cantonese, Mandarin, or a regional dialect. Most were Buddhists, Taoists, or Confucians; and when they did adopt Christianity, they retained the detached, practical, and eclectic attitudes of Chinese religion. And they still took Chinese husbands and wives. Beneath all their American ways, they remained a distinct people.

The Japanese

Japanese America was also changing. In the early years of the twentieth century the Issei had confronted a completely alien culture, and the rise of Japan as a Pacific power had created much fear in the United States. Many Americans doubted whether the Japanese would ever be able to assimilate. After Pearl Harbor these fears reached an emotional frenzy.

Japanese Americans fought valiantly, in part to prove how loyal they were. (The Bettmann Archive)

But attitudes changed by the early 1950s. Hundreds of thousands of GIs returned from the occupation of Japan impressed with the stability of Japanese society, and more than twenty thousand brought back Japanese wives. Americans were amazed at Japanese tenacity and economic skill, at their ability to rise from the ashes of World War II to economic independence. Old stereotypes of treacherous, disloyal, and depraved Japanese gave way to a new consensus about loyal, hardworking, well-educated, and law-abiding Japanese. In 1952, the McCarran-Walter Act permitted Issei to apply for citizenship, and the Immigration and Nationality Act of 1965 ended the Japanese quota. Between 1945 and 1990 nearly 190,000 Japanese immigrated to the United States, and the Japanese-American community, composed of perhaps 280,000 people in 1941, grew to 465,000 in 1960, 750,000 in 1979, and more than 800,000 in 1990. The Supreme Court ruled that California's Alien Land Laws violated the Fourteenth Amendment, and they were repealed in 1956. And in the 1980s, Congress began paying damages of more than $1 billion to the Japanese Americans who had lost so much because of the relocation experience of World War II. Japanese Americans were living in a society that was increasingly open to them.

Tolerance gave full reign to Japanese Americans' cultural impulses. Most Issei who came to America were educated, and they passed on to the Nisei, Sansei, and Yonsei a profound respect for learning. Now they poured into the state colleges, and by 1979 educational achievement among Japanese Americans was second only to that of the Jews. Unskilled workers had dropped from 25 percent to only 3 percent, and the median Japanese-American income was far above the national average. Occupational and educational success did not reduce the level of community integrity; crime, delinquency, divorce, and indigence were far less likely to occur among Japanese Americans than in the society at large. The willingness of the Japanese family to care for its sick, poor, and aged was unsurpassed in the United States.

Given their economic condition in 1945, such achievements were even more remarkable. When the army rounded them up for the relocation camps in 1942, they were permitted to take with them only what they could carry. Doctors, dentists, and medical technicians lost their professional equipment; lawyers their law libraries; fishermen their boats, nets, poles, and tackle; businesspeople their inventories, buildings, and fixtures; farmers their land, leases, and implements; and families their homes, cars, and insurance policies. Congress passed the Japanese Evacuation Claims Act in 1948 to compensate them, but until the payments of the 1980s, only $38 million was ever awarded in damages, while conservative estimates place prewar Japanese property at over $400 million. Thus after the war most Japanese Americans had to start all over again. Despite this, they reached a prosperous middle-class status by the 1990s.

Unlike the Chinese, the Japanese did not experience cultural conflict with new immigrants after 1945. Japan was a remarkably homogeneous society, and the new Issei shared much with the older Issei. Although differences with the Nisei, Sansei, and Yonsei were substantial, the cultural gap was not nearly as great as it was between the older Cantonese settlers and the new immigrants from northern and central China. Still, Nisei did not feel close to Issei prefectural groups or the Japanese Association that represented them, and although their ties to such traditional Japanese values as family loyalty and duty were strong, they were far more acculturated than their parents. They wore shoes indoors, used knives and forks instead of chopsticks, played American sports, and selected marriage partners for romantic rather than family or economic reasons.

All this troubled Issei parents, but they were especially upset by the Nisei tendency to view themselves as a national rather than a prefectural group. In 1930, the Nisei had formed the Japanese-American Citizens League (JACL) to promote their interests, and prefectural origins were ignored. But while the Chinese-American Citizens Association had to compete with the Six Companies and family associations representing the foreign born, the World War II relocation had destroyed Issei influence. By 1945 the Issei-dominated prefectural associations and the old Japanese Association were all but extinct. In the camps the JACL spoke for the incarcerated people, and the Issei, lacking citizenship or recognition from officials of the War Relocation Authority, could do little about their status. After the war the JACL led the campaign against the Alien Land Laws and for evacuation compensation and urged the Nisei to work hard and be "good Americans." It was the Nisei, the "quiet" Americans, who fulfilled the new stereotypes of the Japanese after 1945.

But in the 1960s, 1970s, and 1980s, signs of Sansei and Yonsei restlessness with Nisei values appeared, just as the Nisei had tired of Issei parochialism in the 1920s and 1930s. Most Sansei and Yonsei still reflected the norms of Japanese culture as hardworking, upwardly mobile people; but, unlike the Issei and Nisei, they did not necessarily accept the wisdom of conformity, collective dependence on family and community, a high tolerance for frustration and work, a yearning for achievement, and a willingness to suppress their complaints. Most Sansei and Yonsei still adhered to some or all these values to a degree, but they were questioning them too. Juvenile crime was higher among them than it had been among the Issei or Nisei, and they could not understand the passive way Issei and Nisei had accepted their treatment during World War II. For many Sansei and Yonsei, the Japanese-American Citizens League had sold its birthright in 1942, losing its self-respect and pride.

For the Sansei and Yonsei youth of the 1960s, 1970s, and 1980s, the relocation camps represented a historical event that became a distinguishing feature of ethnicity. Sensitive to discrimination and stereotyping, they protested both. Searching for their own roots, they demanded Japanese studies programs in schools and colleges, and militant Sansei talked of "yellow power" and "yellow pride," community action, and even a revolution of "Third World peoples." While liberal Sansei and Yonsei demanded cultural pluralism, radicals questioned the foundation of capitalism and liberal democracy. It was a futile line of questioning, of course, because so many Japanese Americans were enjoying middle-class prosperity. Nevertheless, the new attitudes clearly spelled the end of Issei isolation and Nisei submission.

The demise of those social values were all but inevitable, and Japanese Americans, like so many previous immigrant groups in the United States, faced powerful assimilationist pressures. Because of political stability and economic prosperity in Japan, emigration was extremely small. During the decade of the 1980s, only 37,000 people came to the United States from Japan. In 1960, Japanese Americans had constituted more than half of all Asians in the United States, but by 1991 that figure had dropped to only 11 percent. Economic success combined with declines in new immigration from Japan accelerated the assimilation process. By the early 1990s, more than half of Japanese Americans were marrying exogamously to non-Japanese, and they were rapidly moving along the road to assimilation.

The Filipinos

After Congress passed the Immigration and Nationality Act of 1965, immigration from the Philippines accelerated, and by the 1980s and early 1990s the Filipinos were among the most rapidly growing of the Asian immigrant groups in the United States. During the 1980s the Philippines had one of the world's most rapidly growing populations, and because of the extensive American military presence there and the historical ties between the United States and the Philippines, the immigration network was well established. American servicemen at Clark Air Base and the Subic Bay Naval Base often married Filipino women and returned with them to the United States; the women's families then began the immigration and naturalization process as well. During the 1960s, nearly 102,000 Filipinos settled in the United States, and those numbers increased to 360,000 immigrants in the 1970s and nearly 500,000 in the 1980s. By 1991, Filipino Americans numbered more than 1.4 million people, and they constituted 20 percent of all Asians in America.

Like so many other ethnic groups, the Filipinos became more politically active in the 1960s. The Filipino Federation of America, founded in 1925 by Hilario Camino Moncado, still offered legal aid and employment assistance, but Filipino activism took the form of a workers' movement. When white growers cut wages for asparagus workers, Filipino immigrants had organized the Filipino Agricultural Labor Association and won several strikes in the late 1930s and 1940s. In 1959, just when Cesar Chavez was forming the National Farm Workers Association for Mexican-American laborers, the AFL-CIO founded the Agricultural Workers Organizing Committee (AWOC). Led by Larry Itlion, the AWOC was primarily a Filipino union, but in 1966, after lengthy strikes against individual growers and the agribusiness corporations, the AWOC and Chavez's union merged into the United Farm Workers Organizing Committee and successfully struck the Di Giorgio Corporation in Kern County, California. Cesar Chavez remained head of the new union, but Philip Vera Cruz, a Filipino, was named vice-chairman. During the 1980s, those labor organization and union contract drives continued to make modest improvements in the living standards of poor Filipino workers.

The Filipino communities in West Coast cities continued to expand in the 1980s, but they continued to have difficulty lifting themselves out of poverty. Large-scale immigration in the 1980s guaranteed that the majority of Filipino Americans were newcomers with extremely limited resources, and unlike the Chinese and Japanese immigrants, the Filipinos did not enjoy the benefit of ethnic institutions imbued with at least some financial resources. They did not have organizations like the hui kuan or the kenjinkai to provide capital for establishing a business foothold, and racist attitudes in many unions sealed off access to skilled jobs. Also, the Filipino-American community was extremely heterogeneous. The Philippines themselves consisted of thousands of islands inhabited by people speaking hundreds of languages. Linguistic differences divided the Filipino community internally, and it was difficult for them to marshal group resources for self-help. In the early 1990s, most Filipinos remained unskilled workers with median incomes among the lowest in the nation.

The Koreans

Korean immigration to the United States was quite limited until recent decades. Korean society enjoyed a good deal of stability, and because Korea was little more than a Japanese colony until after World War II, immigration to the United States was quite restricted. Like the Filipinos and Japanese, some Koreans migrated to the sugarcane fields of Hawaii in the late nineteenth century, and when Hawaii was annexed by the United States in 1898, they became Korean Americans. After 1900, several thousand Koreans came to the mainland to work on commercial farms and as construction workers building the railroad trunk lines in the American West. But by 1945 there were only 9,000 Koreans living in the United States, the vast majority of them in California.

The real boost to Korean immigration came in the wake of the Korean War. At the end of World War II, Korea was divided at the 38th parallel between North Korea, which was a Communist-bloc country, and South Korea, whose ties to the United States were very close. In 1950, North Korean troops invaded South Korea, and under the auspices of the United Nations, American troops commanded by General Douglas MacArthur were deployed to Korea to stop the invasion. The war eventually broadened to include the Chinese, and it was not until 1953 that a ceasefire was negotiated. Hundreds of thousands of American troops remained in South Korea as a defensive force during the 1950s, and as late as the early 1990s there were still more than forty thousand of them stationed there.

Thousands of the American soldiers married Korean women and brought them to the United States when their tours of duty ended. Those women then brought many of their family members to the United States, and by 1960 the Korean-American community had increased to more than 50,000 people. The wives of the servicemen wrote home about opportunities in the United States, and Korean newspapers told similar stories. The book *Day and Night of Komericans*, published in 1976, became a best-seller in Korea and fueled the desire of many Koreans to come to the United States. Under the Immigration and Nationality Act of 1965, Korean nurses, physicians, and professionals settled here first, and they soon brought their families as well.

But the real boom in Korean immigration came in the 1970s and 1980s. Although Korean Americans experienced a good deal of anti-Asian prejudice and discrimination, they were nonetheless impressed with the economic opportunities of life in the United States. In the 1970s, more than 272,000 Koreans settled here, and that number increased to more than 320,000 in the 1980s. By 1991 they constituted 11 percent of the Asian population in the United States and totaled more than 750,000 people. The largest Korean-American community was in Los Angeles, with more than 300,000 living there, but there were also large Korean settlements in New York City and Chicago.

A distinguishing feature of Korean life in the United States was their entrepreneurial success. Like earlier generations of Chinese and Japanese immigrants, the Koreans had family-based revolving credit associations—the *kye*—that provided them with the capital they needed to establish small businesses. They also settled in sections of Los Angeles, New York, and Chicago that were being abandoned by an earlier generation of Jewish, Italian, Polish, and Irish small businessowners. With loan money from their ethnic credit unions and loan associations they purchased liquor stores, dry-cleaning establishments, fast-food restaurants, coin-operated laundries, stationery stores, small grocery stores, pawnshops, sporting-goods stores, floral shops, and video arcades. They carved out a niche for themselves in the retail service and convenience economy that large corporations ignored, and by 1991 there were more than 15,000 Korean-owned businesses in Los Angeles County.

But that very success posed a serious challenge to the immigrants. Most of their businesses served an African-American clientele, who came to increasingly resent Korean prosperity. Many African Americans were dumbfounded at how such a recent group of immigrants had managed to do so well. Unfounded rumors that the federal government was bankrolling immigrant businesses only intensified the resentment, as did the fact that the Korean businesses employed so few African-American workers. Actually, the capital to start the businesses came from ethnic Korean organizations, and the personnel to work the stores came from family members willing to labor for long hours at well below minimum wage. The Korean businesses succeeded because they had very low overhead. They enjoyed financing at below-market interest rates, labor at below-level wage rates, and below-average rents in the depressed commercial real estate markets of the inner cities.

The depth of African-American frustration with the Korean entrepreneurial economy exploded into the national limelight with the Los Angeles riots of 1992. Ironically, the triggering event for the riot did not involve Korean Americans at all. When an all-white jury in Simi Valley, California, acquitted the Los Angeles police officers accused of beating Rodney King, enraged African Americans hit the streets in an orgy of looting and arson. Looters began targeting Korean-owned businesses, stealing their contents and then setting them on fire. When the Los Angeles police proved unable to provide protection to business owners, they hired private Korean security groups, complete with automatic weapons, to protect their property. In the wake of the riots, groups like the Korean Association of Southern California, the Korean Chamber of Commerce, and the Korean National Association all protested the treatment they had received, and at the same time began trying to reach out to representatives of the African-American community to prevent such violence in the future. The images of the riots, however, had a chilling effect on people back in Korea, who began to wonder about the reality of stability and opportunity in America.

The Indochinese

One of the most dramatic outcomes of the Vietnam War was the series of demographic changes that occurred throughout Indochina. Social scientists around the world have long realized that immigration does not begin in a vaccuum; long before people begin moving across continents, they begin moving within their own countries because of major social and economic changes occurring around them. The great migration of people from Indochina to the United States in the late 1970s and 1980s fits that demographic pattern. During the 1950s and 1960s, the American presence in Indochina stimulated monumental demographic changes. In 1954, nearly one million Roman Catholics from North Vietnam relocated to South Vietnam under protocols established by the Geneva Accords. As more and more American money poured into South Vietnam beginning in the early 1960s and especially after 1964, the country's economy changed. South Vietnamese gravitated toward Saigon looking for jobs spawned by the American war machine. Between 1960 and 1970, the population of Saigon increased from just over one million to nearly four million people. Most were peasants who had lived their lives in rural villages. The sheer destructiveness of the war, in which thousands of villages throughout South Vietnam were blown up, set in motion a vast migration within South Vietnam, as did United States policies to resettle peasants into militarily secure areas. Even in Thailand, which was not directly part of the Vietnam War (at least not in the same way Vietnam, Cambodia, and Laos were), the economic impact triggered a large emigration to the United States.

Similar demographic changes came to Laos and Cambodia. The American invasion of Cambodia in 1970 drove large numbers of Vietcong and North Vietnamese soldiers deeper into Cambodia, and it had the same effect on Cambodian peasants. The population of Phnom Penh grew dramatically in the 1960s and 1970s as peasants headed for the city where they thought they might be free of military action at the hands of American soldiers and bombers and various factions of Cambodian guerrillas. In Laos, the Central Intelligence Agency recruited an army among the Hmong tribe to fight the Vietcong and North Vietnamese along the Ho Chi Minh trail. The combined American–South Vietnamese invasion of Laos in 1971 also destabilized hundreds of communities throughout the country.

The war in Southeast Asia and its aftermath stimulated the exodus of more than one million people to the United States. Between 1970 and 1992, approximately 120,000 people came from Thailand, and nearly 140,000 came from Cambodia. Laos sent aproximately 190,000 people to the United States, and more than 550,000 Vietnamese crossed the Pacific to America.

The story of the Indochinese migration to the United States is still incomplete, although historians now identify three basic stages of the immigration process. Until the early 1960s, there were only a handful of Vietnamese, Cambodians, and Laotians in the United States. Most of them were students enrolled in scientific and engineering programs at American universities. Those numbers increased along with the American escalation of the war in the 1960s, but even then the number of permanent Indochinese immigrants living in the United States numbered only a few thousand people. Many of them were the wives of American soldiers who had completed a tour of duty in South Vietnam. By 1975 a total of only 20,038 Indochinese immigrants had settled in the United States within the previous decade. The vast majority were Vietnamese. The Immigration and Naturalization Service did not even keep track of the number of Laotians and Cambodians because there were so few of them.

The second wave of Indochinese immigrants began in 1975 when North Vietnam completed its conquest of South Vietnam, the Khmer Rouge overran Phnom Penh, and the Pathet Lao assumed power in Laos. Indochina had fallen to the Communists, and those Indochinese who came to the United States consisted of the people most closely associated, politically and economically, with the anticommunist regimes of Nguyen Van Thieu in South Vietnam, Lon Nol in Cambodia, and Souvanna Phouma in Laos. The initial wave of Indochinese immigrants after the Communist takeover totaled approximately 170,000 people, of whom 155,000 were Vietnamese, 7,500 were Cambodians, and 7,500 were Laotians. The vast majority were former employees of the United States or of the previous regimes. More than 40 percent of the Vietnamese were Roman Catholics who had been born in North Vietnam, migrated south in 1954, and then worked for South Vietnam during the intervening twenty years. Most of the Laotian immigrants were Hmong tribespeople who had cooperated with the CIA in attacking the North Vietnamese during the war. By the end of 1975, the United States had received 130,000 Indochinese refugees at receiving centers in Guam and the Philippines, while another 60,000 were waiting in refugee camps in Hong Kong and Thailand.

This second wave of Vietnamese immigrants tended to be well educated and blessed with good job and professional skills. Back in South Vietnam they had been large landowners, physicians, dentists, attorneys, civil servants, small businesspeople, and employees of large United States corporations doing business in South Vietnam; when they settled in the United States, they brought their educations and entrepreneurial skills with them. Many were Roman Catholics and already spoke English, or at least understood English. They were accustomed to the economic and social rhythms of modern industrial society, and they had enjoyed substantial contact with Americans during the previous ten years. Their culture shock on arrival, though considerable, was less dramatic than what subsequent waves of Vietnamese immigrants would undergo.

The third wave of Indochinese immigrants began arriving in the United States in the late 1970s and continued throughout the 1980s. They were political and economic refugees from the brutal and ineffective policies imposed by the Communist regimes after 1975 in Vietnam, Laos, and Cambodia. North Vietnam reunited the country under the name Socialist Republic of Vietnam, and political authorities in Hanoi implemented sweeping collectivization schemes all over the economy of the former South Vietnam. The economies of Vietnam and Cambodia (Kampuchea) went into tailspins. Gross national product fell dramatically, as did labor productivity. Income levels fell precipitously as capital and the countries' most talented people fled. In addition to the Communists' policies, the economies of Indochina were suffering from rapid drop in American spending, which had fueled income and employment for the previous decade. Large numbers of Vietnamese and Cambodians suddenly found themselves living in cities but out of work.

The Communist takeover also led to a variety of ethnic discriminations throughout Indochina. In Laos, the Hmong and Mien tribespeople who had cooperated with the Americans found themselves the objects of discrimination. In Cambodia, the Vietnamese and Cham Muslims became the objects of scorn by the ruling Khmer majority. The ethnic Chinese in Saigon, as well as the ethnic Khmers in the Mekong Delta, were targeted for discrimination by the Vietnamese government. Also, the rural mountain peoples of Laos and Vietnam, particularly those who were living in the cities, were treated as second-class citizens by the more urbane groups in Cambodia and Vietnam. Because of the ethnic discrimination, there were strong pockets of discontented people anxious to leave their respective countries.

In addition to severe economic and social problems imposed by Communist economic dictates and the end of United States military spending there, the people of Indochina were also suffering from severe political problems. The government of the Socialist Republic of Vietnam began relocating large numbers of southern Vietnamese out of Saigon back to the countryside, and many former employees of the United States and South Vietnam who had not been able to escape in 1975 found themselves subject to political "re-education." Politically suspect individuals were forced into re-education camps in rural areas where they engaged in hard manual labor, received political indoctrination, and participated in mortification programs where they confessed their sins. Once political authorities decided they were "rehabilitated," they were reassigned to new jobs, usually where their skills could be employed effectively. International human rights authorities protested the entire business, but to little avail.

However, the violation of civil rights in Vietnam was nothing compared to the genocidal rage that swept through Cambodia in the late 1970s. Pol Pot and the Khmer Rouge came to power and launched a liquidation campaign aimed at eliminating everyone who had ever held political power in Cambodia, who had worked as a professional or intellectual, who had owned a small business, or who had worked for a foreign entity—in short everyone except peasants. Declaring "Year Zero," Pol Pot and the Khmer Rouge virtually depopulated the cities and major towns of Cambodia and went on a killing rampage. Some scholars and American intelligence experts estimate that between 1975 and 1979, when Vietnam invaded Cambodia in order to stop the slaughter, the Khmer Rouge assassinated more than one million people, including the elite and middle-class of the entire country.

It was these economic, social, and political disasters in the late 1970s and 1980s that produced the third wave of Indochinese immigration to the United States. These immigrants tended to be less educated than the original wave, and they were more ethnically diverse, often consisting of Vietnamese, Cambodians, Cham, Hmong, Mien, Chinese, and a variety of other tribal people from the highlands. Comparatively few of them were Roman Catholics. They were desperate to escape the political oppression and economic blight of Indochina. Many of them also had family members who had already escaped to the United States with the earlier immigrants. They came out of Vietnam, Cambodia, and Laos illegally, either crossing overland through the mountains and jungles into Thailand, where they ended up in refugee camps or escaped by sea in boats.

By far most of the Indochinese who got away after 1976 left by sea in small boats, hoping to make it to Indonesia, Thailand, Malaysia, or the Philippines. Demographers now estimate that as many as 1.3 million people fled Indochina by boat, earning the title "boat people." Their voyages were beset with danger. Pirates in the South China Sea regularly victimized them, and Indonesia and Malaysia, and later Hong Kong, frequently rejected them even when they did make landfall. Most historians suspect that only half of those who left Indochina in boats survived the journey.

At first the United States welcomed the new immigrants. Congress passed the Indochinese Migration and Refugee Assistance Act of 1975; renewed in 1977, it provided unprecedented economic assistance to the immigrants. The United States government took a systematic approach to the settlement of the Indochinese refugees, making sure that they were not concentrated in any single geographic location. Thousands of small and large communities throughout the United States were asked to sponsor immigrant families, and the government often employed the services of local charitable organizations and churches in settling the immigrants into apartments, jobs, and schools. Most Americans, even those who opposed the war, felt a certain responsibility toward its victims. The government paid for their air fare to the United States, extended loans for those who wanted to start businesses of their own, and provided scholarship assistance for Vietnamese children wishing to attend college. The federal government also provided funds to local school districts to assist them in teaching the Vietnamese immigrants.

But that assistance was not permanent. The third-wave immigrants who came to the United States in the late 1970s and 1980s were not as well educated or as well off as the first immigrants. They came from rural backgrounds and did not adjust as well to economic life in America. Because they came in such large numbers, they raised nativist concerns in the United States. The country was full of American veterans who did not like the Vietnamese anyway, and economic problems in the United States created fears that the immigrants would take jobs from natives and lower the prevailing wage levels. Another problem involved the definition of a refugee. The term "refugee" in United States immigration refers to an individual who is fleeing his or her homeland to escape political repression and persecution. The United States does not recognize poverty or economic suffering, at least in terms of conferring refugee status, and the Immigration and Naturalization Service began denying entry to many Vietnamese in the 1980s on the grounds that they were not true political refugees.

For some of the immigrants, especially uneducated rural peasants and mountain people from the Central Highlands of South Vietnam and Laos, the adjustment was particularly difficult. By 1992 there were more than 250,000 Hmong and Mien tribespeople from Laos and Montagnards from South Vietnam living in the United States. The Laotian tribespeople were concentrated in Fresno, Sacramento, and Oakland, California, while thousands of Montagnards settled in North Carolina. Because most of them were essentially a premodern people practicing an animistic religion before the Vietnam War, their arrival in California in the late 1970s was an especially wrenching experience. Many of the mountain people went into clinical depressions after their arrival in the United States, and an astonishingly large number of them died of a type of sudden-death syndrome.

Like other immigrants who came before them, the Indochinese have created a vibrant community life in the United States. During the 1980s, most of them gravitated to urban centers, especially in the West and Southwest, where the presence of tens of thousands of other Indochinese gave them a sense of community and security. They formed Buddhist churches or groups within Roman Catholic parishes, and they established a variety of community groups, such as the Cambodian Association of San Diego, California, and the Association for the Positive Promotion of Lao Ethics. Vietnamese newspapers like *Dat Lanh* and *Thong Bao* and *Chan Troi Moi* appeared. The Vietnamese are unique among Asian immigrants—not nearly as clannish as the Chinese, but not as assimilationist as the Japanese.

In 1992, only seventeen years had passed since the end of the Vietnam War and the beginning of the large-scale Indochinese migration to the United States. A total of more than one million people from Indochina had settled here. Like other immigrant groups, the Indochinese had stirred up resentment as well as admiration among Americans, and they had established the necessary ethnic institutions to maintain their personal identity and begin the assimilation process in the United States. At the present time there are tens of thousands of Vietnamese languishing in refugee camps in Thailand, Malaysia, Indonesia, and Hong Kong waiting for the chance to come to the United States; hundreds of thousands more in Vietnam are hoping for the same opportunity.

Yellow Power: The Asian-American Movement

In the 1970s Asian Americans still felt the pull of family and tradition. The Asian family had always been the basic institution of society; power flowed from a patriarchal father and loyalty was authoritarian. Individual behavior was a reflection on the family, and children were expected to be ambitious and successful. Independence was discouraged. Peace and harmony were primary values, and family members were expected to contain disruptive feelings. Throughout much of Asian America the traditional values of formal personal relations, inhibition of strong feelings, obedience to authority, loyalty to family, and high educational and occupational achievement continued to be important.

But in American society the emphasis was on individualism, freedom of expression, and equality, even though discrimination often contradicted those values. Equality for Asian Americans seemed to require a movement against Old World values as well as against American discrimination. As a result, Asian Americans in the 1970s and 1980s underwent an identity crisis, and when some groups began demanding equality, their approach seemed more subdued than that of other ethnic groups. Although they tried to create a pan-Asian spirit that crossed cultural lines, the basic differences among Japanese, Chinese, Koreans, Filipinos, and Indochinese were impossible to overcome. Differences in their social and economic condition also helped to prevent the growth of a unified movement for yellow power. While many native-born Chinese Americans and nearly all Japanese Americans had achieved middle-class prosperity, the Filipinos, Khmers, Hmongs, and Vietnamese were still poor, as were the new immigrant Chinese.

The yellow-power movement, then, was handicapped from the beginning, especially by its inability to appeal to influential Japanese and Chinese Americans. Still, there were manifestations of Asian-American discontent. On Hawaii in the 1970s militant Polynesians in the Protect Kahoolawe Ohana occupied parts of the island of Maui, sacred homeland of their rain goddess Hina, and demanded the end of

U.S. Navy test bombings there. In California, Filipino farm workers continued their labor union activities. The Asian-American Political Alliance, a largely Japanese group, worked to create Asian studies programs on college campuses, as did the Intercollegiate Chinese for Social Action. In the 1980s both of those groups, as well as more traditional Asian-American organizations, also protested policies in California state universities that placed informal quotas on the numbers of Asian being admitted. The SAT scores of Chinese, Japanese, Korean, and Vietnamese high school seniors were high enough that they alone could fill most of the freshman classes at the major California universities. And a few minor radical groups such as the Red Guards and the Third World Liberation Front advocated violence to redesign society. Their appeal was hopelessly limited and their clientele small. But even if the yellow-power movement had no real hope of effecting revolutionary change, Asian Americans in general were more concerned about equality than ever before and less willing to return to the submissive collective conformity of earlier years.

Chapter Fifteen

The Newest Arrivals

Historians now identify four general periods of immigration to the United States. Although each period reflected unique circumstances, the primary reason for the mass movement of more than fifty million people in the past three hundred years has been economic. During the colonial period, some groups of English Puritans and German Quakers came to the New World in order to worship as they saw fit, but most of the English, Scots Irish, Scots, German, and Dutch immigrants simply wanted land of their own. It was economic opportunity, not religion, that brought most colonial immigrants to America.

The second wave of immigration to the United States began in the 1790s once the political instability following the American Revolution abated. Rapid population increases in Europe, the industrialization of production, and the commercialization of agriculture combined to create a large group of highly mobile workers searching for jobs and/or land. The flow of immigrants from Germany accelerated dramatically, as did the arrival of Swedish, Norwegian, and Danish settlers, all of whom wanted land. The potato famine drove more than 2 million people out of Ireland and toward the New World in the 1840s and 1850s. A powerful anti-Catholic movement emerged in the United States because of the Irish and German immigrants. During these years, approximately 300,000 Chinese immigrants came to the United

States as well, until the protests of labor unions restricted that movement after 1882. Except for the Chinese and the Irish, most of the immigrants were Protestants who found farmland in America. The second period of American immigration has been known as the Old Immigration.

The third wave, the so-called New Immigration, began in the 1880s when economic changes reached eastern and southern Europe. Millions of Poles, Czechs, Russians, Jews, Slovaks, Italians, Slovenians, Croatians, Serbians, and Ukrainians came to the United States, as did several hundred thousand Japanese. Most of these immigrants were Roman Catholics or Jews, and they arrived after the best land had already been taken. Taking up residence in cities and jobs in the mines and mills of industrial America, they were highly visible and inspired a nativist reaction from Protestant working-class groups. The nativist fears eventually lead to the National Origins Act of 1924, which severely limited immigration. Indeed, through the use of quotas, this law practically stopped the flow of immigrants from eastern and southern Europe and from Japan.

But in the last twenty years, a new shift has occurred in American immigration patterns, with the number of people from Europe steadily declining and the numbers from the rest of the world increasing dramatically. Throughout United States history, Americans have struggled to come to terms with their diversity. Except for the racial division between Africans and whites, the vast majority of those immigrants shared a broad cultural heritage based on a European background and a Judeo-Christian tradition, but despite this they have had difficulty reconciling their differences.

Those differences of the past, however, pale in comparison to the diversity of contemporary American immigrants. Less than 10 percent of the twelve million immigrants coming to the United States between 1980 and 1992 were Europeans. The fourth, or contemporary, wave of immigration has consisted primarily of Hispanic Americans (Mexicans, Puerto Ricans, Cubans, Central Americans, and Caribbean immigrants) and Asians (Chinese, Vietnamese, Koreans, Filipinos, Cambodians, and Asian Indians) who have fled from political instability and economic oppression to the New World. Many of them come from Muslim, Buddhist, Hindu, and animist religious traditions, and their languages and cultural traditions are non-Western. And like every other wave of immigrants, they challenge the prevailing consensus that the United States is a land of tolerance and opportunity.

The Haitians

In recent years, the most controversial of the new immigrants have been coming from Haiti. Although official statistics from the Immigration and Naturalization Service indicate that some 250,000 Haitians have legally entered the United States since 1960, there are today approximately a million Haitians and their American-born children living in the country. At least half of the Haitians living in the United States are undocumented workers who came here via Puerto Rico, Bermuda, Barbados, the Bahamas, Canada, Dominican Republic, or Mexico, where they first went to find jobs. From those regions they have steadily migrated to the United States.

The large-scale Haitian migration to the United States had its origins in 1957, when François Duvalier came to power and inaugurated a brutally repressive political regime. A substantial number of urban professionals and small business entrepreneurs left the island late in the 1950s and early in the 1960s to escape the regime, and most of them settled in New York City. Other Haitian communities appeared in Montreal, Boston, Philadelphia, Washington, and Miami. Economic life in Haiti continued to deteriorate throughout the 1960s and early 1970s and worsened under the political leadership of President-for-Life Jean-Claude Duvalier. By then increasingly large numbers of the urban and rural poor were leaving what had become the poorest country in the Western Hemisphere.

The Haitian immigrants developed a number of important strategies for surviving and succeeding in the United States. They maintained extremely strong kinship systems on the island and used them to their advantage when moving to the United States. Whole extended families would save every penny they could to prepare for the migration, and they then would collectively select the one member of the family most likely to succeed in the United States. That individual would then work in America and send money home to finance the emigration of other family members. The Haitians also established rotating credit pools— similar to those of the Chinese, Japanese, Koreans, and West Indians— to assist people in starting small businesses.

Although life in the United States is far better than the unmitigated economic and political misery endemic to the island, the Haitians nevertheless have faced a variety of challenges here. Because they are African Americans, they encounter the problem of racism that so many immigrants from Africa and the Caribbean have faced. But because they speak a French dialect, not Spanish, they are linguistically separate from the Puerto Ricans, Cubans, and Dominicans in the United States.

Also, many Americans from diverse ethnic backgrounds have found Haitian culture different and peculiar. Haitian religion, for example, has retained powerful African roots and a strong voodoo connection. From the mid-1600s, when the ancestors of present-day Haitians were first transported from Africa to Haiti as slaves, they were forbidden to practice tribal religions. Forced converts to Roman Catholicism, the Haitians refused to abandon voodoo, instead fusing the two into a single religion. Afro-Haitian Catholicism acknowledges God as the creator of heaven and earth, the *Gran Met*, a deity powerful but remote who delegated the mundane management of human affairs to intermediary spirits called *Loa*. Haitians see those spirits everywhere, in trees, ponds, rivers, waterfalls, caves, springs, lakes, valleys, groves. Competition between good and evil spirits is the essence of life, and voodoo Catholicism maintains harmony in the world. Every July 16, Haitians celebrate the *Vyej Marik*, or the apparition of the Virgin of Miracles, Our Lady of Mount Carmel, on top of a palm tree at Ville Bonheur. The annual pilgrimage brings tens of thousands of people into the village—priests and nuns, rich and poor, voodoo practitioners, and wealthy businesspeople—all to propitiate the *Loa Legba* (St. Peter), known as the master of roads and pathways, to make ritual stops at sacred trees, and to wash themselves in the sacred Saut d'Eau waterfalls of the Tombe River. Such voodoo spirits as *Danbala Wedo*, the snake symbol, or *Aida Wedo* or *Ezili Freda* possess the bodies of the worshipers. On the following morning, the pilgrims return to the village square to hear the standard Catholic Mass delivered from the church balcony.

Ever since their first efforts to convert the African slaves, Roman Catholic authorities in Haiti have attempted to suppress the Old World religion. Periodically over the centuries, the church has waged political campaigns against African Catholic syncretic beliefs, the most recent in 1941 when the Haitian government spearheaded an "antisuperstition" crusade involving destruction of temples and sacred natural settings. To the French and Irish priests serving in Haiti throughout the past 350 years, the mixture of formal religion and voodoo was the epitome of sacrilege. The drinking of bull and chicken blood at religious ceremonies, the identification of St. Jacques with the African god of war *Ougou Feray*, the mud baths, and the hexes and charms all alienated the priests, but the traditions survived and came into the dioceses of the American church, especially in Florida, with the wave of Haitian immigrants in the early 1980s.

Many Cuban-American Catholics in Miami and Irish- and Italian-American Catholics in the Northeast felt culturally alienated from the Haitian immigrants, and they resented their arrival, as did many other

Americans concerned in the 1970s and 1980s about Haitians taking jobs from the native born. The Carter administration, and subsequently the Reagan and Bush administrations, refused to acknowledge the Haitians as political refugees, even after the Refugee Act of 1980 defined refugee as any individual with a well-founded fear of discrimination on the basis of race, religion, nationality, or politics. The federal government argued that the Haitians were simply escaping economic poverty, which did not exempt them from existing United States immigration statutes.

Unable to secure enough emigration visas to satisfy the demand for them, thousands of Haitians set off in small, rickety, and overcrowded boats for an 800-mile journey across the Caribbean to Florida, hoping that if they could just get to the United States they could manage to stay. By some estimates more than 50,000 Haitians perished at sea trying to get to the United States. Unlike the Cuban immigrants, the vast majority of whom were accepted immediately on arrival in Florida, the Haitians were jailed in Florida and Puerto Rico while their claims for refugee status were evaluated. The Immigration and Naturalization Service worked diligently at deporting as many of them as possible.

But the double standard—accepting Cuban refugees while rejecting the Haitians—bothered many civil liberties groups and human rights advocates. Back in 1982 federal court orders had mandated the release of all the Haitian detainees pending individual deportation hearings. Those Haitians who were ordered deported usually disappeared into the 500,000-strong Haitian community in New York City. The 1986 Immigration Reform and Control Act awarded resident alien status to all Haitians who could prove they had been in the United States since 1982. Frustrated that so many Haitians were managing to stay in the United States, the Reagan administration ordered the U.S. Coast Guard to interdict the boat people on the high seas before they ever reached American territorial waters. The Bush administration continued this practice, and throughout the late 1980s and early 1990s, American vessels actually physically returned boat people to Haiti.

The Haitian refugee question became a political issue in the presidential election of 1992. After years of military rule, Haiti had returned to democracy when the popularly elected Jean-Bertrand Aristide came to power in 1990. But several months later, early in 1991, the military deposed Aristide and resumed political control of Haiti. The ensuing political instability inspired tens of thousands of Haitians to attempt a crossing of the Caribbean in hope of settling in the United States. The Bush administration continued the Reagan administration's policy of intercepting the boat people on the high seas and forcibly taking them back to Haiti. Democratic candidate Bill Clinton criticized the policy during the 1992 campaign, promising to evaluate each Haitian's refugee status after his or her arrival in the United States. Clinton's victory in the November election inspired hundreds of thousands of Haitians to plan a move to the United States, and all along the coast of the island boats were under construction from November 1992 to January 1993. In a January accident, more than 400 Haitians died when their ship sank in the Caribbean.

When Clinton took office on January 20, the imminent arrival of so many poor Haitian immigrants created a political crisis. The Immigration and Naturalization Service insisted that most of the Haitians entering the United States were fleeing economic hardship, not political persecution. As such, they were not entitled to refugee status and could be deported. With unemployment still a serious problem, as well as racism, there was little sympathy in the United States for the Haitians. Clinton quickly announced his intention to continue the Bush-Reagan policy.

The Muslims

An Arabic-speaking community has existed in the United States since the 1870s, but the vast majority of its members were not Muslims. Perhaps 200,000 Syrians and Lebanese left the Ottoman Empire between 1877 and 1924, most from what became Lebanon in 1945. Most were members of the Syrian Orthodox church or were Roman Catholics of the Uniate tradition, and their faith was blended with ethnic nationalism. They yearned for independence from Turkey, and in the absence of a Syrian nation the Syrian Orthodox church symbolized Syrian patriotism. To discourage nationalism, the Turks had turned on them as they had turned on the Armenians and had slaughtered thousands of people.

The Syrians and Lebanese who escaped to America settled in the cities. The mill towns of New England and New Jersey, the automobile factories of Detroit, the steel centers of western Pennsylvania and eastern Ohio, and the garment districts of New York City all employed Syrian and Lebanese workers. Independent and self-reliant, they became a blue-collar, lower-middle-class community. They had come to America with a talent for enterprise that traced directly back to their great, ancient Aramaean heritage as commercialists in the Fertile Crescent. Thousands worked as peddlers and salesmen, and tiny Syrian and Lebanese communities appeared in most major cities. After saving money and settling down, they often made the transition to shopkeepers, wholesalers, and department-store owners. (By the 1980s, Detroit would become the Arab capital of America with 170,000 Syrians living there.) These Syrians became a middle and upper-middle class in the United States.

In the Old World, Syrian culture had revolved around the extended patriarchal family, the local village, and the church. Immigrants looked on themselves not as Arabs but as Aleppo Melkites (Melkite Uniates from the Aleppo region), or Beirut Maronites (Maronite Uniates), or Zahleh Orthodox. Each family, village, and religion had a value of its own, and people felt comfortable only with their own family, neighbors, and parishioners. America provided them a larger consciousness. Since Melkites, Maronites, and Orthodox Syrians from many villages lived together in ethnic enclaves, many Americans lumped them together as Turks. The Arabic language united them, and village loyalties survived: the Damascus Club, the Aleppian Fraternity, the Becharre Welfare Society attested to the tenacity of community perspectives. But first-generation immigrants also began to see themselves as Syrian Americans.

For thousands of years Syrians had feared "outsiders" and desperately wanted their children to marry people from their own villages. But in the United States, with small clusters of Syrians living in a sea of real outsiders, Syrians in general became insiders, suitable marriage partners for young people. A sense of being Syrian rather than being from a particular village developed among them. The Melkite and Maronite Syrians (Uniate Catholics) gradually accepted Roman Catholicism in the United States: Latin liturgies displaced the Eastern rites in some parishes, and as Melkites and Maronites gained more in common religiously, Syrian ethnicity grew broader.

The Muslim migration to the United States took place in several stages. Between 1875 and 1924 several thousand single, unskilled Arabic-speaking men came from the Ottoman Empire—Syria, Jordan, Palestine, and Lebanon—because they had heard of the success of the Syrian and Lebanese Christians in the United States. They often returned to the Middle East several times before finally settling permanently in the urban areas of the upper Midwest, where they took jobs in mines, mills, and factories. These Arabs constituted the nucleus of the Muslim community in the United States, and between 1924 and 1945 their numbers were augmented by the arrival in America of many of their relatives.

After World War II, the composition of the Muslim community began to change with the arrival of more and more people from India, Pakistan, Yugoslavia, Albania, Bulgaria, and Soviet Central Asia. Although they shared a broad Islamic heritage with the Arab Muslims already in the United States, they were linguistically, racially, and often religiously—Sunnis, Shiites, and Ismailis—different from their Muslim predecessors. Those differences became even more pronounced after 1960 when the number of Muslim immigrants from non-Arabic-speaking regions became dominant. In the 1960s, a total of 34,000 Muslims came to the United States from the Arabic-speaking Middle East, while only 24,000 came from Afghanistan, Turkey, Pakistan, Iran, and Iraq. Those numbers changed in the 1970s to 89,000 Arabic-speaking Muslim immigrants and 130,000 Muslims from the other regions of the Near East, Central Asia, and South Asia. But in the 1980s, while 84,000 Arabic-speaking Muslims settled here, more than 260,000 Muslims came to America from Turkey, Afghanistan, Pakistan, India, Iran, Iraq, and the Soviet Union. Today the Muslim community in the United States includes Albanians, Bosnians, Bulgarians, Libyans, Moroccans, Egyptians, Jordanians, Palestinians, Somalians, Nigerians, Indonesians, Filipinos, Pakistanis, Indians, Afghans, Kazakhs, Turkmen, Kyrgyzians, Turks, Syrians, Lebanese, Azerbaijanis, Caucasians, Iranians, Iraqis, and a host of others.

Life in the United States was a socially complicated matter for Muslim Americans. Although they constituted less than one percent of the American population, foreign affairs in the 1970s, 1980s, and 1990s gave them a highly visible profile. Many Americans were suspicious of the Muslim immigrants, and those suspicions were religiously based. During the 1960s, when the Black Muslims came to national attention, millions of Americans were frightened by the antiwhite rhetoric of people like Malcolm X and Elijah Muhammad. The talk of "white devils" was offensive, and many Americans associated the racist rhetoric with Muslims in general, even though Islam includes people of all racial backgrounds.

The prevailing image of Muslim fanaticism was reinforced by Middle East politics. Ever since 1948, most Americans had sympathized with the fortunes of Israel, much to the consternation of the Arab-American community in particular and the Islamic-American community in general. The energy crisis in the 1970s and early 1980s helped the United States re-evaluate its Middle Eastern policies, but most Americans still associated Islam with fanaticism. The images of Yasir Arafat, with his Palestinian headgear and stubble beard, frightened many people in the 1970s, as did the Ayatollah Khomeini and the fundamentalist revolution in Iran. The 1979–1980 hostage crisis in Iran, as well as the years of controversy over the American hostages in Lebanon during the 1980s and early 1990s, made Muslims appear even more fanatical. So did the terrorist attacks of Libyan leader Mu'ammar al-Gadhafi. Finally, the Gulf War of 1991 against Iraq's

Civil rights leader Jesse Jackson meets with PLO chairman Yasir Arafat.
(UPI/Bettmann Newsphoto)

Saddam Hussein helped reinforce the stereotype and perpetuate the anti-Muslim sentiment held by so many Americans. All of these overseas controversies found political expression in the United States when Muslim Americans and their mosques were targeted for verbal and sometimes physical attacks.

Muslim Americans tried to reverse the stereotypes. Groups like the Arab-American Anti-Discrimination Committee protested the stereotyping of Muslims, as did the Muslim Association of America, the Muslim Student Association, the Organization of Islamic Societies, and the Islamic Society of North America. Islamic mosques appeared in every major American city to serve the spiritual needs of the Muslim community, and Islamic religious leaders tried to interact with other community leaders. But the anti-Muslim stereotypes and the negative stereotypes of the Middle East that appeared so regularly in the American media were difficult to combat.

In addition to discrimination, Muslim Americans also encountered the same pressures to assimilate that all immigrants to the United States have faced. In school and in the workplace, it has been very difficult for Muslim Americans to respond to daily prayer calls or to get time off to celebrate Islamic holidays or attend Friday prayer services at their mosques. Observing the fast during Ramadan—an annual month-long observance in which Muslims are not to have food or water during daylight hours—poses challenges, especially when Ramadan falls during summer months when days are long and fellow workers are eating and drinking. Avoiding the use of alcohol and finding foods free of pork have also been problems.

Muslim immigrants have also been confounded by gender values in the United States. Arab values traditionally defined male honor in terms of the responsibility of men to protect women from the threats inherent in the public world of other males. Islamic values provide rigid definitions of the public roles of men and women; problems inevitably result when immigrants arrive in the United States, where women enjoy far more freedom to make their own financial, sexual, and cultural decisions. During the 1970s and 1980s, when Islamic fundamentalism swept the Near East and Middle East, Muslims rejected Western approaches to modesty, honor, and morality; for more recent Muslim immigrants to the United States, the gender values of America seem even more astonishing. It is common in many Muslim homes to blame the problems of teenage pregnancy, divorce, family disintegration, and pornography in America on the public freedom extended to women.

African Americans from the West Indies

Between 1890 and 1930 more than 350,000 West Indian blacks immigrated to the United States, most of them from the British West Indies—Barbados, Bermuda, Jamaica, Trinidad, Tobago, Bahamas, Turks and Caicos, Antigua, Barbuda, Redonda, St. Kitts, the Virgin Islands, Dominica, Grenada, Nevis, St. Lucia, St. Vincent, and the Grenadines. They settled primarily in northeastern cities, especially New York, and worked at a number of different occupations. Although they faced the same prejudice as African Americans from the South, they kept their distance from other blacks because of cultural differences. Coming mostly from British backgrounds, they spoke standard English and shared middle-class traditions with other Americans. Most were Episcopalian or Roman Catholic, status conscious and upwardly mobile, and competitive. West Indians became prominent in the needle trades and clothing workers' unions and were the elite in the cigar-making industry of New York. By the 1930s, most of New York's African-American doctors, dentists, lawyers, and business people were of West Indian descent.

Like the Chinese hui kuan, West Indian rotating credit associations helped immigrant entrepreneurs get a financial start. Those credit associations—called *ensusu*—originated in West Africa in the fifteenth century, and the Africans being taken as slaves to the West Indies managed to bring the institution with them. Because Africans greatly outnumbered the English whites on the islands and were organized into large labor units, the ensusu survived into the present. The West Indians emigrating to the United States brought the ensusu with them to provide the venture capital they needed to establish ethnic businesses. Coming from predominantly African-American cultures in the West Indies, they were generally a proud and secure people.

In the years following World War II, the migration of African Americans from the West Indies accelerated. During the 1950s, approximately 60,000 people immigrated to the United States from the British West Indies, with Barbados, Jamaica, and Trinidad and Tobago contributing the bulk of the immigrants. Between 1960 and 1970, that number increased to 105,000 people; 225,000 people arrived in the 1970s and 240,000 in the 1980s. Most of the West Indians settled in New York and New Jersey, as their predecessors had.

Observers in both the white and African-American communities wondered why the West Indian immigrants and their descendants— from Malcolm X to Colin L. Powell, chairman of the Joint Chiefs of Staff in the 1980s and early 1990s—seemed more likely to succeed in the United States than African Americans whose ancestors had spent their lives in the South. Although both groups had their origins in the same tribal societies of West Africa in the seventeenth and eighteenth centuries, and both groups encountered racial prejudice, a West-Indian African American was ten times more likely than an African American from the South to own a successful business or secure a professional education, and family incomes were three times as high.

The reasons for the discrepancy seemed clear to many ethnographers. The British West Indies were for the most part all-black societies, even during the centuries of slavery when whites were absentee owners who used resident African Americans to run their sugar plantations. Black slaves on those plantations functioned in all-African societies and did not have to spend their lives responding to the daily whims of white people who looked down on them as inferiors. Also, Great Britain abolished slavery in 1830 and then introduced relatively high-quality public schools to the islands. By the time the West Indians began immigrating to the United States, they were well educated, success-oriented, and accustomed to making their own decisions. Black people from the South, on the other hand, had spent their lives in the presence of their white owners with little freedom or opportunity to make their own decisions. Although slavery was abolished in the United States in 1865, African Americans in the South endured another century of brutal oppression, poor educational systems, and lack of economic opportunity. It was hardly surprising that the West Indians were more prepared for success in urban America than their brothers and sisters from the American South.

Asian Indians

Another major new immigrant group to arrive in the United States during the 1970s and 1980s came from India. Initially these settlers were called Hindus by some Americans, but scholars referred to them as East Indians to differentiate them from native Americans, who for centuries were known as American Indians. By the early 1990s the term Asian Indians was most commonly used to describe immigrants from India. Many scholars include them in discussions of other Asian immigrants such as the Chinese, Japanese, Koreans, and Vietnamese, but unlike those groups, the Asian Indians did not come from a Buddhist culture. They were either Hindus, Sikhs, or Muslims, and their historical experience was quite unlike that of East Asians and Southeast Asians. During the 1960s, approximately 31,000 Asian Indians came to the United States, but those numbers jumped to 177,000 in the 1970s and 270,000 in the 1980s.

During the 1860s and 1870s, labor recruiters from sugar plantations in Hawaii began recruiting workers from India, most of whom were Sikh farmers from the Punjab region. That recruitment process ended in the 1880s when Hawaiian planters started recruiting Japanese workers. By the early 1900s some of those Asian Indians had left Hawaii for jobs on the mainland, where they worked in railroad construction, the timber industry, and commercial agriculture. The 1920 census placed the number of immigrant Asian Indians living in the United States at approximately 6,400 people.

But like the Chinese and then the Japanese immigrants, the Asian Indians soon found themselves the objects of intense discrimination. Since most of them were Sikhs, they stood out because of their obligatory "five Ks"—*kes* (unshorn hair and beard), *kacch* (knee-length trousers), *kara* (iron bangle), *kirpan* (sword) and *khanga* (hair comb). Asian Indians were universally recognizable by their turbans. Although they were a Caucasian people with roots in Aryan India, their dark skins brought intense racial discrimination. The American Federation of Labor began protesting Indian immigration in the early 1900s, and white workers frequently rioted against them. In September 1907, for example, hundreds of white workers attacked the Asian-Indian community in Bellingham, Washington, and drove several hundred Asian Indians across the border into Canada. The Asian Exclusion League also began targeting them for immigration restriction on the grounds that they were a nonwhite and non-Christian people. In 1917, Congress enacted legislation designating India as one of the Asian countries in a "barred zone" and prohibited the entry of new Asian Indian workers. The 1923 Supreme Court decision in *U.S. v. Bhagat Singh Thind* ruled that Indians were not really Caucasians "except in the dim past," and that therefore immigration restriction was justified. Between 1920 and 1940 more than 3,000 Asian Indians returned home to India. By 1945, there were only 1,500 of them left in the United States.

During the 1950s and early 1960s a trickle of Indian immigrants continued to the United States, and by the time of the Immigration and Nationality Act of 1965, they numbered 10,000 people. But the legislation led to a veritable explosion in Asian-Indian immigration. By 1970, more than 20,000 immigrants from Pakistan—most of them Sikhs from the Pakistan Punjab—had arrived in the United States, and another 450,000 people, mostly from India, had arrived by 1990.

The second wave of Indian immigration, however, was quite different from the first. Instead of being farm laborers, most immigrants were highly educated professionals from urban areas. They were English-speaking, middle-class people who had been to college and were used to life in modern economic society. The problem they faced in India involved underemployment and even unemployment of college-educated people. India could not absorb economically all of the physicians and engineers it was producing. They came to the United States primarily for economic reasons, and they made the most of their opportunities. By 1992 more than half the Asian Indians living in the United States were business managers and professionals. Among them were more than 30,000 physicians and dentists, 50,000 engineers and computer-science professionals, 20,000 scientists with doctoral degrees, and several thousand attorneys and accountants. Tens of thousands of Indian immigrants launched their own small businesses—travel agencies, newsstands, fast-food restaurants, luncheonettes, sari shops, gas stations, independent convenience stores, and motels.

Unlike many other immigrant groups, the Asian Indians were not as likely to concentrate demographically in one region. More than one-third of them live in the cities of the Northeast, and one-fifth live in the New York City–New Jersey corridor. Several blocks of Sixth Street in New York City are known today as "Little India." But because of their business and professional skills, the Asian Indians have settled near their careers, and that has dispersed them across the urban landscape of the United States. In spite of their demographic dispersal and economic success, however, the Asian Indians have encountered a good deal of prejudice and discrimination, especially in the Northeast. Their dark skins have set them apart from the surrounding working-class white population, and their Hindu, Muslim, and Sikh faiths have distinguished them from local Jews and Christians. Many whites and African Americans resent the economic success of the Asian Indians, and there have been hate crimes committed against them in New York City and New Jersey as recently as 1993. The Indian Association of America has protested those attacks and is working diligently to make sure that Asian Indians enjoy the full benefit of civil liberties in the United States.

Chapter Sixteen

Native Americans in the Modern World

Following World War II, native Americans, like everyone else, were trying to cope with changes in political and social affairs as well as in their own circumstances. In 1945, they were still recovering from the wars of the nineteenth century and the Dawes Act; and although the Indian Reorganization Act of 1934 had restored tribal autonomy and tried to revive the reservation economy, poverty continued to plague them. Most still lived on the reservations, but by 1990 nearly 900,000 would be living in urban areas. Native America remained a diverse collection of cultures, but important and inevitable changes were occurring. One was the decline of native American languages. Every immigrant coming to America had watched the Old World language weaken and disappear after the first generation, and a similar, if slower, trend was taking place in native America. By 1990, of more than six hundred languages once spoken, only forty—including Cherokee, Creek, Crow, and Navajo—had more than a thousand fluent adherents. The disappearance of native tongues by no means signaled the end of tribal ethnicity, but the widespread use of English indicated an increasing accommodation to white society.

Some native American nations were more acculturated than others. The Hupas of California, for example, turned from traditional rites and subsistence living and adopted the tastes of white society, buying cars, television sets, appliances, and fast-food meals with money from tribal timber leases. The native language disappeared along with the old ways of hunting, fishing, dancing, and worshiping. Other nations were hardly acculturated at all. The Hopis isolated themselves, nurtured traditional ceremonies, and kept their links to the past through reservation institutions including museums and cultural centers. Some native Americans lived in cities and had no manifest ties to their ancestral civilization, preferring instead to function exclusively in white society. Some nations mixed the two worlds. On the Blackfoot reservation, acculturated native Americans working in the white economy lived as neighbors to others who rarely left the reservation. On the Sioux reservation at Pine Ridge, South Dakota, there were tribal murals and symbols inside the Catholic church, tribal signs on priestly vestments, and a mass with a sacred peace-pipe ceremony in place of the traditional Eucharist. No statement can describe the degree of acculturation for all native America, but it was continuing if only at the most primitive levels. Searching for their identity in the midst of vast changes, native Americans would join white liberals in opposing discrimination, but they would lack the political power of other minorities. While African Americans numbered more than 30 million people in 1990 and Mexican Americans more than 18 million, there were only 1.8 million native Americans. African Americans and Mexican Americans had some political power because of the votes they could mobilize, but native American power was much more ephemeral, highly dependent on white opinion. Much of white liberalism in the 1960s rose from a sense of guilt about past sins. While African Americans and Mexican Americans were able to exploit the repentant attitudes of whites as well as exercise their own political power, native Americans had to rely on white help alone to generate social and political change. When ethnic activism became strong in the 1960s, other minorities broke with white liberals and took control of their own movements, but native Americans could ill afford to alienate white supporters. That fact alone made the 1970s and 1980s a period of confusion and stress, with native Americans wondering if they could maintain the modest gains of recent years.

The Termination Program

After World War II, a conservative mood blanketed America, and people yearned for more tranquil times when change had been slower and values more constant. Voices from the past sounded again. The National Council of Churches had commissioned a study of its mission system in 1944, and talk of assimilating native Americans reemerged. Anglo-conformity had returned to Indian affairs. At the same time, the postwar boom in recreational camping turned the attention of white developers back to the reservations. They wanted to turn native American land into large commercial farms or resort developments, to employ it "productively." Ever since 1934, western congressmen had unsuccessfully tried to repeal the Indian Reorganization Act, dissolve the tribes, nullify their corporate authority, and remove native American land from its trust status.

Conservative whites wanted to resolve all native American land claims against the federal government and assimilate the native American people. Some native American nations had been trying for years to recover damages from the federal government for fraudulent treaty arrangements; to settle those disputes, Congress created the Indian Claims Commission in 1946. Native Americans immediately filed 852 claims for more than $1.2 billion, each claim arguing that the government had undervalued the land when the first treaties were negotiated. The Creeks, for example, had received $600,000 for Civil War property losses, and the Kiowas, Apaches, and Comanches a total of $2 million for undervalued real estate. Responding to a claim initiated by the Utes in the 1930s, the Indian Claims Commission awarded them $32 million in 1951. Except for the Ute settlement, however, the commission had awarded only $17.7 million by 1959. When the commission ceased to operate in 1978, over $800 million had been awarded on 285 claims out of the 852 originally filed. Like the Utes, some nations received very large settlements. The eight claims of the California nations resulted in a $29 million payment, while $16 million went to the Chiricahua Apaches, $14,364,000 to the Oklahoma Cherokees, $10,242,000 to the Crows, $15 million to the Cheyennes-Arapahos, $8,500,000 to the Mescalero Apaches, and $15,790,000 to the northern Paiutes. Other settlements were quite small; for example, the Poncas received only $2,500.

It became obvious that satisfactory settlement of all the claims would be impossible, but the attempt did pave the way for the so-called termination program. In 1950, President Truman appointed Dillon S. Myer commissioner of Indian affairs. Previously employed by the War Relocation Authority, Myer was an assimilationist who had tried to scatter Japanese Americans among the general population in 1945. He brought that same commitment to the Bureau of Indian Affairs, hoping to dissolve the reservations and disperse native Americans throughout the country. On August 1, 1953, Congress inaugurated the termination program, passing resolutions removing federal authority over all native Americans, ending their status as wards of the United States and granting them all the privileges of citizenship. State and local governments were to take legal jurisdiction over the reservations, and federal authority would be terminated.

During the Eisenhower administration, Congress terminated several nations in western Oregon, the Alabama-Coushattas in Texas, the Utes and Paiutes in Utah, the Klamaths in Oregon, and the Menominees in Wisconsin. More than 1.6 million acres of reservation land fell into white hands between 1953 and 1956. Without federal funds and with tribal corporate power negated, terminated native Americans had no means of livelihood and sold their land to support themselves. The Klamaths and Menominees suffered especially heavy losses. In 1953, about two thousand Klamaths owned more than 700,000 richly forested acres on the Oregon coast. When termination began, each Klamath could choose to leave his share of the property in a tribal trust or accept its cash value of $44,000. Most took the money and surrendered their claims in tribal property. Some of the land was sold to private interests, some reverted to the federal government, and local Oregon businesses leased the rest. The Menominees numbered more than three thousand people and owned 234,000 acres of prime timber land in 1953. They controlled the reservation completely; produced lumber through their own logging and sawmill operations; supported their own schools and hospitals; maintained roads, plants, and buildings; and sustained their own police department. But termination created a new county for them and a corporation to manage assets; it also subjected the Menominee nation to local and state taxes, ended federal assistance, and destroyed the reservation lumber industry. Poverty and unemployment ensued. Termination was a step backward, an assault on tribalism reflecting the values of the nineteenth rather than the twentieth century. Native Americans and white liberals bitterly protested the program. Earl Old Person, head of the Blackfoot tribe, said:

> It is important to note that in our Indian language the only translation for termination is to "wipe out" or "kill off". . . how can we plan our future when the Indian Bureau threatens to wipe us out as a race? It is like trying to cook a meal in your tipi when someone is standing outside trying to burn the tipi down. *

Ralph Nader denounced termination while he was editor of the *Harvard Law School Record* in 1957, and a number of liberal journals, including *Christian Century*, *Harper's*, and *Nation*, openly criticized government policy. The National Congress of American Indians, a native American lobbying group formed in 1944, condemned termination, as did the Indian Rights Association and the Association of American Indian Affairs. By 1956 the antitermination movement had become so strong that President Eisenhower called a halt to the termination program except in cases where individual nations requested it. Once again the federal government was supporting tribal control of Indian land.

*Quoted in Angie Debo, A *History of the Indians of the United States* (Norman, Okla., 1970), p. 307.

The New Native American Movement

After more than three hundred years, white society still failed to grasp the essence of native American life. Poverty stalked the reservations, and nearly three out of four individuals had incomes below the national average. Infant mortality rates were twice the national average; tuberculosis seven times as high; and life expectancy nearly ten years lower. By most economic indicators native Americans were far worse off than other Americans, and white liberals as well as native Americans blamed the federal government for their plight. But while whites looked on reservation life in terms of the pathology of poverty, native Americans remained drawn irresistibly to the security of that environment. Whites were sympathetic about native American poverty, but native Americans had always been nonmaterialistic and noncompetitive, more concerned with the spiritual than the temporal. They had found freedom and tolerance within their communities, where they were at peace with their environment. True, they were poor by general standards, but they still nurtured a positive self-image based on a rich cultural heritage. And when white liberals proposed the same job-training programs for them that they proposed for African Americans—preparation for jobs that would incorporate native Americans into the white economy— many objected, arguing that they were more interested in making the reservations self-sufficient than in joining white society.

But there was one major change in native American attitudes. For the first time they began transcending tribal cultures for an "Indian" ethnicity. At the turn of the century peyotism, the Ghost Dance, the Sun Dance, and the Society of American Indians had brought some spirit of pan-Indian ethnicity. The formation of the National Congress of American Indians represented a more advanced stage of the movement, even though tribal differences were still too powerful to allow a self-conscious sense of interrelationship among all native Americans. Then, as part of the termination program, the Bureau of Indian Affairs (BIA) relocated thousands to the cities where more economic opportunities supposedly existed. The BIA's goal, of course, was for native Americans to acculturate into American society. Instead of assimilating, however, they congregated in ghetto colonies in Los Angeles, San Francisco, Salt Lake City, Phoenix, Denver, Chicago, and dozens of smaller cities. In the cities they also associated closely with native Americans from other native American nations. Facing poverty, discrimination, and the anonymity of urban life, yet detached from normal tribal relationships, they began to develop a group unity that crossed tribal lines and laid the foundation for the broad native American organizations that would emerge in the 1960s, 1970s, and

1980s. Marriages between members of different native American nations also became common in the cities and helped generate a pan-Indian perspective.

The civil rights movement made white people more sensitive to native American culture and society. Universities such as Stanford and Dartmouth abandoned the name "Indians" as titles for their sports teams. Stereotypical stories about native Americans, in which white successes were always "victories" and Indian successes always "massacres," appeared less frequently in the media. Films such as *Little Big Man* (1970) and *A Man Called Horse* (1972) showed native Americans in a sympathetic light, as did the Advertising Council's antipollution commercials featuring an Indian disappointed at civilization's rape of the land. Individual episodes of television programs like "The Waltons" and "Little House on the Prairie" presented positive images of native American values. Books critical of white history and attitudes, including Dee Brown's *Bury My Heart at Wounded Knee* (1970) and Vine Deloria's *Custer Died for Your Sins* (1969), became best-sellers. Guilty about past discriminations and prepared for change by the black rebellions of the 1960s, white Americans had become more sympathetic to native Americans than ever before.

Other books and pamphlets extolling native American values appeared as Indians explained their point of view to the public. In his book *God Is Red* (1973), Vine Deloria, a Sioux, argued that the spirit of Christianity, its communal brotherhood and condemnation of materialism, had more in common with native American values than with white religions. Native Americans affirmed life over death, place over time, and the spiritual over the material, he argued, and offered much to the troubled psyches of industrialized society. Charles A. Eastman, a Santee Sioux and one of the founders of the Society of American Indians, had made a similar case for native American values in *The Soul of an Indian* (1911), but it was more than sixty years before those ideas took hold in America.

The time was ripe for major changes in native American affairs. Termination and relocation, blanketed as they were in the rhetoric of assimilation, had occurred so subtly and so closely behind the reforms of the Indian Reorganization Act, that native Americans realized they would have to keep a constant vigil against "developing" reservation land and "assimilating" the tribes. Building on the new pan-Indian spirit, white liberalism, and the renaissance of native American values, they began organizing to promote civil rights, economic opportunity, and cultural autonomy. At the 1961 Chicago Indian Conference, 420 representatives of sixty-seven native American nations met to promote cultural pluralism. For years white groups like the Indian Rights

Acclaimed native American artist Blackbear Bosin works on his 8′ x 40′ mural "From Whence All Life," which now hangs in the lobby of a Wichita bank. Native Americans, long relegated to second-class citizenship, are uniting to awaken the country to their needs. (UPI/Bettmann)

Association and the American Indian Defense Association had led the struggle for native American rights, but in the 1960s native Americans took control of the movement themselves.

Individual tribal organizations such as the Iroquois League, DNA (a Navajo legal aid society), the All-Pueblo Council, the United Sioux Tribes, the United Southeast Tribes, and the Columbian Powhatan Confederacy increased their activities. In the cities groups like the Southeast Council of Federated Eastern Indians in New York and the San Francisco Indian Cultural Center worked to keep Indians in touch with their past. And several pan-Indian associations developed in the 1960s. Among the most moderate of them, counterparts of the NAACP and LULAC, were the American Indian Civil Rights Council, the American Indian Women's League, and Indians, Inc. More militant groups included the United Native Americans, the Young American Indian Council, the Organization of Native American Students, and the American Indian Movement (AIM).

Native American groups supported the civil rights movement and the War on Poverty, but some, such as AIM, also demanded the return of all land taken from them and complete tribal autonomy. It was an impossible crusade. By 1990, 260 million Americans depended on land once owned by native Americans, and regardless of the justice of their

A native American demonstration in Washington, D.C. (Spia Press/Black Star)

demands, the welfare of the white majority was too immediate. Surrendering the land would have thrown the economy into chaos. It would also have required a complete alteration of federal policy, as would giving native American nations total autonomy. Such demands pitted native American activists against the BIA, the white community, and more moderate tribal leaders.

Whites viewed the AIM demands as hopelessly naive, and many native Americans were afraid of AIM. Despite past abuses, native Americans were still the only group in the United States enjoying tax-exempt claims to a large body of land, independent tribal organizations free of state and local authority, and a cultural isolation protected by law and the social atmosphere. Moderates sympathized with the feelings of the radicals but feared they would alienate whites, destroy federal control of the reservations, and open native American land to white interest groups, thus completing the process begun three hundred years ago.

The most pressing militant demand was the restoration of tribal lands. In western Nevada the Paiutes wanted Pyramid Lake and the land surrounding it, all of which had been guaranteed them in 1859, long before whites had seen any economic use for it. But later the Department of the Interior had constructed a dam on the Truckee River, and since then the lake had declined in size and the fish population had dwindled. In 1969, California negotiated an agreement with Nevada to divert the Truckee River, which would have destroyed Pyramid Lake. Paiute representatives fought the agreement, and in 1972 and 1973 court orders required the stabilization of Pyramid Lake at a size large enough to sustain tribal fishing needs. Paiute militance had succeeded.

The Taos had similar claims on Blue Lake, an ancient tribal religious shrine in northwestern New Mexico. In 1906, the federal government had incorporated Blue Lake into the Carson National Forest, and since then the Forest Service had opened up the area to recreational hunting, fishing, and camping. But for the Taos, the lake was the source of life and final resting place for the spirits of the dead. At a 1961 meeting of the Association on American Indian Affairs a Taos spokesman said:

> We don't have gold temples in this lake, but we have a sign of a living God to whom we pray—the living trees, the evergreen and spruce and the beautiful flowers and the beautiful rocks and the lake itself. . . . We are taking that water to give us strength so we can gain in knowledge and wisdom. . . . That is the reason this Blue Lake is so important to us.*

Late in the 1960s the Taos demanded the return of the lake. The Department of Agriculture, fearing the implications of returning land to the Indians, offered the Taos a cash payment instead, but they refused. President Richard Nixon sympathized with their demands, and in 1970 Congress returned the lake and 48,000 acres of land to them.

The Pit River nation of northern California had lost all its land in the gold rush of 1849 and in the 1950s demanded the return of 3,368,000 acres. The Indian Claims Commission decided in 1956 that the land had been taken illegally, and in 1963 the federal government awarded the Pit River nation forty-seven cents per acre. Members refused the money, insisting on the return of the land. In June 1970, more than 150 Pit Rivers, impatient with government policy, occupied portions of Lassen National Park and Pacific Gas & Electric Company land that they claimed was their property. Dozens were arrested for trespassing. The dispute was not resolved until 1986 when the Pit Rivers accepted a cash settlement. There were other examples. The Passamaquoddies claimed much of the state of Maine, the Wampanoags much of central

---

*Quoted in Angie Debo, A *History of the Indians of the United States* (Norman, Okla., 1970), pp. 354–355.

Massachusetts, and the Eklutnas of Alaska more than 378,000 acres there. The Seminoles of Florida refused a congressional offer of $12 million for their land. In Littleton, Colorado, native Americans occupied a BIA office to protest discrimination and corruption, and Sioux camped on top of Mount Rushmore to claim it as tribal land. In 1969, a group called Indians of All Tribes occupied Alcatraz Island in San Francisco to dramatize their claims to it; in 1970, others occupied Ellis Island in New York City and Fort Lawson in Puget Sound. In upstate New York the Iroquois fought to deny recreational hunting and fishing rights on their lands, and along the Puyallup River in Washington, state troopers drove native Americans off fishing grounds they claimed as their own. More than 250 Chippewas occupied a lighthouse along Lake Superior in Michigan, and Menominees in 1975 took over a Roman Catholic monastery that was on former reservation land. Repossession of ancient tribal lands was the main objective of native American activism in the 1970s.

Activists were also determined to reform the Bureau of Indian Affairs and regain as much tribal autonomy as possible. Since 1824, the BIA had coordinated the reservation, allotment, termination, and relocation programs, and militant native Americans felt that it had engineered the loss of tribal lands and sovereignty. To the militants, tribal leaders who cooperated with the BIA were either naive dupes of white rhetoric or traitors to their birthright. The BIA was charged with insensitivity to tribal needs, a history of graft and corruption in shipping supplies to the reservations, a willingness to lease reservation resources at cheap rates to white interests, and a constant effort to force white education and values on native Americans. In 1972, AIM members raided the BIA headquarters in Washington, D.C., to publicize their disgust for everything the bureau represented.

Then, in 1973, AIM leaders Russell Means and Dennis Banks headed for the Sioux reservation at Pine Ridge, South Dakota, took over the trading post, and expelled BIA officials. They demanded return of all Sioux land, destruction of the BIA, removal of such tribal leaders as Richard Wilson of the Sioux Tribal Council, and a return to complete tribal sovereignty. Shots were exchanged, and an FBI agent was killed. The incident alienated some whites and upset most middle-aged and older native Americans who felt that destruction of the BIA would only bring them under the purview of local authorities and end in another termination program. Demands for the return of tribal land and tribal sovereignty were as likely to succeed as Marcus Garvey's hope for a separate black state or Reies Tijerina's call for Mexican-American secession from the Southwest. AIM radicalism had polarized both white and native American opinion. The charges against Means and Banks were dismissed in their 1974 trial when a federal judge ruled that

Sioux stand guard outside the Sacred Heart Catholic church at Wounded Knee during their occupation of the area. (UPI/Bettmann)

government prosecutors had tried improperly to influence the jury. More acculturated and yet more vocal about their plight than ever before, native Americans in the late 1970s were still a diverse and separate people in the United States.

Change and Continuity in Modern America

During the 1970s, 1980s, and early 1990s, native Americans continued their quest to regain control over tribal resources and their own cultural future. Most whites remained sympathetic to Indian concerns. Although the 1990 census placed the Indian population at 1.8 million people, nearly 7 million whites claimed to have at least some native American ancestry. Kevin Costner's 1991 film *Dances With Wolves*, the story of a white cavalry officer's interaction with the Lakota Sioux in the 1870s, was the year's most popular film and won several Academy Awards. The combination of white liberal sympathies and native American militancy resulted in a number of economic and political achievements during the 1970s and 1980s.

A key element in the drive for native American self-determination is control of tribal economic resources. The skyrocketing prices of oil, coal, uranium, and natural gas after 1973 have placed a new premium on the value of reservation land, as well as put new pressures on water supplies needed to develop those resources. Peter MacDonald, chairman of the Navajo Tribal Council until 1983, was concerned about the economic colonization of reservations by private corporations and the federal government. He played a key role in organizing in 1975 the Council of Energy Resource Tribes (CERT), a consortium of twenty-three western tribes representing more than 600,000 native Americans. CERT was designed to prevent environmental damage to reservation land, preserve water supplies, protect energy resources from outside exploitation, maximize tribal profits by controlling individual leases, guarantee a fair return on assets, and make sure that revenues from energy resources would be used to convert the reservations into self-sustaining communities.

During the 1980s CERT assisted a number of groups in managing their resources. In Montana, for example, the Crows were able to renegotiate their coal leases with the Westmoreland Resources Company, raising the tribal royalty from 17.5 cents to 40 cents per ton; CERT helped the Crows do the same with older leasing agreements for 30,248 acres held by the Shell Oil Company, 14,237 acres held by the Amax Coal Company, 86,122 acres held by the Peabody Coal Company, and 73,293 acres held by the Gulf Oil Corporation. In each instance the Crows were certain that the leases were anachronistic because world oil and coal prices had risen so dramatically since 1973.

Many native American nations that were not part of CERT made similar demands for resource control and environmental protection. In 1991, for example, gravel miners began cutting into Arizona land that the Hopis considered sacred. Even though the land was located more than fifty miles from the Hopi reservation, the Hopis managed to secure a restraining order to stop the gravel extraction. In upstate New York, despite intense opposition from whites, the Senecas managed to secure substantial profits when new leases came due. Back in 1892, the Senecas signed a 99-year lease with the town of Salamanca, New York, allowing businesses and homes to be built on tribal property. When the lease expired, the Senecas demanded new payments for new leases. White businesses and homeowners protested the Seneca demands, but eventually the city agreed to pay more than $600,000 to the Senecas for lease extensions.

Native American activists had long been concerned about the education of their children, and in their commitment to self-determination they were convinced that they must have control of their school systems. The Indian Education Act of 1972 was a major step toward self-determination. Tribal leaders applauded the law. It mandated parental and tribal participation in all federal aid programs to public schools; allocated funds to encourage the establishment of community-run schools; provided funds to state and local education agencies, colleges, universities, and tribes for new native American history, culture, and bilingual curricula; appropriated money for tribal use in adult education projects; established an Office of Indian Education, controlled by the National Advisory Council on Indian Education (staffed entirely by native Americans), to administer the programs of the Indian Education Act; and allocated funds for teacher training at BIA schools. Herschel Sahmaunt, a Kiowa and president of the National Indian Education Association, hailed the law as "the first piece of legislation enacted into law that gives Indian people on reservations, in rural settings, and in the cities control over their own education."

Congress also approved several other measures supporting the basic concept of self-determination. The Indian Finance Act of 1974 provided new assistance to enterprises and development projects by enlarging revolving funds, creating a new loan guaranty and insurance fund, partially subsidizing loan costs, and providing grants for businesses. The Education Amendments Act of 1978 made major changes in the administration of education programs by giving controlling authority to local communities. Policy setting and program guidance became the responsibility of local school boards. Finally, the Indian Child Welfare Act of 1978 was designed to restrict the placement of native American children by outside social agencies in other than native American homes and environments. The act declared the federal government's intention to promote the stability of tribes and families by establishing minimum standards for any removal of children from the family and for placement, when needed, in homes reflecting the values of native American culture. The law also made it clear that tribal courts had jurisdiction over children living on reservations.

The greatest victory for pan-Indian activists in American history came in 1975 when the Indian Self-Determination and Education Assistance Act went into effect. The act established a new relationship between federal agencies and tribal authorities. By permitting tribal governments to negotiate and contract directly with the Bureau of Indian Affairs and the Department of Health and Human Resources, the act restored tribalism in an important legal sense and gave to native Americans a greater measure of control over federal programs. Tribal governments can set goals, priorities, and administrative procedures for social and educational programs, and tribal governments can restructure and even reject those programs when they conclude that tribal needs are not being met. The act also permitted the federal government to make direct cash payments to tribal governments for personnel training programs and for the construction of health facilities. Tribal leaders are to be in direct control of all programs. Finally, the law stipulated that any public school in the United States receiving federal funds for native American education must use that money exclusively for native American children.

There were, to be sure, critics of self-determination. Some militants were concerned about self-determination lest outsiders interpret it as dominance by elected tribal leaders; people in groups such as the American Indian Movement refuse to recognize the legitimacy of any decisions made by BIA-approved leaders or leaders elected in BIA-supervised elections. They favor self-determination as long as their own organizations enjoy enough power to dictate the planning and implementation of government native American programs. Others fear that legislation supporting self-determination has been just another subterfuge, a subtle way of removing the federal government from native American affairs in one more move toward assimilation.

But if current self-determination programs are not a panacea to all native Americans, they nevertheless signal a major change in native American history, considering the probability that for the first time officials of the federal government are dealing honestly with native American concerns and demands. The most recent experiment under the Indian Self-Determination and Education Assistance Act came in 1991 when the Bureau of Indian Affairs launched a trial program with a number of native American nations. The Quinnalt Nation of Washington, for example, started a three-year process of severing its connection with the BIA. The federal government is now negotiating with the Quinnalts, treating them as a sovereign nation.

The native American struggle for self-determination and respect continues today. The Zuñis and others have launched nationwide campaigns to recover sacred bones and artifacts from museums, for example. Many native American groups led by activist Sioux campaigned throughout the 1980s to rename the Custer National Battleground in Montana, believing Custer to be no hero. In 1991, the federal government surrendered to their demands and labeled the region the Little Big Horn National Battleground. Like the Chippewas of Wisconsin, many native Americans continue to demand exemption from state hunting and fishing regulations on the grounds that only white people are guilty of hunting and fishing species to extinction. And during 1991 and 1992, native American activists condemned the "Tomahawk Chop" used by Atlanta Braves fans as being racist and insensitive.

Chapter Seventeen

White Ethnics in Modern America

The search for community since 1945—the quest for equality, security, and stable neighborhoods—continued the most compelling urge in American history. But in a "nation of nations," as the ethnologist Louis Adamic once called it, the quest for community seemed elusive, and its pursuit often resulted in competition and confrontation. While the headlines concentrated on native and African and Hispanic Americans, white ethnics were equally interested in making American values work for them. After decades of acculturation and some assimilation, several broad white ethnic groupings—Protestant, Jewish, Catholic, and Orthodox—had emerged in the United States, and their needs for security and equity would also help shape social and political life.

The White Protestants

The largest of the white subcommunities was made up of white Protestants. It is difficult to generalize about white Protestants because there has been so much conflict and competition among various groups divided by national origins, language, class, religion, occupation, and religious denomination. In 1850, a Dutch farmer in Michigan and a New England Yankee were both white Protestants but hardly members of the same ethnic group. English, Welsh, Scots, Dutch, German, and Scandinavian Americans were national, language, and religious groups rather than a single ethnic community. But throughout American history, at different stages in different places, white Protestant communities began to emerge. In New York, after several generations, Dutch Reformed settlers began to marry people of English descent to the point where early in the nineteenth century Dutch culture began to disappear. In the German triangle, people from various German backgrounds intermarried until a larger German-American community developed, and members of that community in turn became close to people of British and Scandinavian backgrounds. In the colonial South the English, Scots, Scots-Irish, French Huguenots, and Germans slowly melted into a larger community based on race and religion.

White Protestants shared a host of values that served as the foundation for their community. Race and color were one bond. In the colonial period and early nineteenth century, race had been significant only in a negative sense. Being white brought German, English, and Scots-Irish Southerners together because of the large number of African Americans. The same was true of the English, Germans, and Scandinavians in the Midwest who feared the Indians, or the whites of the Southwest who disliked Mexicans and Indians. Later in the nineteenth century, when pseudoscientific racist theories were put forward, the notion that Anglo-Saxon, Nordic, and Teutonic people were inherently superior to blacks, Indians, Asians, Jews, and Slavs became popular. All whites did not, of course, articulate such ideas clearly, but the feeling became common that whites, especially northern and western European whites, were better than other people.

Religious concerns similarly brought white Protestants together. Throughout American history Protestants argued incessantly over doctrine, but a common front, this time against Roman Catholicism, bound them together. From the anti-Catholic crusades of the 1840s, through the antics of the American Protective Association in the 1890s and the Ku Klux Klan in the 1920s, to the election of 1960, American Protestants have been linked by an uneasiness about, or even fear of, the Catholic church. Beyond that negative bond there were positive values shared by most Protestants. Because they had rejected centralized authority for some form of denominational or congregational autonomy, Protestants tended to be antiauthoritarian, suspicious of concentrated political or religious power. In their view religious sovereignty flowed up from the people through bureaucracies rather than down to the people from a king or a pope. Out of such beliefs came the individualistic ethos of Protestantism. While the Catholic church insisted that man could be saved only through the church, the Protestants—whether in the predestination of the Calvinists, the Inner Light of the Quakers, or the "saving grace" of the evangelicals—believed people could be saved outside the church because the personal relationship with God transcended all institutions.

From that individualistic ethos came Protestant views of success and community. The development of capitalism in premodern Europe had given rise to an ambitious entrepreneurial class who resented Catholic restrictions on business enterprise. Businesspeople saw in Protestantism a liberating force. Eventually Protestant theology not only liberated the entrepreneurial spirit from medieval restrictions but justified material success. Success became a sign of election and divine grace; the striving for success permeated Protestant values, not as a necessary evil but as a positive good.

Finally, Protestant individualism generated a new vision of community. While the older Catholic view of society had seen the whole as more important than any of its parts, Protestants elevated the individual and argued that the community was only a tool to promote individual goals. Once the community stopped serving individual needs, people were justified in breaking away. Therefore Protestants became as mobile geographically as they were economically, willing to sever roots and move on to new opportunities whenever necessary, even if it meant leaving friends, relatives, and familiar places. Most early Protestant immigrants had left peasant villages in Europe for rural America, but industrialization and urbanization had then pushed them into American cities. After World War II they moved on to the suburbs. Each time their roots and commitment to particular communities weakened, and to give themselves a sense of community the Protestants became "joiners," forming clubs and associations. Even their churches were essentially products of individual initiative, of new settlers starting their own independent congregations. In America a whole range of associational activities—YMCA, YWCA, Masons, Odd Fellows, Elks, Lions, Eagles, Moose, Kiwanis, Optimists, Rotary, Salvation Army, Gideons, Daughters of the American Revolution, country clubs, chambers of commerce, and professional groups—were overwhelmingly Protestant in composition, attempts to reconstruct community life.

Although white Protestants, because of their numbers, were scattered throughout society, they dominated elite groups during most of American history. In the largest banks, insurance companies, foundations, universities, and industrial corporations, Protestants controlled the boards of directors, and until 1945 they were dominant in the sciences, professions, and government. Even when they were not well-to-do, as in the case of farmers and skilled workers in the AFL, they often supported conservative values, especially in social, moral, and political affairs. That was an irony of white Protestant history. Extremely flexible and adventurous in economic matters, and in the vanguard of the

Industrial Revolution, at the same time they favored prohibition, immigration restriction, and Sunday blue laws, and opposed gambling, prostitution, and parochial schools. In the nineteenth century most of the German, Scandinavian, and British Protestants in the North joined the Republican party, which was rural, abolitionist, and anti-Catholic. And even in the South, where white Protestants stayed in the Democratic party, they remained rural and conservative in their approach to social affairs. Individualistic, independent, democratic, ruralistic, anti-authoritarian, opportunistic economically, but conservative socially—these were the characteristics of Protestants.

It was only natural that as assimilation blurred the hard lines of national origin, language, and denomination, German, Dutch, British, and Scandinavian Americans would begin to form a more collective identity. It occurred slowly. In the second generation, as English became the main language of the communities, social relations among Protestants became easier. When industrialization and the two world wars attracted rural Protestants to the cities and disrupted kinship networks, they became more willing to associate with other Protestants from different backgrounds and did so frequently in their secular organizations. After World War II mass culture and mass consumerism gave them even more in common. And as they maintained their commitment to geographical and occupational mobility, Protestants from different national and denominational backgrounds found themselves in the same schools, neighborhoods, churches, clubs, and jobs. More important, shared Protestant values and rapid mobility had led to ethnic and denominational intermarriage. British Americans in Nebraska, for example, married endogamously (i.e., within the ethnic community) 49 percent of the time in 1909–1913, but only 37 percent of the time in 1921–1925. British in-marriage rates in New Haven, Connecticut, fell from 72 percent in 1900 to 54 percent in 1950. Among Nebraska and Wisconsin Germans, endogamous marriages dropped from 81 percent in 1910 to 61 percent in 1925. German in-marriages in New Haven declined from 55 percent in 1900 to 40 percent in 1930 to 27 percent in 1950. Among Scandinavians in New York endogamous marriages declined from 61 percent in 1908 to 44 percent in 1921 to 40 percent in 1939. In New Haven, Scandinavian intermarriages increased from only 17 percent in 1900 to 67 percent in 1930 to 78 percent in 1950. Nearly 60 percent of all Finnish marriages in Ohio in 1895 were endogamous, but only 25 percent were in 1935.

Those who intermarried almost always married other Protestants—the Dutch preferring Germans or Scandinavians; the Finns other Scandinavians or Germans; and the English other British Protestants, then Scandinavians and Germans. As this occurred in generation after generation between 1840 and 1990, the descendants of mixed ethnic and denominational marriages acquired a sense of identity based on being white and Protestant. After World War II, as mass education, mass culture, and mobility became even more extensive, intermarriage rates increased and national origin visions blurred even more.

Lutheran churches provide a good example of the blurring of national origin perspectives. During the nineteenth century the German, Swedish, Danish, Norwegian, and Finnish Lutheran churches constantly fragmented over language and doctrinal questions. But in the twentieth century a number of mergers took place. In 1917, several Norwegian churches united into the Norwegian Lutheran Church; in 1918, the United Lutheran Church of America was formed; in 1960, the Norwegian Lutheran Church, the American Lutheran Church, and several evangelical Danish Lutheran churches merged together as the American Lutheran Church; and in 1962, the United Evangelical Danish Lutheran Church, the Finnish Apostolic Lutheran Church, the Augustana (Swedish) Lutheran Church, and a German and Norwegian Lutheran synod formed the Lutheran Church in America. People of Germanic and Scandinavian backgrounds, after generations of intermarriage, had come to view themselves as white Protestants and Lutherans as well as Germans or Scandinavians. Similar feelings developed among English and Welsh Methodists, Scots and Scots-Irish Presbyterians, Scandinavian and British Mormons, Episcopalians, and Congregationalists. To a lesser extent this was also true of Baptists, Disciples of Christ, Pentecostals, and Dutch and German Reformed.

Episcopalians, Methodists, Reformed, Presbyterians, and Congregationalists had high rates of intermarriage to other Protestants; and although most of them were still aware of ethnic roots, tens of millions had also acquired identities based on church, class, occupational, regional, and social loyalties as well as an increasing sense of being part of the white Protestant community. More than 900,000 Germans, 560,000 British, and 1 million Canadians immigrated after 1945 and nurtured the old ethnic cultures, but by the late 1980s nearly 125 million Americans identified with a white Protestant community, although only 70 million claimed a specific church membership.

The Jews

Although Sephardic and Chassidic Jews remained aloof, German, Russian, Polish, Hungarian, and Romanian Jews were all merging into a larger Jewish-American community by 1945. Many came from urban environments, and unlike some other immigrants, they were permanent residents from the beginning. Arriving with their families, they wanted economic security; and immediately after settling into the tenements, they set up businesses serving the Jewish community or found jobs in the skilled trades, providing a solid foundation for the Jewish business elite and the urban labor movement. While other immigrants moved slowly from unskilled to skilled and white-collar jobs, the Jewish reverence for education and the interest of parents in the success of their children lifted them quickly out of working-class life. In the early 1990s more than 90 percent of college-age Jews were enrolled in colleges and universities; more than 80 percent of Jewish men were professionals, businessmen, or sales personnel; less than 10 percent were in blue-collar jobs; and Jewish family incomes were among the highest in the country.

Out of the Jewish community came the Lehmans and Seligmans in finance; the Altmans and Gimbels in merchandising; Sidney Hillman and David Dubinsky in the labor movement; Irving Shapiro of Du Pont and William Paley of CBS; and the remarkable Jewish intellectual community, including such writers as Norman Mailer, Philip Roth, Alfred Kazin, Saul Bellow, and Bernard Malamud; the historians Oscar Handlin and Richard Hofstadter; scientists such as Jonas Salk; film producer Stanley Kubrick; and symphony conductor Leonard Bernstein. Also to be noted are Jacob Javits, Abraham Ribicoff, and Bella Abzug in politics; Fanny Brice, Sophie Tucker, Groucho Marx, Joan Rivers, Milton Berle, Jack Benny, George Burns, Lenny Bruce, Beverly Sills, and Barbra Streisand in entertainment; and Lillian Wald and Elizabeth Stern in social work. The transplanted ghetto, so close in time and spirit to the Old World, was the staging area for the most successful immigrant saga in American history.

Success and its implications, however, seemed to destroy the very communities Jews had worked so hard to build. While America offered Jews more security than any other nation, acceptance threatened Jewish ethnicity. Centuries of persecution and visions of being a chosen people had molded a sense of communality, but American prosperity weakened mutual dependence just as secularization was eroding religious ethnocentrism. As more and more successful Jews moved to the suburbs, Jewish life underwent profound changes. In the 1970s and 1980s Orthodox synagogues in the urban centers seemed far away, and suburban temples, Reform or Conservative, became the focus of social life. The modern, tastefully appointed buildings staffed by American-trained rabbis, however, were more social than religious centers—secularized community headquarters for fund drives, lectures, social gatherings, and clubs. Familiarity with spoken Yiddish and older religious ceremonies lagged, as did attendance at services. Intermarriage with non-Jews climbed steadily after World War II. Most of the more than six million American Jews still valued family life, respectability, pacific conduct, philanthropy, education, and their Jewish identities in the 1980s, but many worried about whether Jewish ethnicity could survive another century in the United States.

Roman Catholic and Orthodox Americans

Two more melting pots in white America consisted of nearly 57 million Roman Catholics and 5 million Eastern Orthodox in the late 1980s. Most Catholic and Orthodox immigrants had left peasant villages, and except for temporary stays in European cities they had had only limited contact with urban life. In the United States they accepted low-paying, unskilled jobs in mines, foundries, mills, and factories. With deep ties to land, village, and family, most of them, except the Irish and German Catholics, planned to work here for a little while, save their money, and return home to pay off mortgages, buy new land, and reconstruct Old World communities. At first they were relatively unconcerned about getting ahead in America, not caring for skilled jobs or success as long as thoughts of going home dominated daily life. Crowded into wretched tenements, laboring in dead-end jobs, cut off from friends and family, they had difficult beginnings in America.

But they rose above that poverty. After a few years they realized that Old World villages were gone forever. The Slavs, Magyars, Italians, Greeks, Romanians, Syrians, and Armenians planted permanent roots and reconstructed village perspectives in the New World. They worked hard, saved money to purchase homes, and donated money to build urban parishes. Their ghetto communities were mixed neighborhoods where other ethnic groups lived, shopped, worked, and went to school. Ethnic-language churches, parochial schools, mutual aid societies, ethnic businesses, and parish organizations circumscribed life in the Catholic and Orthodox communities. The move out of poverty was slow and uneven, depending on the group's length of time in the United States and its Old World experiences, but all improved their living standards during the twentieth century.

Advancement was especially difficult for the Irish. There were many success stories—including the Kennedys in Boston and the Buckleys in New York—but work on canals, railroads, and mills, and life in shantytowns did not leave much of an economic base for success. Instead of taking an entrepreneurial route to prosperity, the Irish often turned to politics and the church. Such Irish clerics as James Cardinal Gibbons, John Ireland, Richard Cardinal Cushing, John Hughes, Dennis Cardinal Dougherty, Francis Cardinal Spellman, James Cardinal McIntyre, and John Cardinal Cody controlled Catholic parishes, parochial

President Kennedy (right)
confers with his closest
adviser, brother Robert.
(UPI/Bettmann)

schools, hospitals, and orphanages. Irish bosses dominated politics in
the Democratic wards of major American cities, and the names of
colorful politicians like James Michael Curley of Boston, Tom Pender-
gast of Kansas City, Al Smith of New York, Richard Daley of Chicago,
and of course the Kennedy brothers in Massachusetts became household words. Along with political power went jobs in the police, fire, and
sanitation departments, the civil service, public schools, and public
construction. From there the Irish moved rapidly into middle- and
upper-class life after World War II. Except for pockets of poverty like
parts of South Boston, most Irish Americans had joined the middle
class by 1975.

For the first time since the Great Famine, Irish-American concern
for Ireland waned, particularly after the final separation of Ireland
(except Northern Ireland) and England in 1921 and the decline of Irish
immigration after 1924. The conflict in Northern Ireland during the
1960s and 1970s, as well as the visits of Bernadette Devlin to promote
Catholic rights in Ulster, inspired Irish-American sympathy, but it did

not compare with Irish-American nationalism in the nineteenth century. The Irish of the 1930s, after nearly a century in America, had taken advantage of education, and by 1940 Catholic secondary schools were dominated by Irish-American faculties and students. After leaving the service in 1945, hundreds of thousands of Irish GIs went to college on the GI Bill and took up jobs in education, the professions, business, and government. The old ghettos dissolved as southern blacks moved in and Irish Americans headed for the suburbs.

The Italian-American experience was difficult, too, as historian Alexander DeConde said, "half bitter and half sweet." Italians left the grinding poverty of southern Italy, but at first most were single males who eschewed status in America for some savings to take back to Italy. Only when their families began joining them did southern Italians look for skilled jobs and economic security. Their economic success was retarded because first-generation Italians viewed loyalty to the family as the ultimate value. They were suspicious of education because it involved alien ideas, association with strangers, and geographical and occupational mobility. The early immigrants discouraged it, urging their children instead to find a "good job."

The children of immigrants were more likely than their parents to become skilled and white-collar workers, but generational differences were narrower for Italians than for most other new immigrants. The third and fourth generations, however, responded less to old community pressures and more to the American emphasis on competitive achievement. These Italian Americans began to enter the middle class, and, represented by people like Frank Rizzo in Philadelphia, Anthony Imperiale in Newark, and Joseph Alioto and George Moscone in San Francisco, Italian-American political power became a force to be reckoned with. The tenure of Lee A. Iacocca first in the presidency of Ford Motor Company and then at the Chrysler Corporation, and John Riccardo at Chrysler, symbolized the economic arrival of Italian Americans.

Eastern European immigrants—Slavs, Hungarians, Romanians, and Greeks—and Syrians and Armenians also enjoyed success and mobility in postwar America. Most had come with few industrial skills and at first no intention of staying. The Slavs and Hungarians suspected intellectuals and worried about the impact of American education. The original migrations from Europe had been socially complex affairs, often with educated professionals and intellectuals leading the way in the mid-nineteenth century, followed by peasant immigrants after 1890. German Poles preceded the Galician and Russian Poles; Bohemian intellectuals inaugurated the migration from Czechoslovakia; and Louis Kossuth's political refugees arrived ahead of the Magyar peasants. The upper classes valued education, but the peasants suspected it with a hostility bordering on anti-intellectualism, for neither Catholic dogma nor the economic demands of peasant villages had rewarded educational achievement. Transplanting their suspicions to America, they destined themselves and their children to blue-collar occupations. But by the 1980s the eastern European communities were quite different from the earlier ones. No longer unskilled workers living in tenements and worshiping in Irish-dominated parishes, they had skilled jobs and white-collar status (more than 25 percent had become businesspeople, professionals, and technicians), owned their own homes, and attended their own churches.

At first the Catholic and Orthodox immigrants avoided labor unions. But when the Great Depression destroyed whatever economic security they had achieved, they flocked to the unions of the CIO: International Ladies Garment Workers, Amalgamated Clothing Workers, United Automobile Workers, United Mine Workers, United Steel Workers, and the Packinghouse Workers. They generally became loyal Democrats. After 1932 a coalition of Jewish and Catholic immigrants, workers, northern African Americans, southern whites, and intellectuals put Franklin D. Roosevelt in the White House, filled Congress with Democrats, and became the foundation for the New Deal, Fair Deal, New Frontier, and Great Society—the most influential liberal reforms in American history. When John Fitzgerald Kennedy won the presidency in 1960, it seemed that the American gospel of success had fulfilled its promise to the Catholic minority. By the mid-1970s Irish, German, Italian, and Slavic Catholics had achieved educational parity with the American population in general, and the family incomes of European Catholic communities were above the national average.

Sources of Social and Economic Unrest

Successful as they were, Catholics were not far enough from their immigrant past to be complacent. Especially for those in the original settlements—Poles in Chicago, Italians in New York, Irish in Boston, Slovaks in Cleveland—the institutional ghetto was largely intact. Ethnic newspapers were declining and some ethnic associations disappearing, but ethnic consciousness and profound attachments to community and neighborhood survived. So did a certain insecurity about whether Americans were ready to accept cultural pluralism. John Kennedy's victory over Richard Nixon had been perilously narrow, and the issue of religion had never gone away. Anti-Catholicism in 1960 was mild compared with the paranoia surrounding Al Smith's campaign in 1928, but old epithets—Polack, dago, Wop, Hunkie, bohunk—had not disappeared, and the popularity of Polish and Italian jokes revealed a continuing prejudice against eastern and southern Europeans. Italian Americans were particularly irritated about tendencies to link them with organized crime. Consequently, even in the 1970s and 1980s many Catholics remained uneasy about their place in American society. Nor were their economic fortunes guaranteed. Although younger Catholics in the 1970s had surpassed national averages in education and income, older Catholics were still blue-collar workers. Memories of the Great Depression were still vivid, and periodic swings in the business cycle and long stretches of unemployment, such as those resulting from layoffs in the mining, automobile, steel, and textile industries in the 1970s and 1980s made economic security fragile indeed. Changes in the American economy and in the cities were also threatening, for as the economy reached postindustrial maturity, the number of blue-collar jobs declined and white-collar jobs increased. Technological innovations were eliminating more blue-collar jobs, and structural unemployment grew progressively worse. Labor unions were losing power in politics and social affairs. Businesses relocated in the suburbs, city tax bases eroded, and property owners were forced to bear the costs of education and social services. People who had struggled to buy homes for their families resented high property taxes that threatened home ownership itself. And at the same time they had to deal with an inflationary spiral that outpaced wage increases.

Jews too worried about the future. No matter how secure they felt economically, vestiges of anti-Semitism still existed in postwar America. Social and business clubs still refused Jews membership; the great corporate board rooms were still largely without Jewish executives; and some Ivy League universities maintained anti-Jewish admission quotas as late as the 1950s. Central to postwar Jewish ethnicity was the Holocaust; it sensitized Jews to every strain of anti-Semitism, and no group in American society would become more committed to civil liberty and community security. The Holocaust also politicized American Jews, helping to offset the secularizing and assimilating forces in the United States.

Like an older Irish-American nationalism, Jewish ethnicity revolved around another country—Israel. In the late 1940s and early 1950s Israel was settled largely by survivors of the Holocaust. For most American Jews the subtleties of international politics and diplomacy seemed irrelevant to the overwhelming question of Jewish survival, and Israel seemed the only guarantee that world Judaism would endure. Israel became the common ground on which American Jews united, and its cause submerged some of the traditional differences between Jewish businesses and Jewish unions, Jewish socialism and Zionism, and the

Reform, Conservative, and Orthodox sects. For religious Jews Israel represented the fulfillment of prophecy, the final stage in the dynamic of Jewish history, and for secular Jews Israel was an alternative to assimilation, a means of preserving ethnicity outside religion, of sustaining a secular faith in a secular American society.

Not surprisingly, many American Jews were troubled by the changing political relationship between Israel and the United States in the 1980s and early 1990s. The energy crisis of the 1970s and early 1980s made the United States more aware than ever before of the needs and sensitivities of the oil-rich Arab states of the Middle East, and in the process American foreign policy became less patient with Israeli designs in the region. During the years of the Reagan and Bush administrations between 1981 and 1993, the United States cultivated its relationship with Saudi Arabia, Egypt, and the Arab Emirates, and frequently criticized Israeli policies in deporting Palestinian activists or establishing permanent settlements in the occupied territories. The controversy even drove a wedge into the Jewish community—between those who unflinchingly supported Israeli policies and those who felt Israel had become too rigid and too militant in its regional posture.

Finally, Catholics and Jews were troubled about social change in America. Most changes were inevitable transformations of Old World customs in the New World society, but they were unnerving nonetheless. Old World families seemed doomed. When both parents worked to make ends meet, children were naturally more independent and less responsive to parental authority. At the same time, life in an industrialized society made children economic liabilities rather than economic assets. In the old peasant villages children had had specific farming chores to perform, but in American cities, with the obligations of school and social pressure, adolescents were economically dependent on parents for many years. Parents complained about the difficulty of raising children in the United States. After World War II hundreds of thousands of veterans moved out of the old ethnic settlements for the cities of the South and the West, and throughout the 1960s and 1970s that trend continued. Immigration from Europe had disrupted extended families, but total dispersal of the extended family became commonplace in twentieth-century America as children and grandchildren moved far away from home and returned only for occasional holidays and short vacations. Parents realized that college education was important for prosperity and success, but at the same time, especially in the 1960s, colleges seemed to be giving young people strange ideas. They became rebellious, critical of traditional values and of the church.

The two bastions of Old World culture, family and church, both changed in the twentieth century. For Jews and the Catholic and

Orthodox groups, America still held out its promise, but beneath the dream was a troubling reality. Many Jewish leaders were concerned about the fact that nearly two out of every three Jews were marrying non-Jews in the 1980s, and they resented attempts by evangelical Protestant groups such as Jews for Jesus to proselytize and make converts in the Jewish community. Many Catholics grew alarmed about the problems facing the church, particularly declines in the number of available clergy and the casual way in which many Catholics chose to agree or disagree with church teachings.

The Impact of the Civil Rights Movement

Against the background of these fears and successes, the civil rights movement during the 1960s and 1970s created a social and political climate where white ethnicity flourished, acting as a catalyst for cultural controversies. White ethnic groups never opposed the principle of equality; indeed, they were among the earliest supporters of egalitarianism. White Protestants in the Republican party implemented the Thirteenth, Fourteenth, and Fifteenth amendments in the 1860s and 1870s, and white ethnic groups in the CIO unions opened their doors to African-American workers in the 1930s, served as the power base behind Hubert Humphrey's civil rights stand at the Democratic convention of 1948, and provided the margin of victory for the Civil Rights Act of 1964. People close to discrimination themselves proved more than willing to oppose de jure discrimination against others. But when the black-power movement gained momentum, when violence erupted in the streets, and when the federal government turned to quotas and neighborhood engineering, many whites were outraged at what they considered a perversion of liberalism. A political coalition began to emerge between white Protestant Republicans who opposed a large federal government and Jews and Catholics who felt the federal government was becoming invasive and anticommunity.

The problem was that civil rights bills could neither erase the legacy of slavery nor solve the problems of the ghettos; equality and economic security did not materialize overnight, and African Americans began focusing on de facto discrimination. Some blacks took to the streets in the 1960s to protest poverty and discrimination. Concerned about equality and the social order, the federal government began in the 1970s to enforce open housing laws, bus children across district lines to achieve racial integration, redesign electoral districts to achieve racial balances, force employers to subordinate seniority rights to those of recently hired minority workers, and impose racial quotas on the admis-

President Lyndon Johnson hands out pens used during the signing of the Civil Rights Act. Receiving them here are Attorney General Robert Kennedy and (wearing glasses) Senator Edward Brooke of Massachusetts, an African American. (The Bettmann Archive)

sions and promotion policies of universities, local government, and private businesses.

But in attempting to reverse three centuries of discrimination, the government failed to understand the immigrant background and white ethnicity. Profoundly committed to homes, families, and neighborhoods as part of a peasant heritage—to houses, parishes, synagogues, schools, and playgrounds—white ethnic groups felt threatened by expanding African-American ghettos and the arbitrary busing of children. Insecure about their jobs in a troubled economy, they viewed union seniority rights as natural laws and were incensed at even the suggestion of modification. And in the college quotas and affirmative action programs they saw a future in which the road to affluence might be blocked by the demands of African Americans, Mexican Americans, Asian Americans, Puerto Ricans, and native Americans. Even the Democratic party, their link to political power, had deserted them in 1972 when the delegation from Chicago, led by Mayor Richard Daley, was denied seating at the Democratic convention because it did not meet the racial, age, and gender quotas demanded by the Democratic National Committee and liberal supporters of Senator George McGovern.

When blamed for African-American poverty and inequality, white ethnic groups were quick to reply that they had not been around during slavery and were not responsible for segregation or ghettos. They argued that they had arrived in the cities at the same time as most African Americans and Mexican Americans were settling there and that they had encountered a good deal of discrimination themselves. They simply refused to be blamed, and instead of viewing the later phase of the civil rights movement as a legitimate campaign for equality, many saw it as an illegitimate attempt to destroy their neighborhoods. While African Americans saw "law and order" as a euphemism for prejudice, white ethnics viewed it as a means of preserving their neighborhoods from violence. When the Catholic parents of Detroit or South Boston protested busing, or when the Chassidic Jews of New York complained about federally mandated electoral redistricting, or when labor unions sued to protect seniority rights, or when the whole Jewish community raised its voice against university quotas, or when the Irish, Polish, and Lithuanian people of Marquette Park, Illinois, opposed civil rights marches, it was not simply prejudice. Some racism was involved because few circles in white society were free of bias, but for the most part the white ethnic groups were protesting what they saw as the imposition of reverse discrimination.

Among Jews as well as Catholics a new sense of community, and a readiness to express it, emerged in the 1960s and 1970s. Ethnic studies programs, first confined to schools and colleges attended by members of racial minorities, spread across the country in the 1970s and 1980s and embraced many white ethnic groups. Meir Kahane formed the Jewish Defense League in 1968 to denounce anti-Semitism, condemn Jewish impulses to assimilate, and radicalize American support of Israel. Joseph Colombo established the Italian-American Civil Rights League, which attacked negative Italian stereotypes and the tendency to associate Italian Americans with organized crime. Anthony Imperiale of Newark organized the North Ward Cultural and Educational Center late in the 1960s to dramatize Italians' commitment to their own neighborhoods. In 1978 Anthony Krzywicki led the Polish American Affairs Council in demanding the resignation of Attorney General Griffin Bell for repeating Polish jokes. The Committee for the Defense of the Polish Name announced that although slandered,

> ridiculed, and misrepresented in the media as "dumb Polacks," Polish Americans have, for the most part, remained silent. This silence, with all its

implications of ineffectuality, fear and intimidation, is the greatest problem facing the Polish-American community today. . . . What the Polish-American community needs more than anything else is an effective process of consciousness raising . . . *

Bumper stickers proclaiming "Polish power" or "Slovak power" or "Irish power" began to appear around the country, as did "I'm Proud to Be Polish" clubs and "I'm Proud to Be Irish" clubs. With the unprecedented popularity of Alex Haley's novel *Roots* and its 1977 ABC serialization on television, as well as NBC's 1978 presentation of "Holocaust," whites as well as blacks turned toward personal histories in search of their origins. The age of white ethnicity had arrived. Beneath the rhetoric of pride and power, several concrete assumptions formed the ideological core of white ethnicity. Most important, ethnic groups argued that pluralism was not just a racial phenomenon but an ethnic one as well, that a large melting pot even among whites would not emerge in the near future. They demanded respect from society, insisting that social engineering should not destroy community institutions and neighborhoods. Implicit in this point of view was a conviction that all racial and ethnic groups maintain themselves voluntarily and that the government should take the approach it has traditionally assumed toward religions—doing nothing either to promote or to destroy them. For white ethnic groups who valued community so highly, it was not the purpose of the government to sponsor residential, educational, or occupational dispersion programs, especially when there was little evidence of overt discrimination.

Along with a broad view of cultural pluralism, these whites opposed political and economic discrimination, but they also interpreted the First, Fifth, and Fourteenth amendments on individual rather than community lines. While working to end discrimination against individuals, the government must not accept a partnership with formally organized ethnic groups and must never give exclusive benefits to particular groups at the expense of other groups. When Alan Bakke sued the University of California at Davis for denying him admission to the medical school because sixteen places had been reserved for members of minority and disadvantaged groups, the white ethnic community rallied to his defense. Legal briefs were filed on his behalf by the American Jewish Committee, the American Jewish Congress, the Italian American Foundation, the Polish-American Affairs Council, the Polish-American Educators Association, the Hellenic Bar Association, and the Ukrainian Congress Committee of America. Most white ethnic

*Quoted in Helen Z. Lopata, *Polish Americans* (Englewood Cliffs, N.J., 1976), p. 77.

groups agreed that discrimination against individuals on the basis of race, religion, or national origins was wrong, but they also protested arbitrary government quotas that discriminated against individuals not included in the arrangement. They were committed to equality and pluralism, but not to a system in which the government obliterated communities, neighborhoods, and individual futures in the name of freedom. Now more vocal than ever before, they were unwilling to accept either ridicule or discrimination.

The traditional white ethnic groups were also alarmed about changing immigration patterns in the 1980s. During the decade more than ten million people entered the United States, but only ten percent of the immigrants were Europeans. They came from Mexico, Central America, the Caribbean, East Asia, South Asia, the Middle East, Southeast Asia, the Pacific, and Africa. Most of them crowded into ethnic enclaves around the country, and when the economy slipped into recession in the early 1990s, resentment of the newcomers intensified. Many Americans resurrected the call for immigration restriction, and the Immigration Act of 1990 was actually biased in favor of Europeans.

During the 1980s, because of the social tensions they felt, a substantial number of white ethnics became known as Reagan Democrats. They deserted the Democratic party to support Ronald Reagan in 1980 and 1984 and George Bush in 1988. They celebrated the weakening of affirmative action enforcement procedures and the demise of forced busing to achieve school integration. But their faith in Republican social values lasted only as long as the economy held strong. When the persistent recession of the early 1990s cost many of them their jobs, they returned to the Democratic fold, reviving the traditional white ethnic–African-American voting coalition that had put Franklin D. Roosevelt, Harry Truman, John F. Kennedy, Lyndon B. Johnson, and Jimmy Carter in the White House. In the presidential election of 1992, Bill Clinton won the presidency, and George Bush lost it, because of their political shift.

smile, never betraying my sense of irony: I was not proud of my mother and father. I was embarrassed by their lack of education. . . . I heard my father speak to my teacher and felt ashamed of his labored, accented words. Then felt guilty for the shame. I felt such contradictory feelings.*

In the later generations increasingly large numbers of people had entered influential middle and professional classes. Economically successful, several decades removed from the Old World, and no longer plagued by internal doubts and self-consciousness, the grandchildren and great-grandchildren of the immigrants regained an interest in their heritage, wondering about Old World values, perhaps visiting Europe or Latin America or enrolling in language classes. They were conscious of their heritage but not desperate about it like the immigrants nor as afraid of it as the second and sometimes third generations. They were comfortable in their identity as English-speaking Americans with an "Old World" nationality. From those positions of security they were prepared to move beyond acculturation to assimilation—the voluntary social mixing with people from other nationality and language groups, which sometimes eventually led to the marriage bed where culture and history fused. Some groups—among them the colonial Dutch, Scots-Irish, Welsh, and French Huguenots—have virtually disappeared as conscious entities.

What emerged out of modernization, acculturation, and assimilation was a series of melting pots based on race and religion. The nationality and linguistic dimensions of ethnic identity were usually the first to go, often in a few generations, but race and religion remained powerful and influential. By the third and fourth generations, the descendants of the Roman Catholic immigrants were expanding their network of social contacts, voluntarily reaching out to the descendants of other Catholic immigrant groups for friends, associates, working and business partners, and eventually wives and husbands. The vast majority of white immigrants married within racial lines, rarely venturing out to the African-American or Hispanic-American communities. Within the boundaries of race and color, they usually married within religious lines even while marrying exogamously in terms of nationality and language. Slowly and almost imperceptibly, Protestant, Catholic, and Jewish melting pots began appearing a few generations after the mass migrations from Europe had ended.

The most important step in acculturation was the loss of the Old World language as English became the language of home, church, school, and commerce. Although some members of white ethnic

*Richard Rodriguez, *Hunger of Memory* (New York, 1982), pp. 51–52.

groups are acquainted with the spoken word of their ancestors, they are rarely able to read or write it. To function in public society, the immigrants and their children had to learn English. Parishes, parochial schools, and ethnic societies tried to counter the public language in private settings, but by the time the second generation had established its own families, English had become the language of intimacy at home. For third-generation children, English was usually the mother tongue, and whatever familiarity they had with the Old World language was a consequence of formal instruction at school. Even then, what connection they had with their grandparents' language was cultural rather than functional bilingualism.

The rate of language loss or gain varied from group to group and depended on several circumstances, including the strength of the churches and ethnic organizations, the extent of recent immigration, demographic residential patterns, occupational and geographic mobility, education, and levels of ethnic nationalism. The accompanying table indicates the extent of language losses or language gains for various Roman Catholic immigrant groups between 1940 and 1960. The uprising in Hungary in 1956, which sent thousands of Magyar refugees to the United States, accounts for the very modest decline in the number of people speaking Magyar in the country. Large-scale immigration of Ukrainians after World War II also explains the dramatic increase in that language.

Not surprisingly, the foreign language press has dropped in circulation and publications by 90 percent since 1920; the nationality-parish issue no longer causes contention within the Catholic Church; ethnic-language parochial schools are almost extinct; and associations based on Old World origins, except among the most recent immigrants, are

TABLE 3
LANGUAGE LOSS IN ETHNIC AMERICA

Language	1940 Speakers	1960 Speakers	Percent Change
French	1,412,060	1,043,220	−26.1
German	4,949,780	3,145,772	−36.4
Polish	2,416,320	2,184,936	−9.6
Czech	520,440	217,771	−58.2
Slovak	484,360	260,000	−46.3
Magyar	453,000	404,114	−10.8
Serbo-Croatian	153,080	184,094	+20.3
Slovenian	178,640	67,108	−62.4
Ukrainian	83,600	252,974	+202.6
Lithuanian	272,680	206,043	−24.4
Italian	3,766,820	3,363,141	−2.5
Spanish	1,861,400	3,335,961	+79.2
Portuguese	215,660	181,109	−16.0

dying. Although recent Supreme Court decisions and federal legislation require public schools to offer bilingual education, English will no doubt continue to replace other languages in the United States.

In addition to losing their languages, the peasant immigrants also surrendered many traditional family values; indeed, the changes had already begun when economic change undermined the nuclear family and forced peasants to reach out to one another in extended kinship associations. The peasant family was quite resilient, and even into the 1990s—especially in groups such as the Italian Americans—ethnic roots of gender roles, generational relationships, kinship networks, property control, and emotional expression remained visible. Differences in family values directly affected immigrant life, explaining why Italians remained aloof from secular and religious institutions, why *zadruga*-raised Croations experimented with extended communal property ownership, and why Irish women played leadership roles in the home. But despite the vitality of peasant families, four generations of life in the United States inevitably altered Old World relationships, certainly not creating monolithic families but generating new family similarities that had not existed in Europe.

For all immigrant families, certain patterns emerged. The peasant tradition of *paterfamilias*, in which fathers ruled their homes with divine authority, slowly changed in the United States. Virtually every group of immigrants complained that their American-born children were unruly and lacking in proper respect for their elders. Immigrant men often registered the same complaint about their wives or the wives of their sons, especially in the 1970s and 1980s when changing social values opened new economic opportunities for women outside the home. Nor could Old World fertility patterns survive. In the economic atmosphere of urban America, children were liabilities; so family size gradually declined over the course of several generations. Because of geographic mobility in America, extended kinship ties, so recently forged in Europe, proved difficult to maintain. All these changes had specific influences on particular groups. Among Puerto Ricans, impersonal norms gradually replaced personalist values as the focus of individual and group relationships. Among Mexican-American families in Los Angeles, extended family living arrangements disappeared in favor of nuclear family arrangements. French-Canadian families experienced a dramatic increase in illegitimate pregnancies and early marriages. Increasing rates of divorce affected Portuguese families. Few families were immune from change. The democratization and shrinkage of the family, the separation of work and home, the compulsory education of children, and the cult of individualism in the United States took their toll on all of the immigrants.

Other institutions have promoted acculturation. Newspapers before World War I, and radio and films before World War II, constituted the communications media, but after 1945 television became the most potent medium. All over America, in practically every home, people from different backgrounds absorb a single mass-consumer culture as large corporations bombard them with slick commercials and bland programming. As parochial schools declined and public schools assumed the responsibility for mass education, Anglo-American values were further reinforced. And as junior, senior, and technical colleges mushroomed after World War II, higher education took on the aura of a natural right and a consensus of values spread throughout the country. Although Americans have by no means become homogenized, similar customs, role models, and values permeate nationality groups to one degree or another. Commercial advertisers have encouraged uniform tastes for housing, cars, clothes, and consumer goods; television and films have made actors, actresses, professional athletes, and entertainers familiar to everyone and role models for young people; American celebrations for Christmas, Thanksgiving, and the Fourth of July are observed by most Americans regardless of cultural background, and older Puritan values of material success and competitive achievement are widely accepted.

The immigrant communities also experienced dramatic changes in occupation and education, especially after World War II. For generations, the ethnic Catholics had been a blue-collar people, both institutionally and philosophically, valuing hard work as honorable and suspecting education and mobility for the threat they posed to religion and community life. While Anglo-Protestants equated success with individual wealth and mobility, ethnic Catholics had opted for family stability and community integrity. By 1950, for example, nearly half the Slovaks in Cleveland were still working at blue-collar jobs, living in the original neighborhoods, and praising the virtues of home, family, and community. They were alienated from the constant change and "progress" of Anglo-America. "Success" for them was a religious and cultural issue rather than a social and economic one. If he wasn't careful, an individual could easily make huge sums of money while losing his family and his own soul.

But after World War II, besides moving to the suburbs, the children and grandchildren of the immigrants began looking at success in increasingly material terms, putting a new premium on educational achievement and occupational advancement. In a comparison of Catholic educational and occupational levels of immigrants' children with those of their parents in the late 1960s, Professor Harold Abramson noted dramatic changes over the course of a single generation. The extent of the changes, of course, varied from group to group, depending on how long each had resided in the United States, how large and

TABLE 4
OCCUPATIONAL MOBILITY: OCCUPATION

Ethnic Group	Father's Occupation			Son's Occupation		
	WHITE COLLAR	BLUE COLLAR	FARM	WHITE COLLAR	BLUE COLLAR	FARM
English	39	57	4	66	31	3
Irish	38	55	7	66	31	3
Italian	26	71	3	48	52	0
French Canadian	23	67	10	32	67	1
German	22	47	31	46	42	12
Lithuanian	19	74	7	45	55	0
East European	16	73	11	24	74	2
Hispanic	16	45	39	18	73	9
Polish	12	77	11	34	65	1
Total	24	62	14	43	54	4

TABLE 5
OCCUPATIONAL MOBILITY: EDUCATION

Ethnic Group	Father's Education				Son's Education			
	8TH GRADE OR LESS	SOME HIGH SCHOOL	HIGH SCHOOL	POST HIGH SCHOOL	8TH GRADE OR LESS	SOME HIGH SCHOOL	HIGH SCHOOL	POST HIGH SCHOOL
Hispanic	84	9	5	2	72	22	18	10
Lithuanian	80	14	0	6	22	21	21	16
Italian	83	10	3	4	20	32	31	17
East European	80	9	7	4	27	24	33	16
Polish	85	8	5	2	25	24	27	24
French Canadian	70	8	10	12	28	29	26	17
German	74	6	13	7	26	13	25	36
English	60	11	20	9	4	29	33	34
Irish	52	17	16	15	3	13	35	49
Total	74	10	9	7	22	23	29	26

demographically concentrated the population was, and how effective nationality parishes and community institutions had been. But for all the groups, increasing educational levels and white-collar jobs were replacing blue-collar and farm labor. Tables 4 and 5 provide examples of occupational and educational mobility among various immigrant groups.

Descendants of Catholic and Jewish immigrants have gone on to higher education in such large numbers that family income for them has reached, and for Jews and Irish Catholics surpassed, the national average. Education reshapes perspectives, challenges traditions, and creates new loyalties. Educated people tend to discard old prejudices and are more willing to move to new places. In the newer suburbs or cities of the Sunbelt, the families, parishes, synagogues, and neighborhoods of the North and East can no longer pull on loyalties, and national origins perspectives must compete with other social divisions. Instead of revolving around questions of nationality, politics there revolves around local issues such as schools, zoning, and taxes, and federal policies such as busing—concerns that affect the community. Generally successful and far from their old ethnic neighborhoods, Protestants, Catholics, and Jews have lost some of the overt manifestations of national origins ethnicity. When people move to new locales and associate with new people in church, school, and on the job, intermarriage and the subsequent dilution of national origins values is inevitable.

Among racial minorities, intermarriage is still uncommon, but even there its frequency is rising. By the late 1980s Japanese Americans were marrying exogamously half of the time, Puerto Ricans in the second generation nearly 45 percent of the time, and Mexican Americans nearly 35 percent of the time. Among whites, intermarriage is fast becoming the norm. When ethnic groups are near their primary settlements— French Canadians in New England, Cubans in Miami, Cajuns in Louisiana, Mexican Americans in the Southwest, native Americans on the reservations, Poles in Chicago, Jews and Italians in New York City—endogamous marriages are still common because most social relationships are confined to neighborhood, parish, synagogue, or parochial school. For the nation as a whole, however, intermarriage rates climbed rapidly in the 1980s: nearly 75 percent for Irish and German Catholics, 60 percent for Poles, Czechs, and Italians, and 50 percent for French Canadians. In 1940, more than 80 percent of Protestants, 84 percent of Roman Catholics, and 94 percent of Jews were marrying within those broad religious groupings, and some scholars were concluding that three melting pots—Protestant, Catholic, and Jewish—were emerging in the United States. But by the late 1980s nearly 50 percent of Jews and Roman Catholics were out-marrying. More acceptable than ever before, national origins and religious inter-marriages have become a common part of American life and are the primary measure of assimilation.

And yet, four centuries into the American experience, the proverbial melting pot still seems far away. More than 60 percent of German Americans today live in the German triangle and German belt of the North and Midwest; 70 percent of Jews are still in the Northeast; 60 percent of the Irish reside in northern cities; 80 percent of Italian Americans remain in the northern and mid-Atlantic states; and 85 percent of the Poles and 75 percent of the other Slavic Catholics are still living in the urban neighborhoods of the mid-Atlantic and upper mid-western states. Ethnic holidays are still celebrated: St. Patrick's Day for the Irish, Columbus Day and Our Lady of Mt. Carmel for the Italians, Orange Day for Irish Protestants, Volkfest and Steuben Day for the Germans, Cinco de Mayo for the Mexicans, Midsummer for some Scandinavians, Kossuth Day for the Magyars, Pulaski Day or St. Stanislaus Day for the Poles, Mardi Gras for the Cajuns, New Year's for the Chinese and Vietnamese, Chrysanthemum Festivals or Doll Day for the Japanese, and Chanukah and Israeli Independence Day for the Jews.

Even the ethnic characteristics of certain disease patterns persist for a variety of genetic, cultural, and environmental reasons. Ashkenazic Jews have high incidences of Tay-Sachs disease, Neimann Pick disease, Gaucher's disease, dysantonomia, and Bloom's syndrome. Sickle-cell anemia most often strikes African Americans. Greeks, Sicilians, and Mediterranean Arabs suffer from high rates of Cooley's anemia. Cystic fibrosis, skin cancer, and such skin disorders as psoriasis are usually confined to white Europeans. And phenylketonuria (PKU) seems to strike the Irish more frequently than other groups. Japanese Americans have high rates of stomach cancer but very low rates of colon and rectal cancer. Jews, Poles, and Russians contract adult leukemia more frequently than most Americans, and Jewish women have inordinately high rates of breast cancer. Tuberculosis, of course, still afflicts poor people in America, especially African Americans, Mexican Americans, Puerto Ricans, Indians, and whites in Appalachia.

Ethnicity survives in America because all of its ingredients—color, nationality, religion, language, and class—persist to one degree or an-other. For those Americans who still experience some discrimination based on color—and that means 30 million African Americans, 18 million Mexican Americans, 3 million Asians, 2 million Puerto Ricans, 1.8 million native Americans, 1 million Cubans, and 500,000 Asian Indians—ethnic identifications are strong and clear. The color line in America, so powerful throughout United States history, remains the most potent social force in the country, a fundamental means by which most Americans identify themselves and direct their community life. For African Americans, Hispanics, and Asians, as well as for 185 million people of European descent, color is the critical key to social groupings. In the late 1980s, only two percent of working-class African Americans were marrying nonblacks, and only 5 percent of middle-class African Americans were marrying outside their ethnic group.

Within these color lines, and despite the forces of assimilation, certain levels of nationality consciousness still survive. In varying degrees perhaps 36 million people claim a British heritage; 30 million a German heritage; 18 million an Irish heritage; 11 million an Italian heritage; 7 million a Scandinavian heritage; and 5 million a Cajun, French, or French Canadian heritage. More than 6 million people are aware of their roots as American Jews; another 17 million as descendants of eastern European Catholics; and perhaps 4 million as children of Orthodox immigrants from eastern and southern Europe. In a total population of 260 million people, the United states may have more than 200 million people who are at least aware of their racial and nationality backgrounds.

The relationship between ethnicity and religion in the United States is as powerful today as it has been throughout American history. As sociologist Andrew Greeley has written, the United States is a denominationalist society for which religion has been a centrifugal rather than unifying force. The more than 6 million American Jews remain divided among the Reform, Conservative, Orthodox, Chassidic, and Sephardic traditions; nearly 60 million Roman Catholics, though united in their devotion to Rome, are divided between the Latin and Uniate traditions as well as by the folk elements of Irish, Slavic, Italian, and Hispanic culture; the 5 million people faithful to Eastern Orthodoxy are usually loyal to the Armenian, Syrian, Russian, or Greek tradition; and more than 160 million Protestants are divided by sectarian loyalties to the Baptist, Methodist, Episcopalian, Lutheran, Reformed, Presbyterian, Pentecostal, Congregational, Unitarian-Universalist, and pietistic churches. To that group can be added millions of Mormons, Seventh Day Adventists, Disciples of Christ, Jehovah's Witnesses, Christian Scientists, Buddhists, and Muslims. Like no other society in human history, the United States is divided into hundreds of religious communities, each offering its members a sense of identity and belonging.

Foreign languages still provide identity and community to many Americans. For Mexican Americans, Puerto Ricans, and Cubans, Spanish still exists as the primary language for many and a secondary language to most. Italian is still widely spoken in New York City, Polish in Chicago, German in Milwaukee, French in Louisiana and upper

New England; Chinese is spoken in San Francisco, New York, and Honolulu; and Japanese in San Francisco, Honolulu, and Los Angeles. Even where English has triumphed, distinctive accents characterize many groups and become a dimension of ethnic identity. The Irish brogue in places such as New York or Boston is still clear, as is the drawl of the English and Scots-Irish in the South. Texmex and Calo are powerful among Mexican Americans, as is black English for many African Americans. Distinctive phonologies still exist for the English spoken by Yankees in New England, Jews and Italians in New York City, Polynesians in Hawaii, and Cajuns in Louisiana. If not an overpowering badge of identity any more, language still serves to unify groups of people.

Finally, class divisions divide America into distinctive communities. The upper classes with inherited wealth enjoy a sense of permanent security that insulates them from the fears of uncertainties of economic survival. Professional classes—physicians, dentists, lawyers, engineers, pharmacists, professors—enjoy unprecedented levels of material prosperity and are highly committed to their occupations as part of their identities. Blue-collar Americans struggle to make ends meet and constantly worry about their economic future. And there is an underclass of chronic ghetto poverty in urban centers and reservations, where people suffer from a pathology of violence and depression bred from an environment of economic desperation. People in each of these groups feel a kinship with one another that serves to organize American society into yet another set of separate communities.

Social life in the United States revolves around these color, nationality, religious, language, and class values, creating a society of thousands of ethnic subgroups. And beneath conscious ethnicity lies the uncharted world of the unconscious; people who do not think about their roots may still exhibit behavior and values consistent with their ethnic background. These are generalizations, of course, and cannot be universally applied. Nevertheless, certain patterns persist. In Norwegian-American families, husbands remain powerful and wives serve as silent supporters from whom dissent or rebellion is strongly discouraged. Italian Americans still revere *la famiglia* as the only social institution to be trusted, and fathers still mete out discipline and mothers affection. In Ireland, where economic catastrophe destroyed or seriously weakened the male role as provider, mothers became dominant in family life; and although recent Irish-American progress has restored some authority to the father, the mother remains the emotional center of the family. Jewish parents still regard raising children as the purpose of marriage and family, and children are still imbued with the need to become well educated, to work hard, and to succeed. And in Polish

American families fathers are still regarded with special affection by sons as well as daughters.

Other behavior patterns continue. French Canadians in New England and Cajuns in Louisiana still nurture a powerful insularity toward outsiders, as do most Italian Americans. Mexican Americans and Puerto Ricans are still more attuned to the spiritual than to the material, and many are uneasy about the competitive individualism of American life. Most native Americans still live in a world that moves to the rhythms of nature and tribal authority. Many Italian Americans retain the fatalistic view of the Mezzogiorno, and many Irish Americans still have the pessimistic outlook of the Old World. Irish-American Catholicism retains its legalistic values, while Latin Catholicism remains more cultural than institutional. Irish Catholics are still among the most politically active of American ethnic groups; and Episcopalians, Methodists, and Presbyterians are the most likely to be engaged in civic activities. German Americans place great value on order, efficiency, and cleanliness. Scandinavian and German Lutherans tend to be more closely attached to mothers than fathers in family life. Ethnicity survives in America; and even as the forces of assimilation grow stronger in the future, ethnic family values and behavorial patterns, as well as loyalties based on color, nationality, religion, accent and language, and class will continue to be expressed.

A multitude of overt activities in the late 1980s and early 1990s have exposed the degree to which American life revolved around ethnic themes. Jews are concerned about relations between the United States and Israel. Arab Americans are disturbed today, as they have been for years, about how the media portrays them in particular and the Muslim world in general, and about American foreign policy bias in favor of Israel. The United States intolerance for Saddam Hussein's violations of United Nations resolutions, and its punishment of Iraq, contrasted sharply with its patience with Israeli violations of UN resolutions in Palestine. Muslim Americans condemn the unwillingness of American leaders to do anything about the slaughter of Bosnians—Muslim Serbs—in the former Yugoslavia, while Croatian Americans and Slovenian Americans and Serbian Americans and Greek Americans are taking sides in the civil wars erupting throughout the Balkans. Many French-Canadian Americans rejoice at the new political power of French separatists in Quebec and hope for the province's independence from Canada. In Miami, Cuban Americans demand that the Clinton administration keep the political and economic pressure on Cuba so that Fidel Castro will fall. African Americans remain extremely concerned about the reality of racism, poverty, and police brutality, as well as the severe social problems in their own communities and how the government will address them. Illegal immigrants continue to sneak into the country, regardless of existing immigration policies, because conditions back home are so bad. Across the country, native Americans continue to demand control over reservation resources and self-determination in their relationship with the United States government. White intellectuals harangue against what they consider the tyranny of political correctness, while white ethnics worry about reverse discrimination. In short, the ethnic merry-go-around continues to revolve, and the centuries-old question of how to reconcile equality, democracy, and cultural pluralism remains at the heart of public life in America

Today, more than 385 years after those first English colonists at Jamestown confronted members of the Powhatan Confederacy, ethnicity remains the dominant force in American social life; the melting pot is still a dream, not a reality; and cultural pluralism is the most realistic approach to ethnic diversity. Driven by persecution or economic decline, transported as slaves, or attracted by religious toleration, political freedom, and economic opportunity, millions of people have pursued their dreams here in the New World. And although United States history is riddled with examples of racism, discrimination, and bitter competition, most of those millions and their descendants found that dream, or at least enough of it to make the pursuit worthwhile.

Bibliographic Essay

There are a number of excellent books dealing with the history of Americans during the colonial period. The best of them include Wilburn R. Jacobs, *Dispossessing the American Indian: Indians and Whites on the Colonial Frontier* (1972); and Francis Jennings, *The Invasion of America: Indians, Colonialism, and the Cant of Conquest* (1975). For early white attitudes toward native Americans, see Rober Beider, *Science Encounters the Indian, 1820–1880: The Early Years of American Ethnology* (1986); and J. E. Chamberlain, *The Harrowing of Eden: White Attitudes Toward Native Americans* (1975). Early regional perspectives can be seen in David H. Corkran, *The Creek Frontier, 1540–1783* (1967); Wesley Frank Craven, *White, Red, and Black: The Seventeenth Century Virginian* (1971). Also see Margaret Connell Szasz, *Indian Education in the American Colonies, 1607–1783* (1988) and J. Keith Wright, Jr., *The Only Land They Knew: The Tragic Story of the American Indians in the Old South* (1981).

The literature on early immigration to America is even more extensive. Among the best works on the Protestant immigrants from the British Isles are Bernard Bailyn, *Voyagers to the West: A Passage in the Peopling of America* (1986); Rowland Berthoff, *British Immigrants in Industrial America, 1839–1900* (1971); Richard Bushman, *From Puritan to Yankee: Character and Social Order in Connecticut, 1690–1765* (1967); Alan Conway, *The Welsh in America* (1961); R. J. Dickson, *Ulster Emigration to Colonial America, 1718–1775* (1966); Wayland F. Dunaway, *The Scotch-Irish of Colonial Pennsylvania* (1944); David Hackett Fischer, *Albion's Seed: Four British Folkways in America* (1989); Ian C. Graham, *Colonists from Scotland: Emigration to North America, 1707–1783* (1956); and James G. Leyburn, *The Scotch-Irish: A Social History* (1962). There is also a rich literature on the Irish Catholics. For the best of these, see Thomas B. Brown, *Irish-American*

Nationalism, 1870–1900 (1966); Dennis Clark, The Irish in Philadelphia (1973); Steven P. Erie, Rainbow's End: Irish-Americans and the Dilemmas of Urban Machine Politics, 1840–1985 (1988); Andrew M. Greeley, That Most Distressful Nation: The Taming of the American Irish (1972); Lawrence McCaffery, The Irish Diaspora in America (1976); and Kirby A. Miller, Emigrants and Exiles: Ireland and the Irish Exodus to North America (1985).

The other major European ethnic groups in early America were the French, the Scandinavians, the Dutch, and the Germans. For the best works on French culture and ethnicity, see Carl A. Brasseaux, The Founding of New Acadia: The Beginnings of Acadian Life in Louisiana, 1765–1803 (1987); Gerard J. Brault, The French-Canadian Heritage in New England (1986); Raymond Breton and Pierre Savrad, The Quebec and Acadian Diaspora in North America (1982); Jon Butler, The Huguenots in America: A Refugee People in New World Society (1983); James H. Dorman, The People Called Cajuns: An Introduction to an Ethnohistory (1983); W. J. Eccles, France in America (1972); Maurice Violette, The Franco Americans (1976); and Nancy Wartick, The Peoples of North America: The French Canadians (1989). The Scandinavian migrations are best described in Arlow W. Anderson, The Norwegian Americans (1975); Jon Gjerde, From Peasants to Farmers: The Migration from Balestrand, Norway, to the Upper Middle West (1985); Odd S. Lovoll, The Promise of America: A History of the Norwegian-American People (1984); Harald Runblom and Hans Norman, eds., From Sweden to America: A History of the Migration (1976). Robert C. Ostergren, A Community Transplanted: The Trans-Atlantic Experience of a Swedish Immigrant Settlement in the Upper Middle West, 1835–1915 (1988); Frederick Hale, Danes in North America (1984); Arthur Hoglund, Finnish Immigrants in America, 1880–1920 (1960); Kristian Hvidt, Flight to America: The Social Background of 300,000 Danish Immigrants (1975).

Some of the best scholarly work in American immigration and ethnicity has revolved around the Dutch immigrants. See James D. Bratt, Dutch Calvinism in Modern America: A History of a Conservative Subculture (1984); Gerald F. DeJong, The Dutch in America, 1609–1974 (1975); Henry S. Lucas, Netherlands in America: Dutch Immigration to the United States and Canada, 1789–1950 (1955); Oliver A. Rink, Holland on the Hudson: An Economic and Social History of Dutch New York (1986); Lawrence J. Taylor, Dutchmen on the Bay: The Ethnohistory of a Contractual Community (1983); and Jacob Van Hinte, Netherlanders in America: A Study of Emigration and Settlement in the 19th and 20th Centuries in the United States of America (1985).

Germans constituted the largest of the nineteenth-century immigrant groups, and the scholarly work on their sojourn in America is consistent with their size. For the most representative works, see Philip Gleason, The Conservative Reformers: German-American Catholics and the Social Order (1968); Frederick Luebke, Immigrants and Politics: The Germans of Nebraska, 1880–1900 (1969); E. Allen McCormick, Germans in America: Aspects of German-American Relations in the Nineteenth Century (1983); Stanley Nadel, Little Germany: Ethnicity, Religion, and Class in New York City, 1845–1880 (1990); Richard K. Scheuerman and Clifford E. Trafzer, The Volga Germans: Pioneers of the Northwest (1980); Frank Trommler and Joseph McVeigh, America and the Germans: An Assessment of a

Three-Hundred Year History (1985); Mack Walker, *Germany and the Emigration, 1816–1885* (1964). Ralph Wood, *The Pennsylvania Germans* (1942); and Mark Wyman, *Immigrants in the Valley: Irish, Germans, and Americans in the Upper Mississippi Country, 1830–1860* (1984).

Native Americans, Mexican Americans, and Chinese Americans were all affected by the westward movement in the United States. For excellent works describing the West before the arrival of the Anglo multitudes, see Donald W. Meinig, *Southwest: Three Peoples in Geographical Change* (1971); James E. Officer, *Hispanic Arizona, 1536–1856* (1987); and Edward H. Spicer, *Cycles of Conquest: The Impact of Spain, Mexico, and the United States on the Indians of the Southwest, 1533–1960* (1961). Francis Prucha has produced first-rate descriptions of American policy toward the Indians: *American Indian Policy in Crisis: Christian Reformers and the Indian, 1865–1900* (1975) and *The Sword of the Republic: The United States Army on the Frontier, 1783–1846* (1969). Also see Michael Paul Rogin, *Fathers and Children: Andrew Jackson and the Subjugation of the American Indian* (1975). Good examples of the impact of those policies are Ralph K. Andrist, *The Long Death: The Last Days of the Plains Indians* (1964); and Albert L. Hurtado, *Indian Survival on the California Frontier* (1988).

The best works on Mexican Americans in the nineteenth century are Charles Gibson, *Spain in America* (1966); Richard Griswold del Castillo, *The Treaty of Guadalupe Hidalgo, A Legacy of Conflict* (1990); Robert F. Heizer and Alan J. Almquist, *The Other Californians: Prejudice and Discrimination Under Spain, Mexico, and the United States to 1920* (1971); Douglas Monroy, *Thrown Among Strangers: The Making of Mexican Culture in Frontier California* (1990); Arnoldo De Leon, *The Tejano Community, 1836–1900* (1982); and David Montejano, *Anglos and Mexicans in the Making of Texas, 1836–1986* (1987).

There is a growing literature on the history of the Chinese in the United States. Especially good are Gunther Barth, *Bitter Strength: A History of the Chinese in the United States* (1964); Anthony B. Chan, *Gold Mountain: The Chinese in the New World* (1983); Ivan H. Light, *Ethnic Enterprise in America: Business and Welfare Among Chinese, Japanese, and Blacks* (1972); Stuart Miller, *The Unwelcome Immigrant: The American Image of the Chinese, 1785–1882* (1969); Victor G. Nee and Brett de Bary, *Longtime Californin'* (1973); Elmer Sandmeyer, *The Anti-Chinese Movement in California* (1973); Henry Tsai Shi-shan, *China and the Overseas Chinese in the United States, 1868–1911* (1983) and *The Chinese Experience in America* (1986); and John Tchen, *The Chinese Laundryman: A Study of Social Isolation* (1987).

During the past generation, some of the best work on the history of American ethnicity has dealt with slavery. For the African background, see Roger Bastide, *African Civilizations in the New World* (1971); and J. D. Fage, *A History of West Africa* (1969). The best books on the slave trade are Philip Curtin's *The Atlantic Slave Trade: A Census* (1969) and *Black Mother: The Years of the African Slave Trade* (1961). Life in the antebellum North for African Americans is the subject of Leonard P. Curry, *The Free Black in Urban America, 1800–1850, The Shadow of Freedom* (1981); and Leon Litwack, *North of Slavery: The Negro in the Free States, 1790–1860* (1961). Four excellent studies of white racial attitudes are Winthrop Jordan, *White Over Black: American Attitudes Toward the Negro, 1550–1812*

(1968); George M. Frederickson, *The Black Image in the White Mind: The Debate on Afro American Character and Destiny, 1817–1914* (1971); Edmund S. Morgan, *American Slavery, American Freedom: The Ordeal of Colonial Virginia* (1975); and David Brion Davis, *The Problem of Slavery in the Age of Revolution: 1770–1823* (1975). Two classic studies of slavery are Stanley Elkins, *Slavery: A Problem in American Intellectual and Institutional Life* (1959); and Kenneth Stampp, *The Peculiar Institution: Slavery in the Antebellum South* (1956). For the best analyses of African-American culture under slavery, see John W. Blassingame, *The Slave Community: Plantation Life in the Antebellum South* (1972); John Boles, ed., *Masters and Slaves in the House of the Lord: Race and Religion in the American South, 1740–1870* (1988); Eugene Genovese, *Roll, Jordan, Roll: The World the Slaves Made* (1974); Herbert G. Gutman, *The Black Family in Slavery and Freedom, 1750–1920* (1976); Lawrence Levine, *Black Culture and Black Consciousness: Afro-American Folk Thought from Slavery to Freedom* (1977); Mechal Sobel, *The World They Made Together: Black and White Values in Eighteenth-Century Virginia* (1987); and Peter H. Wood, *Black Majority: Negroes in Colonial South Carolina from 1670 Through the Stono Rebellion* (1974).

The so-called New Immigration of the late nineteenth and early twentieth centuries introduced a host of new groups to the United States. James S. Olson, *Catholic Immigrants in America* (1987) provides a good survey. For the best books on the Roman Catholic immigrants from eastern Europe, see June Alexander, *The Immigrant Church and Community: Pittsburgh's Slovak Catholics and Lutherans, 1880–1915* (1987); Josef J. Barton, *Peasants and Strangers: Italians, Rumanians, and Slovaks in an American City, 1890–1950* (1975); Andrzej Brozek, *Polish Americans, 1854–1939* (1985); Gerald Govorchin, *Americans from Yugoslavia* (1961); Victor Greene, *For God and Country: The Rise of Polish and Lithuanian Ethnic Consciousness in America* (1975); Vitaut Kipel, *Byelorussian Americans and Their Communities of Cleveland* (1982); Andrew T. Kopan, *Education and Greek Immigrants to Chicago, 1892–1973: A Study in Ethnic Survival* (1990); Robert Mirak, *Torn Between Two Lands: Armenians in America, 1890 to World War I* (1983); Ewa Morawska, *For Bread with Butter: Life-worlds of East Central Europeans in Johnstown, Pennsylvania, 1890–1940* (1986); Halyna Myroniuk and Christine Worobec, *Ukrainians in North America* (1981); Joseph John Parot, *Polish Catholics in Chicago, 1850–1920: A Religious History* (1981); Bohdan P. Procko, *Ukrainian Catholics in America: A History* (1982); George J. Prpic, *South Slavic Immigrants in America* (1978) and *The Croatian Immigrants in America* (1976); Robert L. Skrabanek, *We're Czechs* (1988); Alice Scourby, *The Greek Americans,* 1984; Mark M. Stolarik, *Growing Up on the South Side: Three Generations of Slovaks in Bethlehem, Pennsylvania, 1880–1976* (1985); W. I. Thomas and Florian Znaniecki, *The Polish Peasant in Europe and America* (1918); Steven Bela Vardy, *The Hungarian-Americans* (1985); Charles A. Ward, Philip Shashko, and Donald E. Pienkos, *Studies in Ethnicity: The East European Experience in America* (1985); and Walter C. Warzeski, *Byzantine-Rite Rusins in Carpatho-Ruthenia and America* (1971).

Of all the new immigrants to the United States, the Italians and the Jews have received the most extensive and sophisticated scholarly examination. Among the most useful works on Italian Americans are Dino Cinel, *From Italy to San Fran-*

cisco: The Immigrant Experience (1982); William M. DeMarco, *Ethnics and Enclaves: Boston's Italian North End* (1981); Donna Rae Gabaccia, *From Sicily to Elizabeth Street: Housing and Social Change Among Italian Immigrants, 1880–1930* (1984) and *Militants and Migrants: Rural Sicilians Become American Workers* (1988); Gary Ross Mormino, *Immigrants on the Hill: Italian-Americans in St. Louis, 1882–1982* (1986); Lydio F. Tomasi, *The Italian American Family: The Southern Italian Family's Process of Adjustment to an Urban America* (1972); Silvano M. Tomasi, *Piety and Power: The Role of the Italian Parishes in the New York Metropolitan Area, 1880–1930* (1976); and Donald Tricarco, *The Italians of Greenwich Village: The Social Structure and Transformation of an Ethnic Community* (1984).

For the origins and history of the Jewish community in the United States, Gary Dean Best, *To Free a People: American Jewish Leaders and the Jewish Problem in Eastern Europe 1899–1914* (1982); Naomi Cohen, *American Jews and the Zionist Idea* (1975); Neil M. Cowan and Ruth Schwartz Cowan, *Our Parents' Lives: The Americanization of Eastern European Jews* (1989); Henry L. Feingold, *Zion in America: The Jewish Experience from Colonial Times to the Present* (1974); Arthur Hertzberg, *The Jews in America: Four Centuries of an Uneasy Encounter* (1989); Irving Howe, *World of Our Fathers: The Journey of the East European Jews to America and the Life They Found and Made* (1976); Thomas Kessner, *The Golden Door: Italian and Jewish Mobility in New York City, 1880–1915* (1977); Deborah Dash Moore, *At Home in America, Second Generation New York Jews* (1981); Milton Plesur, *Jewish Life in Twentieth Century America: Challenge and Accommodation* (1982); Judith E. Smith, *Family Connections: A History of Italian and Jewish Lives in Providence, 1900–1940* (1985); Gerald Sorin, *The Prophetic Minority: American Jewish Immigrant Radicals, 1880–1920* (1981).

The scholarly literature on Asian immigration is much more limited, but there are still a number of valuable works. For two useful surveys, see Sucheng Chan, *Asian Americans: An Interpretive History* (1991); and Ronald Takaki, *Strangers from a Different Shore: A History of Asian Americans* (1989). For a look at ethnic Hawaiians, see Eleanor C. Nordyke, *The Peopling of Hawaii* (1977); Ronald Takaki, *Pau Hana, Plantation Life and Labor in Hawaii* (1983); Edward D. Beechert, *Working in Hawaii: A Labor History* (1985); and Elva Whittaker, *The Mainland Haole: The White Experience in Hawaii* (1986). On Filipino immigration, see Marina Espina, *Filipinos in Louisiana* (1988); B. T. Catapusan, *The Filipino Social Adjustment in the United States* (1972); Bruno Lasker, *Filipino Immigration to the United States* (1969); Antonio J. A. Pido, *The Filipinos in America* (1986); and Jesse Quinsaat et al., eds., *Letters in Exile: An Introductory Reader on the History of Filipinos in America* (1976).

The literature on Japanese Americans is more extensive. For general surveys, see Hilary Conroy, *The Japanese Frontier in Hawaii, 1868–1898* (1953); Hilary Conroy and T. Scott Miyakaka, *East Across the Pacific: Historical and Sociological Studies of Japanese Immigration and Assimilation* (1972); Yukiko Kimura, *The Japanese-Americans: Evolution of a Subculture* (1976); and John Modell, *The Economics and Politics of Racial Accommodation: The Japanese of Los Angeles, 1900–1940* (1977). For descriptions of American attitudes toward the Japanese immigrants, see Roger Daniels, *The Politics of Prejudice: The Anti-Japanese*

Movement in California and the Struggle for Japanese Exclusion (1962); and Dennis Ogawa, *From Japs to Japanese: An Evolution of Japanese-American Stereotypes* (1971). Also see Sylvia Junko Yanagisako, *Transforming the Past: Tradition and Kinship Among Japanese Americans* (1985); Yukiko Kimura, *Issei: Japanese Immigrants in Hawaii* (1988); Daisuke Kitigawa, *Issei and Nisei: The Internment Years* (1967); and Ivan Light, *Ethnic Enterprise in America: Business and Welfare Among Chinese, Japanese, and Blacks* (1972). There is a vast literature on the seminal event in Japanese-American history—the relocation camps of World War II. See Donald E. Collins, *Native American Aliens. Disloyalty and the Renunciation of Citizenship by Japanese Americans during World War II* (1985); Roger Daniels, *Concentration Camps USA: Japanese-Americans and World War II* (1971); and Richard Drinnon, *Keeper of Concentration Camps: Dillon S. Myer and American Racism* (1987).

The nativist reaction to American immigration is the subject of the following works: Ray Allen Billington, *The Protestant Crusade, 1800–1860* (1938); Robert Carlson, *The Quest for Conformity: Americanization Through Education* (1975); David M. Chalmers, *Hooded Americanism: The First Century of the Ku Klux Klan* (1965); Thomas Curran, *Xenophobia and Immigration, 1820–1930* (1975); Lawrence R. Davis, *Immigrants, Baptists, and the Protestant Mind in America* (1973); Leonard Dinnerstein, *The Leo Frank Case* (1968) and *Uneasy At Home: Antisemitism and the American Jewish Experience* (1987); David Gerber, ed., *Anti-Semitism in American History* (1986); John Higham, *Strangers in the Land: Patterns of American Nativism, 1860–1925* (1963); Kenneth Jackson, *The Ku Klux Klan in the City, 1915–1930* (1967); Donald L. Kinzner, *An Episode in Anti-Catholicism: The American Protective Association* (1964); Ira M. Leonard and Robert D. Parmet, *American Nativism, 1830–1860* (1970); Frederick Luebke, *Bonds of Loyalty: German Americans and World War I* (1974); Martin Marty, *Righteous Crusade: The Protestant Experience in America* (1970); Paul McBride, *Culture Clash: Immigrants and Reformers, 1880–1920* (1975); Stanley Schultz, *The Culture Factory: Boston Public Schools, 1789–1860* (1973); and Barbara Solomon, *Ancestors and Immigrants* (1965).

Between the 1880s and the 1940s, American Indians experienced the extremes of the allotment policies and the Indian New Deal. For a look at the impact of allotment, see Leonard Carlson, *Indians, Bureaucrats, and Land: The Dawes Act and the Decline of Indian Farming* (1981); Clyde A. Milner, II, *With Good Intentions: Quaker Work among the Pawnees, Otos, and Omahas in the 1870s* (1982); H. Craig Miner, *The Corporation and the Indian: Tribal Sovereignty and Industrial Civilization in Indian Territory, 1865–1907* (1976); D. S. Otis, *The Dawes Act and the Allotment of Indian Lands* (1973); Francis Paul Prucha, *American Indian Policy in Crisis: Christian Reformers and the Indian, 1865–1900* (1975); and Wilcomb E. Washburn, *The Assault on Indian Tribalism: The General Allotment Law* (1975). For the origins and impact of the Indian Reorganization Act of 1934, see Laurence M. Hauptman, *The Iroquois and the New Deal* (1981); Lawrence C. Kelly, *The Navajo Indians and Federal Indian Policy, 1900–1935* (1968) and *The Assault on Assimilation: John Collier and the Origins of Indian Policy Reform* (1983); Donald L. Parman, *The Navajos and the New Deal* (1976); Kenneth Philip, *John Collier's Crusade for Indian Reform, 1920–1954* (1977); Margaret Szasz, *Education and the*

American Indian: The Road to Self-Determination, 1928–1973 (1974); Robert F. Schrader, *The Indian Arts & Crafts Board: An Aspect of New Deal Indian Policy* (1983); and Graham D. Taylor, *The New Deal and American Indian Tribalism: The Administration of the Indian Reorganization Act, 1934–1945* (1980).

For African-American life in the South after the Civil War, see Pete Daniel, *The Shadow of Slavery: Peonage in the South, 1901–1969* (1972); Jack T. Kirby, *Darkness at Dawning: Race and Reform in the Progressive South* (1972); Henry Allen Bullock, *A History of Negro Education in the South: From 1619 to the Present* (1967); Frank Latham, *The Rise and Fall of Jim Crow, 1865–1964* (1969); C. Vann Woodward, *The Strange Career of Jim Crow* (1965); Vernon Wharton, *The Negro in Mississippi, 1865–1890* (1947); George C. Wright, *Life Behind a Veil: Blacks in Louisville, 1865–1930* (1985); and Herbert Gutman, *The Black Family in Slavery and Freedom, 1750–1920* (1977). Excellent works on the African-American migration to the North are Peter Gottlieb, *Making Their Own Way: Southern Blacks' Migration to Pittsburgh, 1916–1930* (1987); and Florette Henri, *Black Migration: Movement North, 1900–1920* (1975). For works on the development of African-American communities in the North, see Nathan Huggins, *Harlem Renaissance* (1971); Kenneth L. Kusmer, *A Ghetto Takes Shape: Black Cleveland, 1870–1930* (1976); Gilbert Osofsky, *Harlem: The Making of a Ghetto, 1890–1930* (1966); Allan H. Spear, *Black Chicago: The Making of a Ghetto, 1890–1920* (1967); and Joe William Trotter, Jr. *Black Milwaukee: The Making of an Industrial Proletariat, 1915–1945* (1985).

Life in the Southwest after the Treaty of Guadalupe Hidalgo is the subject of Cletus E. Daniel, *Bitter Harvest: A History of California Farmworkers, 1870–1941* (1981); Mario T. Garcia, *Desert Immigrants: The Mexicans of El Paso, 1880–1920* (1982); Robert F. Heizer and Alan F. Almquist, *The Other Californians: Prejudice and Discrimination Under Spain, Mexico, and the United States to 1920* (1971); William A. Kelleher, *Turmoil in New Mexico, 1846–1868* (1952); Howard R. Lamar, *The Far Southwest, 1846–1912: A Territorial History* (1970); Tom Lea, *The King Ranch* (1957); and Leonard Pitt, *The Decline of the Californios: A Social History of Spanish-Speaking Californians, 1848–1890* (1966). The Mexican Revolution and the migration north is the subject of James D. Cockroh, *Intellectual Precursors of the Mexican Revolution* (1969); and Carey McWilliams, *North from Mexico: The Spanish-Speaking People of the United States* (1949). For life in the cities of the Southwest, see Joan Moore et al., *Homeboys: Gangs, Drugs, and Prison in the Barrios of Los Angeles* (1978); John J. Poggie, *Between Two Cultures: The Life of an American Mexican* (1973); and Albert Camarillo, *Chicanos in a Changing Society: From Mexican Pueblos to American Barrios in Santa Barbara and Southern California, 1848–1930*. The following works all deal with the issues surrounding Mexican labor in the United States: Richard P. Craig, *The Bracero Program: Interest Groups and Foreign Policy* (1971); Ernesto Galarza, *Merchants of Labor: The Mexican Bracero Story* (1965) and *Spiders in the House and Workers in the Field* (1970); Abraham Hoffman, *Unwanted Mexican Americans in the Great Depression: Repatriation Pressures, 1929–1939* (1974); Carey McWilliams, *Factories in the Fields: The Story of Migratory Farm Labor in California* (1939); Mark Reisler, *By the Sweat of Their Brow: Mexican Immigrant Labor in the United States, 1900–1940* (1976); and Julian Samora, *Los Mojados: The Wetback Story* (1971).

The modern African-American civil rights movement has captured scholarly attention, and it is the subject of a number of excellent recent works. For the best of them, see Catherine A. Barnes, *Journey from Jim Crow: The Desegregation of Southern Transit* (1983); Numan V. Bartley, *The Rise of Massive Resistance: Race and Politics in the South During the 1950s* (1969); Clayborne Carson, *In Struggle: SNCC and the Black Awakening* (1981); David J. Garrow, *Protest at Selma: Martin Luther King, Jr. and the Voting Rights Act of 1965* (1978) and *Bearing the Cross: Martin Luther King, Jr., and the Southern Christian Leadership Conference* (1986); Steven F. Lawson, *In Pursuit of Power: Southern Blacks and Electoral Politics, 1965–1982* (1985); C. Eric Lincoln, *The Black Muslims in America* (1973); Manning Marable, *Black American Politics: From the Washington Marches to Jesse Jackson* (1985); Doug McAdam, *Political Process and the Development of Black Insurgency, 1930–1970* (1982); Juan Williams, *Eyes on the Prize: America's Civil Rights Years* (1987); Nathan Wright, Jr., *Black Power and Urban Unrest* (1967); and Malcolm X, *The Autobiography of Malcolm X* (1964).

For general works on contemporary Hispanic immigrants in the United States, see David T. Abalos, *Latinos in the United States: The Sacred and the Political* (1987); L. H. Gann and Peter J. Duignan, *The Hispanics in the United States: A History* (1987); Juan Gomez-Quinones, *Chicano Politics: Reality and Promise, 1940–1990* (1990); Martin Ridge, *The New Bilingualism: An American Dilemma* (1981); and Thomas Weyr, *Hispanic U.S.A.: Breaking the Melting Pot* (1988). Good comparative studies are Michael J. McNally, *Catholicism in South Florida, 1868–1968* (1984); Gary R. Mormino and George E. Pozzetta, *The Immigrant World of Ybor City: Italians and Their Latin Neighbors in Tampa, 1885–1985* (1987); Ransford W. Palmer, *In Search of a Better Life: Perspectives on Migration from the Caribbean* (1990); Silvia Pedraza-Bailey, *Political and Economic Migrants in America: Cubans and Mexicans* (1985); and Alejandro Portes and Robert L. Bach, *Latin Journey: Cuban and Mexican Immigrants in the United States* (1985). For studies of individual groups, see Glenn Hendricks, *The Dominican Diaspora: From the Dominican Republic to New York City, Villages in Transition* (1974); Thomas D. Boswell and James R. Curtis, *The Cuban-American Experience: Culture, Images, and Perspectives* (1984); Joseph P. Fitzpatrick, *Puerto Rican Americans: The Meaning of Migration to the United States* (1987); Felix M. Padilla, *Puerto Rican Chicago* (1987); Virginia E. Sanchez-Korrol, *From Colonia to Community: The History of Puerto Ricans in New York City, 1917–1948* (1983); and Clara E. Rodriguez, *Puerto Ricans: Born in the U.S.A.* (1989).

The literature on Mexican Americans is, not surprisingly, the most elaborate of any of the Hispanic communities. See Mario Garcia, *Mexican-Americans: Leadership, Ideology, and Identity, 1930–1960* (1989); Richard Griswold del Castillo, *La Familia: Chicano Families in the Urban Southwest, 1848 to the Present* (1984); Jose A. Hernandez, *Mutual Aid for Survival: The Case of the Mexican American* (1985); Ruth Horowitz, *Honor and the American Dream: Culture and Identity in a Chicano Community* (1983); Martin Sanchez Jankowski, *City Bound: Urban Life and Political Attitudes Among Chicano Youth* (1986); Robert Lee Maril, *Poorest of Americans: The Mexican Americans of the Lower Rio Grande Valley of Texas* (1989); Ricardo Romo, *East Los Angeles: History of a Barrio* (1983); Carlos Vélez-Ibañez, *Bonds of Mutual Trust: The Cultural Systems of Rotating Credit Associations among Urban Mexicans and Chicanos* (1983).

The contemporary explosion of immigrants from Asia is now generating a scholarly literature of its own. The best works on Korean immigrants are Won Moo Hurh, *Assimilation Patterns of Immigrants in the United States: A Case Study of Korean Immigrants in the Chicago Area* (1978); Hyung-chan Kim, *The Korean Diaspora* (1977); Hyung-chan Kim and Wayne Patterson, eds., *The Koreans in America, 1882–1974* (1974); Ilsoo Kim, *New Urban Immigrants: The Korean Community in New York* (1981); Wayne Patterson, *The Korean Frontiers in America: Immigration to Hawaii, 1898–1988* (1989); Ivan Light and Edna Bonacich, *Immigrant Entrepreneurs: Koreans in Los Angeles* (1988); and Pyong Gap Min, *Ethnic Business Enterprise: Korean Small Business in Atlanta* (1988). For recent works on Chinese Americans, see Henry Tsai Shi-shan, *The Chinese Experience in America* (1986); and Betty Lee Sung, *Chinese American Intermarriage* (1990). The best recent work on Japanese Americans is Sylvia Junko Yanagisako, *Transforming the Past: Tradition and Kinship Among Japanese Americans* (1985). Finally, there is an increasing volume of scholarly works on the Indochinese immigrants. See Nathan Caplan, John K. Whitmore, and Marcella Choy, *The Boat People and Achievement in America: A Study of Family Life, Hard Work, and Cultural Values* (1989); Bruce T. Downey and Douglas P. Olney, eds., *The Hmong in the West: Observations and Reports* (1982); James M. Freeman, *Hearts of Sorrow: Vietnamese American Lives* (1989); Bruce Grant, *The Boat People* (1979); Gail P. Kelly, *From Vietnam to America: A Chronicle of the Vietnamese Immigration to the United States* (1977); John K. Leba, et al., *The Vietnamese Entrepreneurs in the U.S.A.: The First Decade* (1985); Paul Rutledge, *The Vietnamese Experience in America* (1992); Paul Strand and Woodrow Jones, Jr., *Indochinese Refugees in America: Problems of Adaptation and Assimilation* (1985); Valerie O'Connor Sutter, *The Indochinese Refugee Dilemma* (1990); and Barry Wain, *The Refused: The Agony of the Indochinese Refugees* (1981).

Of the newer immigrant groups, the Asian Indians have been the most economically successful. See Sripati Chandrasekhar, *From India to America: A Brief History of Immigration, Problems of Discrimination, Admission and Assimilation* (1982); Margaret Gibson, *Accommodation Without Assimilation: Sikh Immigrants in an American High School* (1988); Parmatma Saran and Edwin Eames, *The New Ethnics: Asian Indians in the United States* (1980); and Parmatma Saran, *The Asian Indian Experience in the United States* (1985); Joan Jensen, *Passage from India: Asian Indian Immigrants in North America* (1988); Arthur M. Helweg and Usha M. Helweg, *An Immigrant Success Story: East Indians in America* (1990); and Raymond Brady Williams, *Religions of Immigrants from India and Pakistan: New Threads in the American Tapestry* (1988).

The islands of the Caribbean have also sent a new wave of immigrants to the United States in recent years. For general backgrounds, see Virginia Dominguez, *From Neighbor to Stranger: The Dilemma of Caribbean Peoples in the United States* (1975); Ransford W. Palmer, *In Search of a Better Life: Perspectives on Migration from the Caribbean* (1990); David Reimers, *Still the Golden Door: The Third World Comes to America* (1985); and Bonham C. Richardson, *Caribbean Migrants: Environment and Human Survival on St. Kitts and Nevis* (1983). More specific histories of individual groups from the Caribbean include Glenn Hendricks, *The Dominican Diaspora: From the Dominican Republic to New York City, Villages in Transition* (1974); Michel Laguerre, *American Odyssey:*

Haitians in New York City (1984); Jake C. Miller, *The Plight of the Haitian Refugees* (1984).

For the history of Muslim peoples in the United States, see Barbara C. Aswad, ed., *Arabic Speaking Communities in American Cities* (1974); Abdo A. Elkholy, *The Arab Moslems in the United States* (1966); Yvonne Yazbeck Haddad and Adair T. Lummis, *Islamic Values in the United States: A Comparative Study* (1987); Eric J. Hooglund, *Crossing the Waters: Arabic-Speaking Immigrants to the United States before 1940* (1987); and Earle Waugh, Abu Laban Baha, and Regula Qureishi, *The Muslim Community in North America* (1983).

Several recent works have dealt with the demands of native Americans for self-determination. See Sandra L. Cadwalader and Vine Deloria, Jr., *The Aggressions of Civilization: Federal Indian Policy Since the 1880s* (1984); Stephen Cornell, *The Return of the Native: American Indian Political Resurgence* (1988); Vine Deloria, Jr., *God Is Red* (1973); W. T. Stanbury, *Success and Failure: Indians in Urban Society* (1976); Margaret Szasz, *Education and the American Indian: The Road to Self-Determination, 1928–1973* (1974); and Wilcomb E. Washborn, *The Indian in America* (1975).

A number of books deal with dimensions of the white ethnic movement in the 1970s and 1980s. See Richard Krickus, *Pursuing the American Dream: White Ethnics and the New Populism* (1976); Michael Novak, *The Rise of the Unmeltable Ethnic* (1971); Joseph Ryan, ed., *White Ethnics: Their Life in Working Class America* (1973); Peter Schrag, *The Decline of the WASP* (1973); and Perry Weed, *The White Ethnic Movement and Ethnic Politics* (1973). Also see Richard D. Alba, ed., *Ethnicity and Race in the U.S.A.: Toward the Twenty-First Century* (1988); Harry S. Ashmore, *Hearts and Minds: The Anatomy of Racism from Roosevelt to Reagan* (1982); Nathan Glazer, *Ethnic Dilemmas: 1964–1982* (1983); John Lescott-Leszczynski, *The History of U.S. Ethnic Policy and Its Impact on European Ethnics* (1984); Stanley Lieberson and Mary C. Waters, *From Many Strands: Ethnic and Racial Groups in Contemporary America* (1988); and Paul R. Spickard, *Mixed Blood: Intermarriage and Ethnic Identity in Twentieth-Century America* (1989).

Index